The Fuzzy Bunch

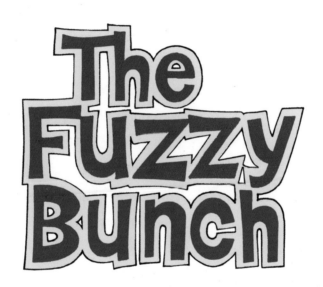

Other *Get Fuzzy* Books

The Dog Is Not a Toy (House Rule #4)

Fuzzy Logic: Get Fuzzy 2

The Get Fuzzy Experience: Are You Bucksperienced

I Would Have Bought You a Cat, But . . .

Blueprint for Disaster

Say Cheesy

Scrum Bums

I'm Ready for My Movie Contract

Take Our Cat, Please!

Ignorance, Thy Name Is Bucky

Dumbheart

Masters of the Nonsenseverse

Survival of the Filthiest

The Birth of Canis

Treasuries

Groovitude: A Get Fuzzy Treasury

Bucky Katt's Big Book of Fun

Loserpalooza

The Potpourrific Great Big Grab Bag of Get Fuzzy

Treasury of the Lost Litter Box

The Stinking

a **GET FUZZY** collection

by darby conley

**Andrews McMeel
Publishing, LLC**
Kansas City • Sydney • London

Andrews McMeel Publishing, LLC
an Andrews McMeel Universal company
1130 Walnut Street
Kansas City, Missouri 64106
www.andrewsmcmeel.com

13 14 15 16 17 RRD 10 9 8 7 6 5 4 3 2 1

ISBN: 978-1-4494-2939-3

Library of Congress Control Number: 2013933851 1

Get Fuzzy can be viewed on the Internet at
www.gocomics.com/getfuzzy

──────── **ATTENTION: SCHOOLS AND BUSINESSES** ────────

Andrews McMeel books are available at quantity discounts with bulk purchase for educational, business, or sales promotional use. For information, please e-mail the Special Sales Department: specialsales@amuniversal.com

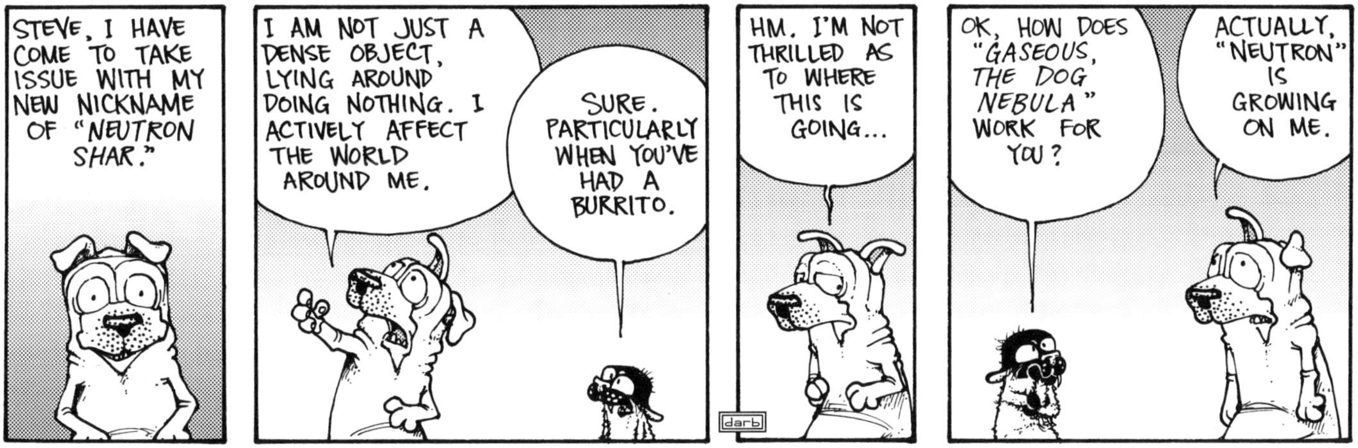
STEVE, I HAVE COME TO TAKE ISSUE WITH MY NEW NICKNAME OF "NEUTRON SHAR."
I AM NOT JUST A DENSE OBJECT, LYING AROUND DOING NOTHING. I ACTIVELY AFFECT THE WORLD AROUND ME.
SURE. PARTICULARLY WHEN YOU'VE HAD A BURRITO.
HM. I'M NOT THRILLED AS TO WHERE THIS IS GOING...
OK, HOW DOES "*GASEOUS, THE DOG NEBULA*" WORK FOR YOU?
ACTUALLY, "NEUTRON" IS GROWING ON ME.

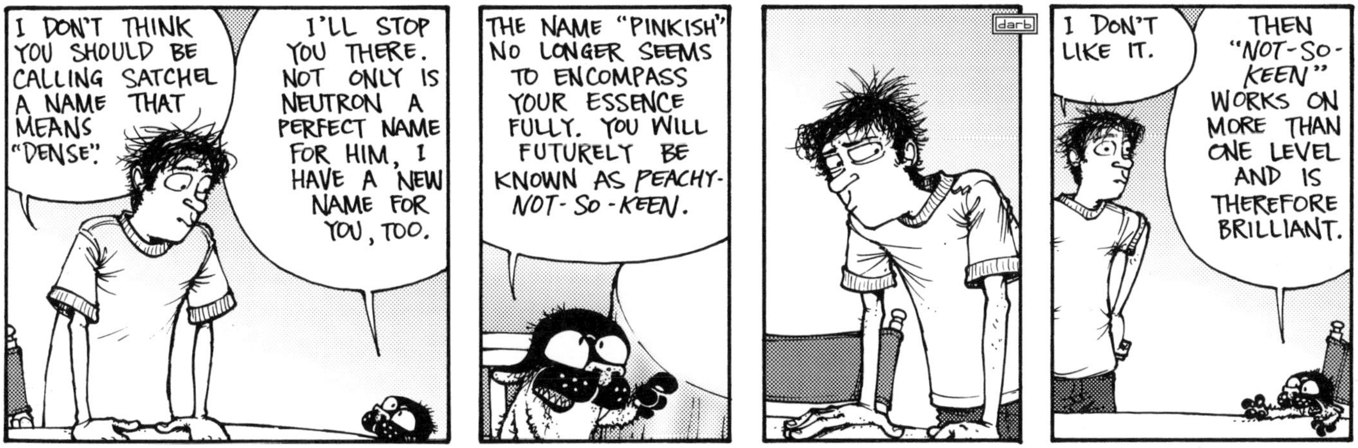
I DON'T THINK YOU SHOULD BE CALLING SATCHEL A NAME THAT MEANS "DENSE."
I'LL STOP YOU THERE. NOT ONLY IS NEUTRON A PERFECT NAME FOR HIM, I HAVE A NEW NAME FOR YOU, TOO.
THE NAME "PINKISH" NO LONGER SEEMS TO ENCOMPASS YOUR ESSENCE FULLY. YOU WILL FUTURELY BE KNOWN AS *PEACHY-NOT-SO-KEEN*.
I DON'T LIKE IT.
THEN "*NOT-SO-KEEN*" WORKS ON MORE THAN ONE LEVEL AND IS THEREFORE BRILLIANT.

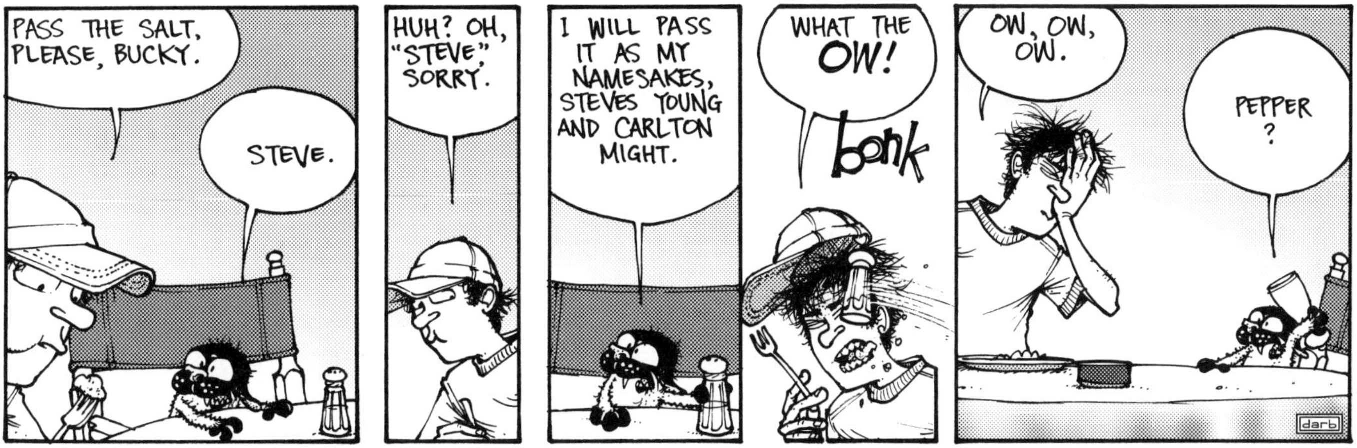
PASS THE SALT, PLEASE, BUCKY.
STEVE.
HUH? OH, "STEVE." SORRY.
I WILL PASS IT AS MY NAMESAKES, STEVES YOUNG AND CARLTON MIGHT.
WHAT THE OW!
bonk
OW, OW, OW.
PEPPER ?

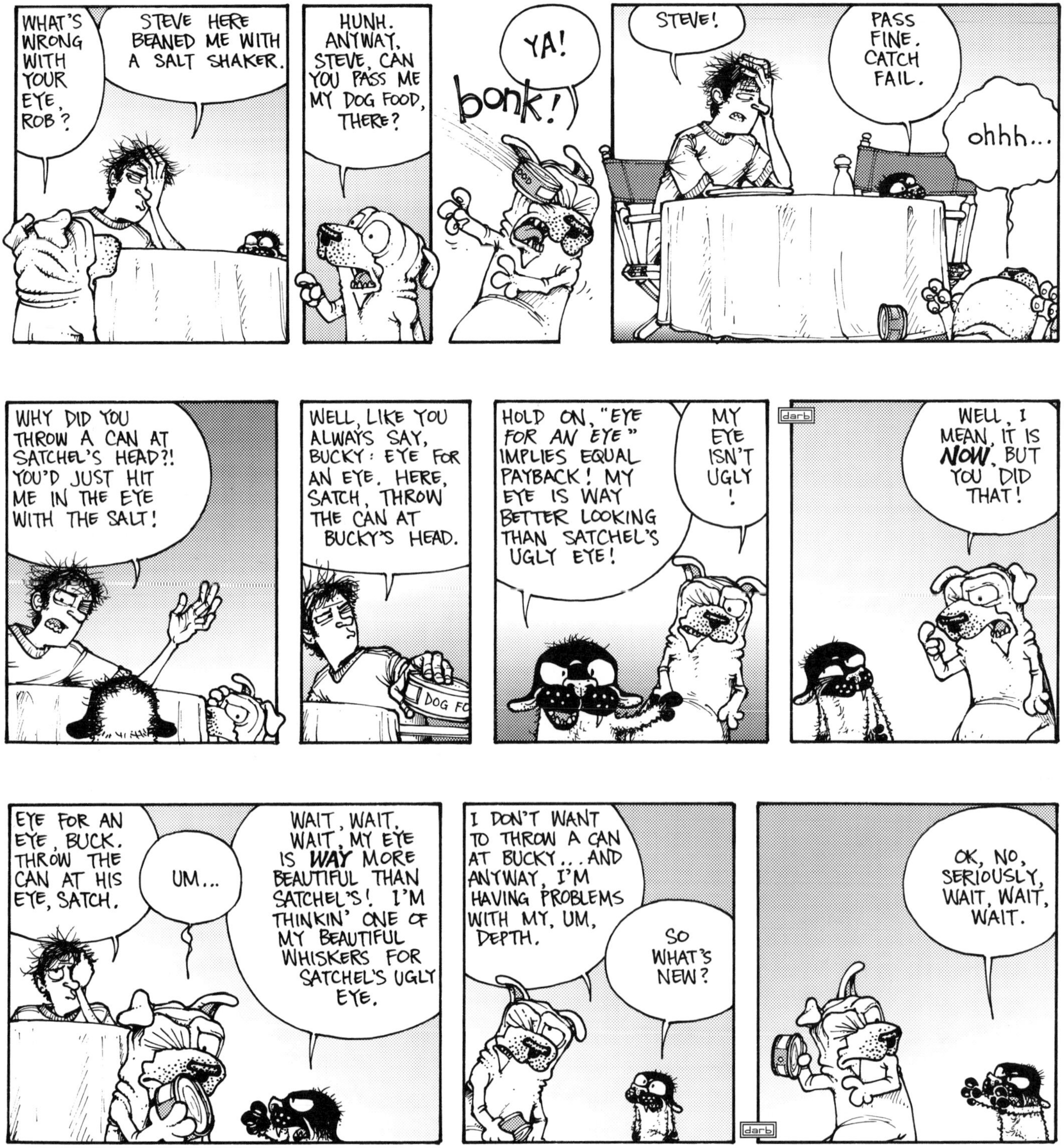
WHAT'S WRONG WITH YOUR EYE, ROB?
STEVE HERE BEANED ME WITH A SALT SHAKER.
HUNH. ANYWAY, STEVE, CAN YOU PASS ME MY DOG FOOD, THERE?
YA!
bonk!
STEVE!
PASS FINE. CATCH FAIL.
ohhh...
WHY DID YOU THROW A CAN AT SATCHEL'S HEAD?! YOU'D JUST HIT ME IN THE EYE WITH THE SALT!
WELL, LIKE YOU ALWAYS SAY, BUCKY: EYE FOR AN EYE. HERE, SATCH, THROW THE CAN AT BUCKY'S HEAD.
HOLD ON, "EYE FOR AN EYE" IMPLIES EQUAL PAYBACK! MY EYE IS WAY BETTER LOOKING THAN SATCHEL'S UGLY EYE!
MY EYE ISN'T UGLY!
WELL, I MEAN, IT IS NOW, BUT YOU DID THAT!
EYE FOR AN EYE, BUCK. THROW THE CAN AT HIS EYE, SATCH.
UM...
WAIT, WAIT, WAIT, MY EYE IS WAY MORE BEAUTIFUL THAN SATCHEL'S! I'M THINKIN' ONE OF MY BEAUTIFUL WHISKERS FOR SATCHEL'S UGLY EYE.
I DON'T WANT TO THROW A CAN AT BUCKY... AND ANYWAY, I'M HAVING PROBLEMS WITH MY, UM, DEPTH.
SO WHAT'S NEW?
OK, NO, SERIOUSLY, WAIT, WAIT, WAIT.
darb

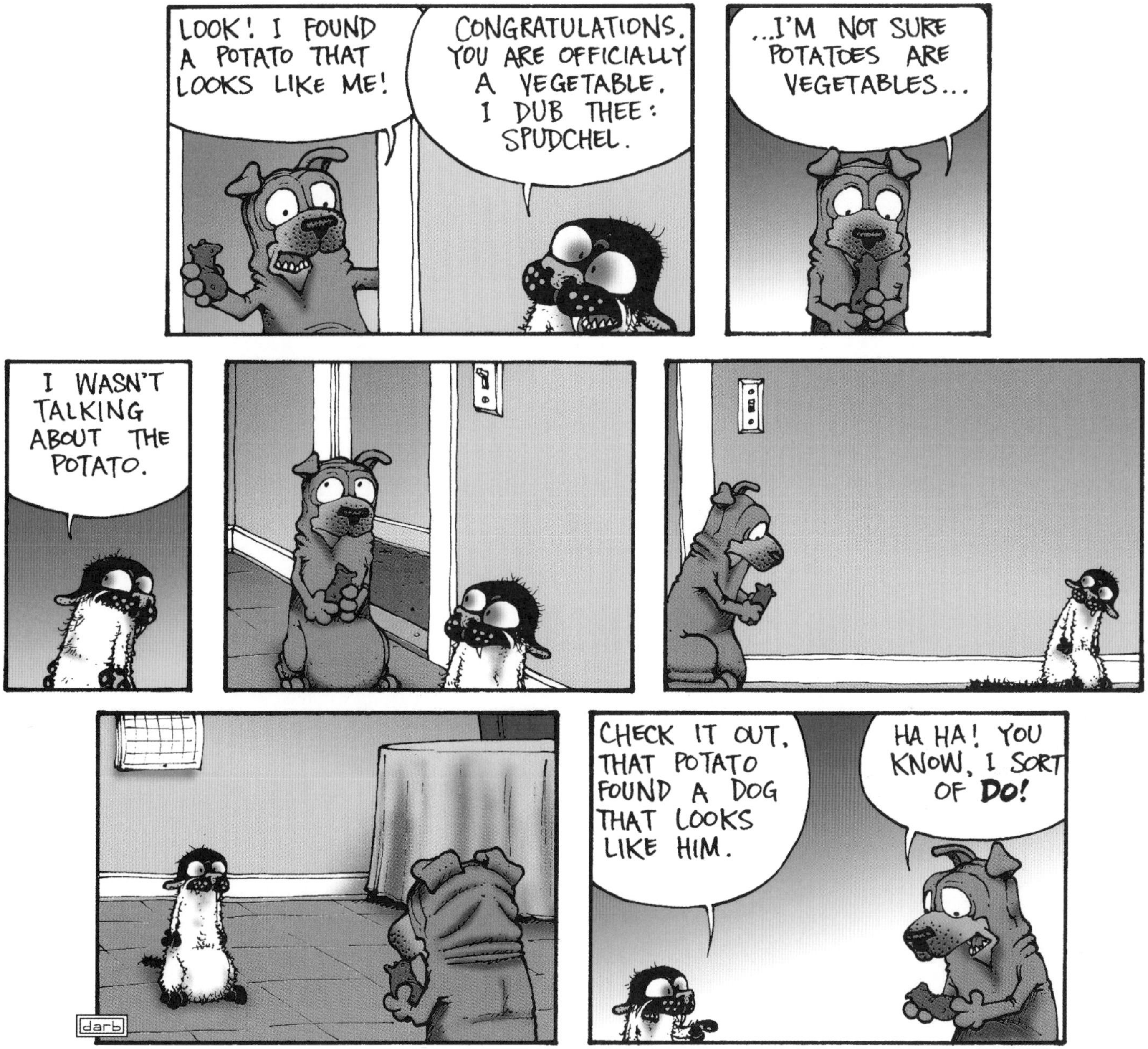
LOOK! I FOUND A POTATO THAT LOOKS LIKE ME!
CONGRATULATIONS. YOU ARE OFFICIALLY A VEGETABLE. I DUB THEE: SPUDCHEL.
...I'M NOT SURE POTATOES ARE VEGETABLES...
I WASN'T TALKING ABOUT THE POTATO.
darb
CHECK IT OUT. THAT POTATO FOUND A DOG THAT LOOKS LIKE HIM.
HA HA! YOU KNOW, I SORT OF **DO!**

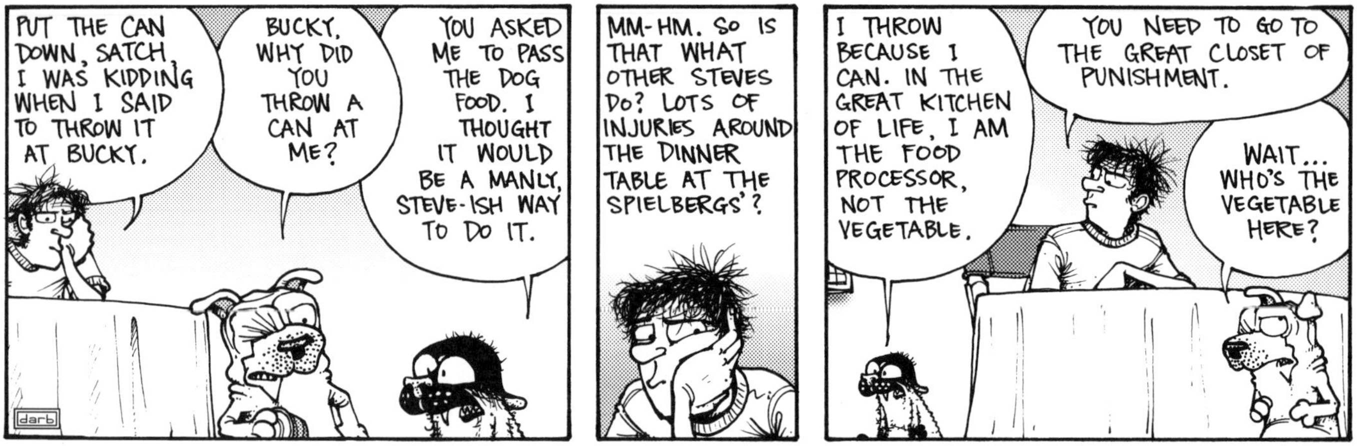
PUT THE CAN DOWN, SATCH. I WAS KIDDING WHEN I SAID TO THROW IT AT BUCKY.
BUCKY, WHY DID YOU THROW A CAN AT ME?
YOU ASKED ME TO PASS THE DOG FOOD. I THOUGHT IT WOULD BE A MANLY, STEVE-ISH WAY TO DO IT.
darb
MM-HM. SO IS THAT WHAT OTHER STEVES DO? LOTS OF INJURIES AROUND THE DINNER TABLE AT THE SPIELBERGS'?
I THROW BECAUSE I CAN. IN THE GREAT KITCHEN OF LIFE, I AM THE FOOD PROCESSOR, NOT THE VEGETABLE.
YOU NEED TO GO TO THE GREAT CLOSET OF PUNISHMENT.
WAIT... WHO'S THE VEGETABLE HERE?

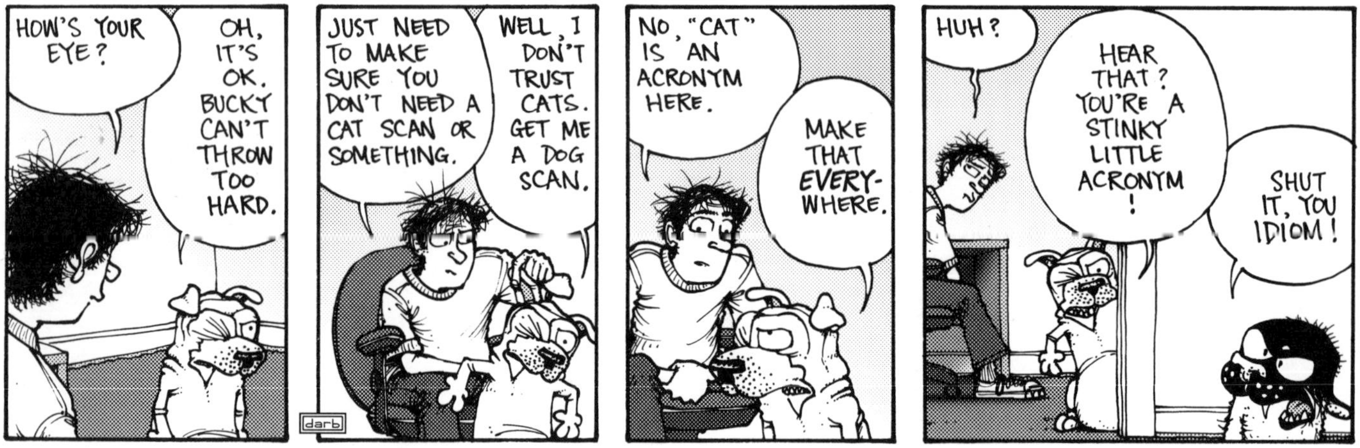
HOW'S YOUR EYE?
OH, IT'S OK. BUCKY CAN'T THROW TOO HARD.
JUST NEED TO MAKE SURE YOU DON'T NEED A CAT SCAN OR SOMETHING.
WELL, I DON'T TRUST CATS. GET ME A DOG SCAN.
darb
NO, "CAT" IS AN ACRONYM HERE.
MAKE THAT EVERY-WHERE.
HUH?
HEAR THAT? YOU'RE A STINKY LITTLE ACRONYM!
SHUT IT, YOU IDIOM!

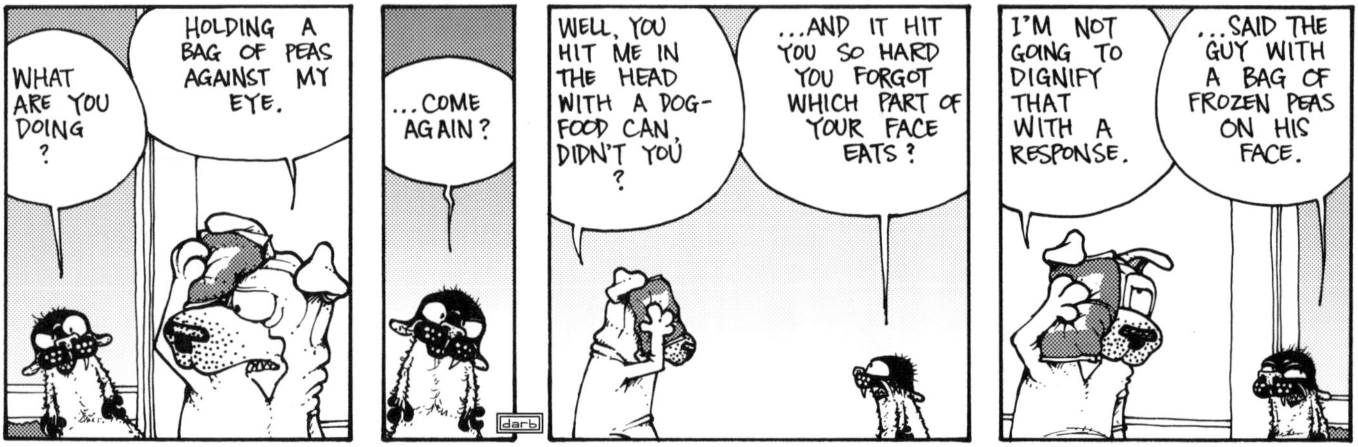
WHAT ARE YOU DOING?
HOLDING A BAG OF PEAS AGAINST MY EYE.
...COME AGAIN?
darb
WELL, YOU HIT ME IN THE HEAD WITH A DOG-FOOD CAN, DIDN'T YOU?
...AND IT HIT YOU SO HARD YOU FORGOT WHICH PART OF YOUR FACE EATS?
I'M NOT GOING TO DIGNIFY THAT WITH A RESPONSE.
...SAID THE GUY WITH A BAG OF FROZEN PEAS ON HIS FACE.

YOU WANNA HELP ME TRAIN?

WHAT WOULD I NEED TO DO?

WHIP THIS STRING AROUND SO I CAN CATCH THE FEATHER.

WHY? THE BIRD IS ALREADY DEAD... ISN'T THAT JUST ADDING INSULT TO INJURY?

SATCHEL, IF THIS FEATHER WAS A METAPHOR, IT'D BE YOUR BRAIN.

HEY, AND IF THE STRING WAS MY BODY, I'D BE LIKE, A **WORM!**

WHAT MAKES YOU THINK YOU CAN WIN A FEATHER-ON-A-STRING TOURNAMENT? I'VE NEVER SEEN YOU DO THAT.

I DON'T HAVE TO PRACTICE ALL THE TIME. I'M A NATURAL TALENT.

MY OLD FEATHER COACH TOLD ME I COULD BE THE NEXT CHEEKY MITTS.

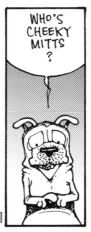

WHO'S CHEEKY MITTS?

WHO'S ...? ONLY THE GREATEST FEATHER-ON-A-STRING PLAYER IN THE HISTORY OF THE ENGLISH LANGUAGE!

I DON'T THINK YOU SAID THAT RIGHT...

RIGHTEOUS BOVINE, HE MUST BE GYRATING IN HIS CRYPT.

SO YOU'RE A GOOD FEATHER-ON-A-STRING PLAYER, EH?

SATCHEL, I COULD BE THE JIMI HENDRIX OF FEATHER-ON-A-STRING IF I WANTED TO BE.

OK, WHO'S JAMES HENDRIX?

FOR THE LOVE OF,... OK, FORGET THAT. I'M THE PAUL McCARTNEY OF FEATHER-ON-A-STRING.

SOMEHOW I DOUBT SIR PAUL PLAYS WITH FEATHERS ON STRINGS... HE'S QUITE WEALTHY. AND A VEGAN.

SATCHEL, YOU ARE THE SPICE GIRL OF INTELLECTUALS.

THANK YOU. AND YOU'RE THE HANSON OF MANNERS.

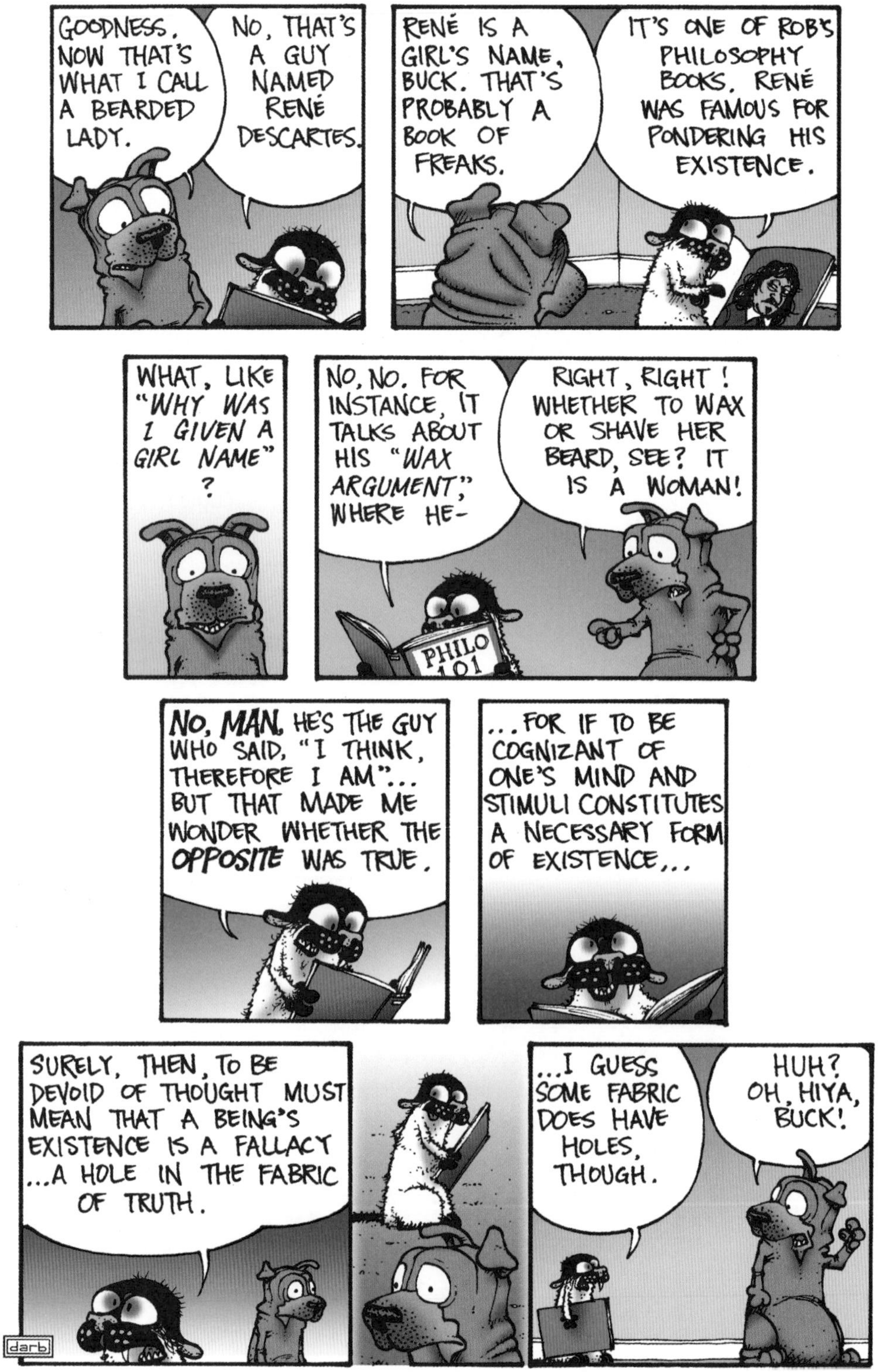
GOODNESS. NOW THAT'S WHAT I CALL A BEARDED LADY.
NO, THAT'S A GUY NAMED RENÉ DESCARTES.
RENÉ IS A GIRL'S NAME, BUCK. THAT'S PROBABLY A BOOK OF FREAKS.
IT'S ONE OF ROB'S PHILOSOPHY BOOKS. RENÉ WAS FAMOUS FOR PONDERING HIS EXISTENCE.
WHAT, LIKE "*WHY WAS I GIVEN A GIRL NAME*"?
NO, NO. FOR INSTANCE, IT TALKS ABOUT HIS "*WAX ARGUMENT*," WHERE HE-
RIGHT, RIGHT! WHETHER TO WAX OR SHAVE HER BEARD, SEE? IT IS A WOMAN!
PHILO 101
NO, MAN. HE'S THE GUY WHO SAID, "I THINK, THEREFORE I AM"... BUT THAT MADE ME WONDER WHETHER THE ***OPPOSITE*** WAS TRUE.
...FOR IF TO BE COGNIZANT OF ONE'S MIND AND STIMULI CONSTITUTES A NECESSARY FORM OF EXISTENCE,...
SURELY, THEN, TO BE DEVOID OF THOUGHT MUST MEAN THAT A BEING'S EXISTENCE IS A FALLACY ...A HOLE IN THE FABRIC OF TRUTH.
...I GUESS SOME FABRIC DOES HAVE HOLES, THOUGH.
HUH? OH, HIYA, BUCK!
darb

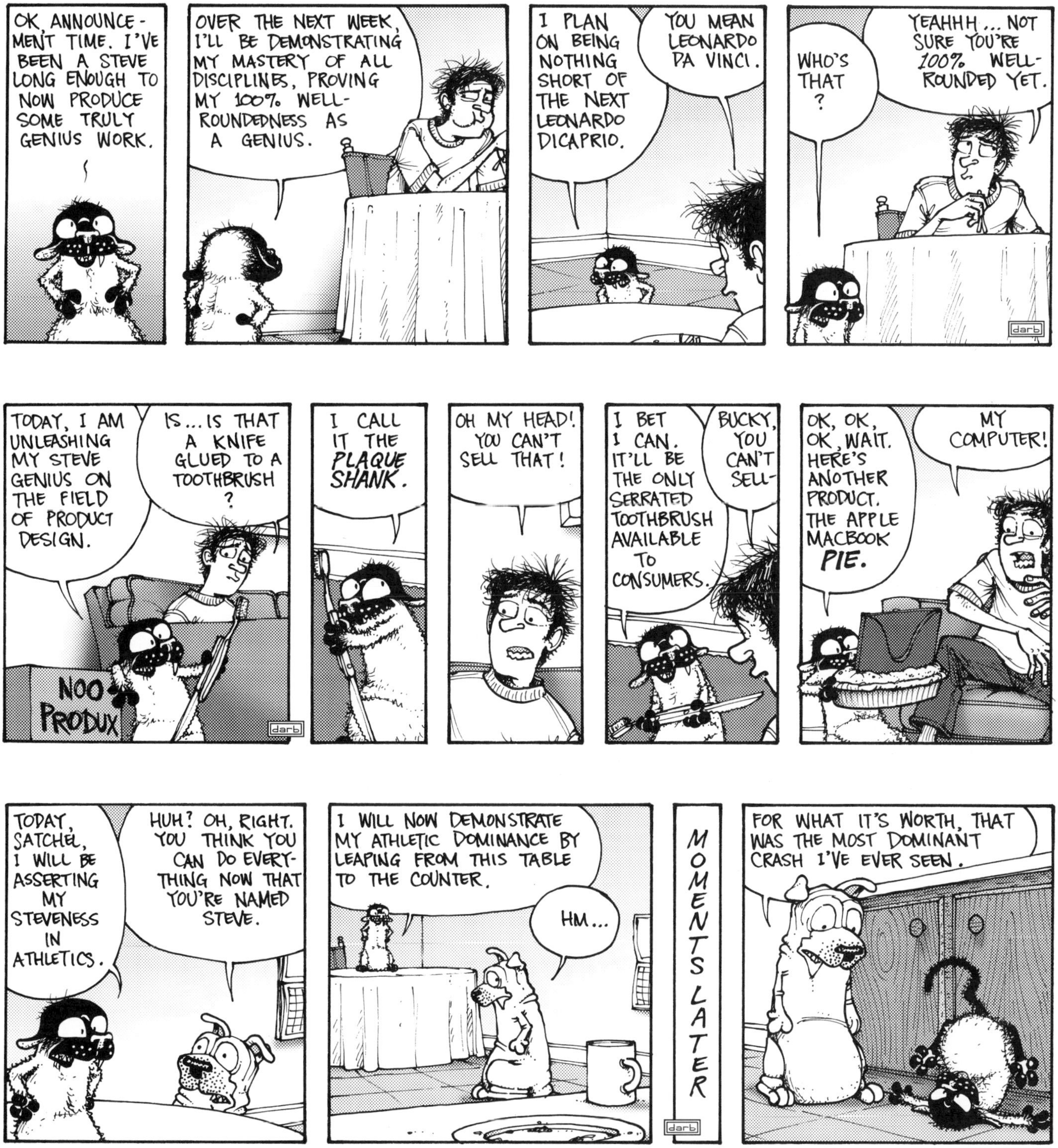
OK, ANNOUNCE-MENT TIME. I'VE BEEN A STEVE LONG ENOUGH TO NOW PRODUCE SOME TRULY GENIUS WORK.
OVER THE NEXT WEEK, I'LL BE DEMONSTRATING MY MASTERY OF ALL DISCIPLINES, PROVING MY 100% WELL-ROUNDEDNESS AS A GENIUS.
I PLAN ON BEING NOTHING SHORT OF THE NEXT LEONARDO DICAPRIO.
YOU MEAN LEONARDO DA VINCI.
WHO'S THAT ?
YEAHHH... NOT SURE YOU'RE 100% WELL-ROUNDED YET.
darb
TODAY, I AM UNLEASHING MY STEVE GENIUS ON THE FIELD OF PRODUCT DESIGN.
IS... IS THAT A KNIFE GLUED TO A TOOTHBRUSH ?
NOO PRODUX
I CALL IT THE PLAQUE SHANK.
OH MY HEAD! YOU CAN'T SELL THAT!
I BET I CAN. IT'LL BE THE ONLY SERRATED TOOTHBRUSH AVAILABLE TO CONSUMERS.
BUCKY, YOU CAN'T SELL-
OK, OK, OK, WAIT. HERE'S ANOTHER PRODUCT. THE APPLE MACBOOK PIE.
MY COMPUTER!
darb
TODAY, SATCHEL, I WILL BE ASSERTING MY STEVENESS IN ATHLETICS.
HUH? OH, RIGHT. YOU THINK YOU CAN DO EVERY-THING NOW THAT YOU'RE NAMED STEVE.
I WILL NOW DEMONSTRATE MY ATHLETIC DOMINANCE BY LEAPING FROM THIS TABLE TO THE COUNTER.
HM...
MOMENTS LATER
FOR WHAT IT'S WORTH, THAT WAS THE MOST DOMINANT CRASH I'VE EVER SEEN.
darb

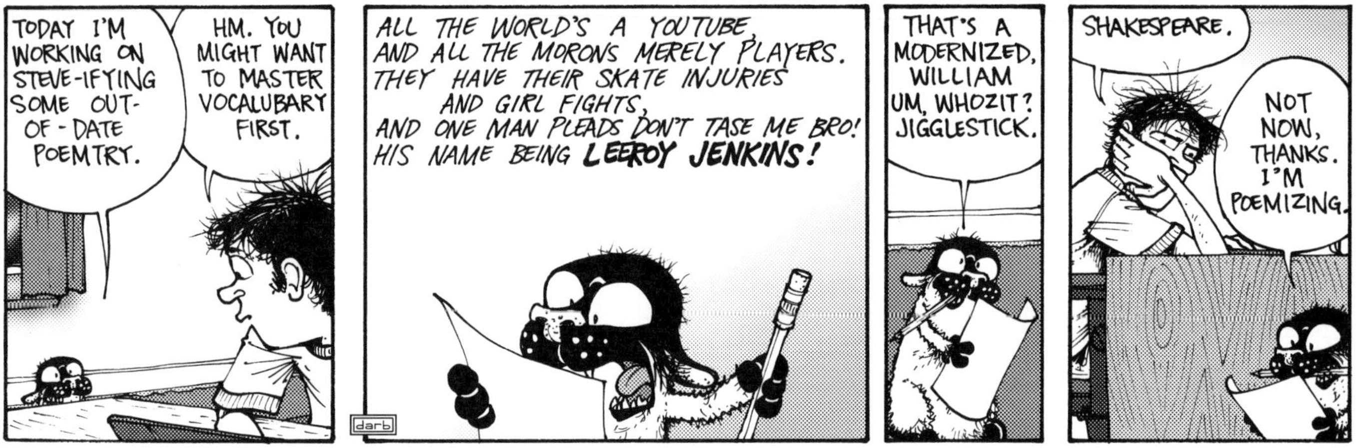
TODAY I'M WORKING ON STEVE-IFYING SOME OUT-OF-DATE POEMTRY.
HM. YOU MIGHT WANT TO MASTER VOCALUBARY FIRST.
ALL THE WORLD'S A YOUTUBE, AND ALL THE MORONS MERELY PLAYERS. THEY HAVE THEIR SKATE INJURIES AND GIRL FIGHTS, AND ONE MAN PLEADS DON'T TASE ME BRO! HIS NAME BEING LEEROY JENKINS!
darb
THAT'S A MODERNIZED, WILLIAM UM, WHOZIT? JIGGLESTICK.
SHAKESPEARE.
NOT NOW, THANKS. I'M POEMIZING.

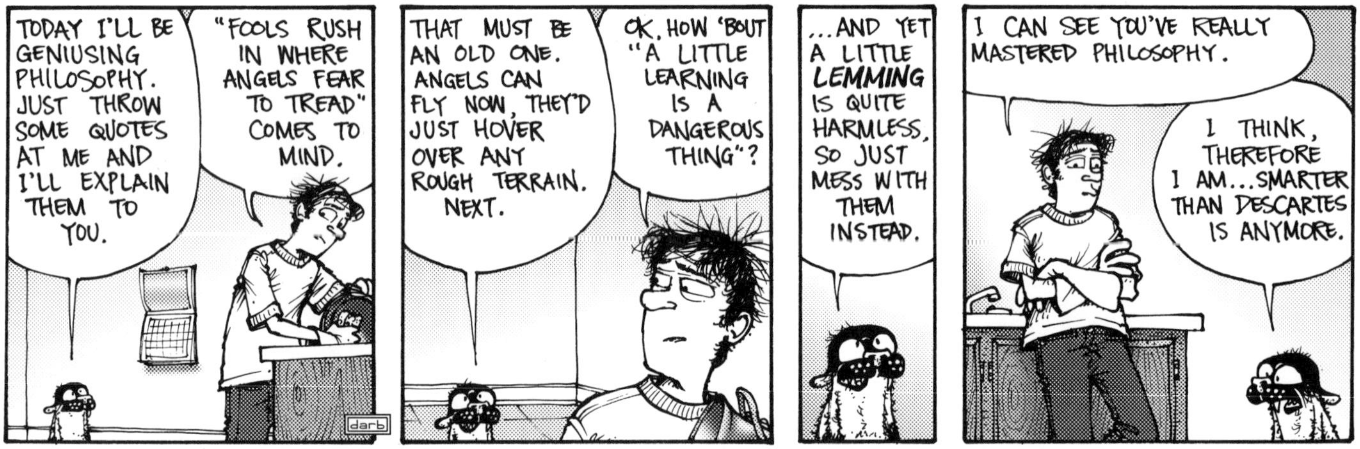
TODAY I'LL BE GENIUSING PHILOSOPHY. JUST THROW SOME QUOTES AT ME AND I'LL EXPLAIN THEM TO YOU.
"FOOLS RUSH IN WHERE ANGELS FEAR TO TREAD" COMES TO MIND.
darb
THAT MUST BE AN OLD ONE. ANGELS CAN FLY NOW, THEY'D JUST HOVER OVER ANY ROUGH TERRAIN. NEXT.
OK, HOW 'BOUT "A LITTLE LEARNING IS A DANGEROUS THING"?
...AND YET A LITTLE LEMMING IS QUITE HARMLESS, SO JUST MESS WITH THEM INSTEAD.
I CAN SEE YOU'VE REALLY MASTERED PHILOSOPHY.
I THINK, THEREFORE I AM...SMARTER THAN DESCARTES IS ANYMORE.

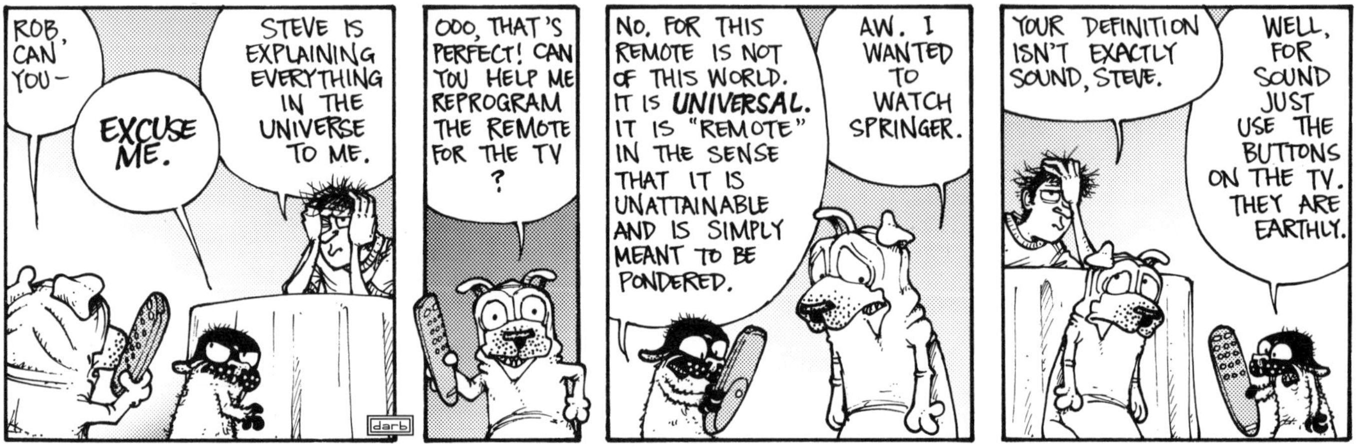
ROB, CAN YOU—
EXCUSE ME.
STEVE IS EXPLAINING EVERYTHING IN THE UNIVERSE TO ME.
darb
OOO, THAT'S PERFECT! CAN YOU HELP ME REPROGRAM THE REMOTE FOR THE TV?
NO. FOR THIS REMOTE IS NOT OF THIS WORLD. IT IS UNIVERSAL. IT IS "REMOTE" IN THE SENSE THAT IT IS UNATTAINABLE AND IS SIMPLY MEANT TO BE PONDERED.
AW. I WANTED TO WATCH SPRINGER.
YOUR DEFINITION ISN'T EXACTLY SOUND, STEVE.
WELL, FOR SOUND JUST USE THE BUTTONS ON THE TV. THEY ARE EARTHLY.

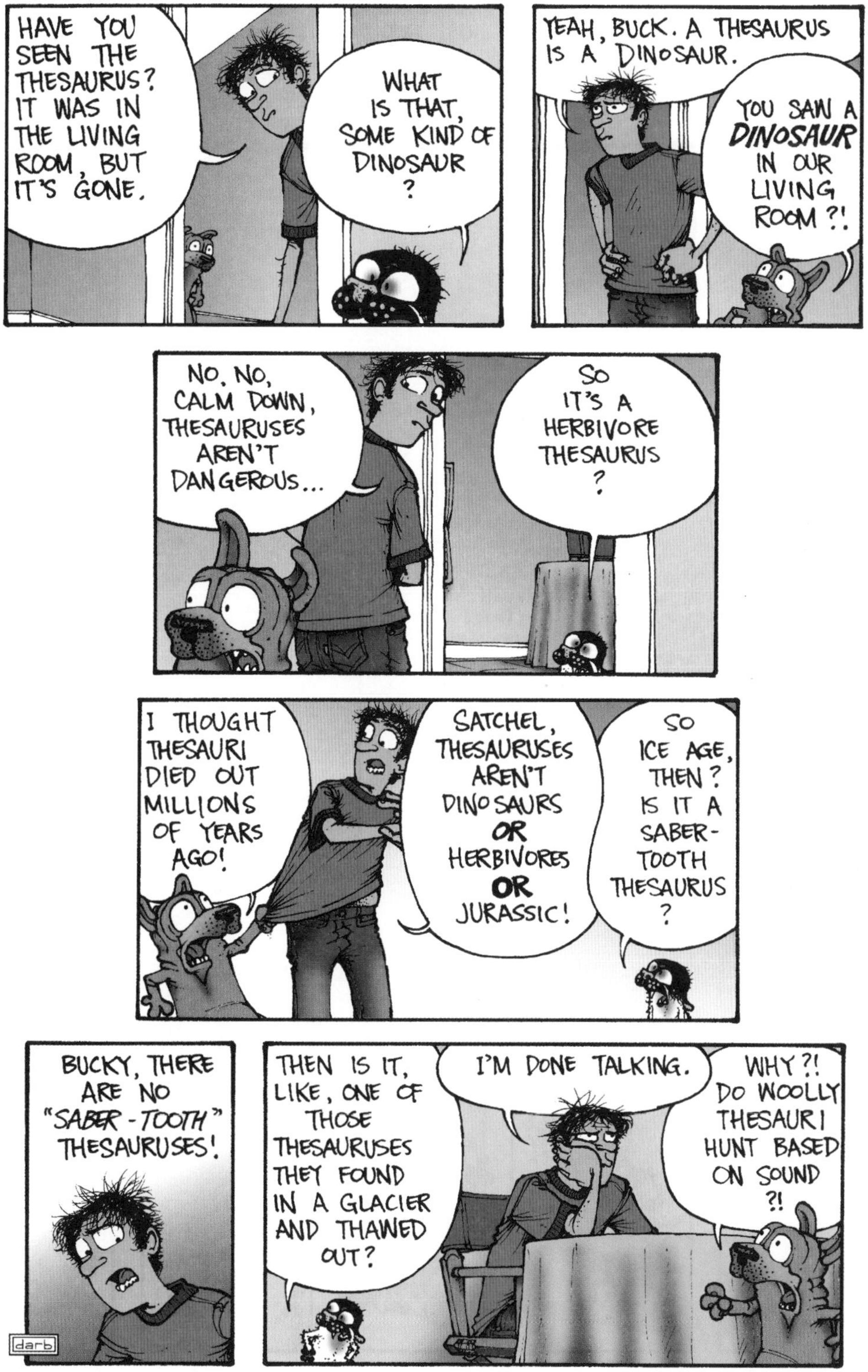
HAVE YOU SEEN THE THESAURUS? IT WAS IN THE LIVING ROOM, BUT IT'S GONE.
WHAT IS THAT, SOME KIND OF DINOSAUR?
YEAH, BUCK. A THESAURUS IS A DINOSAUR.
YOU SAW A DINOSAUR IN OUR LIVING ROOM?!
NO. NO, CALM DOWN, THESAURUSES AREN'T DANGEROUS...
SO IT'S A HERBIVORE THESAURUS?
I THOUGHT THESAURI DIED OUT MILLIONS OF YEARS AGO!
SATCHEL, THESAURUSES AREN'T DINOSAURS OR HERBIVORES OR JURASSIC!
SO ICE AGE, THEN? IS IT A SABER-TOOTH THESAURUS?
BUCKY, THERE ARE NO "SABER-TOOTH" THESAURUSES!
darb
THEN IS IT, LIKE, ONE OF THOSE THESAURUSES THEY FOUND IN A GLACIER AND THAWED OUT?
I'M DONE TALKING.
WHY?! DO WOOLLY THESAURI HUNT BASED ON SOUND?!

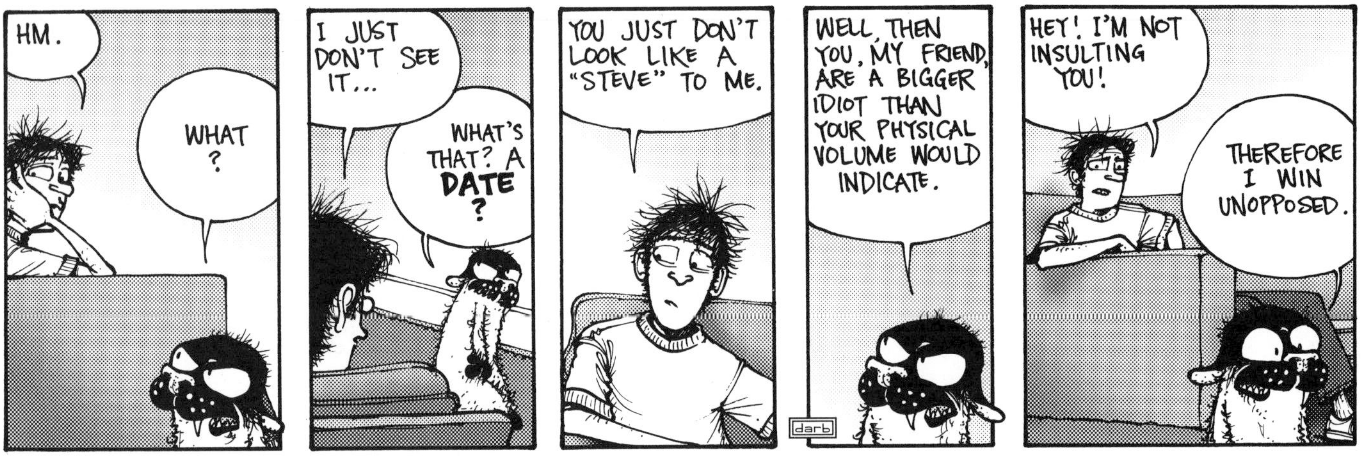

HM.
WHAT ?
I JUST DON'T SEE IT...
WHAT'S THAT? A **DATE** ?
YOU JUST DON'T LOOK LIKE A "STEVE" TO ME.
WELL, THEN YOU, MY FRIEND, ARE A BIGGER IDIOT THAN YOUR PHYSICAL VOLUME WOULD INDICATE.
darb
HEY! I'M NOT INSULTING YOU!
THEREFORE I WIN UNOPPOSED.

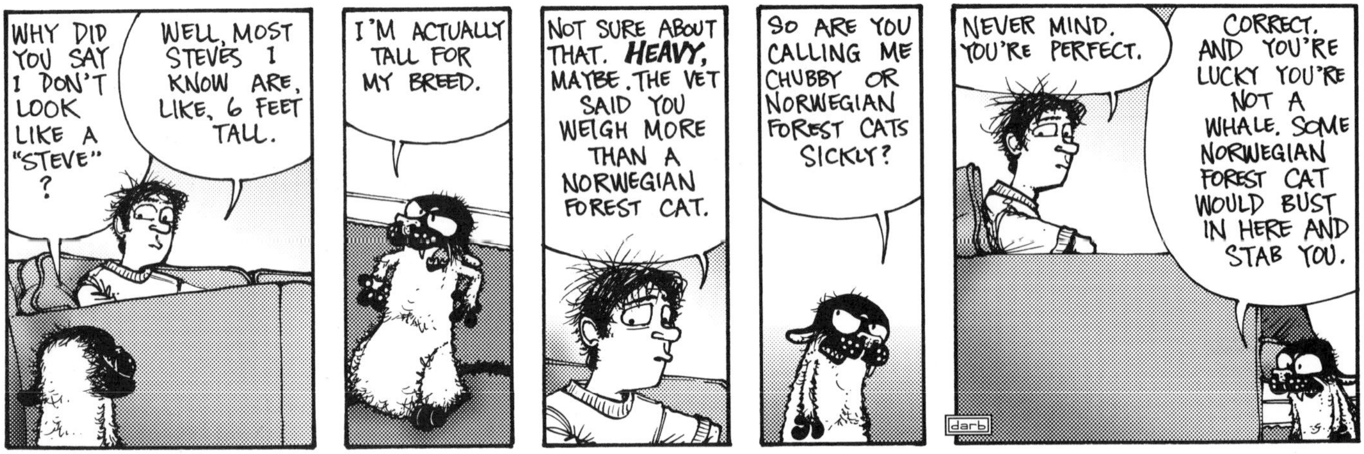

WHY DID YOU SAY I DON'T LOOK LIKE A "STEVE" ?
WELL, MOST STEVES I KNOW ARE, LIKE, 6 FEET TALL.
I'M ACTUALLY TALL FOR MY BREED.
NOT SURE ABOUT THAT. ***HEAVY,*** MAYBE. THE VET SAID YOU WEIGH MORE THAN A NORWEGIAN FOREST CAT.
SO ARE YOU CALLING ME CHUBBY OR NORWEGIAN FOREST CATS SICKLY?
darb
NEVER MIND. YOU'RE PERFECT.
CORRECT. AND YOU'RE LUCKY YOU'RE NOT A WHALE. SOME NORWEGIAN FOREST CAT WOULD BUST IN HERE AND STAB YOU.

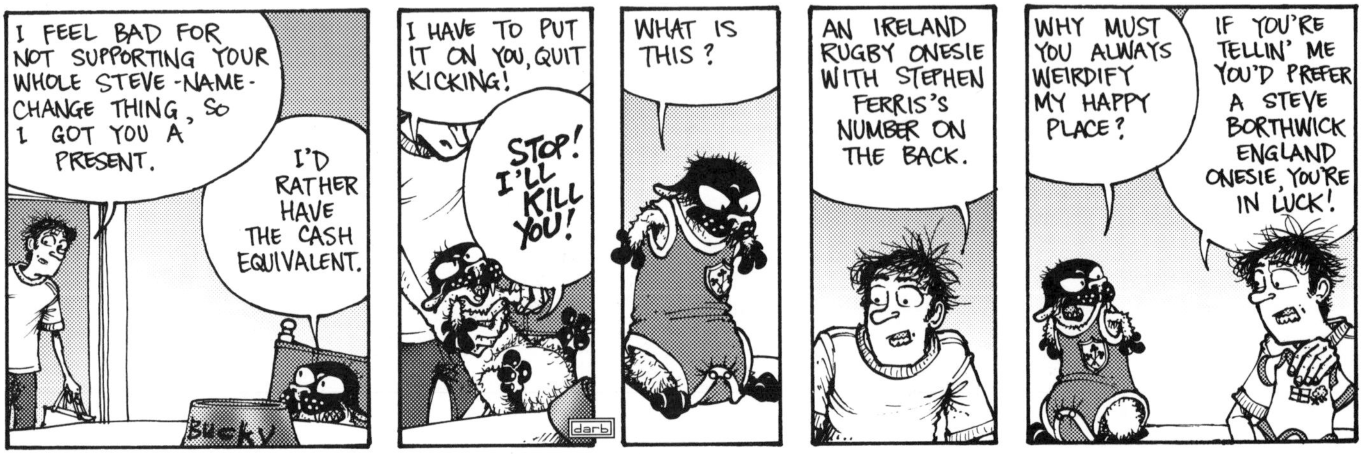

I FEEL BAD FOR NOT SUPPORTING YOUR WHOLE STEVE-NAME-CHANGE THING, SO I GOT YOU A PRESENT.
I'D RATHER HAVE THE CASH EQUIVALENT.
BUCKY
I HAVE TO PUT IT ON YOU, QUIT KICKING!
STOP! I'LL KILL YOU!
darb
WHAT IS THIS ?
AN IRELAND RUGBY ONESIE WITH STEPHEN FERRIS'S NUMBER ON THE BACK.
WHY MUST YOU ALWAYS WEIRDIFY MY HAPPY PLACE?
IF YOU'RE TELLIN' ME YOU'D PREFER A STEVE BORTHWICK ENGLAND ONESIE, YOU'RE IN LUCK!

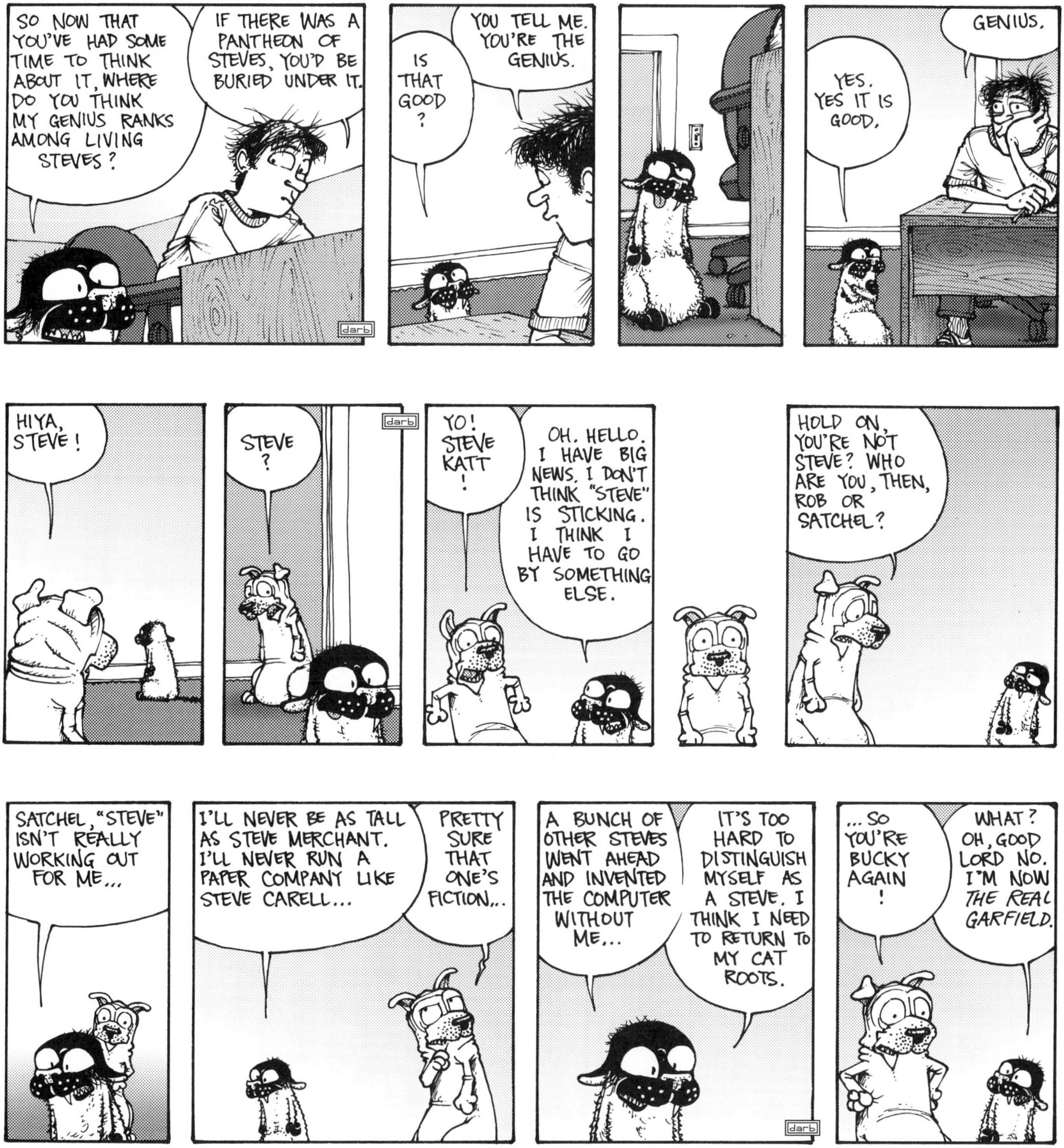

SO NOW THAT YOU'VE HAD SOME TIME TO THINK ABOUT IT, WHERE DO YOU THINK MY GENIUS RANKS AMONG LIVING STEVES?
IF THERE WAS A PANTHEON OF STEVES, YOU'D BE BURIED UNDER IT.
IS THAT GOOD?
YOU TELL ME. YOU'RE THE GENIUS.
YES. YES IT IS GOOD.
GENIUS.
darb
HIYA, STEVE!
STEVE?
YO! STEVE KATT!
OH. HELLO. I HAVE BIG NEWS. I DON'T THINK "STEVE" IS STICKING. I THINK I HAVE TO GO BY SOMETHING ELSE.
HOLD ON, YOU'RE NOT STEVE? WHO ARE YOU, THEN, ROB OR SATCHEL?
darb
SATCHEL, "STEVE" ISN'T REALLY WORKING OUT FOR ME...
I'LL NEVER BE AS TALL AS STEVE MERCHANT. I'LL NEVER RUN A PAPER COMPANY LIKE STEVE CARELL...
PRETTY SURE THAT ONE'S FICTION...
A BUNCH OF OTHER STEVES WENT AHEAD AND INVENTED THE COMPUTER WITHOUT ME...
IT'S TOO HARD TO DISTINGUISH MYSELF AS A STEVE. I THINK I NEED TO RETURN TO MY CAT ROOTS.
...SO YOU'RE BUCKY AGAIN!
WHAT? OH, GOOD LORD NO. I'M NOW *THE REAL GARFIELD*.
darb

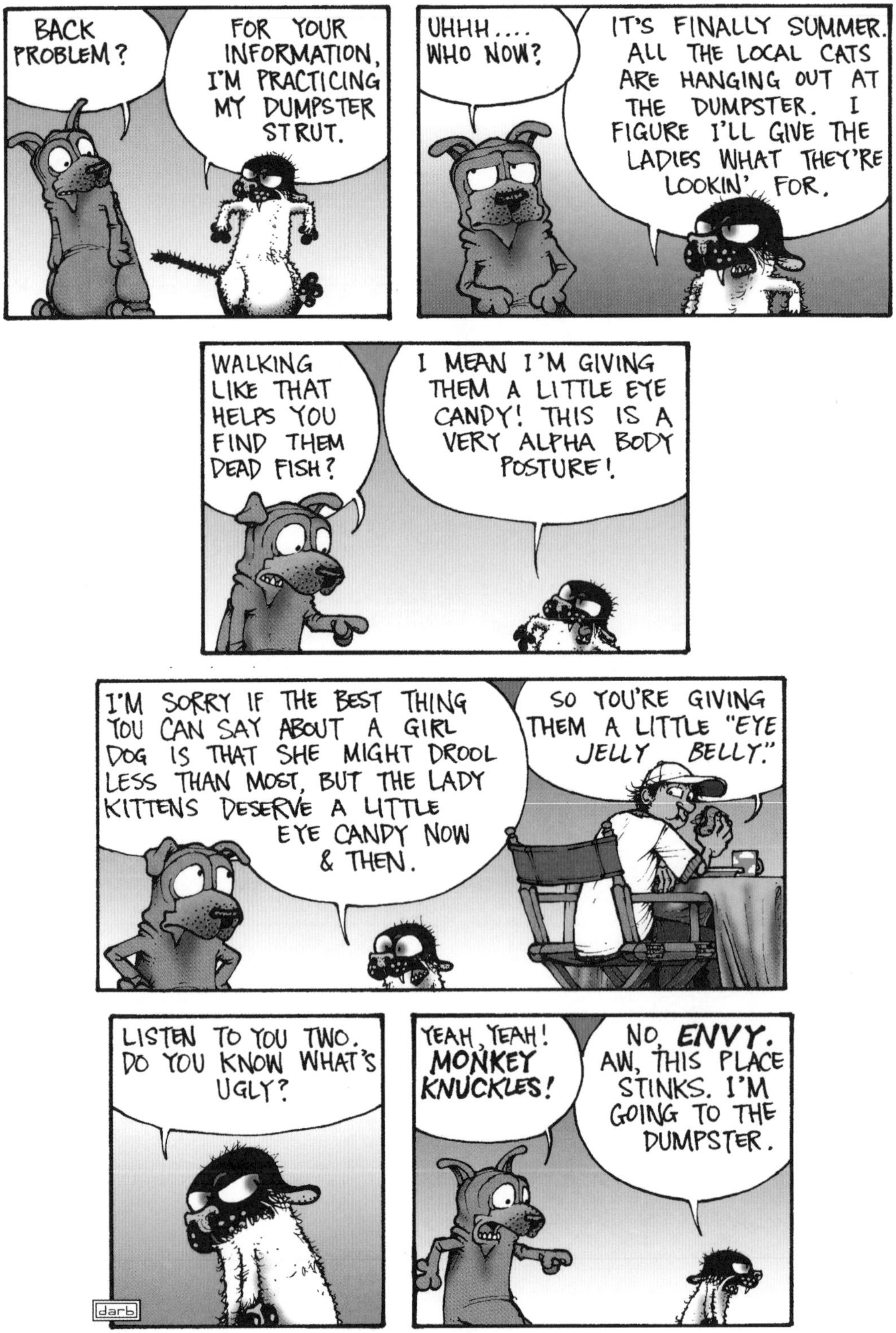
BACK PROBLEM?
FOR YOUR INFORMATION, I'M PRACTICING MY DUMPSTER STRUT.
UHHH.... WHO NOW?
IT'S FINALLY SUMMER. ALL THE LOCAL CATS ARE HANGING OUT AT THE DUMPSTER. I FIGURE I'LL GIVE THE LADIES WHAT THEY'RE LOOKIN' FOR.
WALKING LIKE THAT HELPS YOU FIND THEM DEAD FISH?
I MEAN I'M GIVING THEM A LITTLE EYE CANDY! THIS IS A VERY ALPHA BODY POSTURE!
I'M SORRY IF THE BEST THING YOU CAN SAY ABOUT A GIRL DOG IS THAT SHE MIGHT DROOL LESS THAN MOST, BUT THE LADY KITTENS DESERVE A LITTLE EYE CANDY NOW & THEN.
SO YOU'RE GIVING THEM A LITTLE "EYE JELLY BELLY."
LISTEN TO YOU TWO. DO YOU KNOW WHAT'S UGLY?
YEAH, YEAH! **MONKEY KNUCKLES!**
NO, **ENVY.** AW, THIS PLACE STINKS. I'M GOING TO THE DUMPSTER.
darb

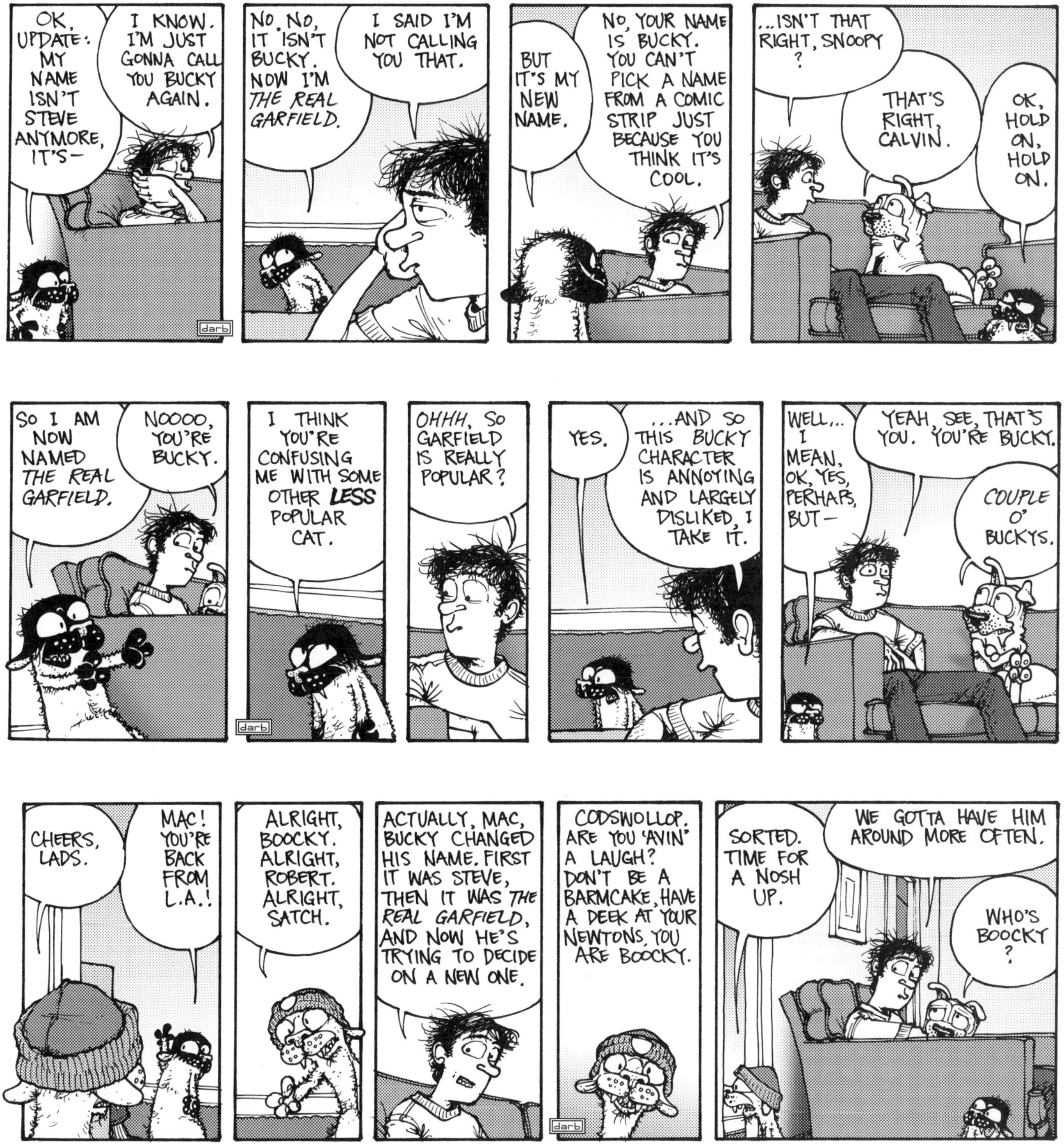
OK. UPDATE: MY NAME ISN'T STEVE ANYMORE, IT'S—
I KNOW. I'M JUST GONNA CALL YOU BUCKY AGAIN.
darb
NO, NO, IT ISN'T BUCKY. NOW I'M *THE REAL GARFIELD.*
I SAID I'M NOT CALLING YOU THAT.
BUT IT'S MY NEW NAME.
NO, YOUR NAME IS BUCKY. YOU CAN'T PICK A NAME FROM A COMIC STRIP JUST BECAUSE YOU THINK IT'S COOL.
...ISN'T THAT RIGHT, SNOOPY?
THAT'S RIGHT, CALVIN.
OK, HOLD ON, HOLD ON.
SO I AM NOW NAMED *THE REAL GARFIELD.*
NOOOO, YOU'RE BUCKY.
I THINK YOU'RE CONFUSING ME WITH SOME OTHER **LESS** POPULAR CAT.
darb
OHHH, SO GARFIELD IS REALLY POPULAR?
YES.
...AND SO THIS *BUCKY* CHARACTER IS ANNOYING AND LARGELY DISLIKED, I TAKE IT.
WELL... I MEAN, OK, YES, PERHAPS, BUT—
YEAH, SEE, THAT'S YOU. YOU'RE BUCKY.
COUPLE O' BUCKYS.
CHEERS, LADS.
MAC! YOU'RE BACK FROM L.A.!
ALRIGHT, BOOCKY. ALRIGHT, ROBERT. ALRIGHT, SATCH.
ACTUALLY, MAC, BUCKY CHANGED HIS NAME. FIRST IT WAS STEVE, THEN IT WAS *THE REAL GARFIELD*, AND NOW HE'S TRYING TO DECIDE ON A NEW ONE.
darb
CODSWOLLOP. ARE YOU 'AVIN' A LAUGH? DON'T BE A BARMCAKE, HAVE A DEEK AT YOUR NEWTONS. YOU ARE BOOCKY.
SORTED. TIME FOR A NOSH UP.
WE GOTTA HAVE HIM AROUND MORE OFTEN.
WHO'S BOOCKY?

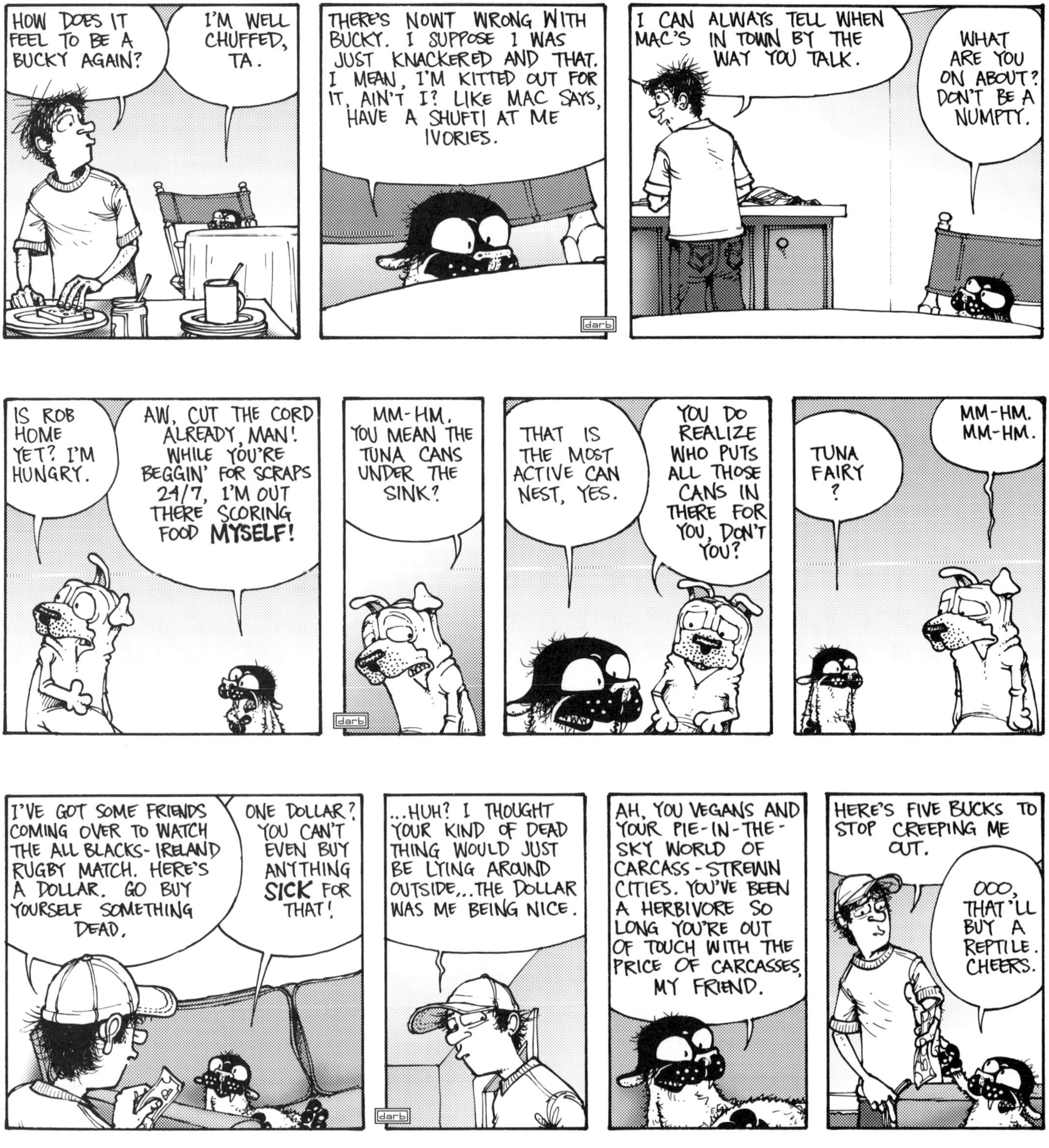
HOW DOES IT FEEL TO BE A BUCKY AGAIN?
I'M WELL CHUFFED, TA.
THERE'S NOWT WRONG WITH BUCKY. I SUPPOSE I WAS JUST KNACKERED AND THAT. I MEAN, I'M KITTED OUT FOR IT, AIN'T I? LIKE MAC SAYS, HAVE A SHUFTI AT ME IVORIES.
darb
I CAN ALWAYS TELL WHEN MAC'S IN TOWN BY THE WAY YOU TALK.
WHAT ARE YOU ON ABOUT? DON'T BE A NUMPTY.
IS ROB HOME YET? I'M HUNGRY.
AW, CUT THE CORD ALREADY, MAN! WHILE YOU'RE BEGGIN' FOR SCRAPS 24/7, I'M OUT THERE SCORING FOOD MYSELF!
MM-HM. YOU MEAN THE TUNA CANS UNDER THE SINK?
darb
THAT IS THE MOST ACTIVE CAN NEST, YES.
YOU DO REALIZE WHO PUTS ALL THOSE CANS IN THERE FOR YOU, DON'T YOU?
TUNA FAIRY?
MM-HM. MM-HM.
I'VE GOT SOME FRIENDS COMING OVER TO WATCH THE ALL BLACKS-IRELAND RUGBY MATCH. HERE'S A DOLLAR. GO BUY YOURSELF SOMETHING DEAD.
ONE DOLLAR? YOU CAN'T EVEN BUY ANYTHING SICK FOR THAT!
...HUH? I THOUGHT YOUR KIND OF DEAD THING WOULD JUST BE LYING AROUND OUTSIDE... THE DOLLAR WAS ME BEING NICE.
darb
AH, YOU VEGANS AND YOUR PIE-IN-THE-SKY WORLD OF CARCASS-STREWN CITIES. YOU'VE BEEN A HERBIVORE SO LONG YOU'RE OUT OF TOUCH WITH THE PRICE OF CARCASSES, MY FRIEND.
HERE'S FIVE BUCKS TO STOP CREEPING ME OUT.
OOO, THAT'LL BUY A REPTILE. CHEERS.

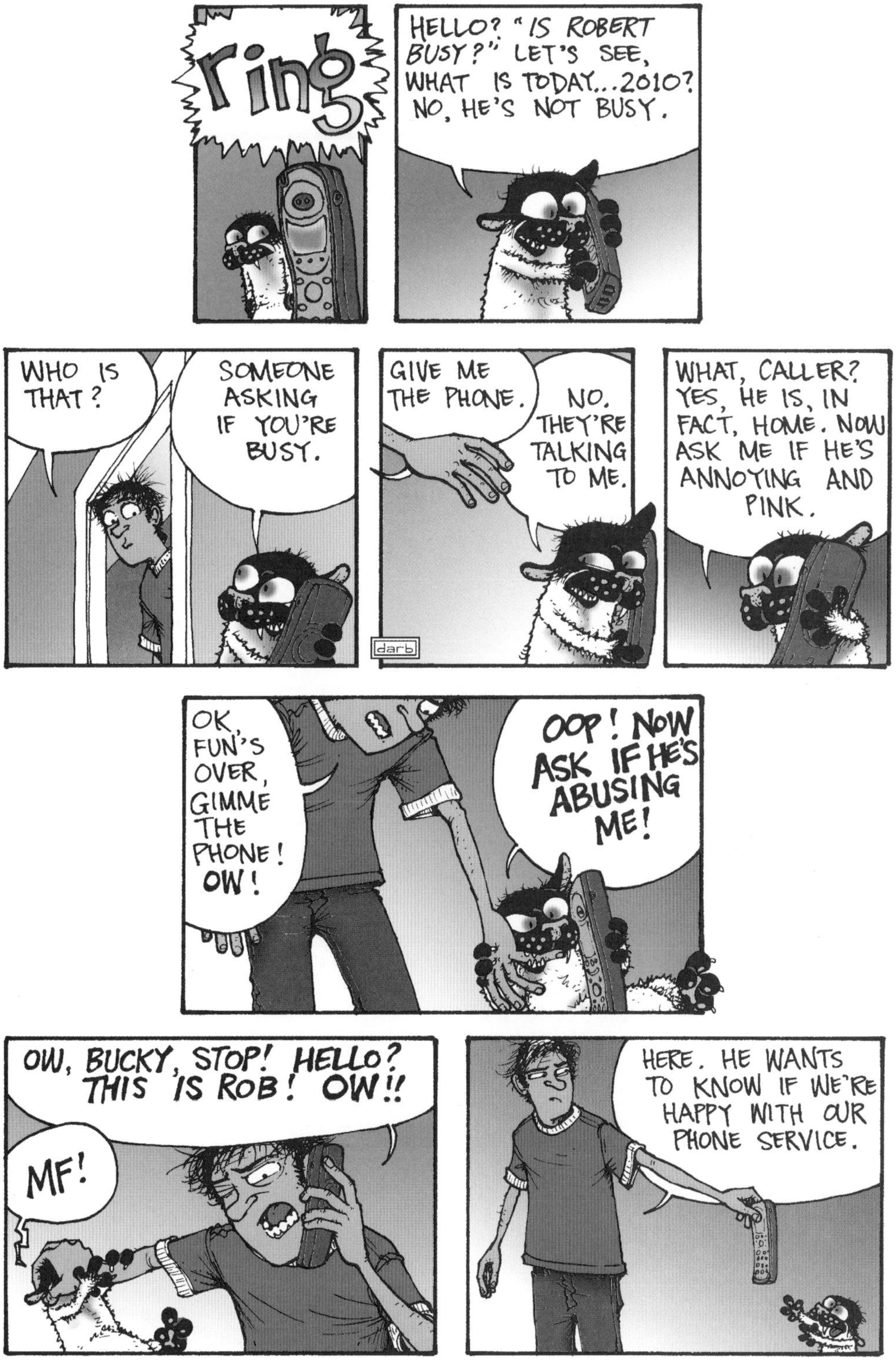
ring
HELLO? "IS ROBERT BUSY?" LET'S SEE, WHAT IS TODAY...2010? NO, HE'S NOT BUSY.
WHO IS THAT?
SOMEONE ASKING IF YOU'RE BUSY.
GIVE ME THE PHONE.
NO. THEY'RE TALKING TO ME.
darb
WHAT, CALLER? YES, HE IS, IN FACT, HOME. NOW ASK ME IF HE'S ANNOYING AND PINK.
OK, FUN'S OVER, GIMME THE PHONE! OW!
OOP! NOW ASK IF HE'S ABUSING ME!
OW, BUCKY, STOP! HELLO? THIS IS ROB! OW!!
MF!
HERE. HE WANTS TO KNOW IF WE'RE HAPPY WITH OUR PHONE SERVICE.

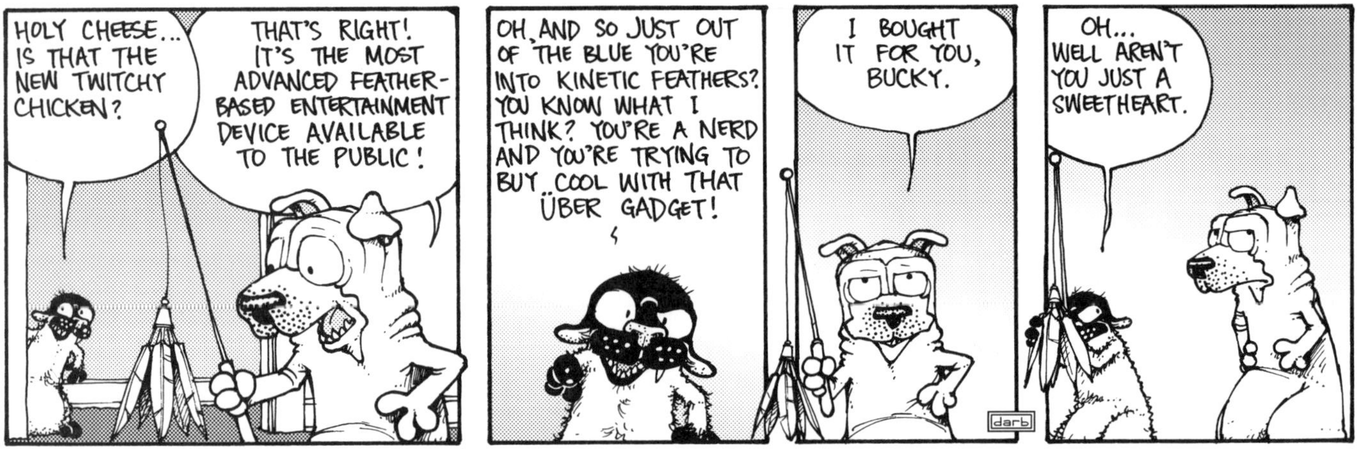
HOLY CHEESE... IS THAT THE NEW TWITCHY CHICKEN?
THAT'S RIGHT! IT'S THE MOST ADVANCED FEATHER-BASED ENTERTAINMENT DEVICE AVAILABLE TO THE PUBLIC!
OH, AND SO JUST OUT OF THE BLUE YOU'RE INTO KINETIC FEATHERS? YOU KNOW WHAT I THINK? YOU'RE A NERD AND YOU'RE TRYING TO BUY COOL WITH THAT ÜBER GADGET!
I BOUGHT IT FOR YOU, BUCKY.
darb
OH... WELL AREN'T YOU JUST A SWEETHEART.

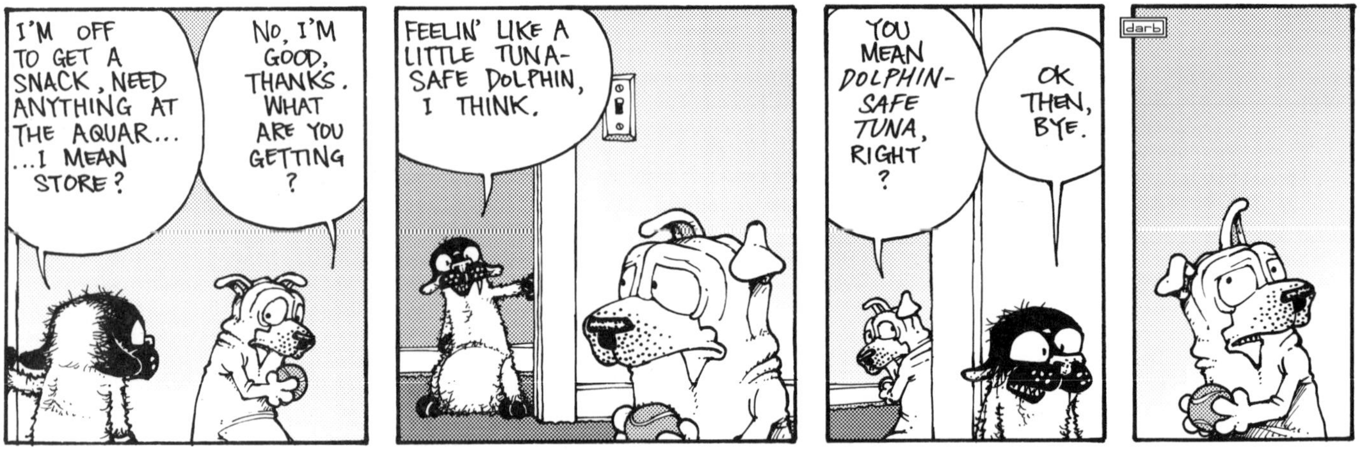
I'M OFF TO GET A SNACK, NEED ANYTHING AT THE AQUAR... ...I MEAN STORE?
NO, I'M GOOD, THANKS. WHAT ARE YOU GETTING?
FEELIN' LIKE A LITTLE TUNA-SAFE DOLPHIN, I THINK.
YOU MEAN *DOLPHIN-SAFE TUNA*, RIGHT?
OK THEN, BYE.
darb

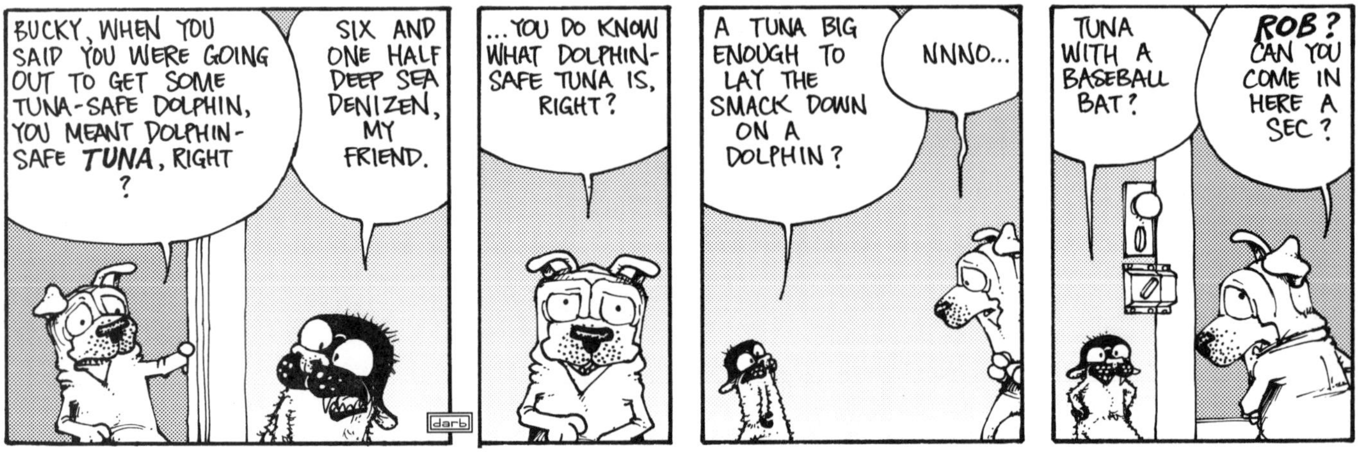
BUCKY, WHEN YOU SAID YOU WERE GOING OUT TO GET SOME TUNA-SAFE DOLPHIN, YOU MEANT DOLPHIN-SAFE **TUNA**, RIGHT?
SIX AND ONE HALF DEEP SEA DENIZEN, MY FRIEND.
darb
...YOU DO KNOW WHAT DOLPHIN-SAFE TUNA IS, RIGHT?
A TUNA BIG ENOUGH TO LAY THE SMACK DOWN ON A DOLPHIN?
NNNO...
TUNA WITH A BASEBALL BAT?
ROB? CAN YOU COME IN HERE A SEC?

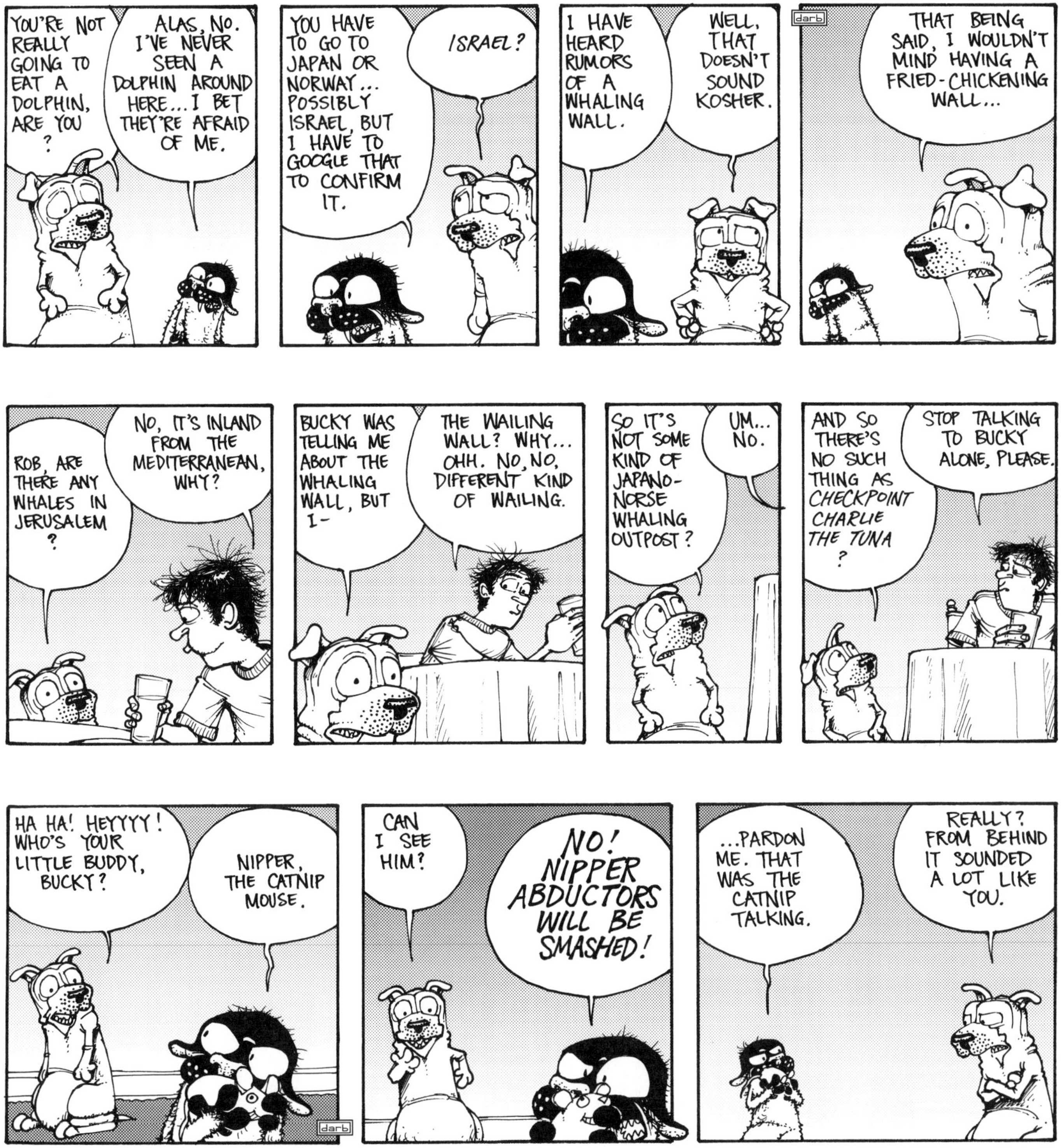

YOU'RE NOT REALLY GOING TO EAT A DOLPHIN, ARE YOU?
ALAS, NO. I'VE NEVER SEEN A DOLPHIN AROUND HERE... I BET THEY'RE AFRAID OF ME.
YOU HAVE TO GO TO JAPAN OR NORWAY... POSSIBLY ISRAEL, BUT I HAVE TO GOOGLE THAT TO CONFIRM IT.
ISRAEL?
I HAVE HEARD RUMORS OF A WHALING WALL.
WELL, THAT DOESN'T SOUND KOSHER.
darb
THAT BEING SAID, I WOULDN'T MIND HAVING A FRIED-CHICKENING WALL...
ROB, ARE THERE ANY WHALES IN JERUSALEM?
NO, IT'S INLAND FROM THE MEDITERRANEAN, WHY?
BUCKY WAS TELLING ME ABOUT THE WHALING WALL, BUT I-
THE WAILING WALL? WHY... OHH. NO, NO, DIFFERENT KIND OF WAILING.
SO IT'S NOT SOME KIND OF JAPANO-NORSE WHALING OUTPOST?
UM... NO.
AND SO THERE'S NO SUCH THING AS CHECKPOINT CHARLIE THE TUNA?
STOP TALKING TO BUCKY ALONE, PLEASE.
HA HA! HEYYYY! WHO'S YOUR LITTLE BUDDY, BUCKY?
NIPPER, THE CATNIP MOUSE.
darb
CAN I SEE HIM?
NO! NIPPER ABDUCTORS WILL BE SMASHED!
...PARDON ME. THAT WAS THE CATNIP TALKING.
REALLY? FROM BEHIND IT SOUNDED A LOT LIKE YOU.

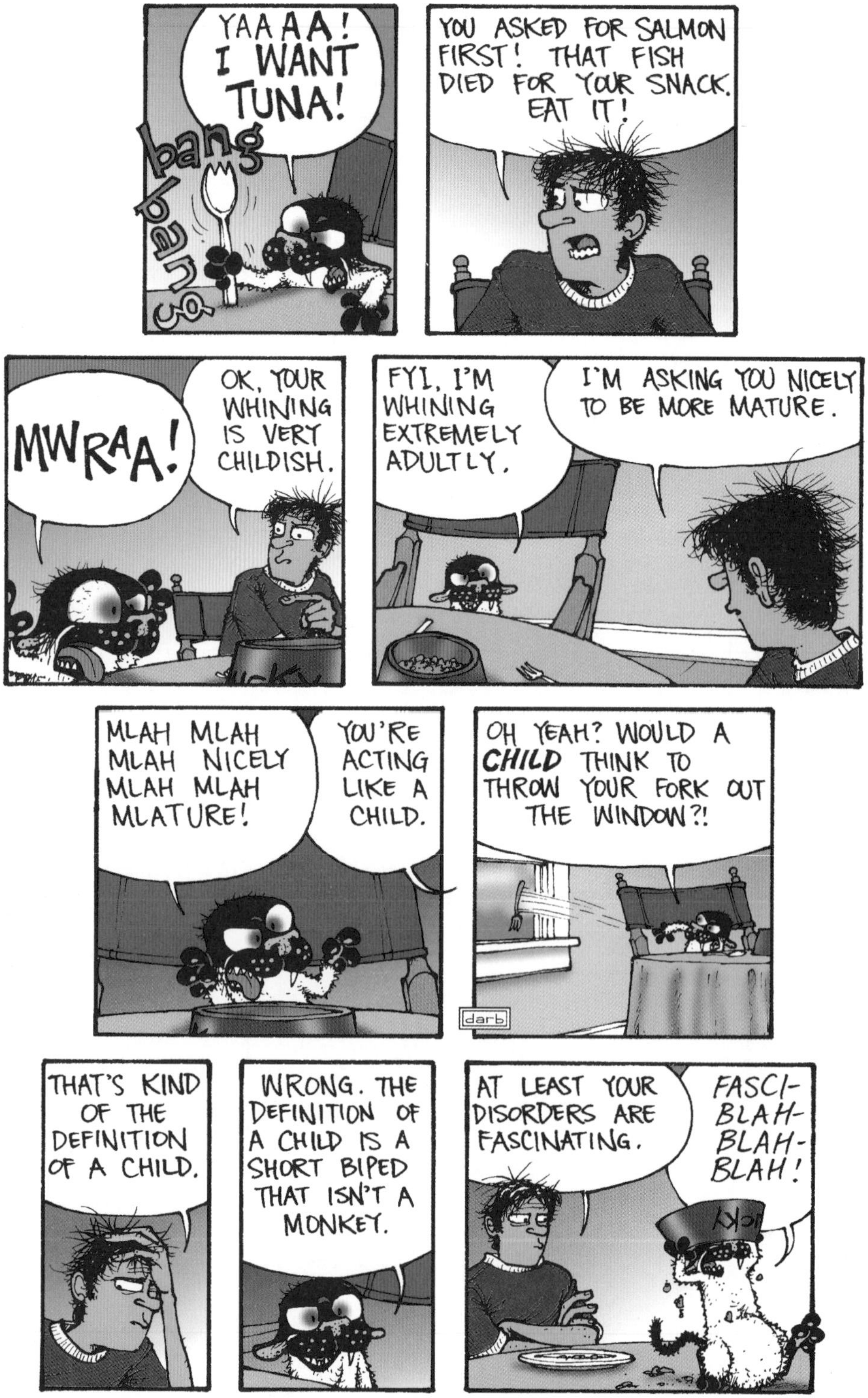
YAAAA! I WANT TUNA!
bang bang bang
YOU ASKED FOR SALMON FIRST! THAT FISH DIED FOR YOUR SNACK. EAT IT!
MWRAA!
OK, YOUR WHINING IS VERY CHILDISH.
FYI, I'M WHINING EXTREMELY ADULTLY.
I'M ASKING YOU NICELY TO BE MORE MATURE.
MLAH MLAH MLAH NICELY MLAH MLAH MLATURE!
YOU'RE ACTING LIKE A CHILD.
OH YEAH? WOULD A CHILD THINK TO THROW YOUR FORK OUT THE WINDOW?!
darb
THAT'S KIND OF THE DEFINITION OF A CHILD.
WRONG. THE DEFINITION OF A CHILD IS A SHORT BIPED THAT ISN'T A MONKEY.
AT LEAST YOUR DISORDERS ARE FASCINATING.
FASCI-BLAH-BLAH-BLAH!

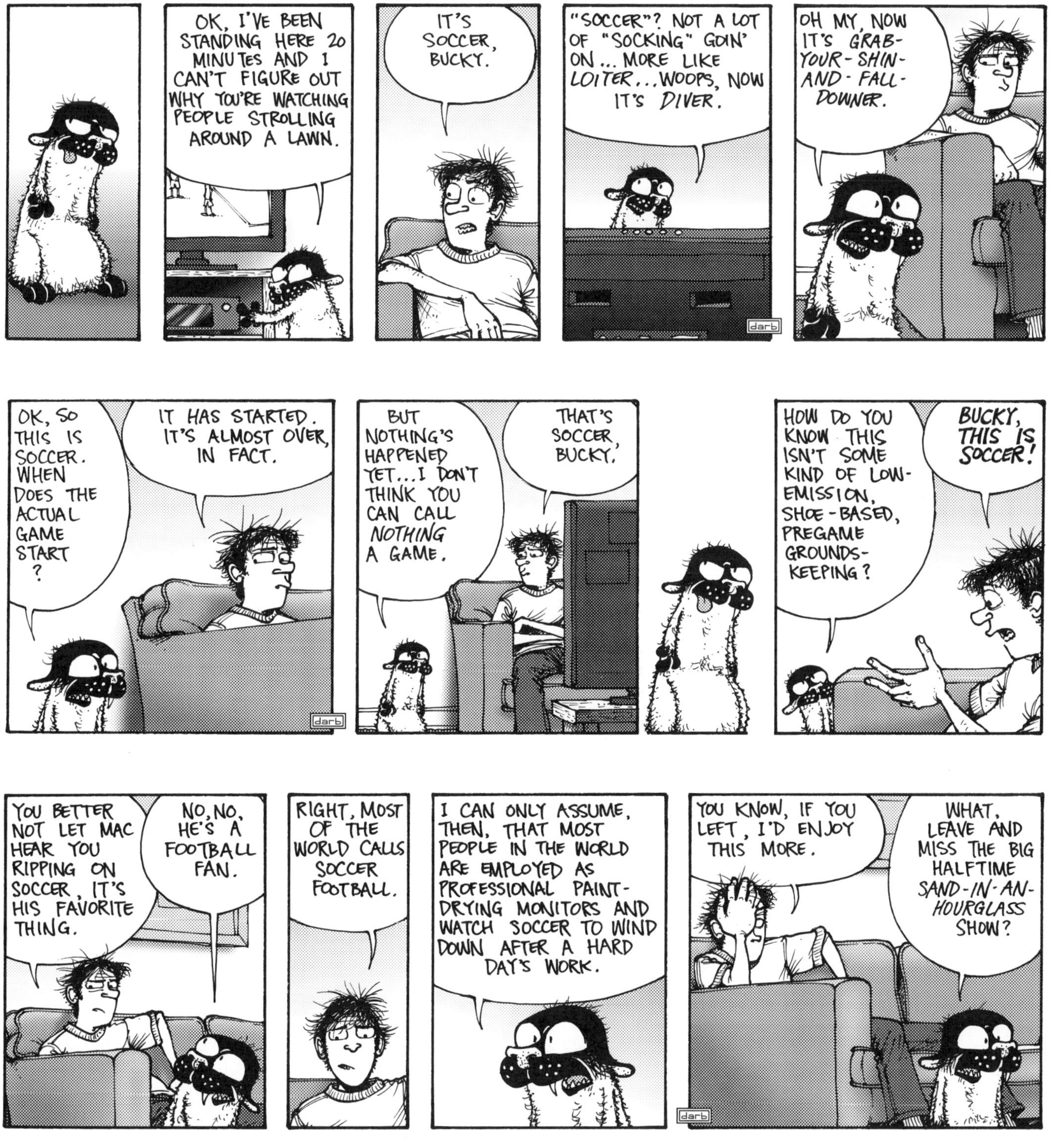
OK, I'VE BEEN STANDING HERE 20 MINUTES AND I CAN'T FIGURE OUT WHY YOU'RE WATCHING PEOPLE STROLLING AROUND A LAWN.
IT'S SOCCER, BUCKY.
"SOCCER"? NOT A LOT OF "SOCKING" GOIN' ON... MORE LIKE LOITER... WOOPS, NOW IT'S DIVER.
OH MY, NOW IT'S GRAB-YOUR-SHIN-AND-FALL-DOWNER.
darb
OK, SO THIS IS SOCCER. WHEN DOES THE ACTUAL GAME START?
IT HAS STARTED. IT'S ALMOST OVER, IN FACT.
BUT NOTHING'S HAPPENED YET... I DON'T THINK YOU CAN CALL NOTHING A GAME.
THAT'S SOCCER, BUCKY.
HOW DO YOU KNOW THIS ISN'T SOME KIND OF LOW-EMISSION, SHOE-BASED, PREGAME GROUNDS-KEEPING?
BUCKY, THIS IS SOCCER!
darb
YOU BETTER NOT LET MAC HEAR YOU RIPPING ON SOCCER, IT'S HIS FAVORITE THING.
NO, NO, HE'S A FOOTBALL FAN.
RIGHT, MOST OF THE WORLD CALLS SOCCER FOOTBALL.
I CAN ONLY ASSUME, THEN, THAT MOST PEOPLE IN THE WORLD ARE EMPLOYED AS PROFESSIONAL PAINT-DRYING MONITORS AND WATCH SOCCER TO WIND DOWN AFTER A HARD DAY'S WORK.
YOU KNOW, IF YOU LEFT, I'D ENJOY THIS MORE.
WHAT, LEAVE AND MISS THE BIG HALFTIME SAND-IN-AN-HOURGLASS SHOW?
darb

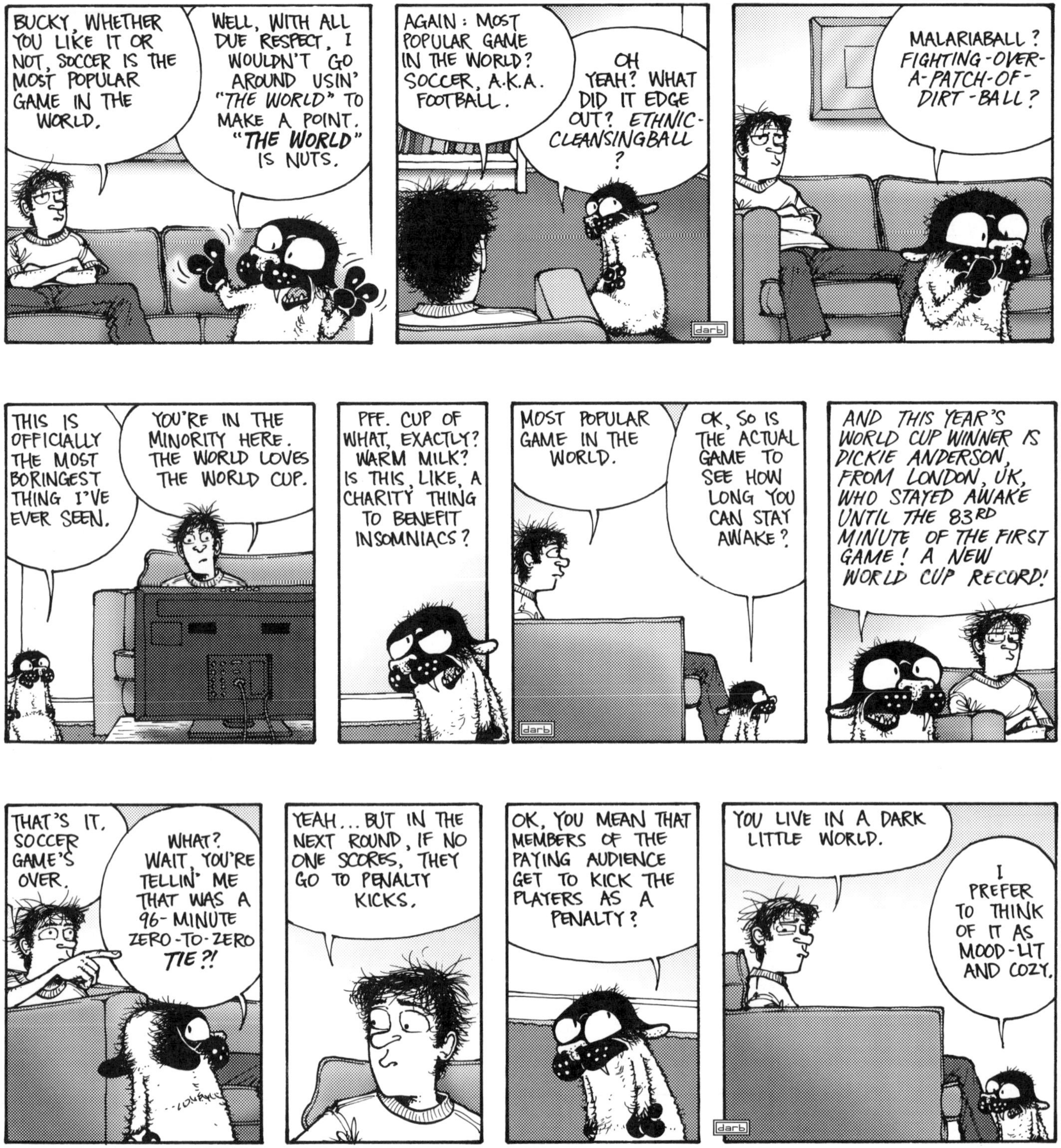
BUCKY, WHETHER YOU LIKE IT OR NOT, SOCCER IS THE MOST POPULAR GAME IN THE WORLD.
WELL, WITH ALL DUE RESPECT, I WOULDN'T GO AROUND USIN' "THE WORLD" TO MAKE A POINT. "THE WORLD" IS NUTS.
AGAIN: MOST POPULAR GAME IN THE WORLD? SOCCER, A.K.A. FOOTBALL.
OH YEAH? WHAT DID IT EDGE OUT? ETHNIC-CLEANSINGBALL?
MALARIABALL? FIGHTING-OVER-A-PATCH-OF-DIRT-BALL?
darb
THIS IS OFFICIALLY THE MOST BORINGEST THING I'VE EVER SEEN.
YOU'RE IN THE MINORITY HERE. THE WORLD LOVES THE WORLD CUP.
PFF. CUP OF WHAT, EXACTLY? WARM MILK? IS THIS, LIKE, A CHARITY THING TO BENEFIT INSOMNIACS?
MOST POPULAR GAME IN THE WORLD.
OK, SO IS THE ACTUAL GAME TO SEE HOW LONG YOU CAN STAY AWAKE?
AND THIS YEAR'S WORLD CUP WINNER IS DICKIE ANDERSON, FROM LONDON, UK, WHO STAYED AWAKE UNTIL THE 83RD MINUTE OF THE FIRST GAME! A NEW WORLD CUP RECORD!
darb
THAT'S IT. SOCCER GAME'S OVER.
WHAT? WAIT, YOU'RE TELLIN' ME THAT WAS A 96-MINUTE ZERO-TO-ZERO TIE?!
YEAH... BUT IN THE NEXT ROUND, IF NO ONE SCORES, THEY GO TO PENALTY KICKS.
OK, YOU MEAN THAT MEMBERS OF THE PAYING AUDIENCE GET TO KICK THE PLAYERS AS A PENALTY?
YOU LIVE IN A DARK LITTLE WORLD.
I PREFER TO THINK OF IT AS MOOD-LIT AND COZY.
darb

OK, SO I'VE BEEN WORKING ON WAYS TO IMPROVE SOCCER SINCE THAT, UH, PLANET MUG THINGY.

WORLD CUP.

ONE: NO GOALIES. YOU SIMPLY PUT ONE OF THE FORWARD'S GRANDMOTHERS IN A DUNKING BOOTH THAT DROPS HER INTO ICE COLD WATER WHENEVER HIS TEAM TAKES A SHOT THAT MISSES THE OPEN GOAL.

TWO: NO CLEATS. EVERYBODY WEARS THOSE LEAD-SOLED FRANKENSTEIN-TYPE BOOTS. THAT SHOULD MAKE #1 MORE INTERESTING, TOO.

THREE: ALL THE SUBSTITUTES ARE KNIFE-WIELDING MONKEYS. EXCEPT THE BACK-UP GOALIE. HE HAS A SLINGSHOT.

FOUR: ALL THE REFS ARE MMA FIGHTERS AND EVERY TIME A PLAYER FALLS DOWN AND FAKES AN INJURY, THE REF STEPS IN AND ADMINISTERS UNTO THAT PLAYER THE VERY INJURY THEY WERE FAKING.

OH MY... THAT'S A REVOLTING IDEA... I MEAN I'D *WATCH* IT, BUT...

...WHICH OF COURSE WOULD RESULT IN TEAMS LIKE, SAY, PORTUGAL FIELDING AN ALL-MONKEY SIDE AFTER EVERY ONE OF THEIR STARTERS HAD FAKED AN INJURY.

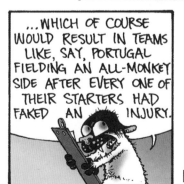

FINISHED?

YEAH, FOR NOW. I HAVE TO GOOGLE THE GENEVA CONVENTION BEFORE I REDEFINE "PENALTY SHOTS."

darb

27

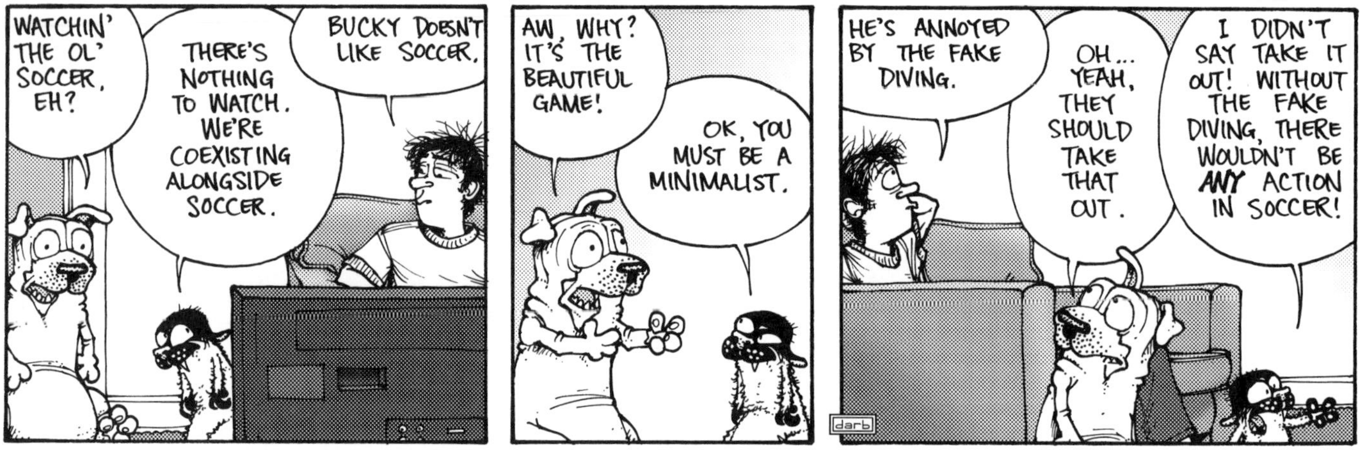
WATCHIN' THE OL' SOCCER, EH?
THERE'S NOTHING TO WATCH. WE'RE COEXISTING ALONGSIDE SOCCER.
BUCKY DOESN'T LIKE SOCCER.
AW, WHY? IT'S THE BEAUTIFUL GAME!
OK, YOU MUST BE A MINIMALIST.
HE'S ANNOYED BY THE FAKE DIVING.
OH... YEAH, THEY SHOULD TAKE THAT OUT.
I DIDN'T SAY TAKE IT OUT! WITHOUT THE FAKE DIVING, THERE WOULDN'T BE ANY ACTION IN SOCCER!
darb

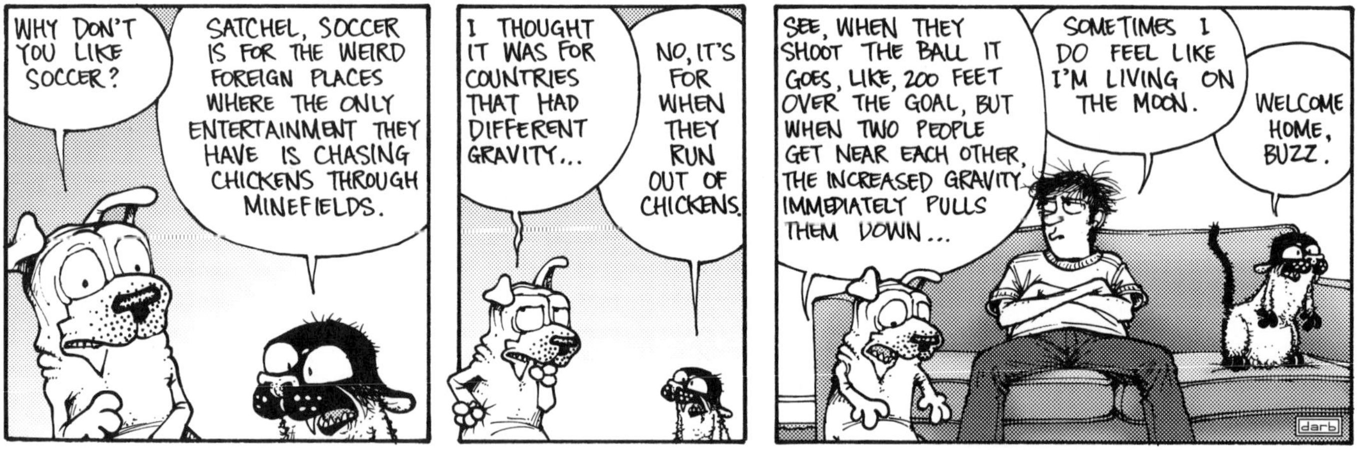
WHY DON'T YOU LIKE SOCCER?
SATCHEL, SOCCER IS FOR THE WEIRD FOREIGN PLACES WHERE THE ONLY ENTERTAINMENT THEY HAVE IS CHASING CHICKENS THROUGH MINEFIELDS.
I THOUGHT IT WAS FOR COUNTRIES THAT HAD DIFFERENT GRAVITY...
NO, IT'S FOR WHEN THEY RUN OUT OF CHICKENS.
SEE, WHEN THEY SHOOT THE BALL IT GOES, LIKE, 200 FEET OVER THE GOAL, BUT WHEN TWO PEOPLE GET NEAR EACH OTHER, THE INCREASED GRAVITY IMMEDIATELY PULLS THEM DOWN...
SOMETIMES I DO FEEL LIKE I'M LIVING ON THE MOON.
WELCOME HOME, BUZZ.
darb

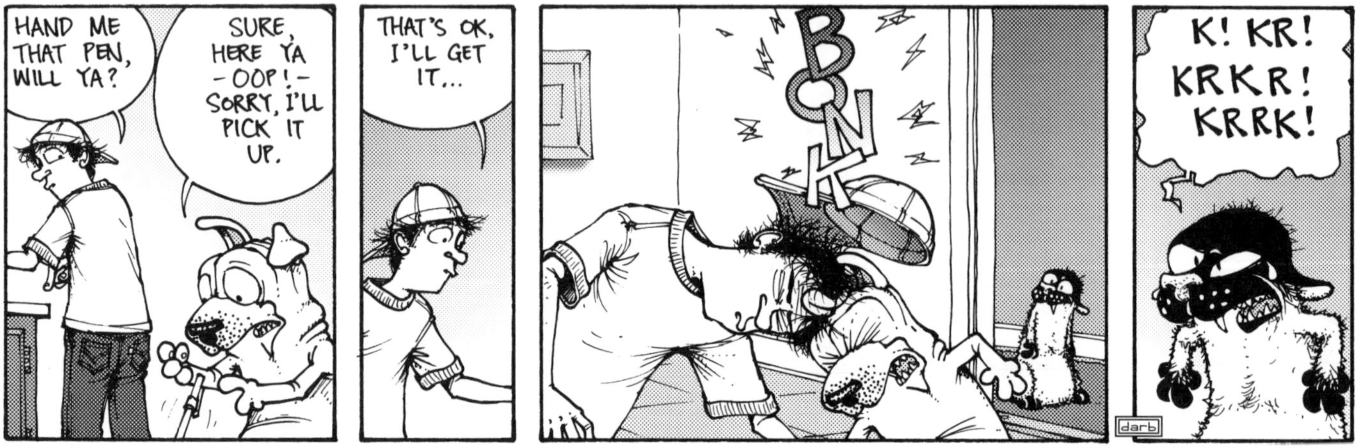
HAND ME THAT PEN, WILL YA?
SURE, HERE YA -OOP!- SORRY, I'LL PICK IT UP.
THAT'S OK, I'LL GET IT...
BONK
K! KR! KRKR! KRRK!
darb

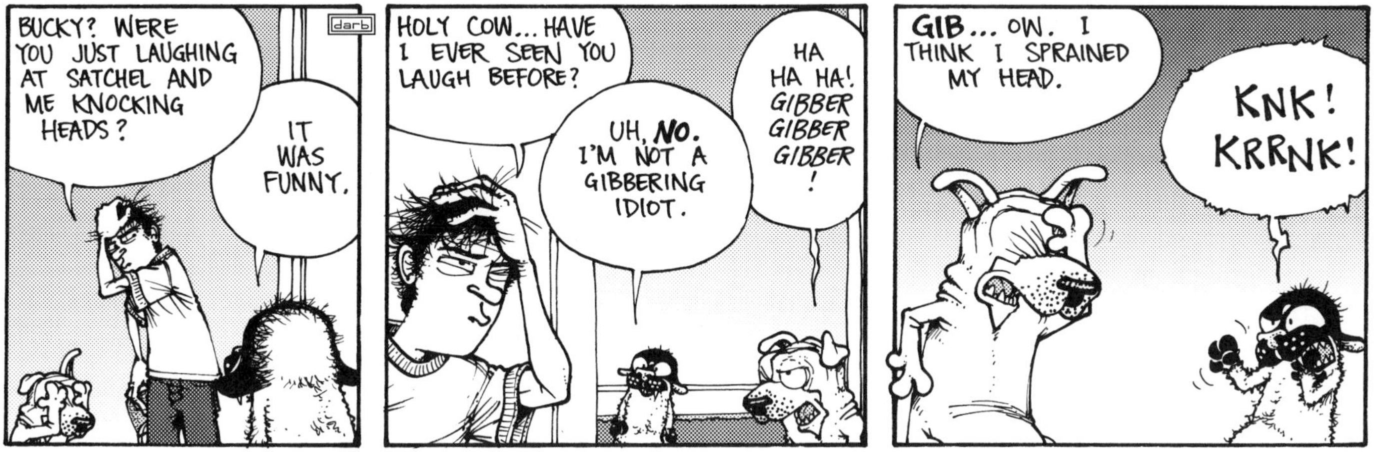
BUCKY? WERE YOU JUST LAUGHING AT SATCHEL AND ME KNOCKING HEADS?
IT WAS FUNNY.
HOLY COW... HAVE I EVER SEEN YOU LAUGH BEFORE?
UH, **NO.** I'M NOT A GIBBERING IDIOT.
HA HA HA! *GIBBER GIBBER GIBBER*!
GIB... OW. I THINK I SPRAINED MY HEAD.
KNK! KRRNK!

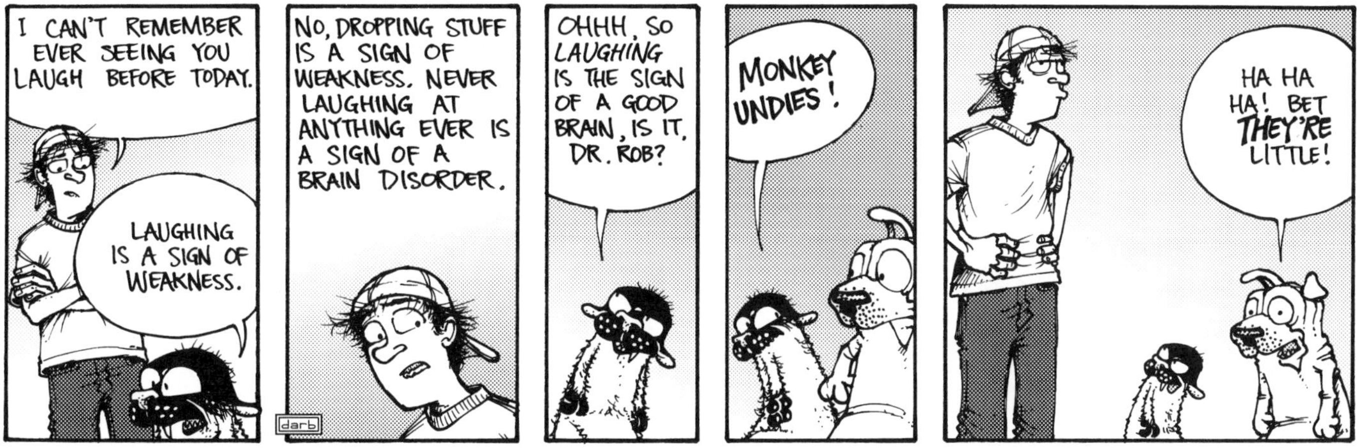
I CAN'T REMEMBER EVER SEEING YOU LAUGH BEFORE TODAY.
LAUGHING IS A SIGN OF WEAKNESS.
NO, DROPPING STUFF IS A SIGN OF WEAKNESS. NEVER LAUGHING AT ANYTHING EVER IS A SIGN OF A BRAIN DISORDER.
OHHH, SO *LAUGHING* IS THE SIGN OF A GOOD BRAIN, IS IT, DR. ROB?
MONKEY UNDIES!
HA HA HA! BET ***THEY'RE*** LITTLE!

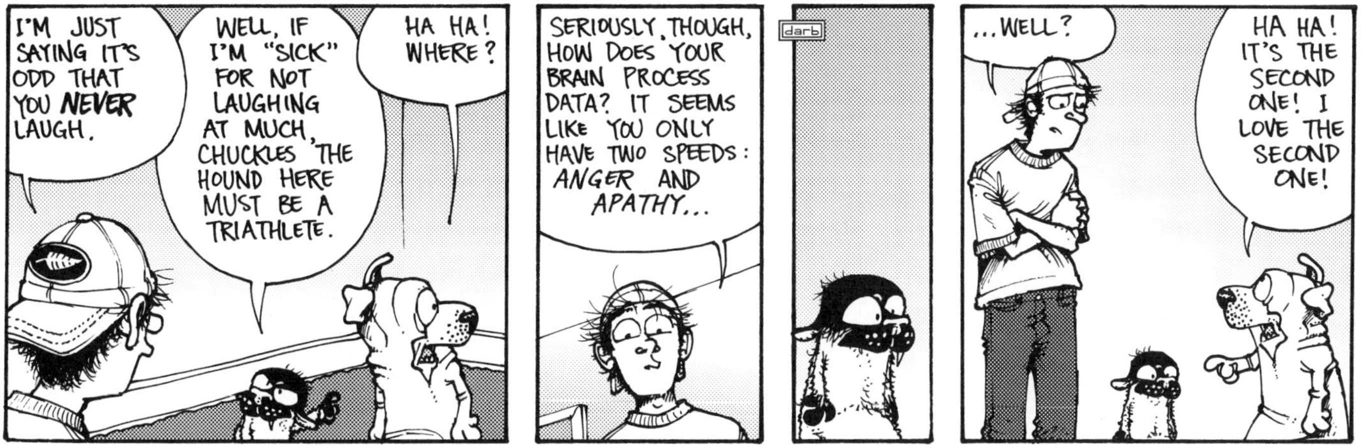
I'M JUST SAYING IT'S ODD THAT YOU ***NEVER*** LAUGH.
WELL, IF I'M "SICK" FOR NOT LAUGHING AT MUCH, CHUCKLES THE HOUND HERE MUST BE A TRIATHLETE.
HA HA! WHERE?
SERIOUSLY, THOUGH, HOW DOES YOUR BRAIN PROCESS DATA? IT SEEMS LIKE YOU ONLY HAVE TWO SPEEDS: *ANGER* AND *APATHY*...
...WELL?
HA HA! IT'S THE SECOND ONE! I LOVE THE SECOND ONE!

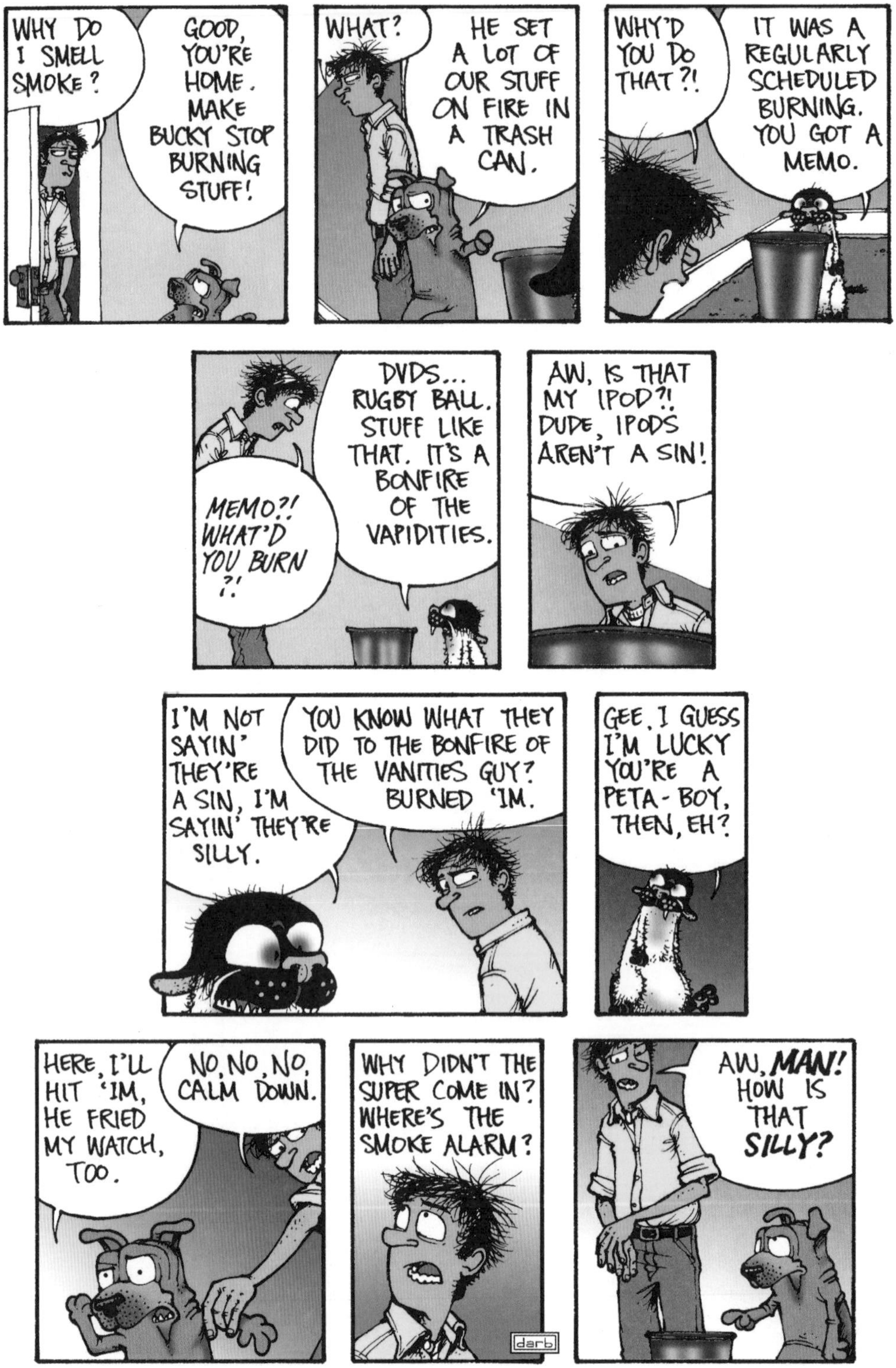
WHY DO I SMELL SMOKE?
GOOD, YOU'RE HOME. MAKE BUCKY STOP BURNING STUFF!
WHAT?
HE SET A LOT OF OUR STUFF ON FIRE IN A TRASH CAN.
WHY'D YOU DO THAT?!
IT WAS A REGULARLY SCHEDULED BURNING. YOU GOT A MEMO.
MEMO?! WHAT'D YOU BURN?!
DVDS... RUGBY BALL. STUFF LIKE THAT. IT'S A BONFIRE OF THE VAPIDITIES.
AW, IS THAT MY IPOD?! DUDE, IPODS AREN'T A SIN!
I'M NOT SAYIN' THEY'RE A SIN, I'M SAYIN' THEY'RE SILLY.
YOU KNOW WHAT THEY DID TO THE BONFIRE OF THE VANITIES GUY? BURNED 'IM.
GEE, I GUESS I'M LUCKY YOU'RE A PETA-BOY, THEN, EH?
HERE, I'LL HIT 'IM, HE FRIED MY WATCH, TOO.
NO, NO, NO, CALM DOWN.
WHY DIDN'T THE SUPER COME IN? WHERE'S THE SMOKE ALARM?
darb
AW, MAN! HOW IS THAT SILLY?

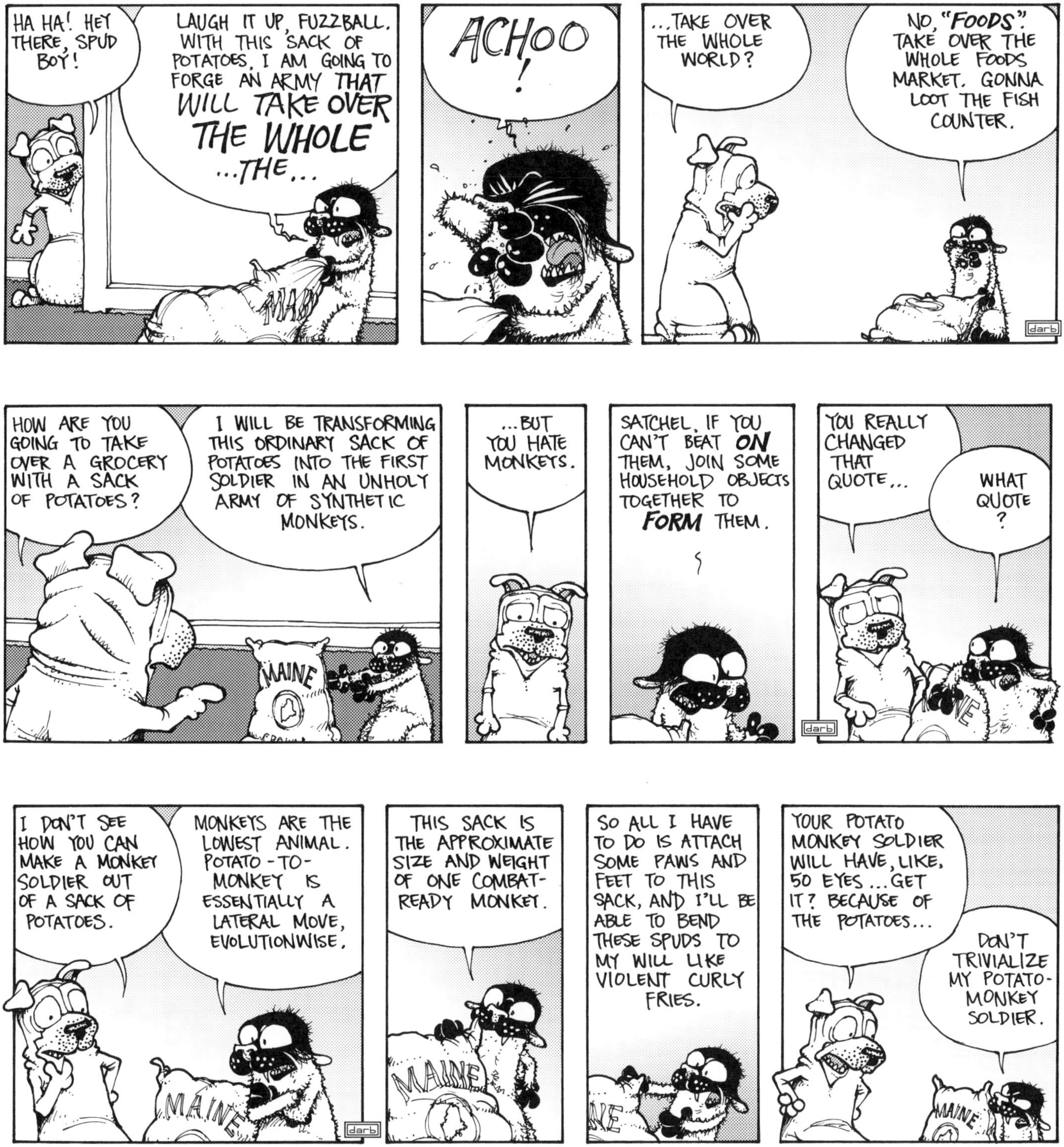
HA HA! HEY THERE, SPUD BOY!
LAUGH IT UP, FUZZBALL. WITH THIS SACK OF POTATOES, I AM GOING TO FORGE AN ARMY THAT WILL TAKE OVER THE WHOLE ...THE...
ACHOO!
...TAKE OVER THE WHOLE WORLD?
NO, "FOODS". TAKE OVER THE WHOLE FOODS MARKET. GONNA LOOT THE FISH COUNTER.
darb
HOW ARE YOU GOING TO TAKE OVER A GROCERY WITH A SACK OF POTATOES?
I WILL BE TRANSFORMING THIS ORDINARY SACK OF POTATOES INTO THE FIRST SOLDIER IN AN UNHOLY ARMY OF SYNTHETIC MONKEYS.
MAINE
...BUT YOU HATE MONKEYS.
SATCHEL, IF YOU CAN'T BEAT ON THEM, JOIN SOME HOUSEHOLD OBJECTS TOGETHER TO FORM THEM.
darb
YOU REALLY CHANGED THAT QUOTE...
WHAT QUOTE?
I DON'T SEE HOW YOU CAN MAKE A MONKEY SOLDIER OUT OF A SACK OF POTATOES.
MONKEYS ARE THE LOWEST ANIMAL. POTATO-TO-MONKEY IS ESSENTIALLY A LATERAL MOVE, EVOLUTIONWISE.
MAINE
darb
THIS SACK IS THE APPROXIMATE SIZE AND WEIGHT OF ONE COMBAT-READY MONKEY.
MAINE
SO ALL I HAVE TO DO IS ATTACH SOME PAWS AND FEET TO THIS SACK, AND I'LL BE ABLE TO BEND THESE SPUDS TO MY WILL LIKE VIOLENT CURLY FRIES.
YOUR POTATO MONKEY SOLDIER WILL HAVE, LIKE, 50 EYES...GET IT? BECAUSE OF THE POTATOES...
DON'T TRIVIALIZE MY POTATO-MONKEY SOLDIER.
MAINE

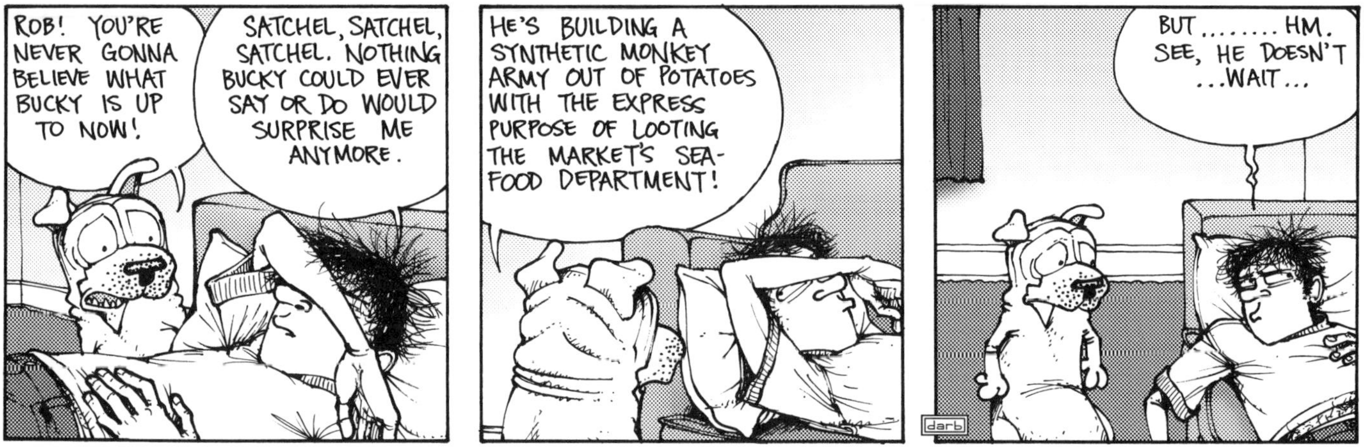
ROB! YOU'RE NEVER GONNA BELIEVE WHAT BUCKY IS UP TO NOW!
SATCHEL, SATCHEL, SATCHEL. NOTHING BUCKY COULD EVER SAY OR DO WOULD SURPRISE ME ANYMORE.
HE'S BUILDING A SYNTHETIC MONKEY ARMY OUT OF POTATOES WITH THE EXPRESS PURPOSE OF LOOTING THE MARKET'S SEA-FOOD DEPARTMENT!
BUT........HM. SEE, HE DOESN'T ...WAIT...
darb

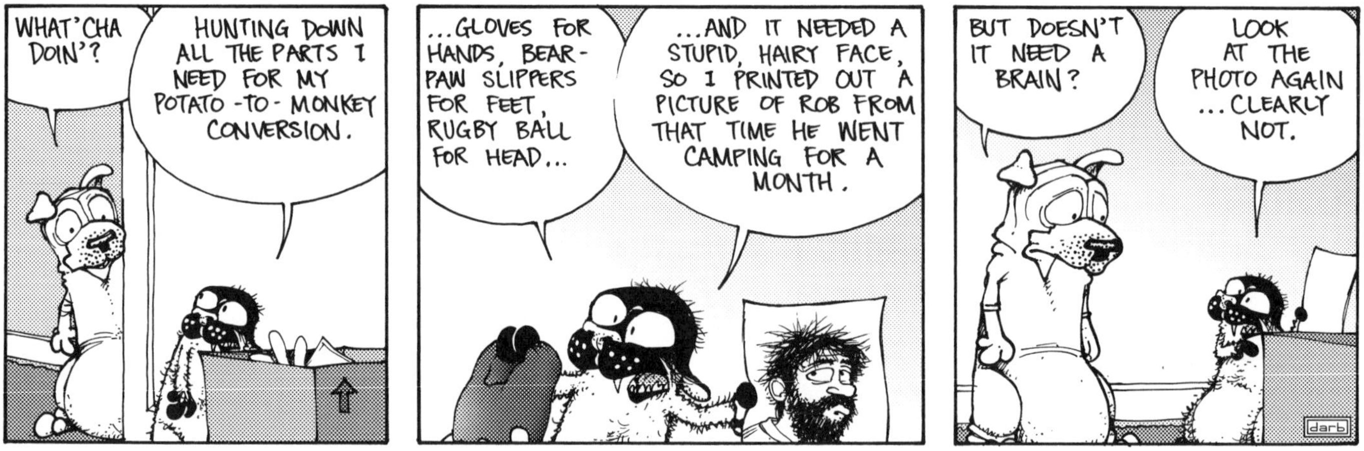
WHAT'CHA DOIN'?
HUNTING DOWN ALL THE PARTS I NEED FOR MY POTATO-TO-MONKEY CONVERSION.
...GLOVES FOR HANDS, BEAR-PAW SLIPPERS FOR FEET, RUGBY BALL FOR HEAD...
...AND IT NEEDED A STUPID, HAIRY FACE, SO I PRINTED OUT A PICTURE OF ROB FROM THAT TIME HE WENT CAMPING FOR A MONTH.
BUT DOESN'T IT NEED A BRAIN?
LOOK AT THE PHOTO AGAIN ...CLEARLY NOT.
darb

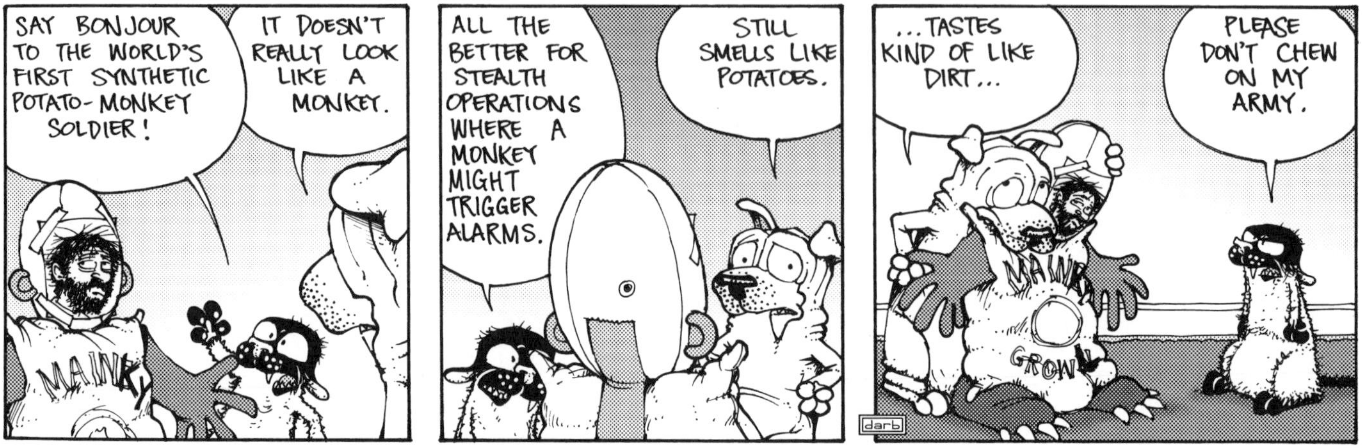
SAY BONJOUR TO THE WORLD'S FIRST SYNTHETIC POTATO-MONKEY SOLDIER!
IT DOESN'T REALLY LOOK LIKE A MONKEY.
MAINKY
ALL THE BETTER FOR STEALTH OPERATIONS WHERE A MONKEY MIGHT TRIGGER ALARMS.
STILL SMELLS LIKE POTATOES.
darb
...TASTES KIND OF LIKE DIRT...
PLEASE DON'T CHEW ON MY ARMY.

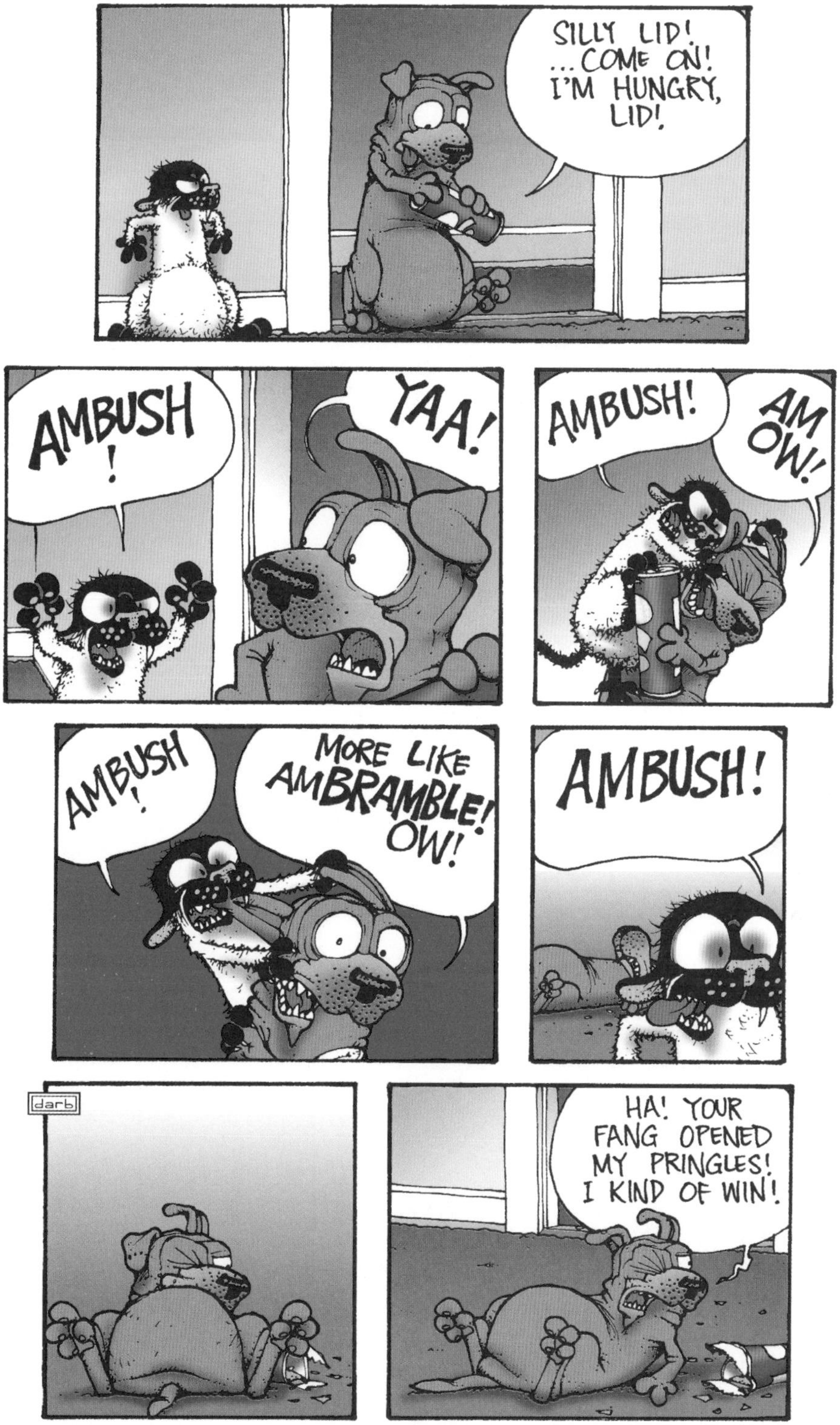
SILLY LID! ...COME ON! I'M HUNGRY, LID!
AMBUSH !
YAA!
AMBUSH!
AM OW!
AMBUSH !
MORE LIKE AMBRAMBLE! OW!
AMBUSH!
darb
HA! YOUR FANG OPENED MY PRINGLES! I KIND OF WIN!

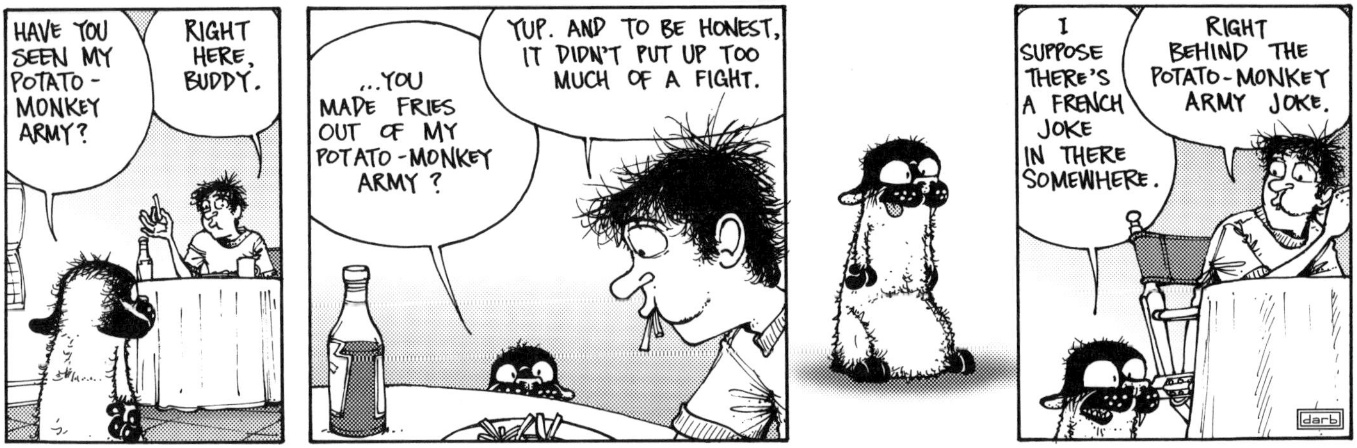
HAVE YOU SEEN MY POTATO-MONKEY ARMY?
RIGHT HERE, BUDDY.
...YOU MADE FRIES OUT OF MY POTATO-MONKEY ARMY?
YUP. AND TO BE HONEST, IT DIDN'T PUT UP TOO MUCH OF A FIGHT.
I SUPPOSE THERE'S A FRENCH JOKE IN THERE SOMEWHERE.
RIGHT BEHIND THE POTATO-MONKEY ARMY JOKE.
darb

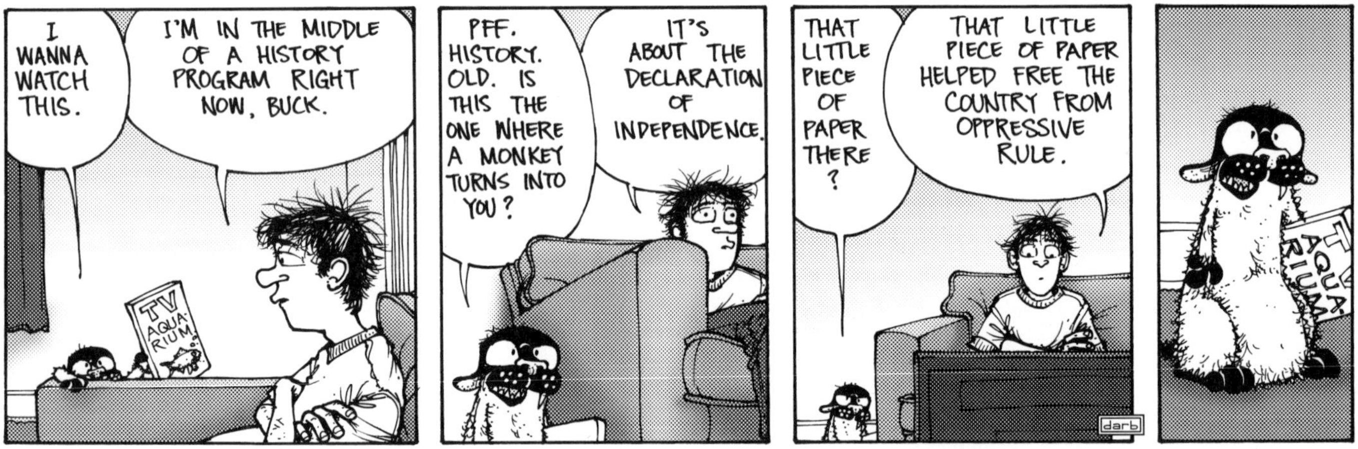
I WANNA WATCH THIS.
I'M IN THE MIDDLE OF A HISTORY PROGRAM RIGHT NOW, BUCK.
TV AQUARIUM
PFF. HISTORY. OLD. IS THIS THE ONE WHERE A MONKEY TURNS INTO YOU?
IT'S ABOUT THE DECLARATION OF INDEPENDENCE.
THAT LITTLE PIECE OF PAPER THERE?
THAT LITTLE PIECE OF PAPER HELPED FREE THE COUNTRY FROM OPPRESSIVE RULE.
darb
TV AQUARIUM

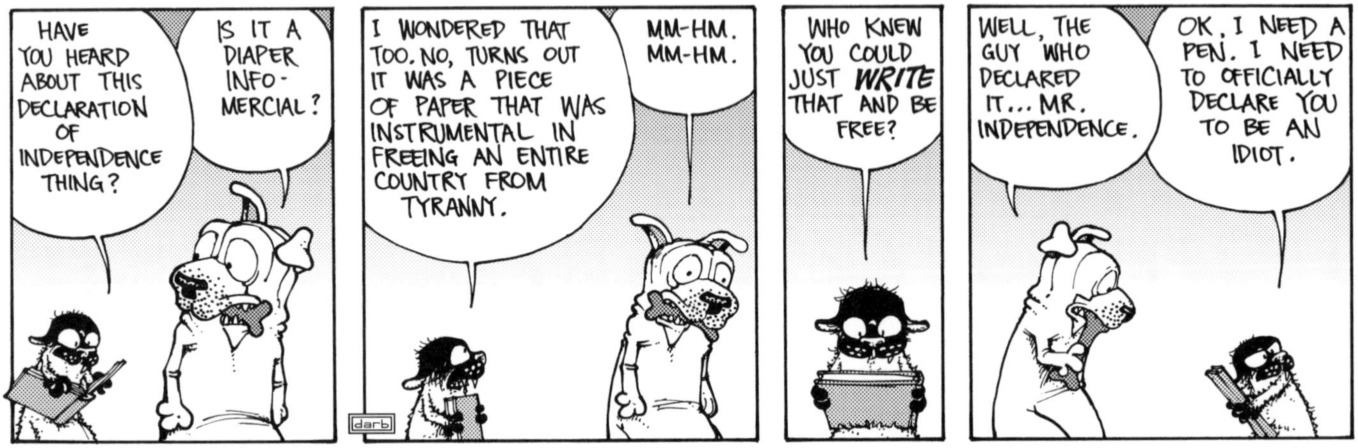
HAVE YOU HEARD ABOUT THIS DECLARATION OF INDEPENDENCE THING?
IS IT A DIAPER INFO-MERCIAL?
darb
I WONDERED THAT TOO. NO, TURNS OUT IT WAS A PIECE OF PAPER THAT WAS INSTRUMENTAL IN FREEING AN ENTIRE COUNTRY FROM TYRANNY.
MM-HM. MM-HM.
WHO KNEW YOU COULD JUST WRITE THAT AND BE FREE?
WELL, THE GUY WHO DECLARED IT... MR. INDEPENDENCE.
OK, I NEED A PEN. I NEED TO OFFICIALLY DECLARE YOU TO BE AN IDIOT.

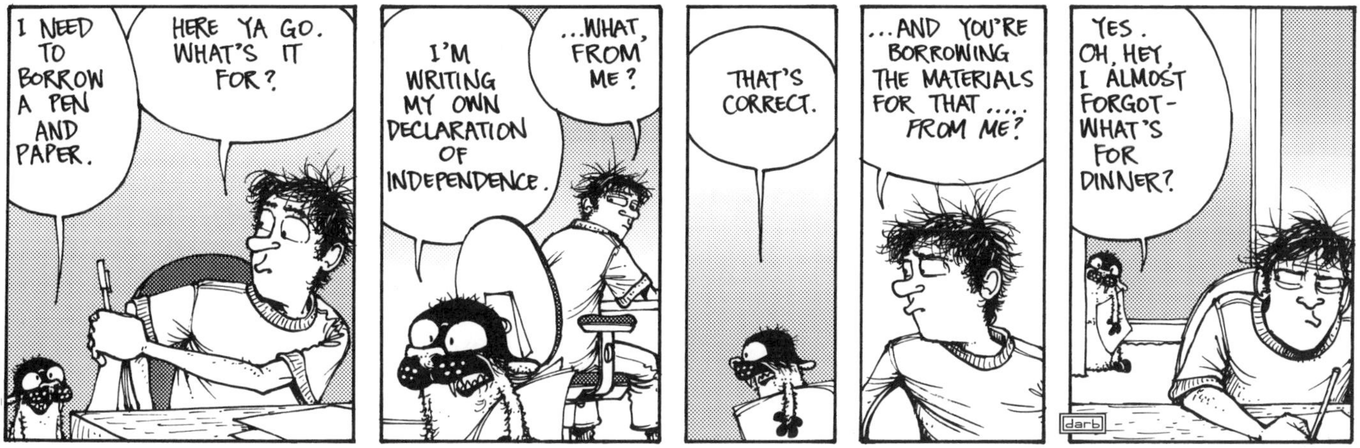
I NEED TO BORROW A PEN AND PAPER.
HERE YA GO. WHAT'S IT FOR?
I'M WRITING MY OWN DECLARATION OF INDEPENDENCE.
...WHAT, FROM ME?
THAT'S CORRECT.
...AND YOU'RE BORROWING THE MATERIALS FOR THAT..... FROM ME?
YES. OH, HEY, I ALMOST FORGOT- WHAT'S FOR DINNER?
darb

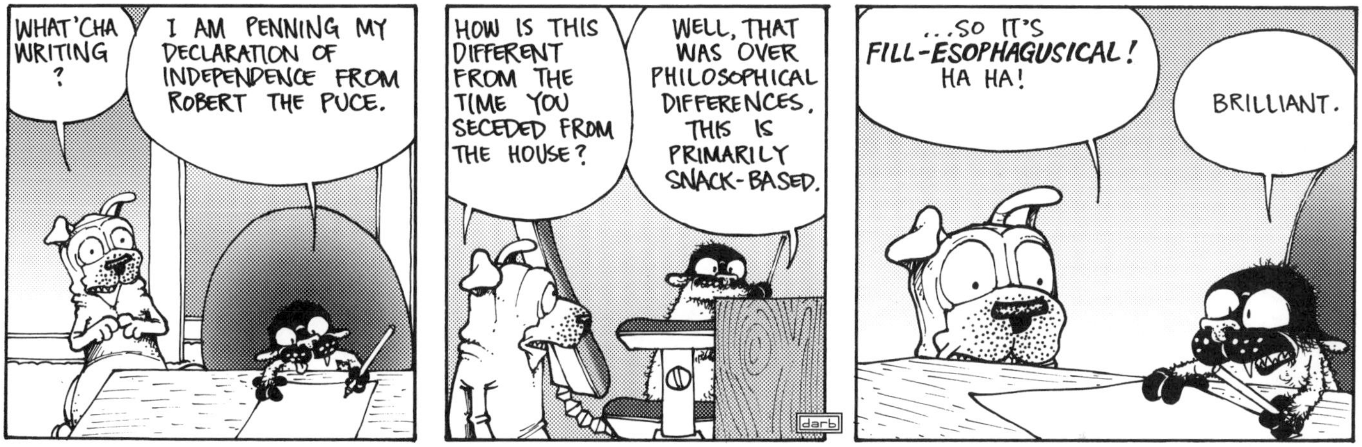
WHAT'CHA WRITING?
I AM PENNING MY DECLARATION OF INDEPENDENCE FROM ROBERT THE PUCE.
HOW IS THIS DIFFERENT FROM THE TIME YOU SECEDED FROM THE HOUSE?
WELL, THAT WAS OVER PHILOSOPHICAL DIFFERENCES. THIS IS PRIMARILY SNACK-BASED.
darb
...SO IT'S FILL-ESOPHAGUSICAL! HA HA!
BRILLIANT.

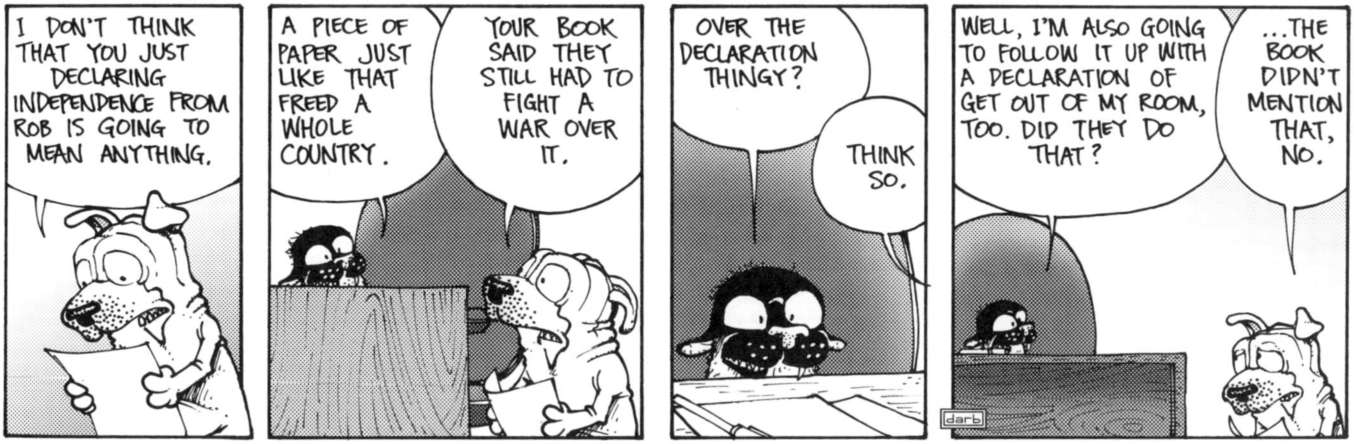
I DON'T THINK THAT YOU JUST DECLARING INDEPENDENCE FROM ROB IS GOING TO MEAN ANYTHING.
A PIECE OF PAPER JUST LIKE THAT FREED A WHOLE COUNTRY.
YOUR BOOK SAID THEY STILL HAD TO FIGHT A WAR OVER IT.
OVER THE DECLARATION THINGY?
THINK SO.
WELL, I'M ALSO GOING TO FOLLOW IT UP WITH A DECLARATION OF GET OUT OF MY ROOM, TOO. DID THEY DO THAT?
...THE BOOK DIDN'T MENTION THAT, NO.
darb

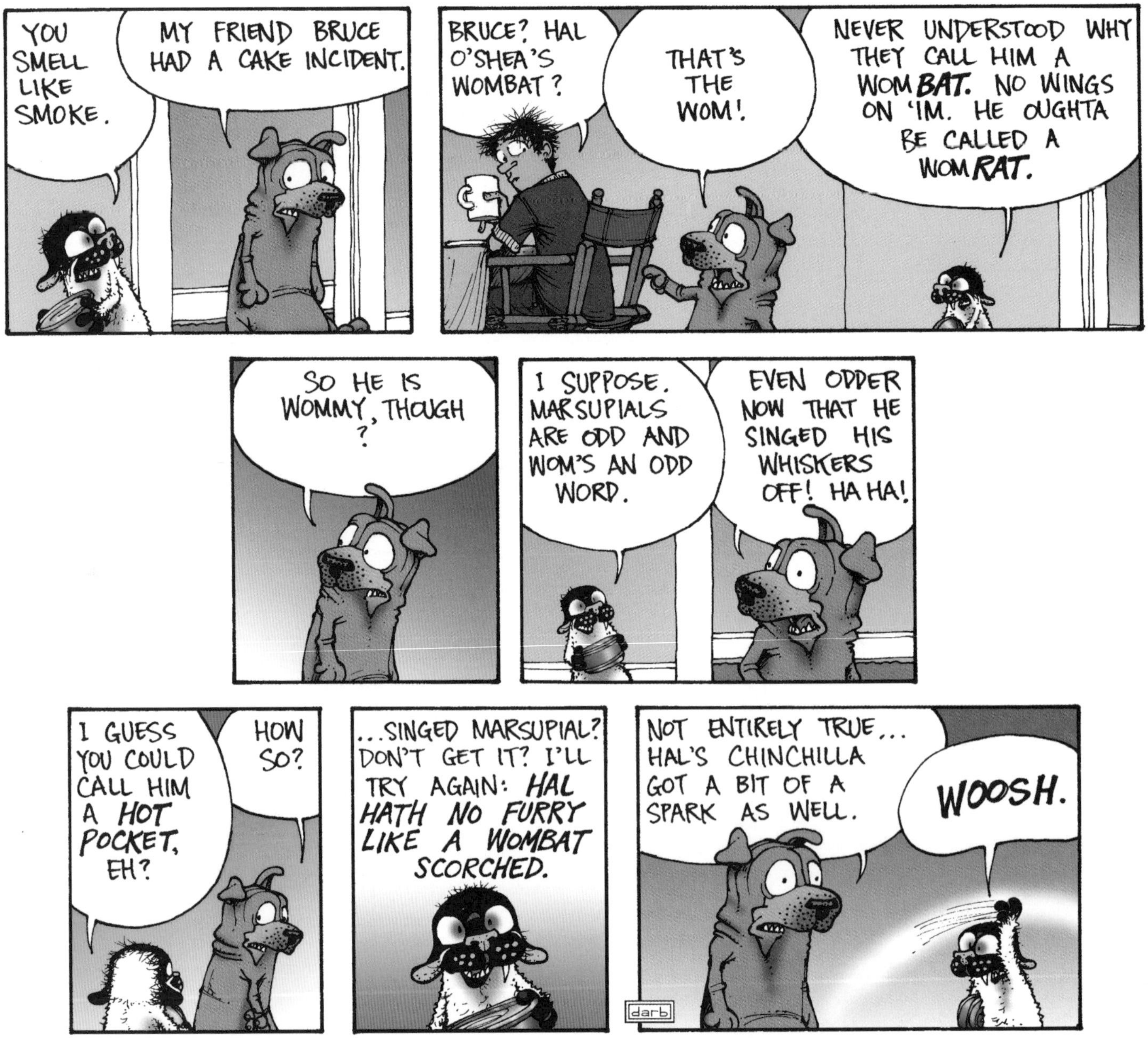
YOU SMELL LIKE SMOKE.
MY FRIEND BRUCE HAD A CAKE INCIDENT.
BRUCE? HAL O'SHEA'S WOMBAT?
THAT'S THE WOM!
NEVER UNDERSTOOD WHY THEY CALL HIM A WOMBAT. NO WINGS ON 'IM. HE OUGHTA BE CALLED A WOMRAT.
SO HE IS WOMMY, THOUGH?
I SUPPOSE. MARSUPIALS ARE ODD AND WOM'S AN ODD WORD.
EVEN ODDER NOW THAT HE SINGED HIS WHISKERS OFF! HA HA!
I GUESS YOU COULD CALL HIM A HOT POCKET, EH?
HOW SO?
...SINGED MARSUPIAL? DON'T GET IT? I'LL TRY AGAIN: HAL HATH NO FURRY LIKE A WOMBAT SCORCHED.
NOT ENTIRELY TRUE... HAL'S CHINCHILLA GOT A BIT OF A SPARK AS WELL.
WOOSH.
darb

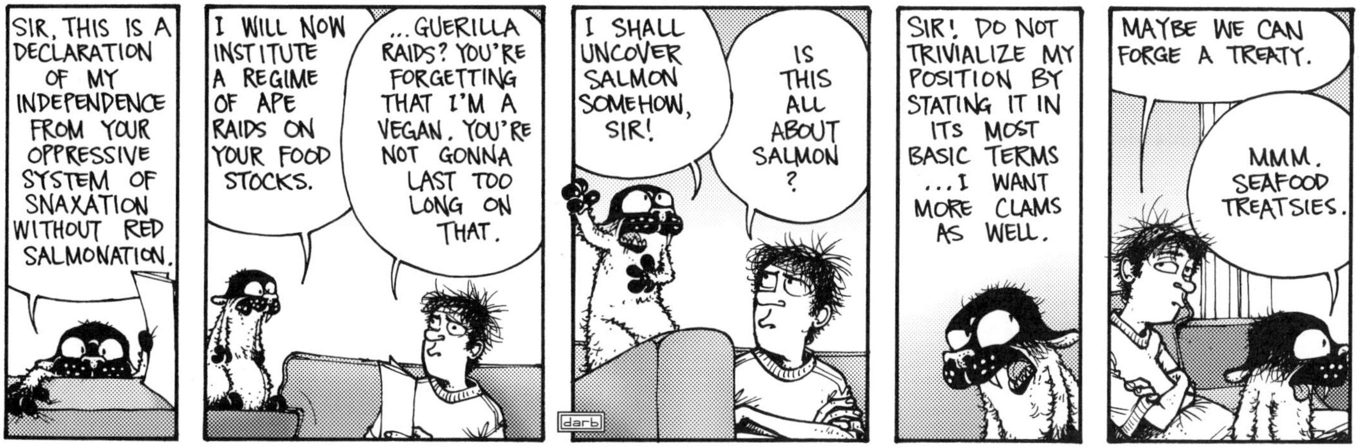
SIR, THIS IS A DECLARATION OF MY INDEPENDENCE FROM YOUR OPPRESSIVE SYSTEM OF SNAXATION WITHOUT RED SALMONATION.
I WILL NOW INSTITUTE A REGIME OF APE RAIDS ON YOUR FOOD STOCKS.
...GUERILLA RAIDS? YOU'RE FORGETTING THAT I'M A VEGAN. YOU'RE NOT GONNA LAST TOO LONG ON THAT.
I SHALL UNCOVER SALMON SOMEHOW, SIR!
IS THIS ALL ABOUT SALMON?
darb
SIR! DO NOT TRIVIALIZE MY POSITION BY STATING IT IN ITS MOST BASIC TERMS ...I WANT MORE CLAMS AS WELL.
MAYBE WE CAN FORGE A TREATY.
MMM. SEAFOOD TREATSIES.

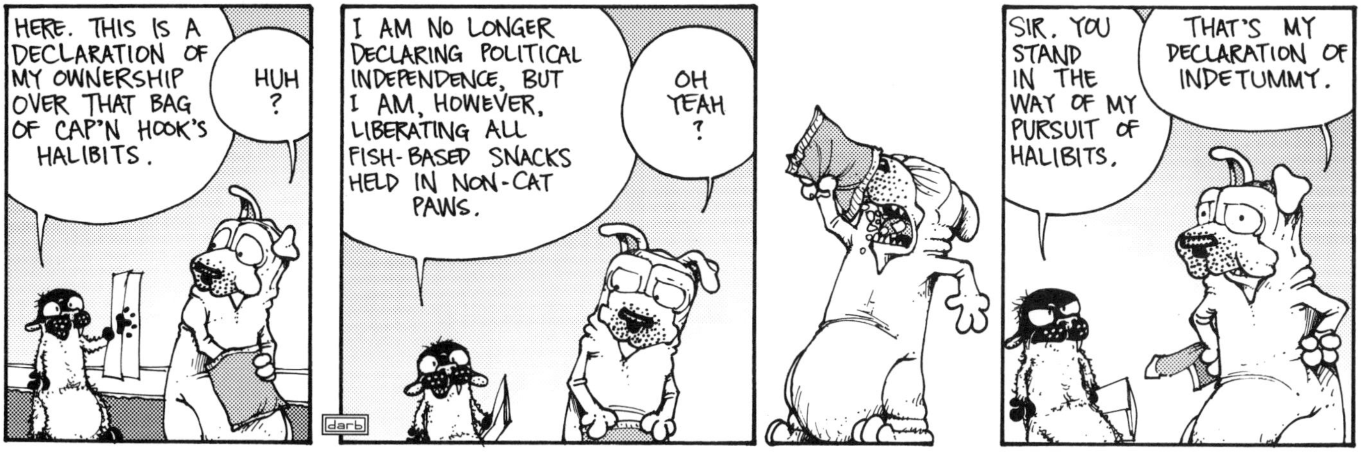
HERE. THIS IS A DECLARATION OF MY OWNERSHIP OVER THAT BAG OF CAP'N HOOK'S HALIBITS.
HUH?
darb
I AM NO LONGER DECLARING POLITICAL INDEPENDENCE, BUT I AM, HOWEVER, LIBERATING ALL FISH-BASED SNACKS HELD IN NON-CAT PAWS.
OH YEAH?
SIR. YOU STAND IN THE WAY OF MY PURSUIT OF HALIBITS.
THAT'S MY DECLARATION OF INDETUMMY.

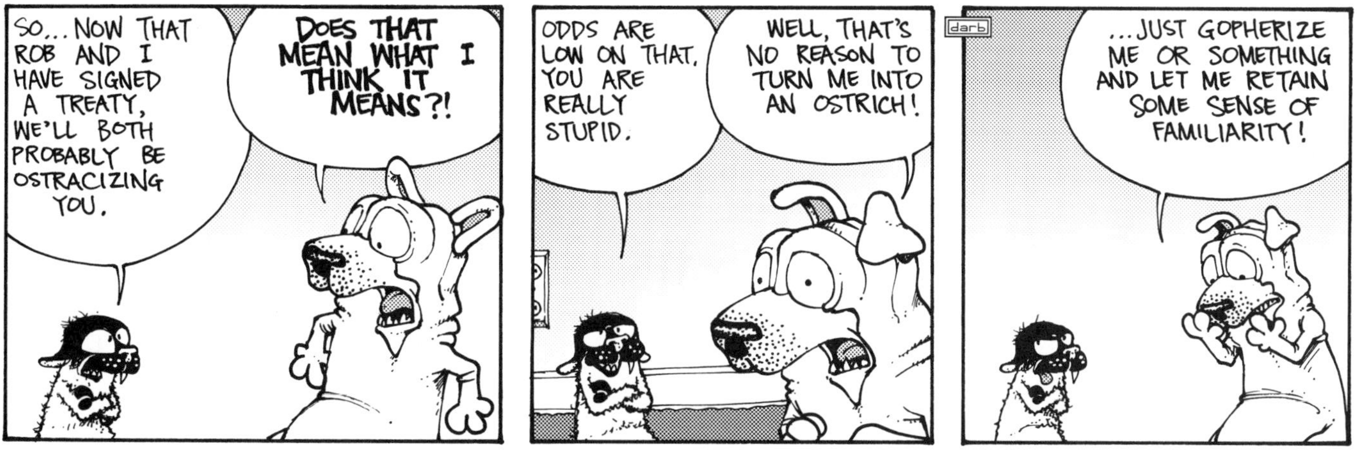
SO... NOW THAT ROB AND I HAVE SIGNED A TREATY, WE'LL BOTH PROBABLY BE OSTRACIZING YOU.
DOES THAT MEAN WHAT I THINK IT MEANS?!
ODDS ARE LOW ON THAT. YOU ARE REALLY STUPID.
WELL, THAT'S NO REASON TO TURN ME INTO AN OSTRICH!
darb
...JUST GOPHERIZE ME OR SOMETHING AND LET ME RETAIN SOME SENSE OF FAMILIARITY!

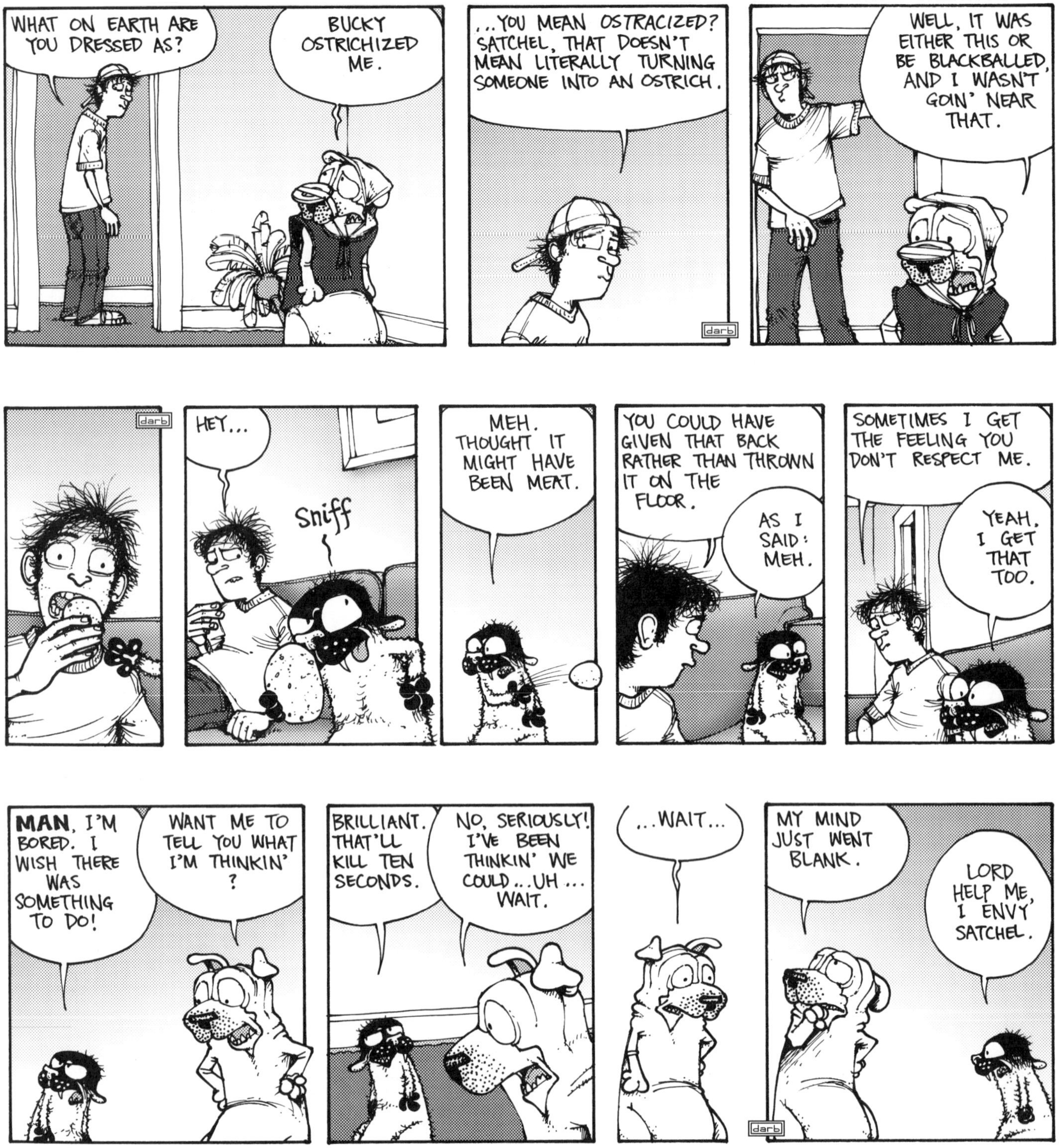
WHAT ON EARTH ARE YOU DRESSED AS?
BUCKY OSTRICHIZED ME.
...YOU MEAN OSTRACIZED? SATCHEL, THAT DOESN'T MEAN LITERALLY TURNING SOMEONE INTO AN OSTRICH.
WELL, IT WAS EITHER THIS OR BE BLACKBALLED, AND I WASN'T GOIN' NEAR THAT.
darb
darb
HEY...
Sniff
MEH. THOUGHT IT MIGHT HAVE BEEN MEAT.
YOU COULD HAVE GIVEN THAT BACK RATHER THAN THROWN IT ON THE FLOOR.
AS I SAID: MEH.
SOMETIMES I GET THE FEELING YOU DON'T RESPECT ME.
YEAH. I GET THAT TOO.
MAN, I'M BORED. I WISH THERE WAS SOMETHING TO DO!
WANT ME TO TELL YOU WHAT I'M THINKIN'?
BRILLIANT. THAT'LL KILL TEN SECONDS.
NO, SERIOUSLY! I'VE BEEN THINKIN' WE COULD... UH... WAIT.
...WAIT...
MY MIND JUST WENT BLANK.
LORD HELP ME, I ENVY SATCHEL.
darb

WHY DOES THIS HISTORY BOOK GO BACK TO YEAR ZERO FOR PART OF THE WORLD AND ONLY 1492 FOR AMERICA?

WELL...HISTORY IS WRITTEN BY THE VICTORS, ISN'T IT?

WHAT DOES THAT MEAN?

IT—

I'LL HANDLE THIS, ROBERT.

SEE, SATCHEL, IT MEANS THAT NO NATIVE AMERICANS WERE NAMED VICTOR. PUBLISHERS HAD TO WAIT FOR EUROPERS TO MOVE HERE AND START WRITING BOOKS.

IT MEANS THAT THOSE WHO ARE VICTORIOUS IN WAR GET TO DOCUMENT EVENTS.

OK, YEAH, THAT TOO. SEE, SATCHEL, ALL THE LOSERS' PRINTING PRESSES WERE BOMBED.

UHH...

IT OBVIOUSLY HAS A TRIPLE MEANING, TOO, IN THAT LOSERS ARE JUST *BAD* AT STUFF... FIGHTING... SPORTS... HYGIENE... WRITING HISTORY BOOKS...

IT'S HARD FOR ME TO TALK ABOUT THINGS WITH YOU...

DUH. YOU'RE A LOSER.

darb

39

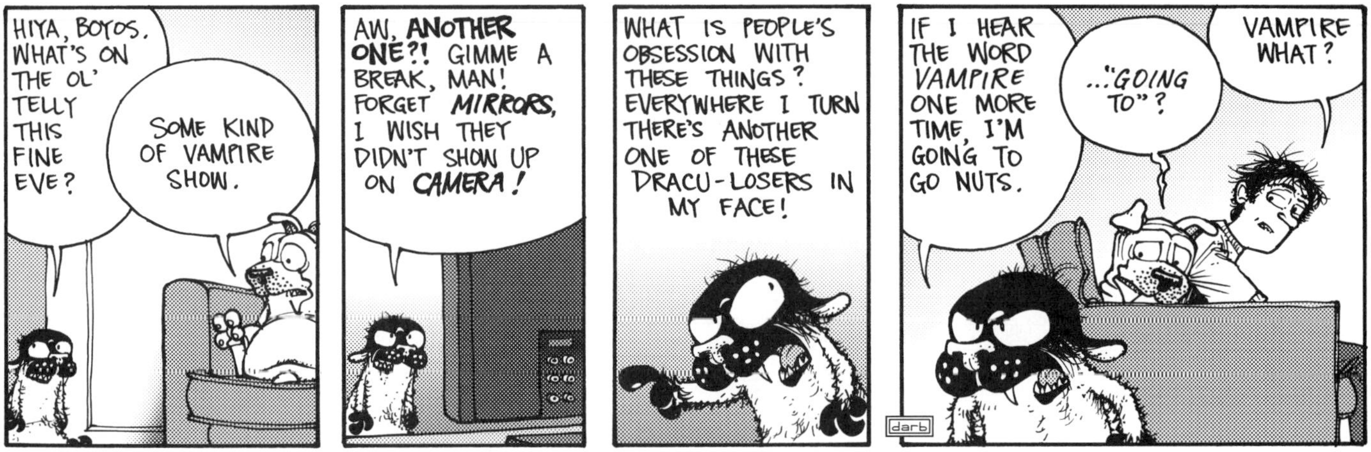
HIYA, BOYOS. WHAT'S ON THE OL' TELLY THIS FINE EVE?
SOME KIND OF VAMPIRE SHOW.
AW, ANOTHER ONE?! GIMME A BREAK, MAN! FORGET MIRRORS, I WISH THEY DIDN'T SHOW UP ON CAMERA!
WHAT IS PEOPLE'S OBSESSION WITH THESE THINGS? EVERYWHERE I TURN THERE'S ANOTHER ONE OF THESE DRACU-LOSERS IN MY FACE!
IF I HEAR THE WORD VAMPIRE ONE MORE TIME, I'M GOING TO GO NUTS.
VAMPIRE WHAT?
..."GOING TO"?
darb

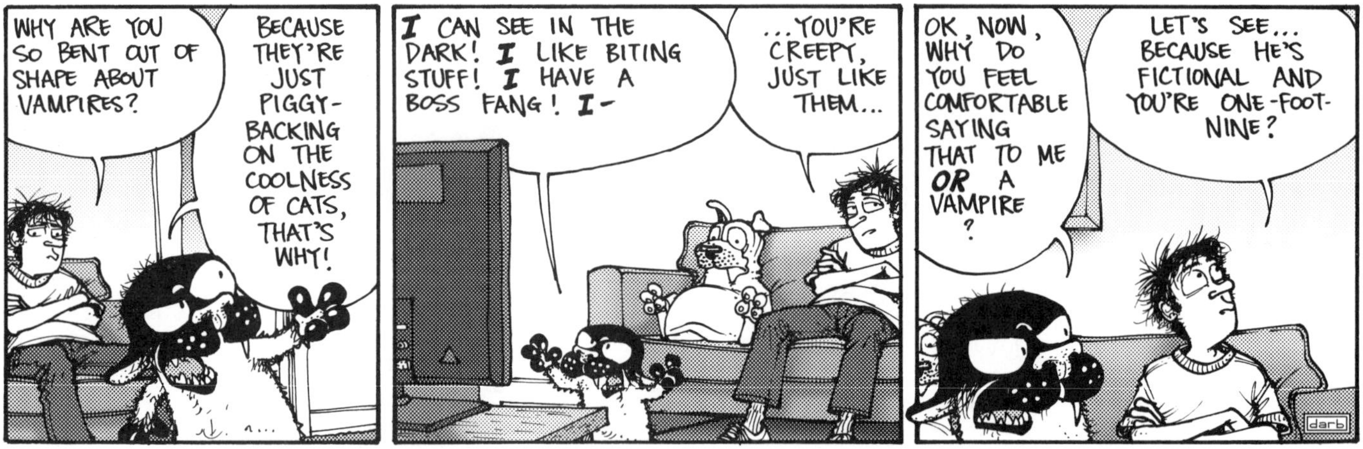
WHY ARE YOU SO BENT OUT OF SHAPE ABOUT VAMPIRES?
BECAUSE THEY'RE JUST PIGGY-BACKING ON THE COOLNESS OF CATS, THAT'S WHY!
I CAN SEE IN THE DARK! I LIKE BITING STUFF! I HAVE A BOSS FANG! I-
...YOU'RE CREEPY, JUST LIKE THEM...
OK, NOW, WHY DO YOU FEEL COMFORTABLE SAYING THAT TO ME OR A VAMPIRE?
LET'S SEE... BECAUSE HE'S FICTIONAL AND YOU'RE ONE-FOOT-NINE?
darb

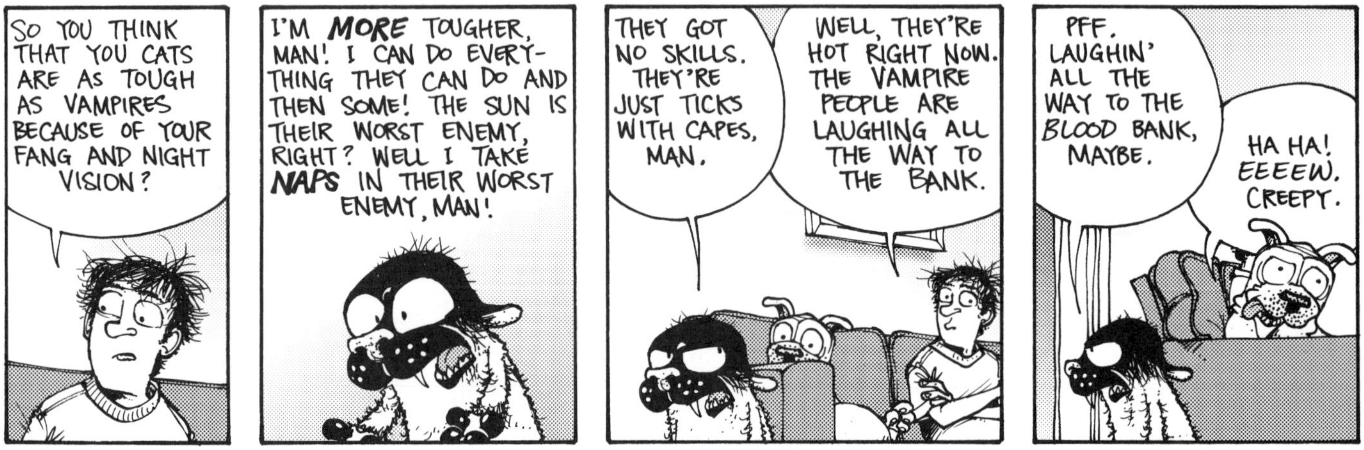
SO YOU THINK THAT YOU CATS ARE AS TOUGH AS VAMPIRES BECAUSE OF YOUR FANG AND NIGHT VISION?
I'M MORE TOUGHER, MAN! I CAN DO EVERY-THING THEY CAN DO AND THEN SOME! THE SUN IS THEIR WORST ENEMY, RIGHT? WELL I TAKE NAPS IN THEIR WORST ENEMY, MAN!
THEY GOT NO SKILLS. THEY'RE JUST TICKS WITH CAPES, MAN.
WELL, THEY'RE HOT RIGHT NOW. THE VAMPIRE PEOPLE ARE LAUGHING ALL THE WAY TO THE BANK.
PFF. LAUGHIN' ALL THE WAY TO THE BLOOD BANK, MAYBE.
HA HA! EEEEW. CREEPY.

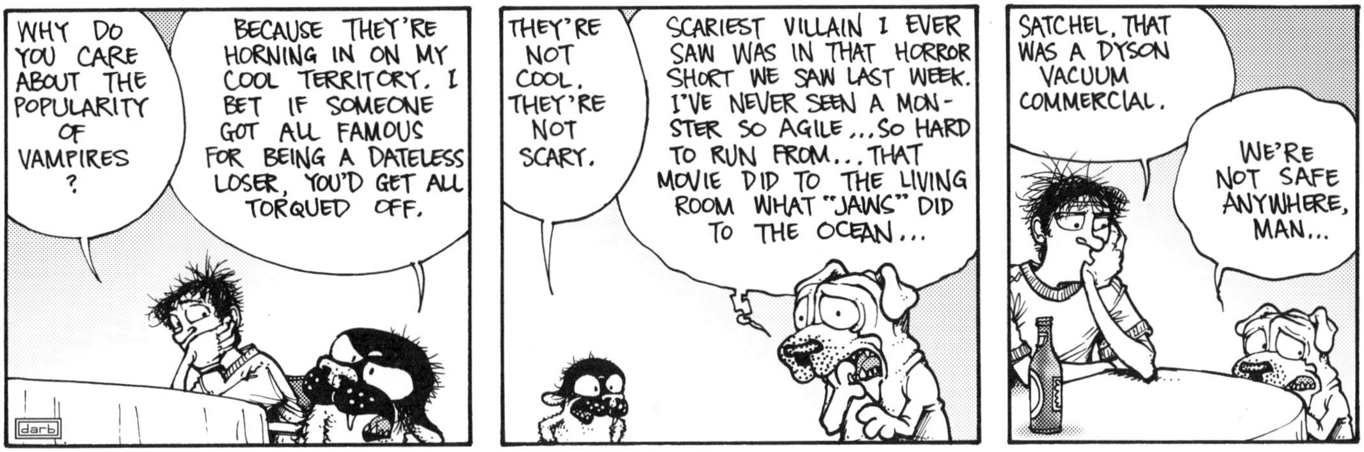
WHY DO YOU CARE ABOUT THE POPULARITY OF VAMPIRES ?
BECAUSE THEY'RE HORNING IN ON MY COOL TERRITORY. I BET IF SOMEONE GOT ALL FAMOUS FOR BEING A DATELESS LOSER, YOU'D GET ALL TORQUED OFF.
THEY'RE NOT COOL. THEY'RE NOT SCARY.
SCARIEST VILLAIN I EVER SAW WAS IN THAT HORROR SHORT WE SAW LAST WEEK. I'VE NEVER SEEN A MON-STER SO AGILE...SO HARD TO RUN FROM...THAT MOVIE DID TO THE LIVING ROOM WHAT "JAWS" DID TO THE OCEAN...
SATCHEL, THAT WAS A DYSON VACUUM COMMERCIAL.
WE'RE NOT SAFE ANYWHERE, MAN...
darb

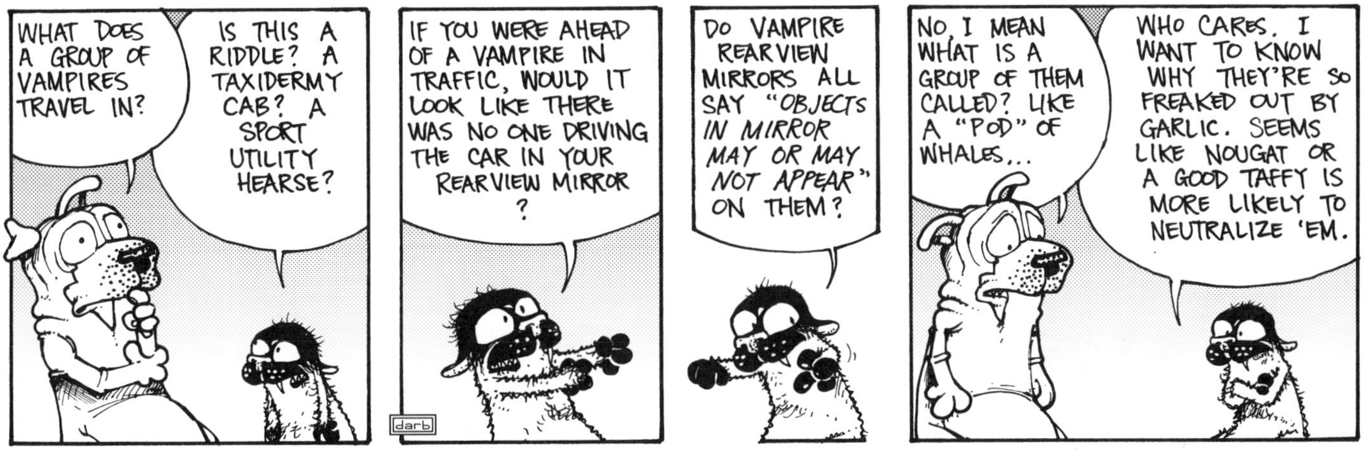
WHAT DOES A GROUP OF VAMPIRES TRAVEL IN?
IS THIS A RIDDLE? A TAXIDERMY CAB? A SPORT UTILITY HEARSE?
IF YOU WERE AHEAD OF A VAMPIRE IN TRAFFIC, WOULD IT LOOK LIKE THERE WAS NO ONE DRIVING THE CAR IN YOUR REARVIEW MIRROR ?
darb
DO VAMPIRE REARVIEW MIRRORS ALL SAY "OBJECTS IN MIRROR MAY OR MAY NOT APPEAR" ON THEM?
NO, I MEAN WHAT IS A GROUP OF THEM CALLED? LIKE A "POD" OF WHALES...
WHO CARES. I WANT TO KNOW WHY THEY'RE SO FREAKED OUT BY GARLIC. SEEMS LIKE NOUGAT OR A GOOD TAFFY IS MORE LIKELY TO NEUTRALIZE 'EM.

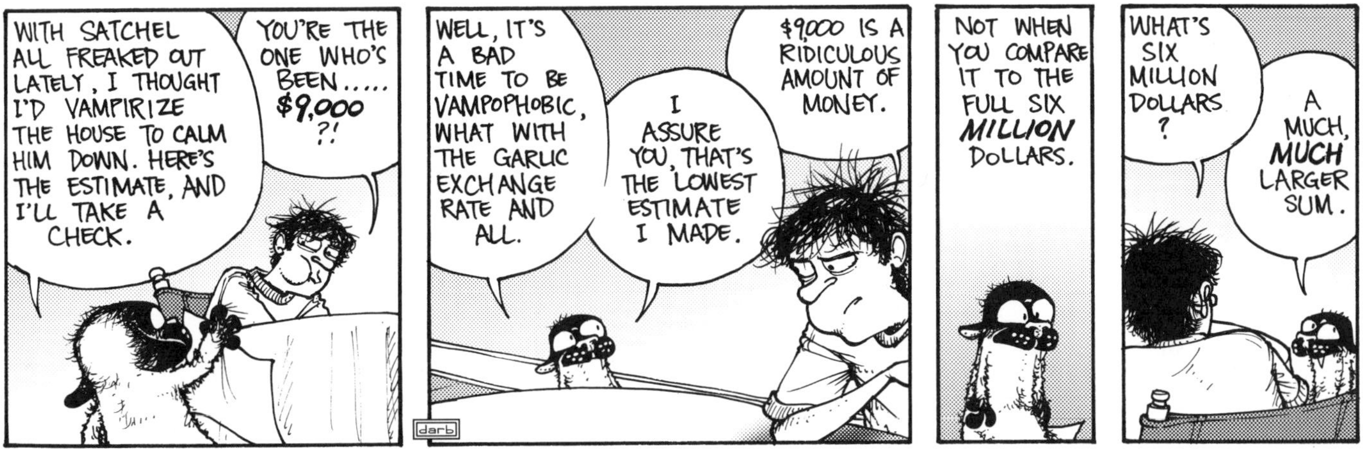
WITH SATCHEL ALL FREAKED OUT LATELY, I THOUGHT I'D VAMPIRIZE THE HOUSE TO CALM HIM DOWN. HERE'S THE ESTIMATE, AND I'LL TAKE A CHECK.
YOU'RE THE ONE WHO'S BEEN..... $9,000 ?!
WELL, IT'S A BAD TIME TO BE VAMPOPHOBIC, WHAT WITH THE GARLIC EXCHANGE RATE AND ALL.
I ASSURE YOU, THAT'S THE LOWEST ESTIMATE I MADE.
$9,000 IS A RIDICULOUS AMOUNT OF MONEY.
darb
NOT WHEN YOU COMPARE IT TO THE FULL SIX MILLION DOLLARS.
WHAT'S SIX MILLION DOLLARS ?
A MUCH, MUCH LARGER SUM.

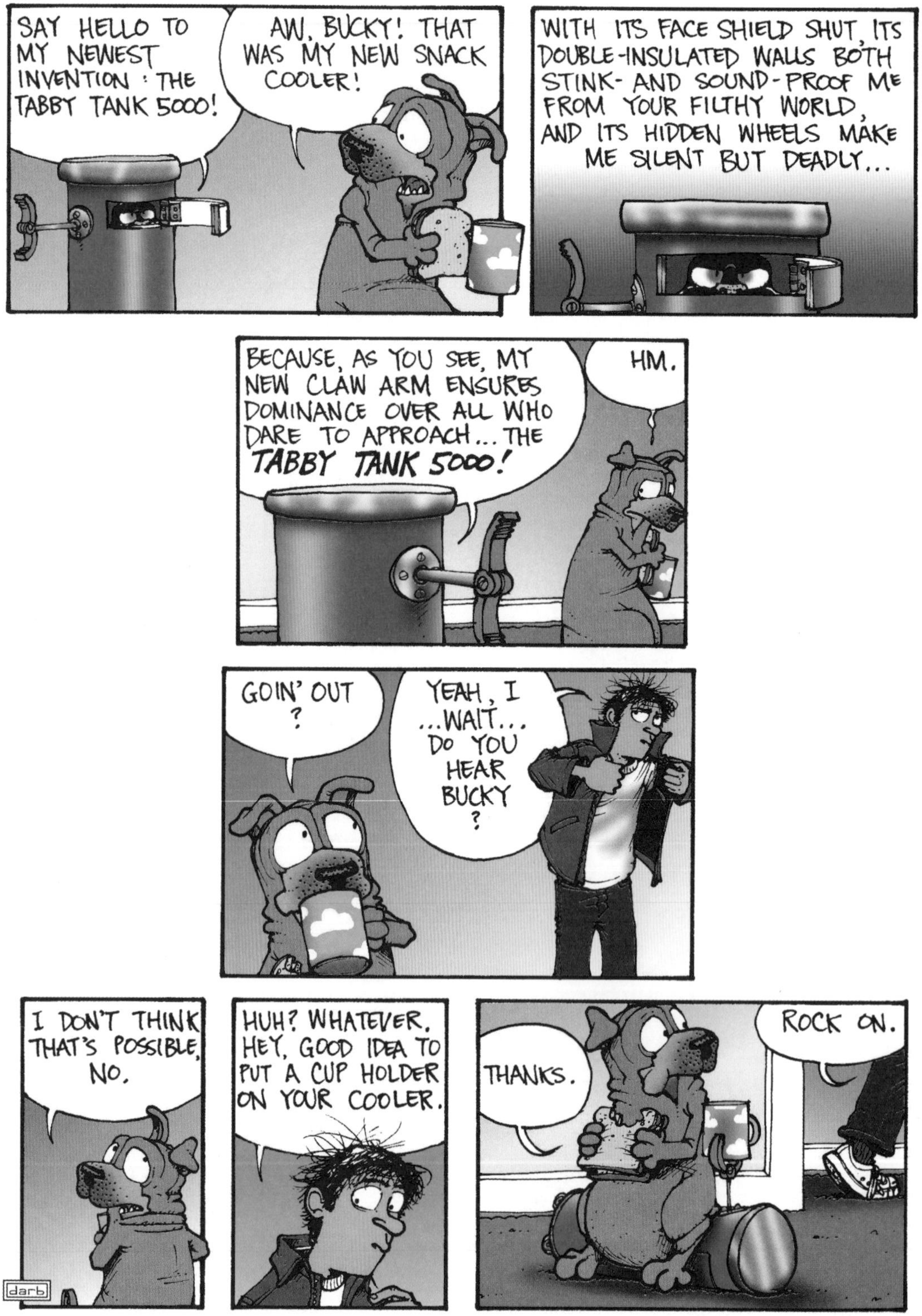
SAY HELLO TO MY NEWEST INVENTION : THE TABBY TANK 5000!
AW, BUCKY! THAT WAS MY NEW SNACK COOLER!
WITH ITS FACE SHIELD SHUT, ITS DOUBLE-INSULATED WALLS BOTH STINK- AND SOUND-PROOF ME FROM YOUR FILTHY WORLD, AND ITS HIDDEN WHEELS MAKE ME SILENT BUT DEADLY...
BECAUSE, AS YOU SEE, MY NEW CLAW ARM ENSURES DOMINANCE OVER ALL WHO DARE TO APPROACH... THE TABBY TANK 5000!
HM.
GOIN' OUT ?
YEAH, I ...WAIT... DO YOU HEAR BUCKY ?
I DON'T THINK THAT'S POSSIBLE, NO.
HUH? WHATEVER. HEY, GOOD IDEA TO PUT A CUP HOLDER ON YOUR COOLER.
THANKS.
ROCK ON.
darb

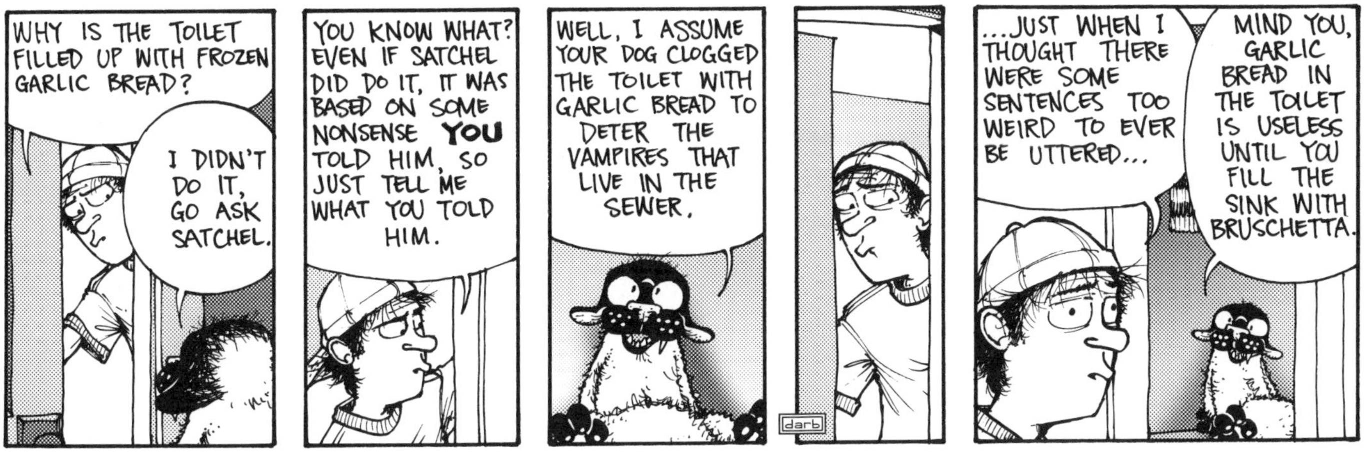
WHY IS THE TOILET FILLED UP WITH FROZEN GARLIC BREAD?
I DIDN'T DO IT, GO ASK SATCHEL.
YOU KNOW WHAT? EVEN IF SATCHEL DID DO IT, IT WAS BASED ON SOME NONSENSE **YOU** TOLD HIM, SO JUST TELL ME WHAT YOU TOLD HIM.
WELL, I ASSUME YOUR DOG CLOGGED THE TOILET WITH GARLIC BREAD TO DETER THE VAMPIRES THAT LIVE IN THE SEWER.
darb
...JUST WHEN I THOUGHT THERE WERE SOME SENTENCES TOO WEIRD TO EVER BE UTTERED...
MIND YOU, GARLIC BREAD IN THE TOILET IS USELESS UNTIL YOU FILL THE SINK WITH BRUSCHETTA.

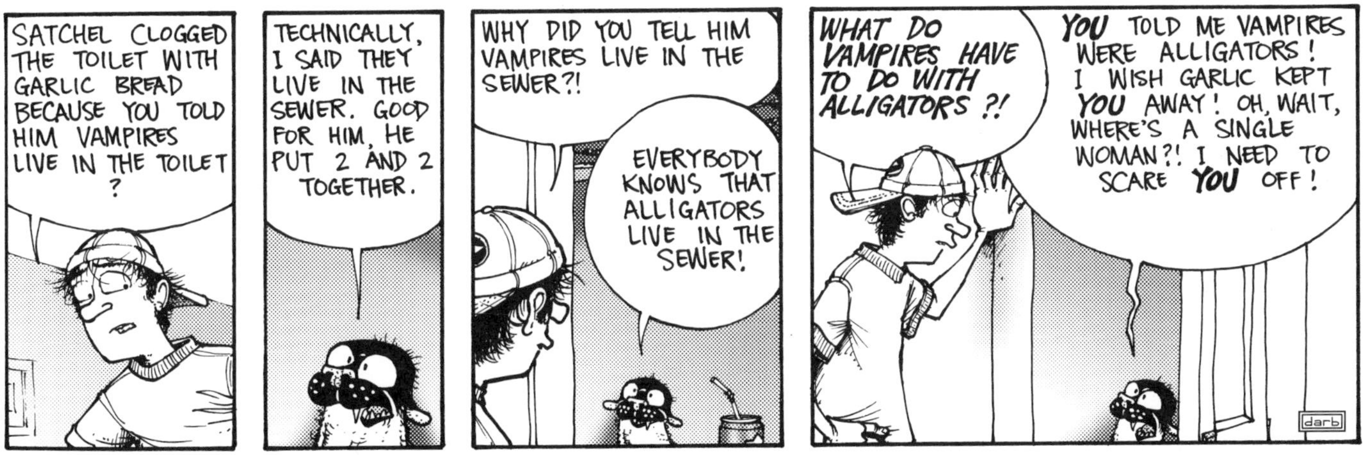
SATCHEL CLOGGED THE TOILET WITH GARLIC BREAD BECAUSE YOU TOLD HIM VAMPIRES LIVE IN THE TOILET?
TECHNICALLY, I SAID THEY LIVE IN THE SEWER. GOOD FOR HIM, HE PUT 2 AND 2 TOGETHER.
WHY DID YOU TELL HIM VAMPIRES LIVE IN THE SEWER?!
EVERYBODY KNOWS THAT ALLIGATORS LIVE IN THE SEWER!
WHAT DO VAMPIRES HAVE TO DO WITH ALLIGATORS ?!
YOU TOLD ME VAMPIRES WERE ALLIGATORS! I WISH GARLIC KEPT **YOU** AWAY! OH, WAIT, WHERE'S A SINGLE WOMAN?! I NEED TO SCARE **YOU** OFF!
darb

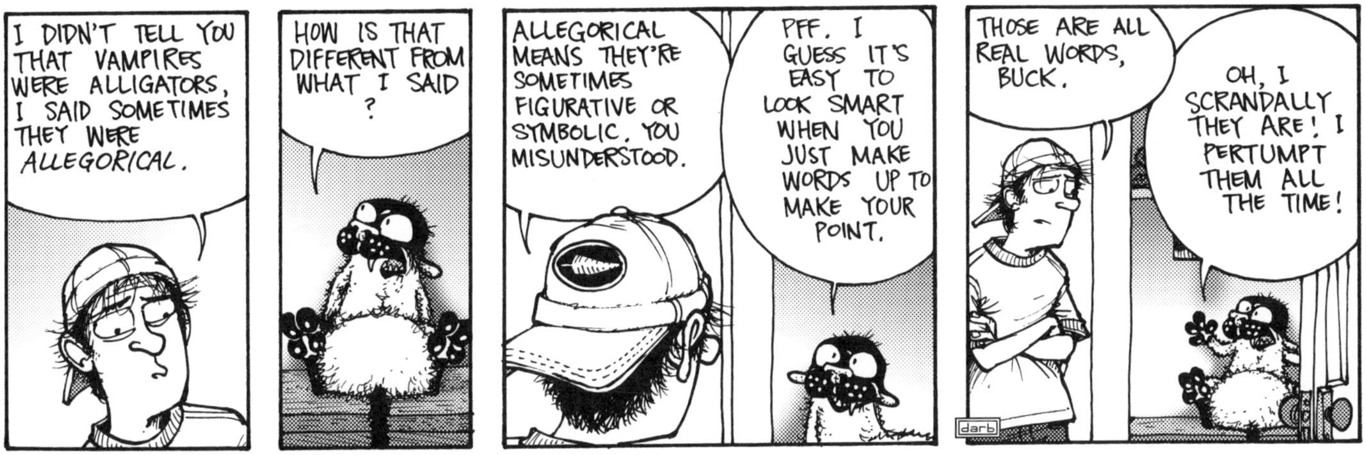
I DIDN'T TELL YOU THAT VAMPIRES WERE ALLIGATORS, I SAID SOMETIMES THEY WERE *ALLEGORICAL*.
HOW IS THAT DIFFERENT FROM WHAT I SAID?
ALLEGORICAL MEANS THEY'RE SOMETIMES FIGURATIVE OR SYMBOLIC. YOU MISUNDERSTOOD.
PFF. I GUESS IT'S EASY TO LOOK SMART WHEN YOU JUST MAKE WORDS UP TO MAKE YOUR POINT.
darb
THOSE ARE ALL REAL WORDS, BUCK.
OH, I SCRANDALLY THEY ARE! I PERTUMPT THEM ALL THE TIME!

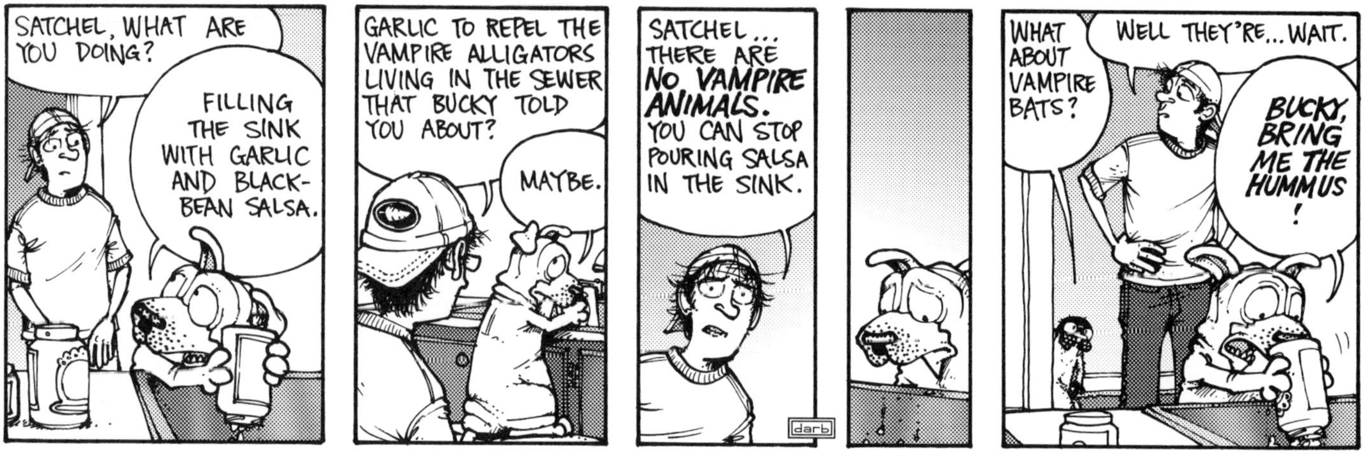
SATCHEL, WHAT ARE YOU DOING?
FILLING THE SINK WITH GARLIC AND BLACK-BEAN SALSA.
GARLIC TO REPEL THE VAMPIRE ALLIGATORS LIVING IN THE SEWER THAT BUCKY TOLD YOU ABOUT?
MAYBE.
SATCHEL... THERE ARE **NO VAMPIRE ANIMALS.** YOU CAN STOP POURING SALSA IN THE SINK.
WHAT ABOUT VAMPIRE BATS?
WELL THEY'RE... WAIT.
BUCKY, BRING ME THE HUMMUS!

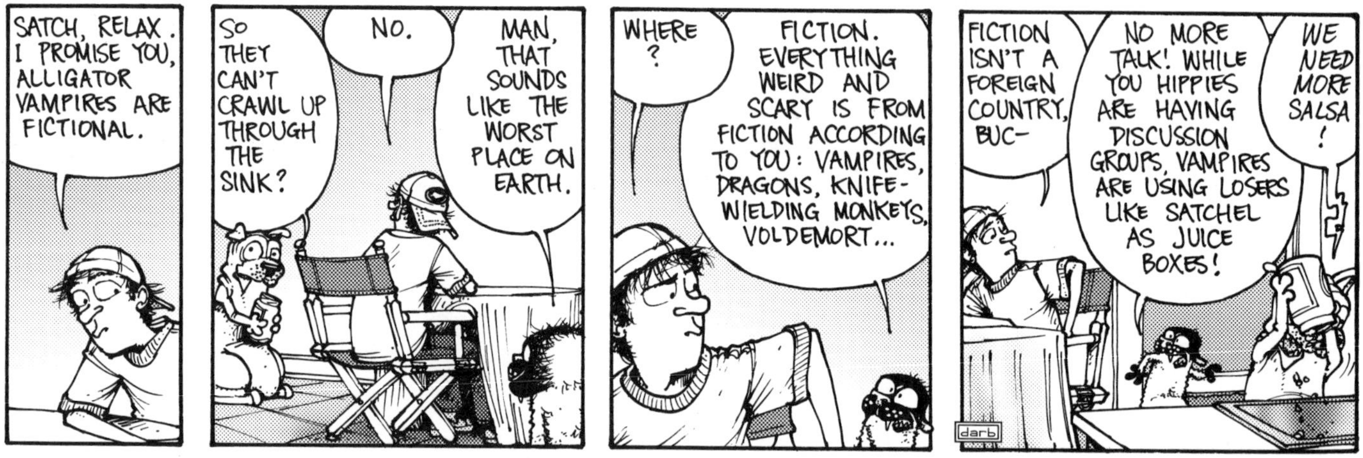
SATCH, RELAX. I PROMISE YOU, ALLIGATOR VAMPIRES ARE FICTIONAL.
SO THEY CAN'T CRAWL UP THROUGH THE SINK?
NO.
MAN, THAT SOUNDS LIKE THE WORST PLACE ON EARTH.
WHERE?
FICTION. EVERYTHING WEIRD AND SCARY IS FROM FICTION ACCORDING TO YOU: VAMPIRES, DRAGONS, KNIFE-WIELDING MONKEYS, VOLDEMORT...
FICTION ISN'T A FOREIGN COUNTRY, BUC-
NO MORE TALK! WHILE YOU HIPPIES ARE HAVING DISCUSSION GROUPS, VAMPIRES ARE USING LOSERS LIKE SATCHEL AS JUICE BOXES!
WE NEED MORE SALSA!

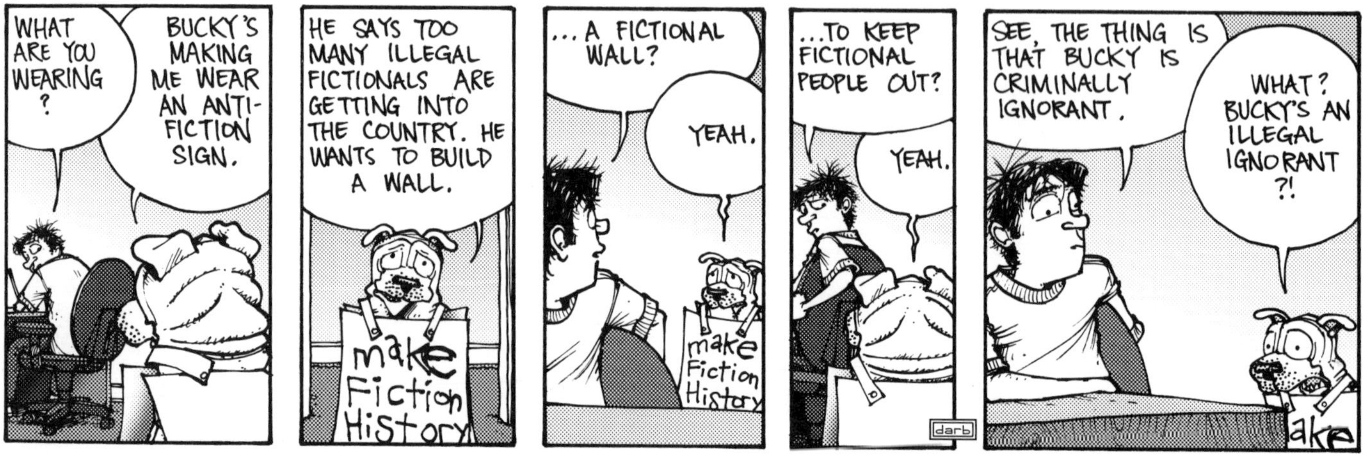
WHAT ARE YOU WEARING?
BUCKY'S MAKING ME WEAR AN ANTI-FICTION SIGN.
HE SAYS TOO MANY ILLEGAL FICTIONALS ARE GETTING INTO THE COUNTRY. HE WANTS TO BUILD A WALL.
make Fiction History
...A FICTIONAL WALL?
YEAH.
make Fiction History
...TO KEEP FICTIONAL PEOPLE OUT?
YEAH.
SEE, THE THING IS THAT BUCKY IS CRIMINALLY IGNORANT.
WHAT? BUCKY'S AN ILLEGAL IGNORANT?!

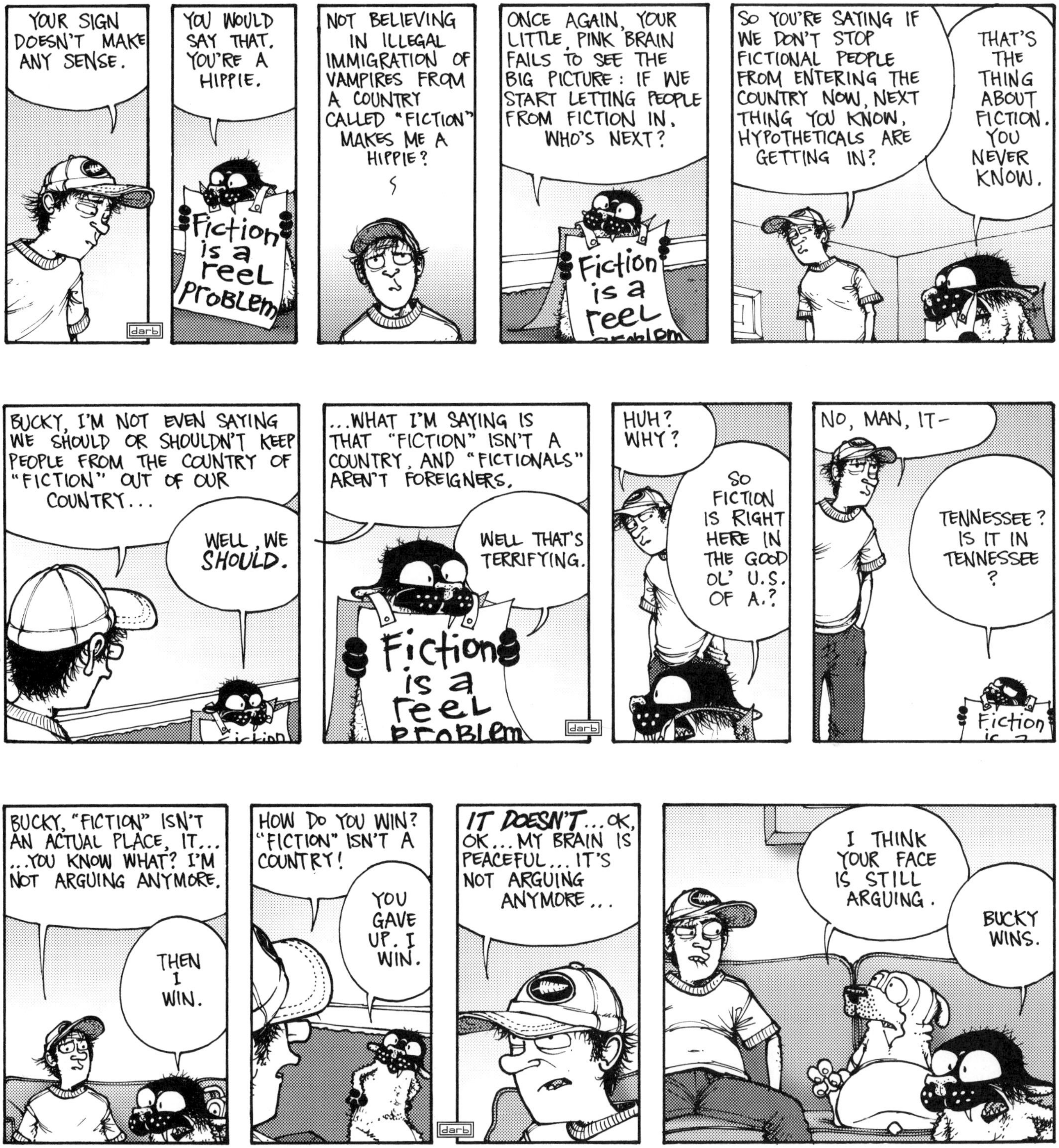
YOUR SIGN DOESN'T MAKE ANY SENSE.
Fiction is a reel problem
darb
YOU WOULD SAY THAT. YOU'RE A HIPPIE.
Fiction is a reel problem
NOT BELIEVING IN ILLEGAL IMMIGRATION OF VAMPIRES FROM A COUNTRY CALLED "FICTION" MAKES ME A HIPPIE?
ONCE AGAIN, YOUR LITTLE, PINK BRAIN FAILS TO SEE THE BIG PICTURE: IF WE START LETTING PEOPLE FROM FICTION IN, WHO'S NEXT?
Fiction is a reel
SO YOU'RE SAYING IF WE DON'T STOP FICTIONAL PEOPLE FROM ENTERING THE COUNTRY NOW, NEXT THING YOU KNOW, HYPOTHETICALS ARE GETTING IN?
THAT'S THE THING ABOUT FICTION. YOU NEVER KNOW.
BUCKY, I'M NOT EVEN SAYING WE SHOULD OR SHOULDN'T KEEP PEOPLE FROM THE COUNTRY OF "FICTION" OUT OF OUR COUNTRY...
WELL, WE SHOULD.
...WHAT I'M SAYING IS THAT "FICTION" ISN'T A COUNTRY, AND "FICTIONALS" AREN'T FOREIGNERS.
WELL THAT'S TERRIFYING.
Fiction is a reel problem
darb
HUH? WHY?
SO FICTION IS RIGHT HERE IN THE GOOD OL' U.S. OF A.?
NO, MAN, IT—
TENNESSEE? IS IT IN TENNESSEE?
Fiction
BUCKY, "FICTION" ISN'T AN ACTUAL PLACE, IT... ...YOU KNOW WHAT? I'M NOT ARGUING ANYMORE.
THEN I WIN.
HOW DO YOU WIN? "FICTION" ISN'T A COUNTRY!
YOU GAVE UP. I WIN.
darb
IT DOESN'T... OK, OK... MY BRAIN IS PEACEFUL... IT'S NOT ARGUING ANYMORE...
I THINK YOUR FACE IS STILL ARGUING.
BUCKY WINS.

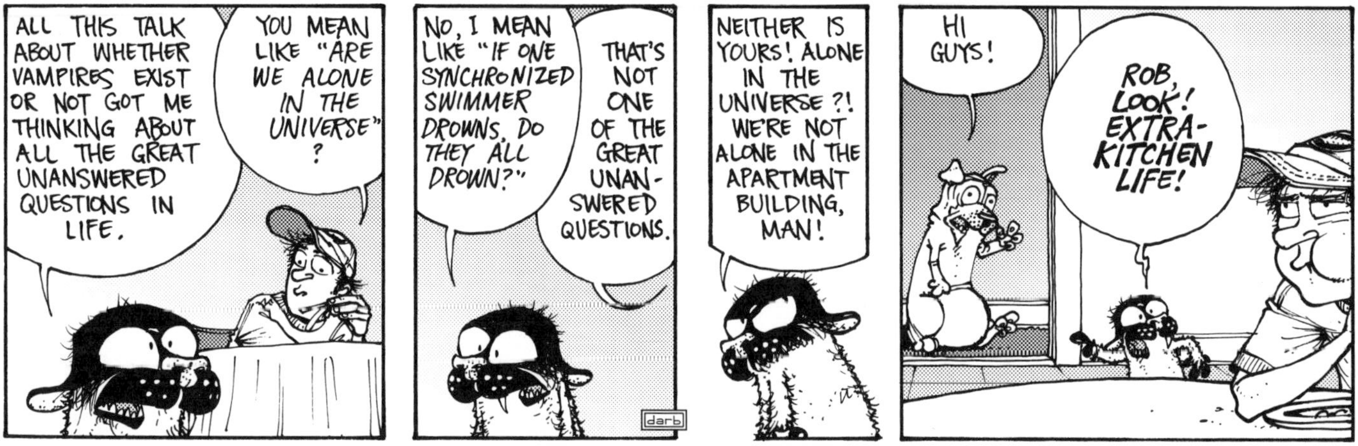
ALL THIS TALK ABOUT WHETHER VAMPIRES EXIST OR NOT GOT ME THINKING ABOUT ALL THE GREAT UNANSWERED QUESTIONS IN LIFE.
YOU MEAN LIKE "ARE WE ALONE IN THE UNIVERSE" ?
NO, I MEAN LIKE "IF ONE SYNCHRONIZED SWIMMER DROWNS, DO THEY ALL DROWN?"
THAT'S NOT ONE OF THE GREAT UNANSWERED QUESTIONS.
darb
NEITHER IS YOURS! ALONE IN THE UNIVERSE?! WE'RE NOT ALONE IN THE APARTMENT BUILDING, MAN!
HI GUYS!
ROB, LOOK! EXTRA-KITCHEN LIFE!

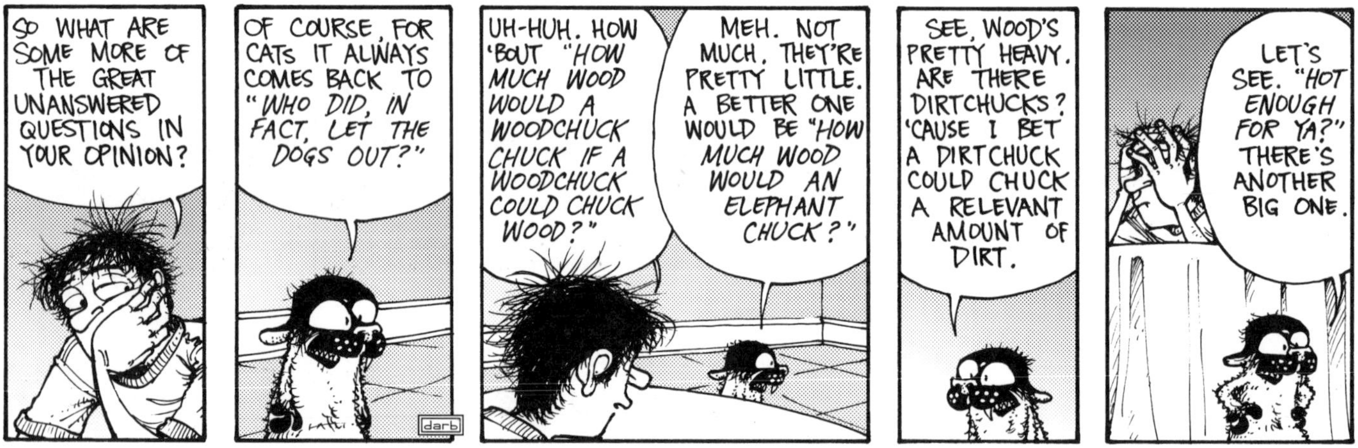
SO WHAT ARE SOME MORE OF THE GREAT UNANSWERED QUESTIONS IN YOUR OPINION?
OF COURSE, FOR CATS IT ALWAYS COMES BACK TO "WHO DID, IN FACT, LET THE DOGS OUT?"
darb
UH-HUH. HOW 'BOUT "HOW MUCH WOOD WOULD A WOODCHUCK CHUCK IF A WOODCHUCK COULD CHUCK WOOD?"
MEH. NOT MUCH. THEY'RE PRETTY LITTLE. A BETTER ONE WOULD BE "HOW MUCH WOOD WOULD AN ELEPHANT CHUCK?"
SEE, WOOD'S PRETTY HEAVY. ARE THERE DIRTCHUCKS? 'CAUSE I BET A DIRTCHUCK COULD CHUCK A RELEVANT AMOUNT OF DIRT.
LET'S SEE. "HOT ENOUGH FOR YA?" THERE'S ANOTHER BIG ONE.

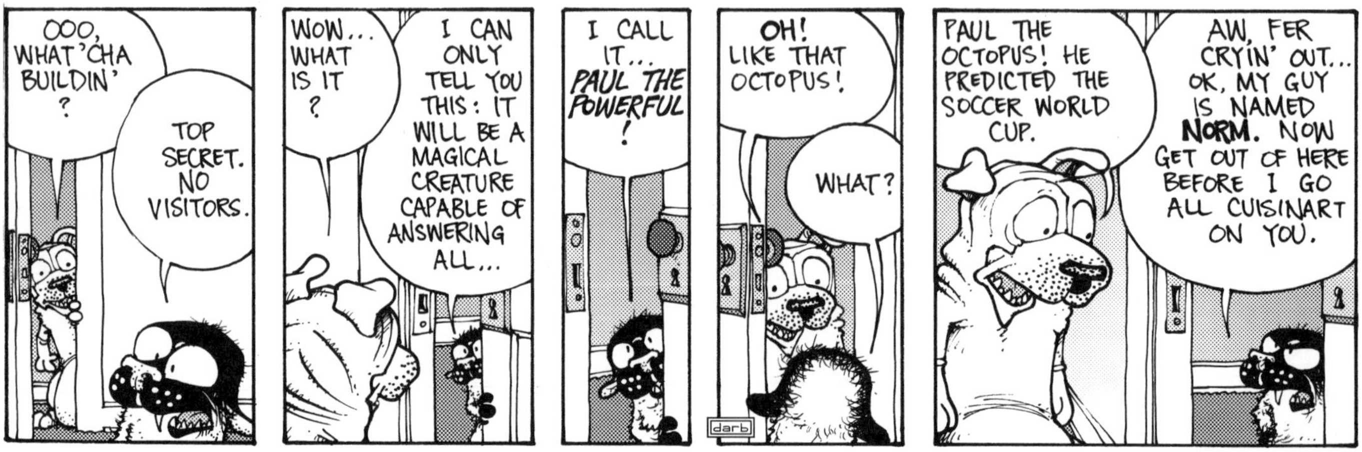
OOO, WHAT'CHA BUILDIN'?
TOP SECRET. NO VISITORS.
WOW... WHAT IS IT?
I CAN ONLY TELL YOU THIS: IT WILL BE A MAGICAL CREATURE CAPABLE OF ANSWERING ALL...
I CALL IT... PAUL THE POWERFUL!
darb
OH! LIKE THAT OCTOPUS!
WHAT?
PAUL THE OCTOPUS! HE PREDICTED THE SOCCER WORLD CUP.
AW, FER CRYIN' OUT... OK, MY GUY IS NAMED NORM. NOW GET OUT OF HERE BEFORE I GO ALL CUISINART ON YOU.

SATCHEL, ARE THERE ANY DOG NAMES THAT RHYME WITH "EDELWEISS"?
UHHH... ODIE? NO...
SEE, I'M ADAPTING "THE SOUND OF MUSIC" FOR CATS. THAT MAKES DOGS THE NAZIS.
darb
THAT'S A BIT LIKE THE POT CALLING THE SNOWBALL BLACK, ISN'T IT?
STAY OUT OF THIS, ROB. OR SHOULD I SAY... GOAT-HERDING PUPPET.
BUT WHY DO YOU ALWAYS MAKE DOGS INTO THE BAD GUYS?
RELAX, YOU'LL HAVE SOME BOSS MUSICAL NUMBERS.
SUCH AS?
WELL, THE FIRST NUMBER IS "HOW DO YOU SOLVE A PROBLEM LIKE DYSPLASIA?"
MM-HM. MM-HM.
UMM... "SCHIPPERKE GOING ON #SEVENTEEN"...
LESS SURE ABOUT THAT ONE.
MY FAVORITE IS "CLIMB EV'RY PANTLEG."
NEXT WEEK: BUCKY SINGS ROE-RAY-FLEA!

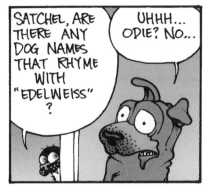

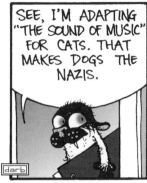

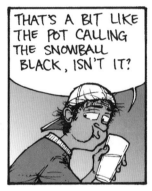

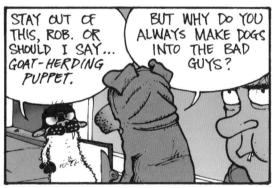

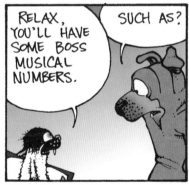

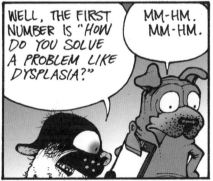

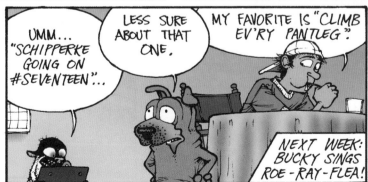

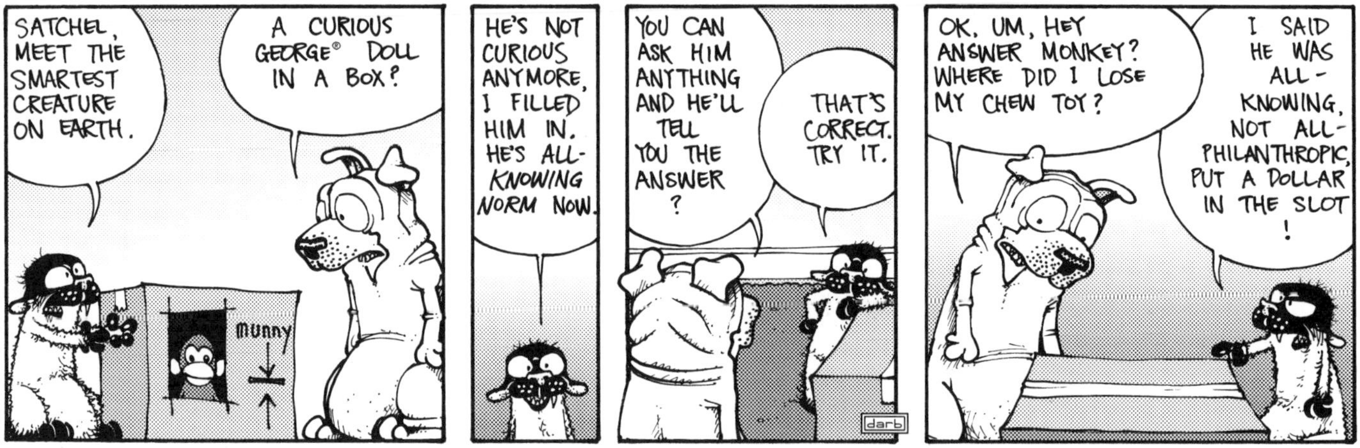
SATCHEL, MEET THE SMARTEST CREATURE ON EARTH.
A CURIOUS GEORGE® DOLL IN A BOX?
munny
HE'S NOT CURIOUS ANYMORE, I FILLED HIM IN. HE'S ALL-KNOWING NORM NOW.
YOU CAN ASK HIM ANYTHING AND HE'LL TELL YOU THE ANSWER?
THAT'S CORRECT. TRY IT.
darb
OK. UM, HEY ANSWER MONKEY? WHERE DID I LOSE MY CHEW TOY?
I SAID HE WAS ALL-KNOWING, NOT ALL-PHILANTHROPIC, PUT A DOLLAR IN THE SLOT!

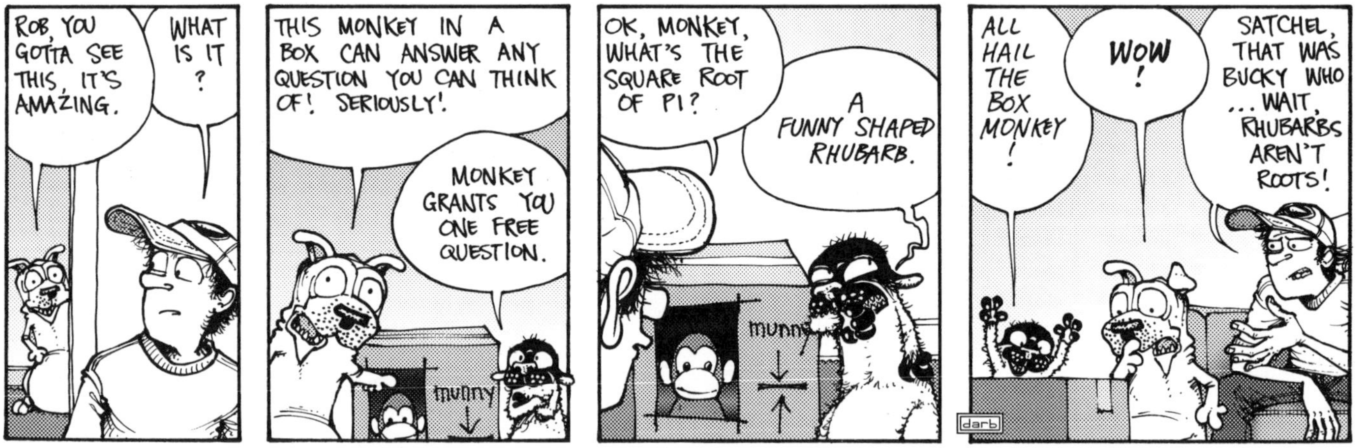
ROB, YOU GOTTA SEE THIS, IT'S AMAZING.
WHAT IS IT?
THIS MONKEY IN A BOX CAN ANSWER ANY QUESTION YOU CAN THINK OF! SERIOUSLY!
MONKEY GRANTS YOU ONE FREE QUESTION.
munny
OK, MONKEY, WHAT'S THE SQUARE ROOT OF PI?
A FUNNY SHAPED RHUBARB.
munny
ALL HAIL THE BOX MONKEY!
WOW!
SATCHEL, THAT WAS BUCKY WHO ... WAIT, RHUBARBS AREN'T ROOTS!
darb

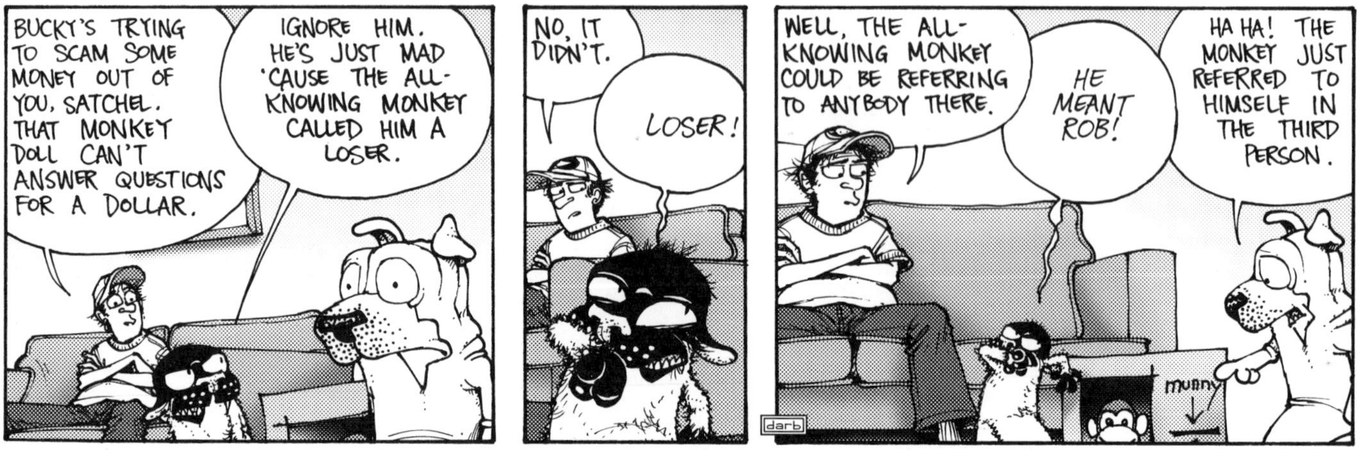
BUCKY'S TRYING TO SCAM SOME MONEY OUT OF YOU, SATCHEL. THAT MONKEY DOLL CAN'T ANSWER QUESTIONS FOR A DOLLAR.
IGNORE HIM. HE'S JUST MAD 'CAUSE THE ALL-KNOWING MONKEY CALLED HIM A LOSER.
NO, IT DIDN'T.
LOSER!
darb
WELL, THE ALL-KNOWING MONKEY COULD BE REFERRING TO ANYBODY THERE.
HE MEANT ROB!
HA HA! THE MONKEY JUST REFERRED TO HIMSELF IN THE THIRD PERSON.
munny

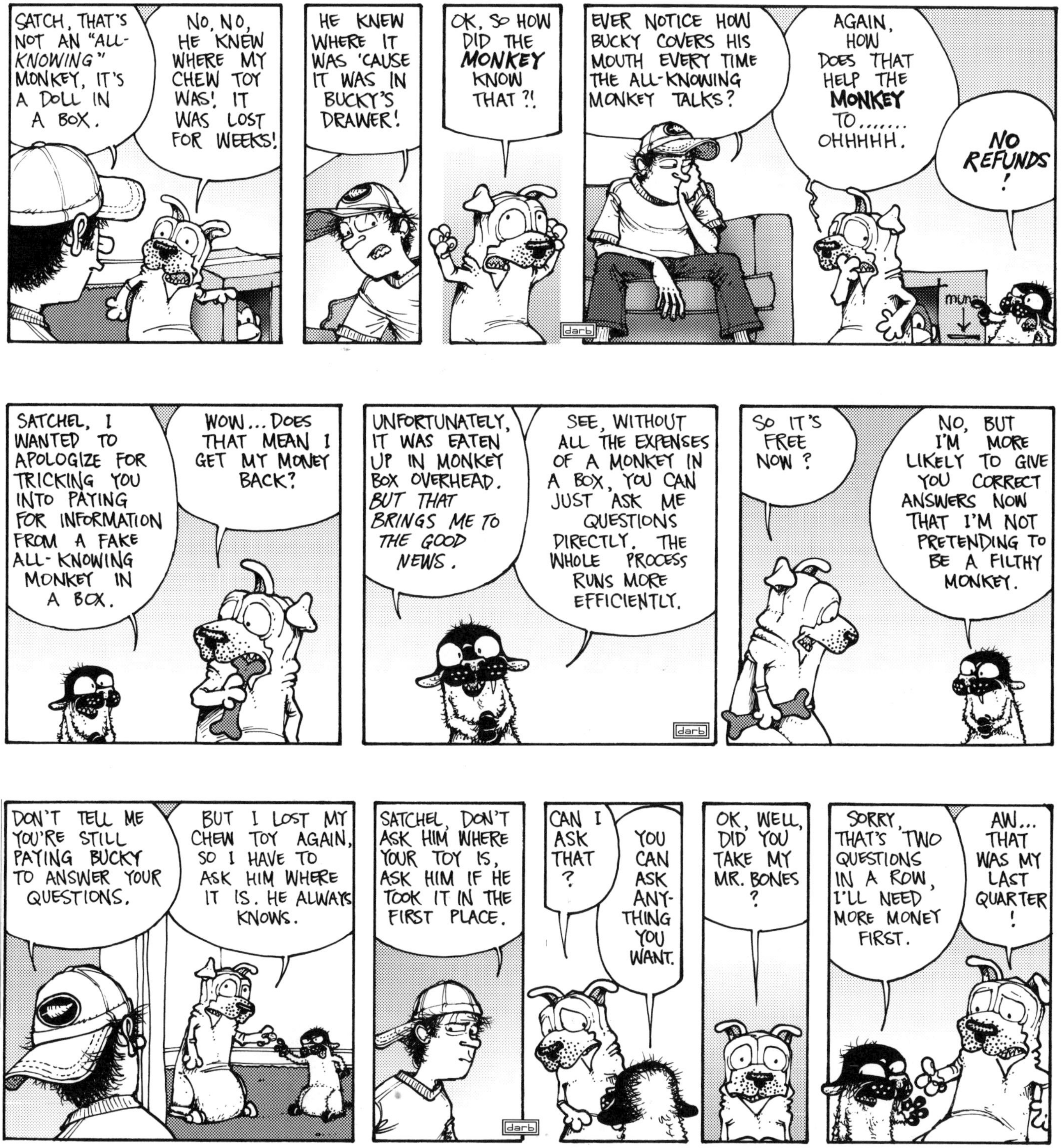

SATCH, THAT'S NOT AN "ALL-KNOWING" MONKEY, IT'S A DOLL IN A BOX.
NO, NO, HE KNEW WHERE MY CHEW TOY WAS! IT WAS LOST FOR WEEKS!
HE KNEW WHERE IT WAS 'CAUSE IT WAS IN BUCKY'S DRAWER!
OK, SO HOW DID THE **MONKEY** KNOW THAT ?!
EVER NOTICE HOW BUCKY COVERS HIS MOUTH EVERY TIME THE ALL-KNOWING MONKEY TALKS?
AGAIN, HOW DOES THAT HELP THE **MONKEY** TO....... OHHHHH.
NO REFUNDS !
SATCHEL, I WANTED TO APOLOGIZE FOR TRICKING YOU INTO PAYING FOR INFORMATION FROM A FAKE ALL-KNOWING MONKEY IN A BOX.
WOW... DOES THAT MEAN I GET MY MONEY BACK?
UNFORTUNATELY, IT WAS EATEN UP IN MONKEY BOX OVERHEAD. *BUT THAT BRINGS ME TO THE GOOD NEWS.*
SEE, WITHOUT ALL THE EXPENSES OF A MONKEY IN A BOX, YOU CAN JUST ASK ME QUESTIONS DIRECTLY. THE WHOLE PROCESS RUNS MORE EFFICIENTLY.
SO IT'S FREE NOW ?
NO, BUT I'M MORE LIKELY TO GIVE YOU CORRECT ANSWERS NOW THAT I'M NOT PRETENDING TO BE A FILTHY MONKEY.
DON'T TELL ME YOU'RE STILL PAYING BUCKY TO ANSWER YOUR QUESTIONS.
BUT I LOST MY CHEW TOY AGAIN, SO I HAVE TO ASK HIM WHERE IT IS. HE ALWAYS KNOWS.
SATCHEL, DON'T ASK HIM WHERE YOUR TOY IS, ASK HIM IF HE TOOK IT IN THE FIRST PLACE.
CAN I ASK THAT ?
YOU CAN ASK ANYTHING YOU WANT.
OK, WELL, DID YOU TAKE MY MR. BONES ?
SORRY, THAT'S TWO QUESTIONS IN A ROW, I'LL NEED MORE MONEY FIRST.
AW... THAT WAS MY LAST QUARTER !

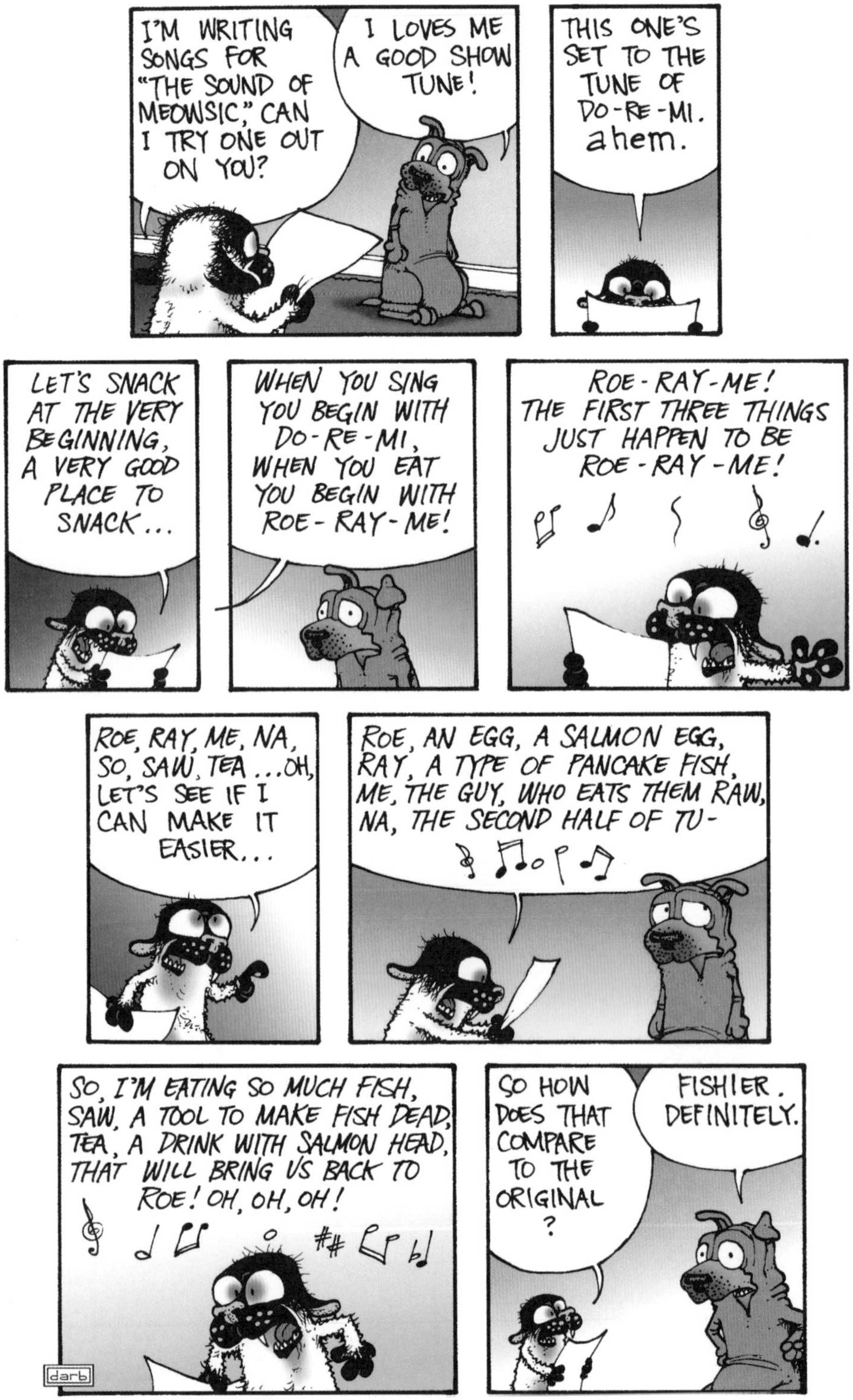
I'M WRITING SONGS FOR "THE SOUND OF MEOWSIC," CAN I TRY ONE OUT ON YOU?
I LOVES ME A GOOD SHOW TUNE!
THIS ONE'S SET TO THE TUNE OF DO-RE-MI. ahem.
LET'S SNACK AT THE VERY BEGINNING, A VERY GOOD PLACE TO SNACK...
WHEN YOU SING YOU BEGIN WITH DO-RE-MI, WHEN YOU EAT YOU BEGIN WITH ROE-RAY-ME!
ROE-RAY-ME! THE FIRST THREE THINGS JUST HAPPEN TO BE ROE-RAY-ME!
ROE, RAY, ME, NA, SO, SAW, TEA ...OH, LET'S SEE IF I CAN MAKE IT EASIER...
ROE, AN EGG, A SALMON EGG, RAY, A TYPE OF PANCAKE FISH, ME, THE GUY, WHO EATS THEM RAW, NA, THE SECOND HALF OF TU-
SO, I'M EATING SO MUCH FISH, SAW, A TOOL TO MAKE FISH DEAD, TEA, A DRINK WITH SALMON HEAD, THAT WILL BRING US BACK TO ROE! OH, OH, OH!
darb
SO HOW DOES THAT COMPARE TO THE ORIGINAL ?
FISHIER. DEFINITELY.

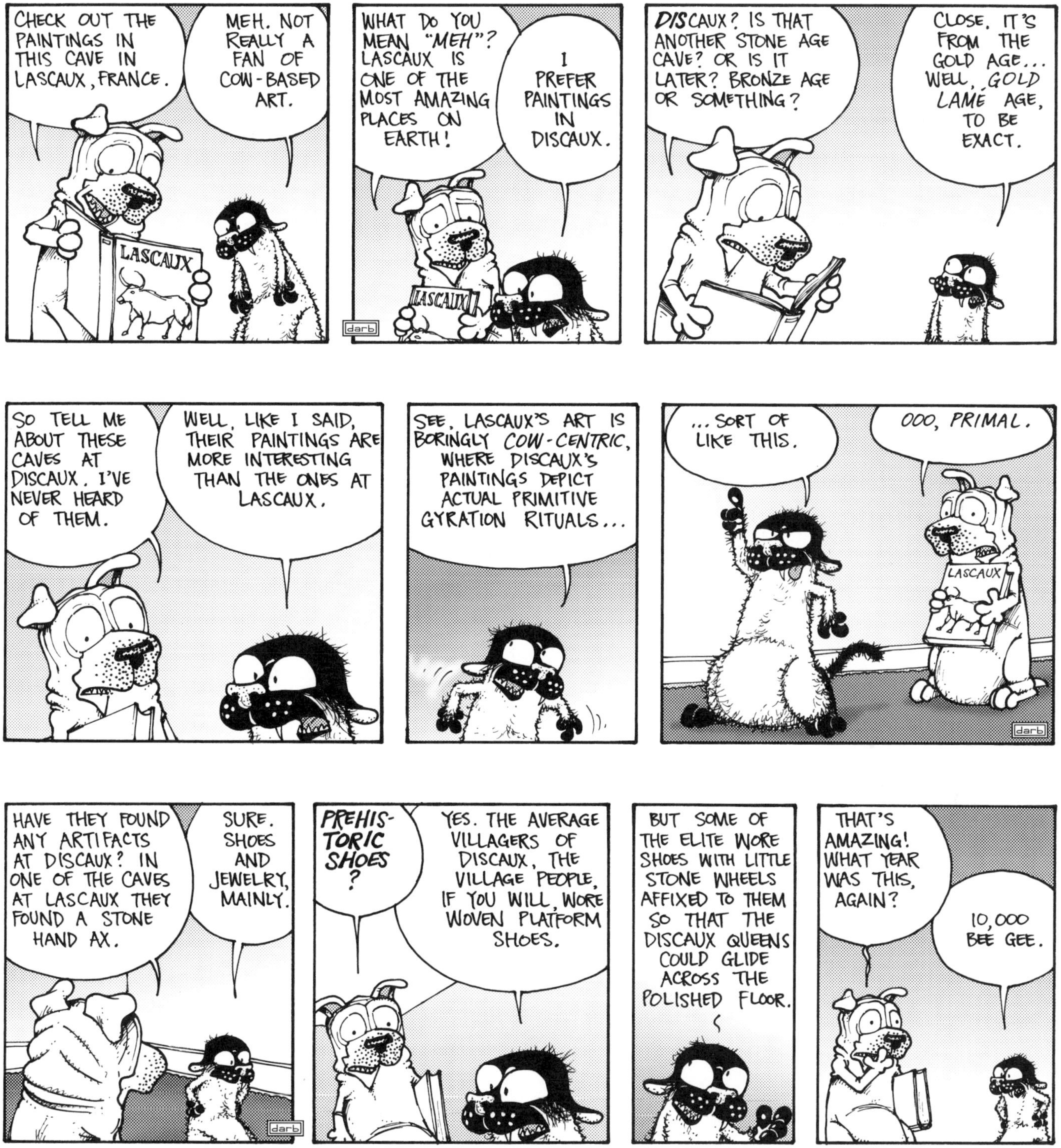
CHECK OUT THE PAINTINGS IN THIS CAVE IN LASCAUX, FRANCE.
LASCAUX
MEH. NOT REALLY A FAN OF COW-BASED ART.
darb
WHAT DO YOU MEAN "MEH"? LASCAUX IS ONE OF THE MOST AMAZING PLACES ON EARTH!
LASCAUX
I PREFER PAINTINGS IN DISCAUX.
DISCAUX? IS THAT ANOTHER STONE AGE CAVE? OR IS IT LATER? BRONZE AGE OR SOMETHING?
CLOSE. IT'S FROM THE GOLD AGE... WELL, GOLD LAMÉ AGE, TO BE EXACT.
SO TELL ME ABOUT THESE CAVES AT DISCAUX. I'VE NEVER HEARD OF THEM.
WELL, LIKE I SAID, THEIR PAINTINGS ARE MORE INTERESTING THAN THE ONES AT LASCAUX.
SEE, LASCAUX'S ART IS BORINGLY COW-CENTRIC, WHERE DISCAUX'S PAINTINGS DEPICT ACTUAL PRIMITIVE GYRATION RITUALS...
...SORT OF LIKE THIS.
OOO, PRIMAL.
LASCAUX
darb
HAVE THEY FOUND ANY ARTIFACTS AT DISCAUX? IN ONE OF THE CAVES AT LASCAUX THEY FOUND A STONE HAND AX.
SURE. SHOES AND JEWELRY, MAINLY.
darb
PREHISTORIC SHOES?
YES. THE AVERAGE VILLAGERS OF DISCAUX, THE VILLAGE PEOPLE, IF YOU WILL, WORE WOVEN PLATFORM SHOES.
BUT SOME OF THE ELITE WORE SHOES WITH LITTLE STONE WHEELS AFFIXED TO THEM SO THAT THE DISCAUX QUEENS COULD GLIDE ACROSS THE POLISHED FLOOR.
THAT'S AMAZING! WHAT YEAR WAS THIS, AGAIN?
10,000 BEE GEE.

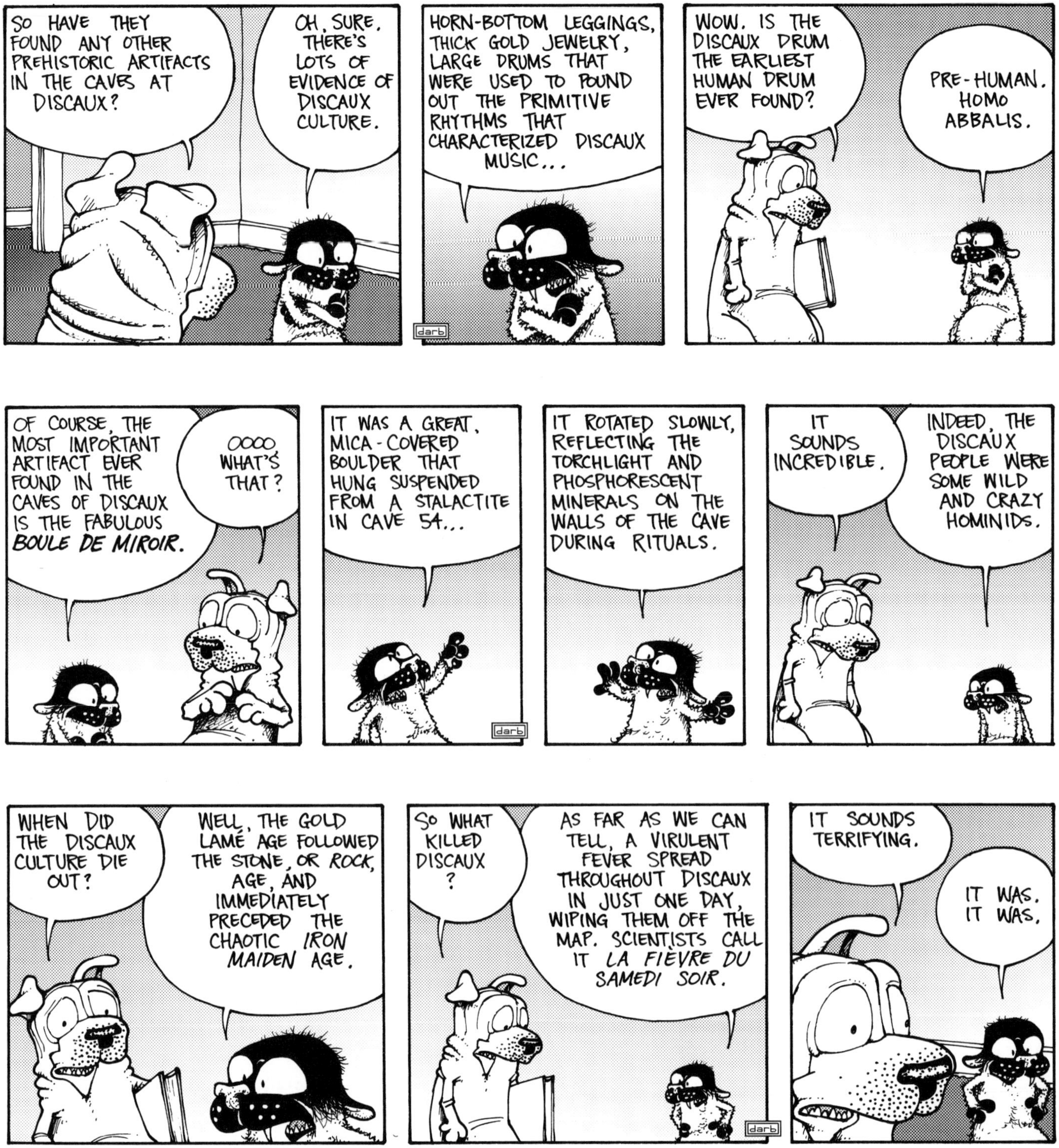
SO HAVE THEY FOUND ANY OTHER PREHISTORIC ARTIFACTS IN THE CAVES AT DISCAUX?
OH, SURE. THERE'S LOTS OF EVIDENCE OF DISCAUX CULTURE.
HORN-BOTTOM LEGGINGS, THICK GOLD JEWELRY, LARGE DRUMS THAT WERE USED TO POUND OUT THE PRIMITIVE RHYTHMS THAT CHARACTERIZED DISCAUX MUSIC...
WOW. IS THE DISCAUX DRUM THE EARLIEST HUMAN DRUM EVER FOUND?
PRE-HUMAN. HOMO ABBALIS.
darb
OF COURSE, THE MOST IMPORTANT ARTIFACT EVER FOUND IN THE CAVES OF DISCAUX IS THE FABULOUS *BOULE DE MIROIR*.
OOOO. WHAT'S THAT?
IT WAS A GREAT, MICA-COVERED BOULDER THAT HUNG SUSPENDED FROM A STALACTITE IN CAVE 54...
IT ROTATED SLOWLY, REFLECTING THE TORCHLIGHT AND PHOSPHORESCENT MINERALS ON THE WALLS OF THE CAVE DURING RITUALS.
IT SOUNDS INCREDIBLE.
INDEED, THE DISCAUX PEOPLE WERE SOME WILD AND CRAZY HOMINIDS.
darb
WHEN DID THE DISCAUX CULTURE DIE OUT?
WELL, THE GOLD LAMÉ AGE FOLLOWED THE STONE, OR *ROCK*, AGE, AND IMMEDIATELY PRECEDED THE CHAOTIC *IRON MAIDEN* AGE.
SO WHAT KILLED DISCAUX?
AS FAR AS WE CAN TELL, A VIRULENT FEVER SPREAD THROUGHOUT DISCAUX IN JUST ONE DAY, WIPING THEM OFF THE MAP. SCIENTISTS CALL IT *LA FIÈVRE DU SAMEDI SOIR*.
IT SOUNDS TERRIFYING.
IT WAS. IT WAS.
darb

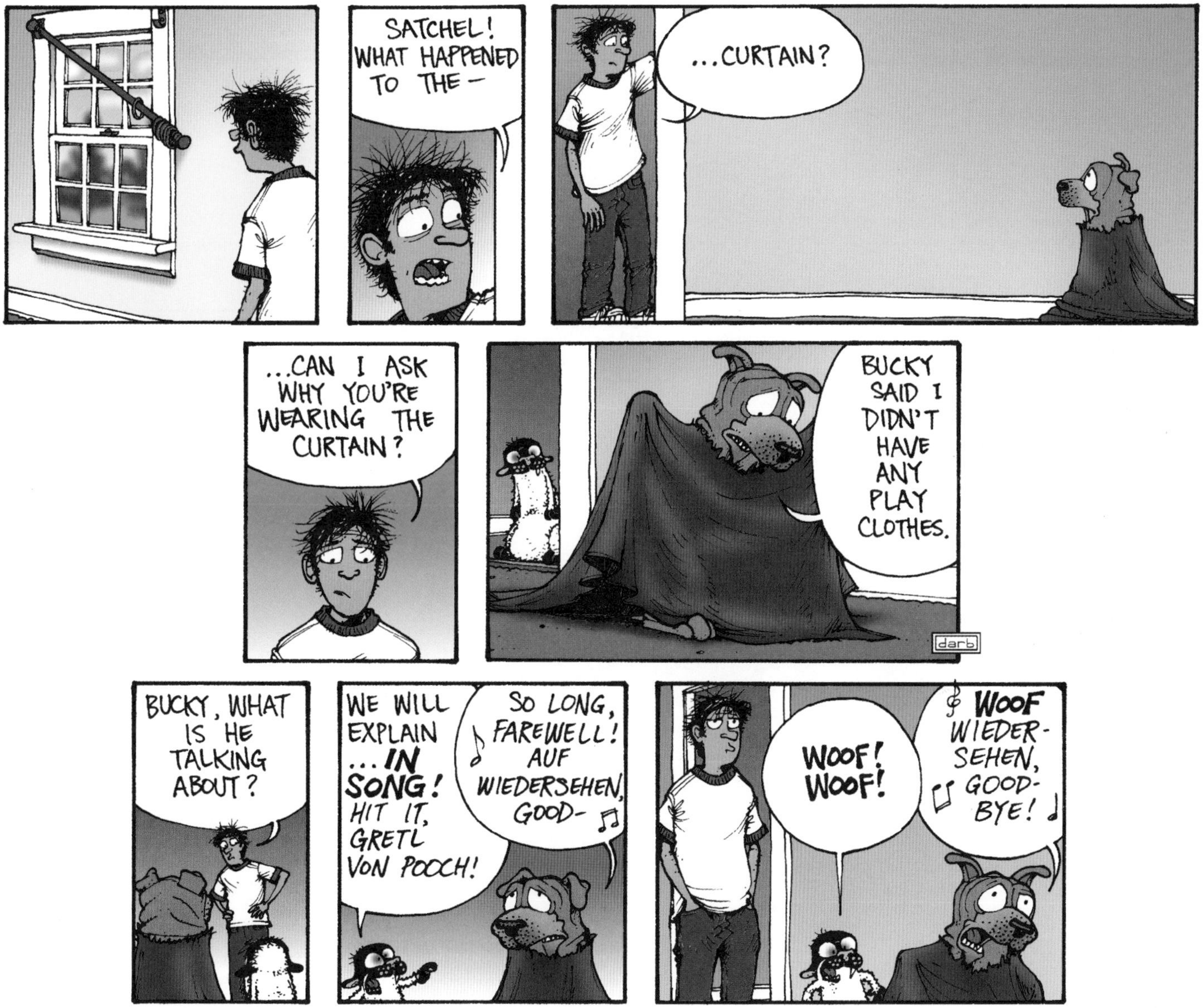
SATCHEL! WHAT HAPPENED TO THE –
...CURTAIN?
...CAN I ASK WHY YOU'RE WEARING THE CURTAIN?
BUCKY SAID I DIDN'T HAVE ANY PLAY CLOTHES.
darb
BUCKY, WHAT IS HE TALKING ABOUT?
WE WILL EXPLAIN ...IN SONG! HIT IT, GRETL VON POOCH!
SO LONG, FAREWELL! AUF WIEDERSEHEN, GOOD-
WOOF! WOOF!
WOOF WIEDER-SEHEN, GOOD-BYE!

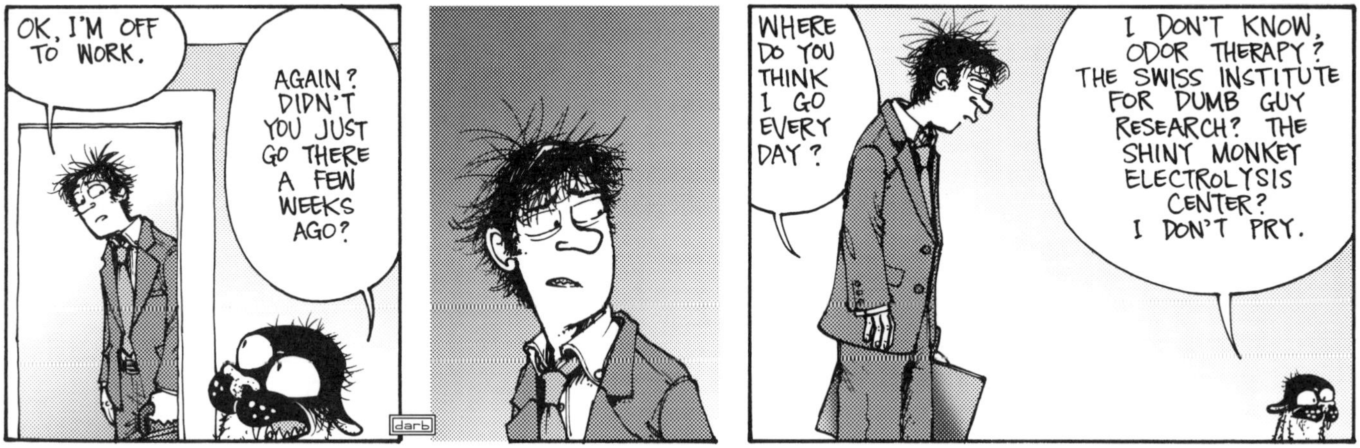
OK, I'M OFF TO WORK.
AGAIN? DIDN'T YOU JUST GO THERE A FEW WEEKS AGO?
WHERE DO YOU THINK I GO EVERY DAY?
I DON'T KNOW, ODOR THERAPY? THE SWISS INSTITUTE FOR DUMB GUY RESEARCH? THE SHINY MONKEY ELECTROLYSIS CENTER? I DON'T PRY.
darb

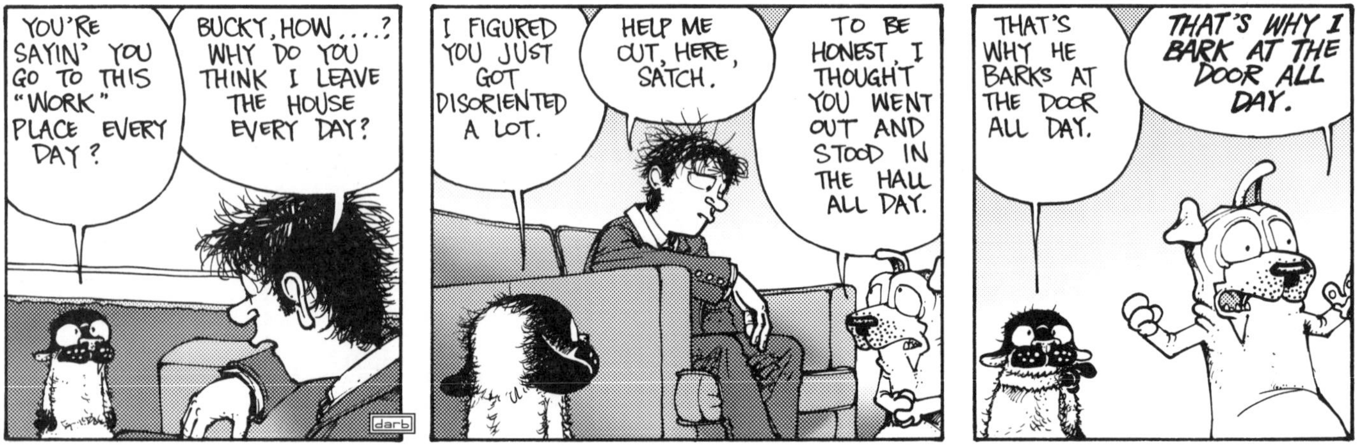
YOU'RE SAYIN' YOU GO TO THIS "WORK" PLACE EVERY DAY?
BUCKY, HOW....? WHY DO YOU THINK I LEAVE THE HOUSE EVERY DAY?
I FIGURED YOU JUST GOT DISORIENTED A LOT.
HELP ME OUT, HERE, SATCH.
TO BE HONEST, I THOUGHT YOU WENT OUT AND STOOD IN THE HALL ALL DAY.
THAT'S WHY HE BARKS AT THE DOOR ALL DAY.
THAT'S WHY I BARK AT THE DOOR ALL DAY.
darb

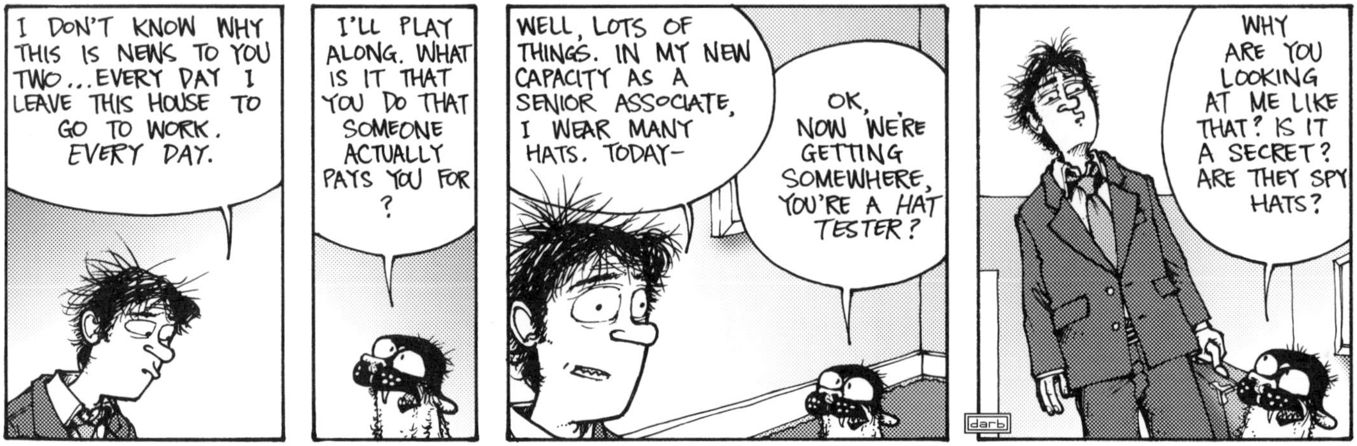
I DON'T KNOW WHY THIS IS NEWS TO YOU TWO... EVERY DAY I LEAVE THIS HOUSE TO GO TO WORK. EVERY DAY.
I'LL PLAY ALONG. WHAT IS IT THAT YOU DO THAT SOMEONE ACTUALLY PAYS YOU FOR?
WELL, LOTS OF THINGS. IN MY NEW CAPACITY AS A SENIOR ASSOCIATE, I WEAR MANY HATS. TODAY-
OK, NOW WE'RE GETTING SOMEWHERE, YOU'RE A HAT TESTER?
WHY ARE YOU LOOKING AT ME LIKE THAT? IS IT A SECRET? ARE THEY SPY HATS?
darb

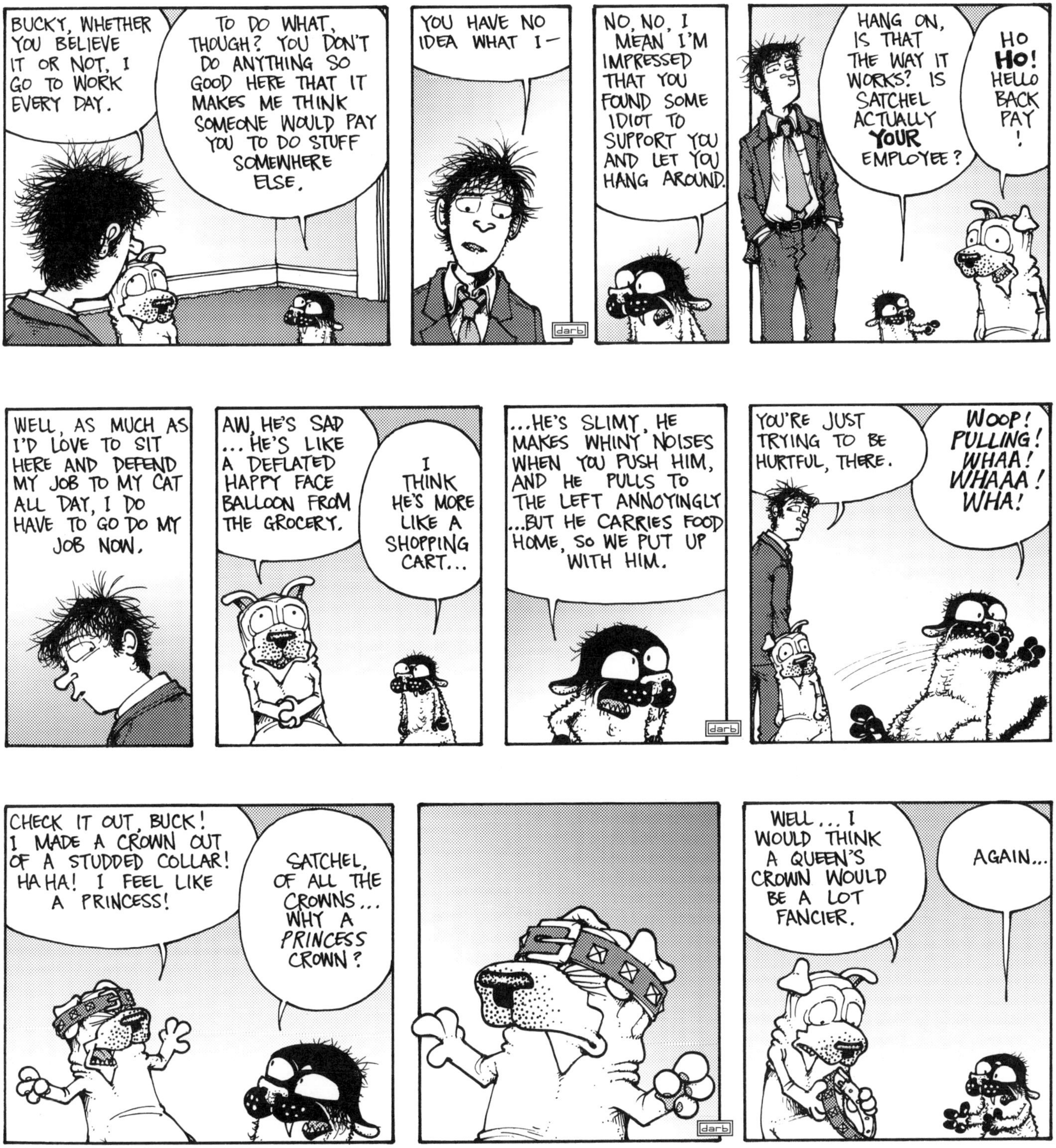
BUCKY, WHETHER YOU BELIEVE IT OR NOT, I GO TO WORK EVERY DAY.
TO DO WHAT, THOUGH? YOU DON'T DO ANYTHING SO GOOD HERE THAT IT MAKES ME THINK SOMEONE WOULD PAY YOU TO DO STUFF SOMEWHERE ELSE.
YOU HAVE NO IDEA WHAT I—
NO, NO, I MEAN I'M IMPRESSED THAT YOU FOUND SOME IDIOT TO SUPPORT YOU AND LET YOU HANG AROUND.
HANG ON, IS THAT THE WAY IT WORKS? IS SATCHEL ACTUALLY YOUR EMPLOYEE?
HO HO! HELLO BACK PAY!
darb
WELL, AS MUCH AS I'D LOVE TO SIT HERE AND DEFEND MY JOB TO MY CAT ALL DAY, I DO HAVE TO GO DO MY JOB NOW.
AW, HE'S SAD ... HE'S LIKE A DEFLATED HAPPY FACE BALLOON FROM THE GROCERY.
I THINK HE'S MORE LIKE A SHOPPING CART...
...HE'S SLIMY, HE MAKES WHINY NOISES WHEN YOU PUSH HIM, AND HE PULLS TO THE LEFT ANNOYINGLY ...BUT HE CARRIES FOOD HOME, SO WE PUT UP WITH HIM.
YOU'RE JUST TRYING TO BE HURTFUL, THERE.
WOOP! PULLING! WHAA! WHAAA! WHA!
darb
CHECK IT OUT, BUCK! I MADE A CROWN OUT OF A STUDDED COLLAR! HAHA! I FEEL LIKE A PRINCESS!
SATCHEL, OF ALL THE CROWNS... WHY A PRINCESS CROWN?
WELL... I WOULD THINK A QUEEN'S CROWN WOULD BE A LOT FANCIER.
AGAIN...
darb

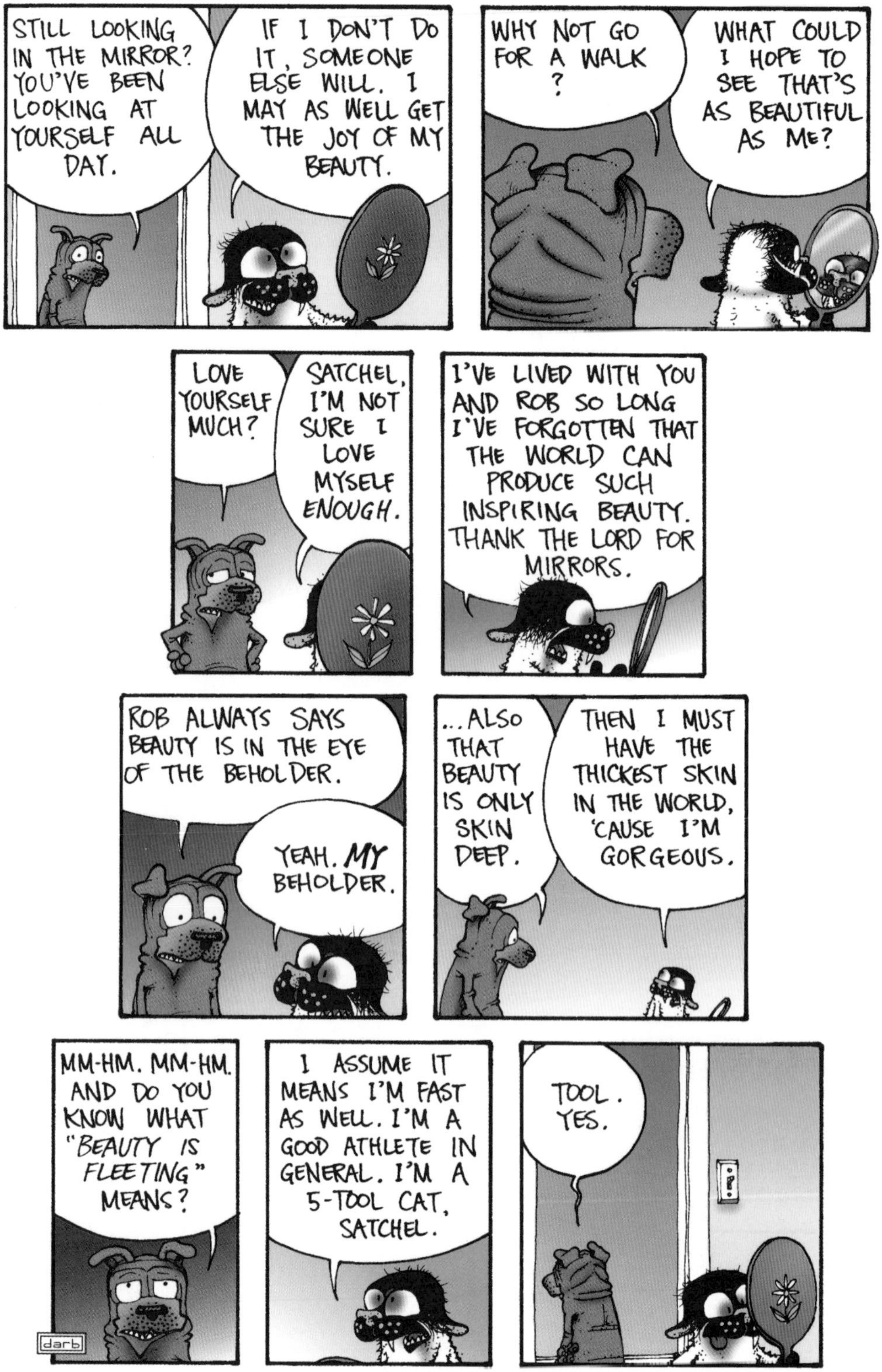
STILL LOOKING IN THE MIRROR? YOU'VE BEEN LOOKING AT YOURSELF ALL DAY.
IF I DON'T DO IT, SOMEONE ELSE WILL. I MAY AS WELL GET THE JOY OF MY BEAUTY.
WHY NOT GO FOR A WALK?
WHAT COULD I HOPE TO SEE THAT'S AS BEAUTIFUL AS ME?
LOVE YOURSELF MUCH?
SATCHEL, I'M NOT SURE I LOVE MYSELF ENOUGH.
I'VE LIVED WITH YOU AND ROB SO LONG I'VE FORGOTTEN THAT THE WORLD CAN PRODUCE SUCH INSPIRING BEAUTY. THANK THE LORD FOR MIRRORS.
ROB ALWAYS SAYS BEAUTY IS IN THE EYE OF THE BEHOLDER.
YEAH. MY BEHOLDER.
...ALSO THAT BEAUTY IS ONLY SKIN DEEP.
THEN I MUST HAVE THE THICKEST SKIN IN THE WORLD, 'CAUSE I'M GORGEOUS.
MM-HM. MM-HM. AND DO YOU KNOW WHAT "BEAUTY IS FLEETING" MEANS?
I ASSUME IT MEANS I'M FAST AS WELL. I'M A GOOD ATHLETE IN GENERAL. I'M A 5-TOOL CAT, SATCHEL.
TOOL. YES.
darb

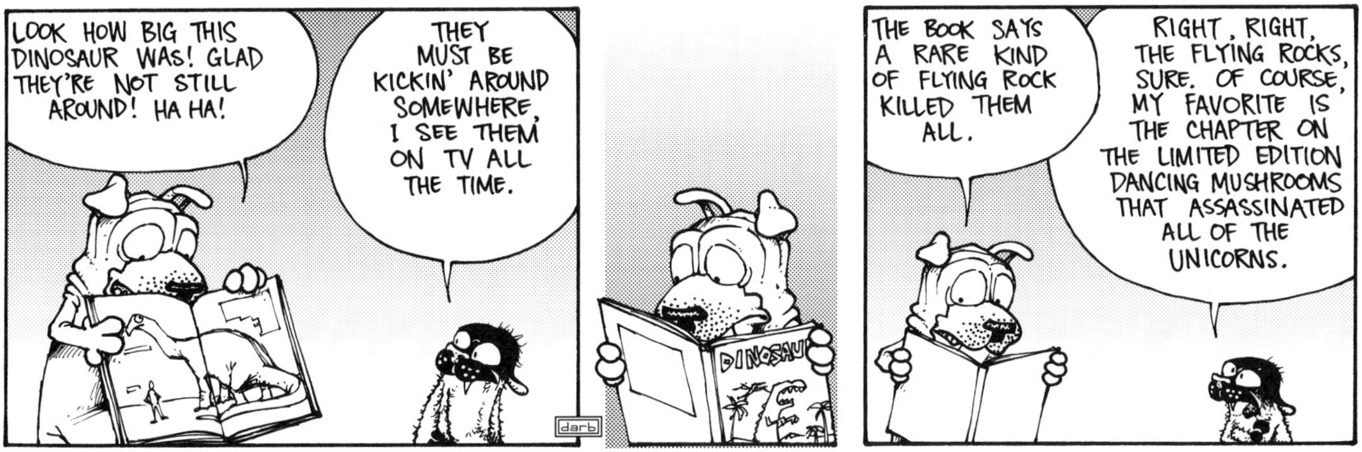
LOOK HOW BIG THIS DINOSAUR WAS! GLAD THEY'RE NOT STILL AROUND! HA HA!
THEY MUST BE KICKIN' AROUND SOMEWHERE, I SEE THEM ON TV ALL THE TIME.
darb
DINOSAUR
THE BOOK SAYS A RARE KIND OF FLYING ROCK KILLED THEM ALL.
RIGHT, RIGHT, THE FLYING ROCKS, SURE. OF COURSE, MY FAVORITE IS THE CHAPTER ON THE LIMITED EDITION DANCING MUSHROOMS THAT ASSASSINATED ALL OF THE UNICORNS.

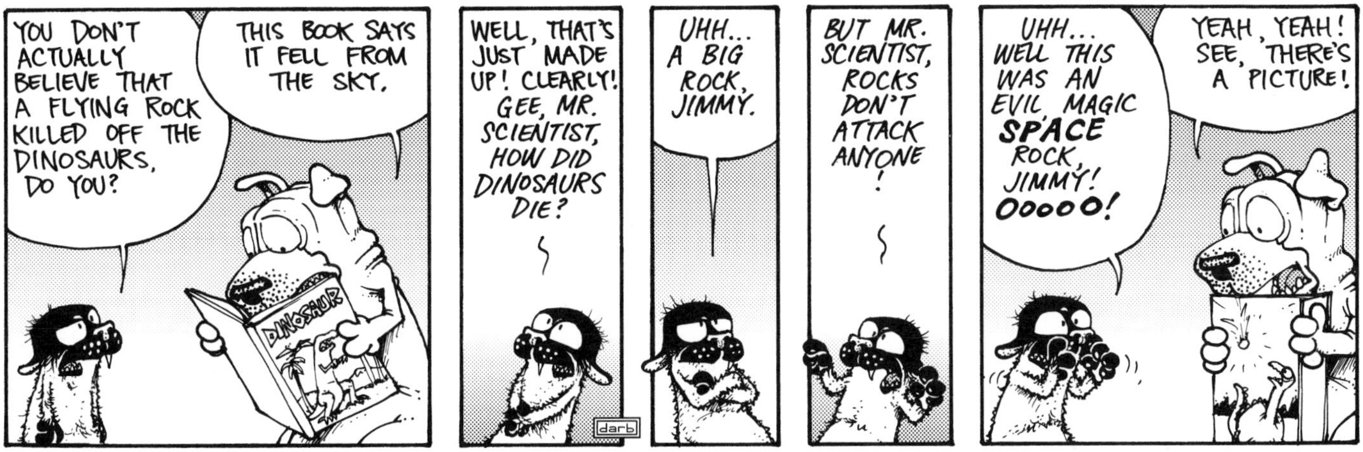
YOU DON'T ACTUALLY BELIEVE THAT A FLYING ROCK KILLED OFF THE DINOSAURS, DO YOU?
THIS BOOK SAYS IT FELL FROM THE SKY.
DINOSAUR
WELL, THAT'S JUST MADE UP! CLEARLY! GEE, MR. SCIENTIST, HOW DID DINOSAURS DIE?
darb
UHH... A BIG ROCK, JIMMY.
BUT MR. SCIENTIST, ROCKS DON'T ATTACK ANYONE!
UHH... WELL THIS WAS AN EVIL MAGIC SPACE ROCK, JIMMY! OOOOO!
YEAH, YEAH! SEE, THERE'S A PICTURE!

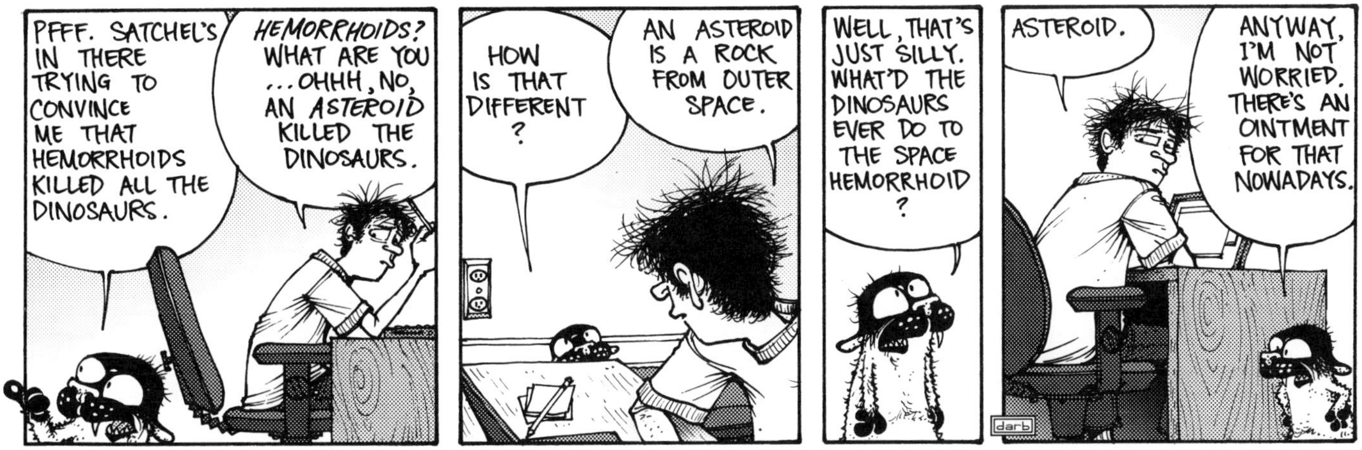
PFFF. SATCHEL'S IN THERE TRYING TO CONVINCE ME THAT HEMORRHOIDS KILLED ALL THE DINOSAURS.
HEMORRHOIDS? WHAT ARE YOU ...OHHH, NO, AN ASTEROID KILLED THE DINOSAURS.
HOW IS THAT DIFFERENT?
AN ASTEROID IS A ROCK FROM OUTER SPACE.
WELL, THAT'S JUST SILLY. WHAT'D THE DINOSAURS EVER DO TO THE SPACE HEMORRHOID?
ASTEROID.
ANYWAY, I'M NOT WORRIED. THERE'S AN OINTMENT FOR THAT NOWADAYS.
darb

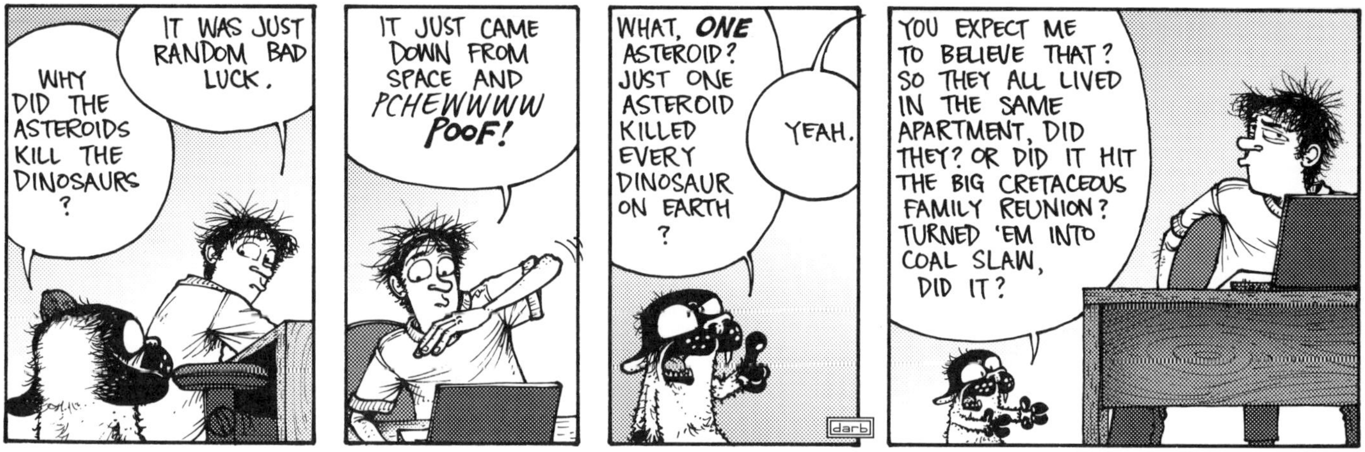
WHY DID THE ASTEROIDS KILL THE DINOSAURS?
IT WAS JUST RANDOM BAD LUCK.
IT JUST CAME DOWN FROM SPACE AND PCHEWWWW POOF!
WHAT, ONE ASTEROID? JUST ONE ASTEROID KILLED EVERY DINOSAUR ON EARTH?
YEAH.
darb
YOU EXPECT ME TO BELIEVE THAT? SO THEY ALL LIVED IN THE SAME APARTMENT, DID THEY? OR DID IT HIT THE BIG CRETACEOUS FAMILY REUNION? TURNED 'EM INTO COAL SLAW, DID IT?

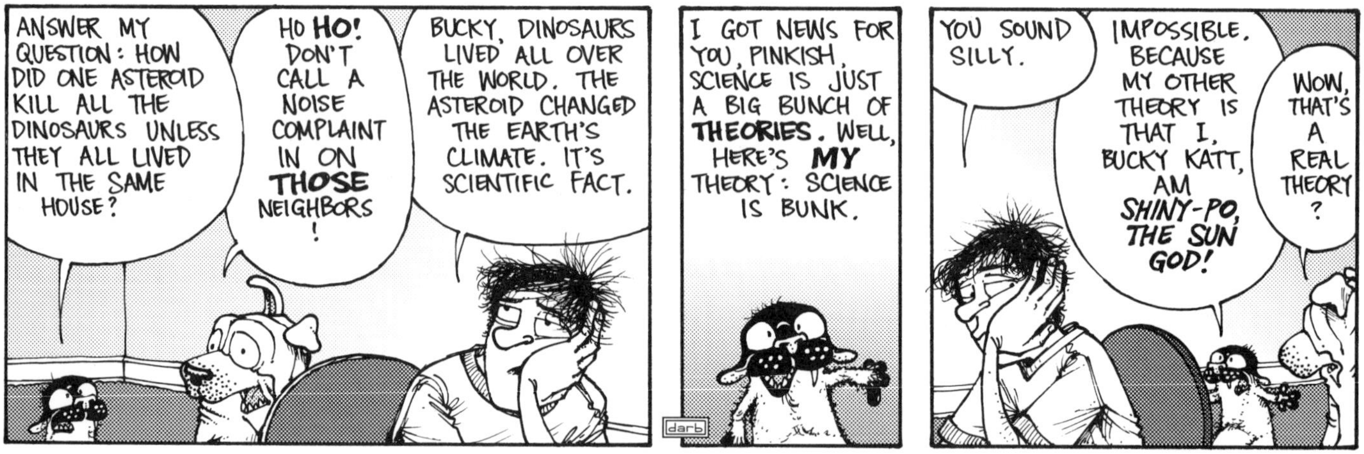
ANSWER MY QUESTION: HOW DID ONE ASTEROID KILL ALL THE DINOSAURS UNLESS THEY ALL LIVED IN THE SAME HOUSE?
HO HO! DON'T CALL A NOISE COMPLAINT IN ON THOSE NEIGHBORS!
BUCKY, DINOSAURS LIVED ALL OVER THE WORLD. THE ASTEROID CHANGED THE EARTH'S CLIMATE. IT'S SCIENTIFIC FACT.
darb
I GOT NEWS FOR YOU, PINKISH, SCIENCE IS JUST A BIG BUNCH OF THEORIES. WELL, HERE'S MY THEORY: SCIENCE IS BUNK.
YOU SOUND SILLY.
IMPOSSIBLE. BECAUSE MY OTHER THEORY IS THAT I, BUCKY KATT, AM SHINY-PO, THE SUN GOD!
WOW, THAT'S A REAL THEORY?

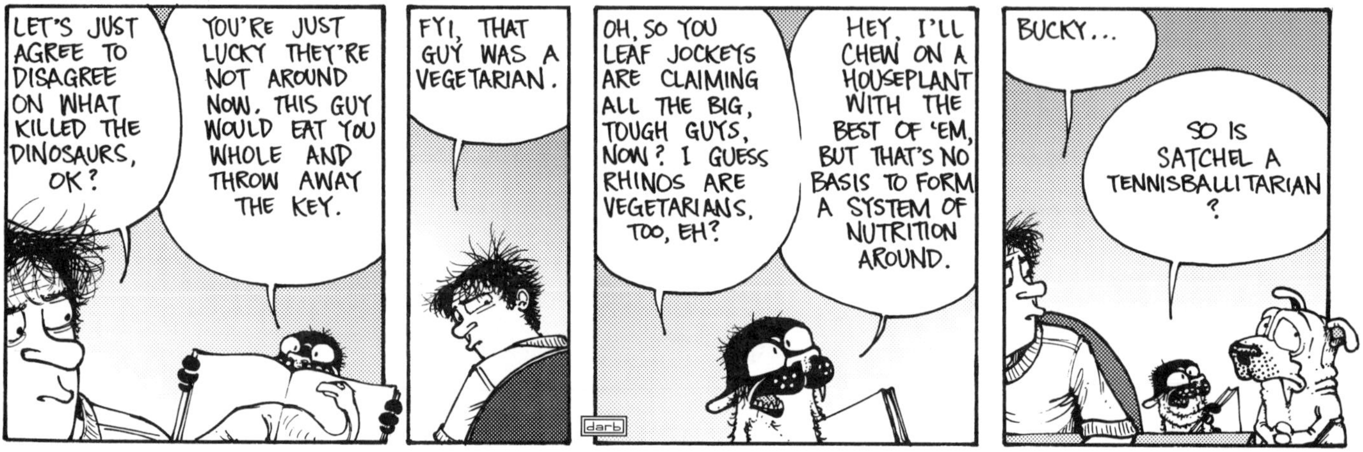
LET'S JUST AGREE TO DISAGREE ON WHAT KILLED THE DINOSAURS, OK?
YOU'RE JUST LUCKY THEY'RE NOT AROUND NOW. THIS GUY WOULD EAT YOU WHOLE AND THROW AWAY THE KEY.
FYI, THAT GUY WAS A VEGETARIAN.
darb
OH, SO YOU LEAF JOCKEYS ARE CLAIMING ALL THE BIG, TOUGH GUYS, NOW? I GUESS RHINOS ARE VEGETARIANS, TOO, EH?
HEY, I'LL CHEW ON A HOUSEPLANT WITH THE BEST OF 'EM, BUT THAT'S NO BASIS TO FORM A SYSTEM OF NUTRITION AROUND.
BUCKY...
SO IS SATCHEL A TENNISBALLITARIAN?

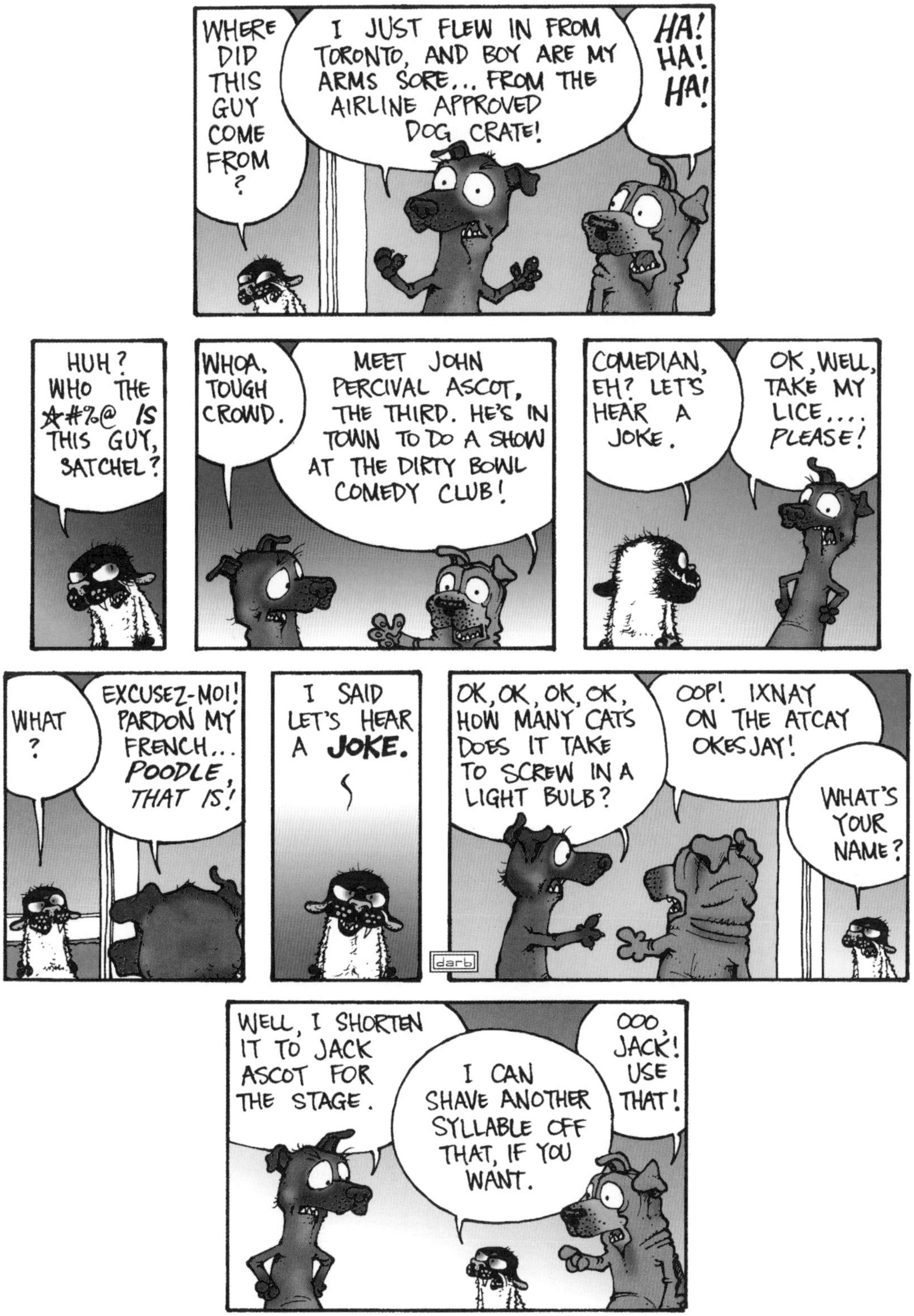
WHERE DID THIS GUY COME FROM?
I JUST FLEW IN FROM TORONTO, AND BOY ARE MY ARMS SORE... FROM THE AIRLINE APPROVED DOG CRATE!
HA! HA! HA!
HUH? WHO THE ✯#%@ IS THIS GUY, SATCHEL?
WHOA. TOUGH CROWD.
MEET JOHN PERCIVAL ASCOT, THE THIRD. HE'S IN TOWN TO DO A SHOW AT THE DIRTY BOWL COMEDY CLUB!
COMEDIAN, EH? LET'S HEAR A JOKE.
OK, WELL, TAKE MY LICE.... PLEASE!
WHAT?
EXCUSEZ-MOI! PARDON MY FRENCH... POODLE, THAT IS!
I SAID LET'S HEAR A JOKE.
OK, OK, OK, OK, HOW MANY CATS DOES IT TAKE TO SCREW IN A LIGHT BULB?
OOP! IXNAY ON THE ATCAY OKESJAY!
WHAT'S YOUR NAME?
darb
WELL, I SHORTEN IT TO JACK ASCOT FOR THE STAGE.
I CAN SHAVE ANOTHER SYLLABLE OFF THAT, IF YOU WANT.
OOO, JACK! USE THAT!

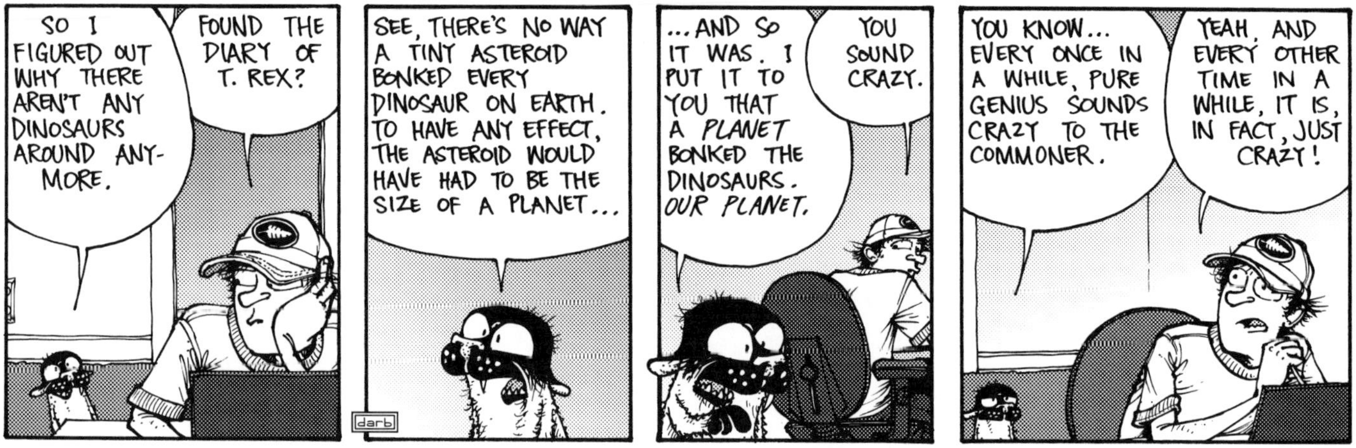
SO I FIGURED OUT WHY THERE AREN'T ANY DINOSAURS AROUND ANYMORE.
FOUND THE DIARY OF T. REX?
SEE, THERE'S NO WAY A TINY ASTEROID BONKED EVERY DINOSAUR ON EARTH. TO HAVE ANY EFFECT, THE ASTEROID WOULD HAVE HAD TO BE THE SIZE OF A PLANET...
...AND SO IT WAS. I PUT IT TO YOU THAT A *PLANET* BONKED THE DINOSAURS. *OUR PLANET.*
YOU SOUND CRAZY.
YOU KNOW... EVERY ONCE IN A WHILE, PURE GENIUS SOUNDS CRAZY TO THE COMMONER.
YEAH, AND EVERY OTHER TIME IN A WHILE, IT IS, IN FACT, JUST CRAZY!

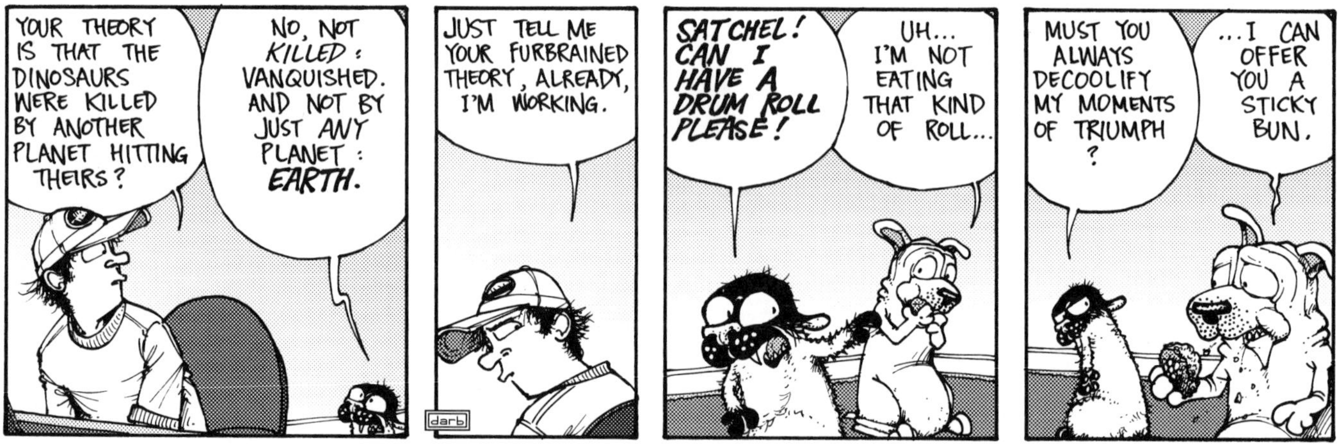
YOUR THEORY IS THAT THE DINOSAURS WERE KILLED BY ANOTHER PLANET HITTING THEIRS?
NO, NOT *KILLED*: VANQUISHED. AND NOT BY JUST *ANY* PLANET: **EARTH**.
JUST TELL ME YOUR FURBRAINED THEORY, ALREADY, I'M WORKING.
SATCHEL! CAN I HAVE A DRUM ROLL PLEASE!
UH... I'M NOT EATING THAT KIND OF ROLL...
MUST YOU ALWAYS DECOOLIFY MY MOMENTS OF TRIUMPH?
...I CAN OFFER YOU A STICKY BUN.

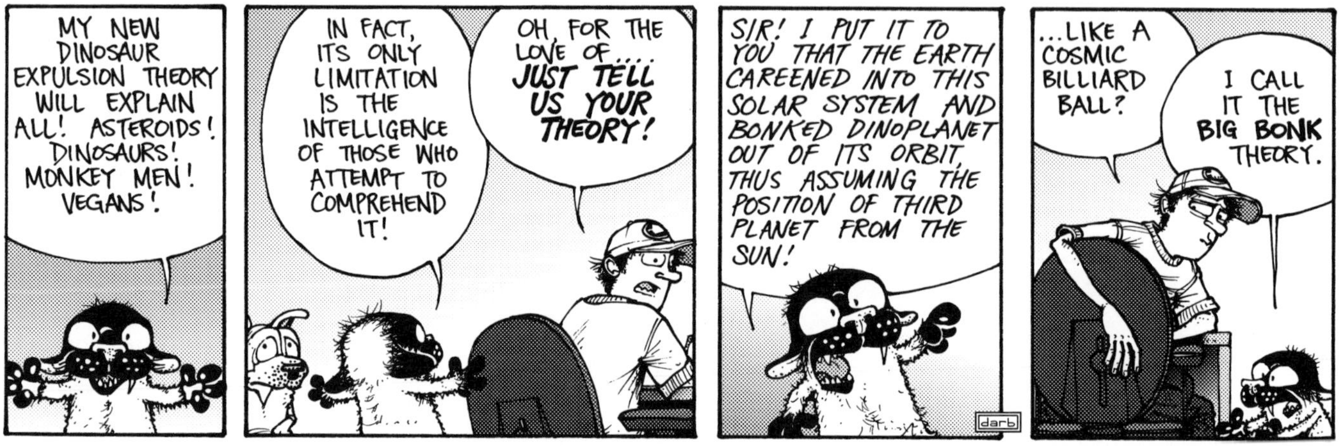
MY NEW DINOSAUR EXPULSION THEORY WILL EXPLAIN ALL! ASTEROIDS! DINOSAURS! MONKEY MEN! VEGANS!
IN FACT, ITS ONLY LIMITATION IS THE INTELLIGENCE OF THOSE WHO ATTEMPT TO COMPREHEND IT!
OH, FOR THE LOVE OF.... **JUST TELL US YOUR THEORY!**
SIR! I PUT IT TO YOU THAT THE EARTH CAREENED INTO THIS SOLAR SYSTEM AND BONKED DINOPLANET OUT OF ITS ORBIT, THUS ASSUMING THE POSITION OF THIRD PLANET FROM THE SUN!
...LIKE A COSMIC BILLIARD BALL?
I CALL IT THE **BIG BONK** THEORY.

Panel 1: SO YOUR THEORY IS THAT THE EARTH HURTLED THROUGH SPACE AND KNOCKED A PLANET FULL OF DINOSAURS OUT OF ITS ORBIT LIKE A BIG CROQUET BALL?

Panel 2: THAT'S CORRECT. / THEN WHY ARE THERE DINOSAUR FOSSILS ON EARTH?

Panel 3: SEE, WHEN TWO OBJECTS COLLIDE, RESIDUE IS ALWAYS TRANSFERRED BETWEEN... WAIT, I'LL SHOW YOU.

Panel 4: SLAP!

Panel 5: WHAT THE...? / SATCHEL'S FUR ON MY PAW. FILTHY PROOF OF THE BIG BONK.

Panel 6: OK, SO PUTTING YOUR THEORY OF THE BIG BONK TOGETHER, ALL DINOSAUR FOSSILS ON EARTH ARE ANCIENT "RESIDUE" FROM WHEN THE EARTH COLLIDED WITH THE DINOSAUR PLANET...

Panel 7: ...AND, AS YOU SAY, THAT'S WHY ALL THE FOSSILS ARE FLAT... BECAUSE THEY WERE CRUSHED IN THE IMPACT? / ...AND STUCK TO THE EARTH LIKE LIZARD PANCAKES, YES.

Panel 8: SO SOMEWHERE OUT THERE DINOSAURS ARE STILL ALIVE? / HURTLING THROUGH SPACE IRATE AND NAUSEATED, YES. / AND TRYING TO FIGURE OUT WHAT ALL THE FLAT, LITTLE HUMAN FOSSILS ARE, PRESUMABLY.

Panel 9: MY BIG BONK THEORY EXPLAINS EVERYTHING. WHERE EARTH HIT THE DINOSAUR PLANET, THERE'S A BIG DENT. THAT'S THE OCEAN. / ...AND DINOPLANET WAS A LOT OLDER THAN EARTH, SO THAT'S WHY WE NOW HAVE MILLION-YEAR-OLD DINOSAUR BONES ON OUR SIX-THOUSAND-YEAR-OLD PLANET.

Panel 10: WOW, ANYTHING ELSE? / A FEW OF THE DINOSAURS THAT STUCK TO THE EARTH SURVIVED THE IMPACT. THAT'S HOW THEY WERE ABLE TO FILM "THE FLINTSTONES." / MM-HM. SO THAT WOULD BE IN THE *FACETIOUS* PERIOD, WHICH FOLLOWED THE CRETACEOUS.

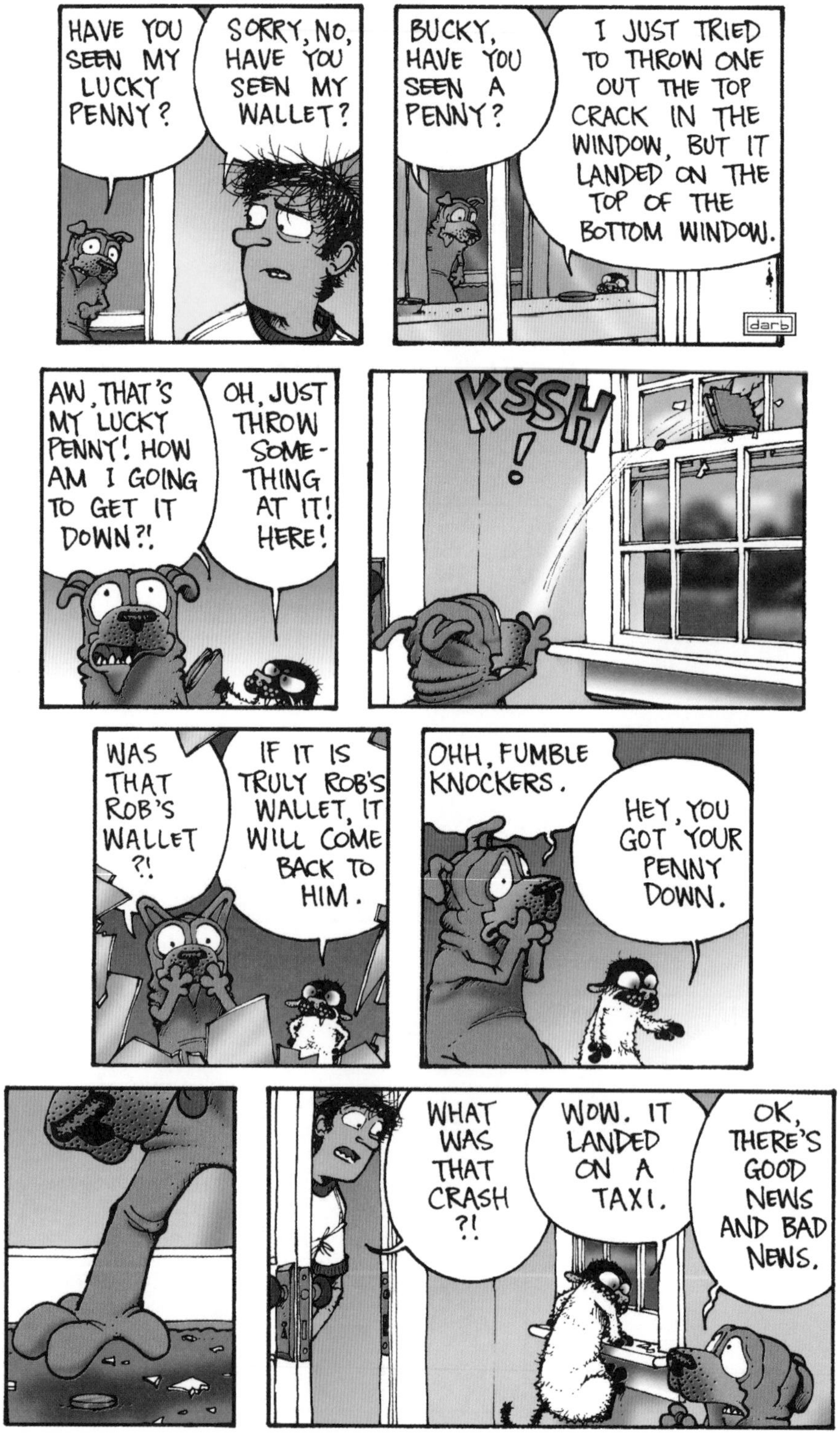
HAVE YOU SEEN MY LUCKY PENNY?
SORRY, NO, HAVE YOU SEEN MY WALLET?
BUCKY, HAVE YOU SEEN A PENNY?
I JUST TRIED TO THROW ONE OUT THE TOP CRACK IN THE WINDOW, BUT IT LANDED ON THE TOP OF THE BOTTOM WINDOW.
darb
AW, THAT'S MY LUCKY PENNY! HOW AM I GOING TO GET IT DOWN?!
OH, JUST THROW SOME-THING AT IT! HERE!
KSSH
!
WAS THAT ROB'S WALLET?!
IF IT IS TRULY ROB'S WALLET, IT WILL COME BACK TO HIM.
OHH, FUMBLE KNOCKERS.
HEY, YOU GOT YOUR PENNY DOWN.
WHAT WAS THAT CRASH?!
WOW. IT LANDED ON A TAXI.
OK, THERE'S GOOD NEWS AND BAD NEWS.

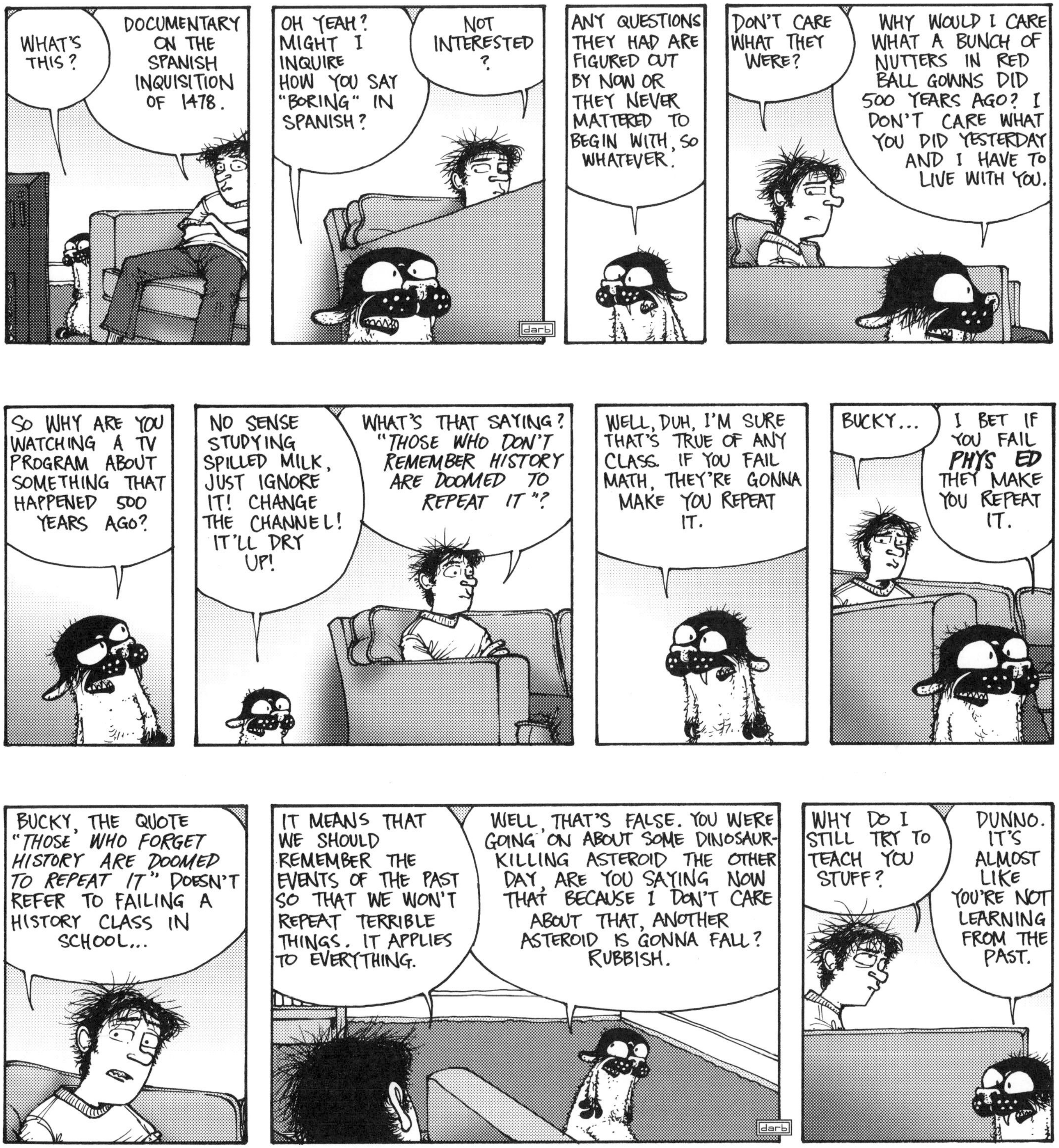
WHAT'S THIS?
DOCUMENTARY ON THE SPANISH INQUISITION OF 1478.
OH YEAH? MIGHT I INQUIRE HOW YOU SAY "BORING" IN SPANISH?
NOT INTERESTED?
ANY QUESTIONS THEY HAD ARE FIGURED OUT BY NOW OR THEY NEVER MATTERED TO BEGIN WITH, SO WHATEVER.
DON'T CARE WHAT THEY WERE?
WHY WOULD I CARE WHAT A BUNCH OF NUTTERS IN RED BALL GOWNS DID 500 YEARS AGO? I DON'T CARE WHAT YOU DID YESTERDAY AND I HAVE TO LIVE WITH YOU.
darb
SO WHY ARE YOU WATCHING A TV PROGRAM ABOUT SOMETHING THAT HAPPENED 500 YEARS AGO?
NO SENSE STUDYING SPILLED MILK, JUST IGNORE IT! CHANGE THE CHANNEL! IT'LL DRY UP!
WHAT'S THAT SAYING? "THOSE WHO DON'T REMEMBER HISTORY ARE DOOMED TO REPEAT IT"?
WELL, DUH, I'M SURE THAT'S TRUE OF ANY CLASS. IF YOU FAIL MATH, THEY'RE GONNA MAKE YOU REPEAT IT.
BUCKY...
I BET IF YOU FAIL PHYS ED THEY MAKE YOU REPEAT IT.
BUCKY, THE QUOTE "THOSE WHO FORGET HISTORY ARE DOOMED TO REPEAT IT" DOESN'T REFER TO FAILING A HISTORY CLASS IN SCHOOL...
IT MEANS THAT WE SHOULD REMEMBER THE EVENTS OF THE PAST SO THAT WE WON'T REPEAT TERRIBLE THINGS. IT APPLIES TO EVERYTHING.
WELL, THAT'S FALSE. YOU WERE GOING ON ABOUT SOME DINOSAUR-KILLING ASTEROID THE OTHER DAY, ARE YOU SAYING NOW THAT BECAUSE I DON'T CARE ABOUT THAT, ANOTHER ASTEROID IS GONNA FALL? RUBBISH.
darb
WHY DO I STILL TRY TO TEACH YOU STUFF?
DUNNO. IT'S ALMOST LIKE YOU'RE NOT LEARNING FROM THE PAST.

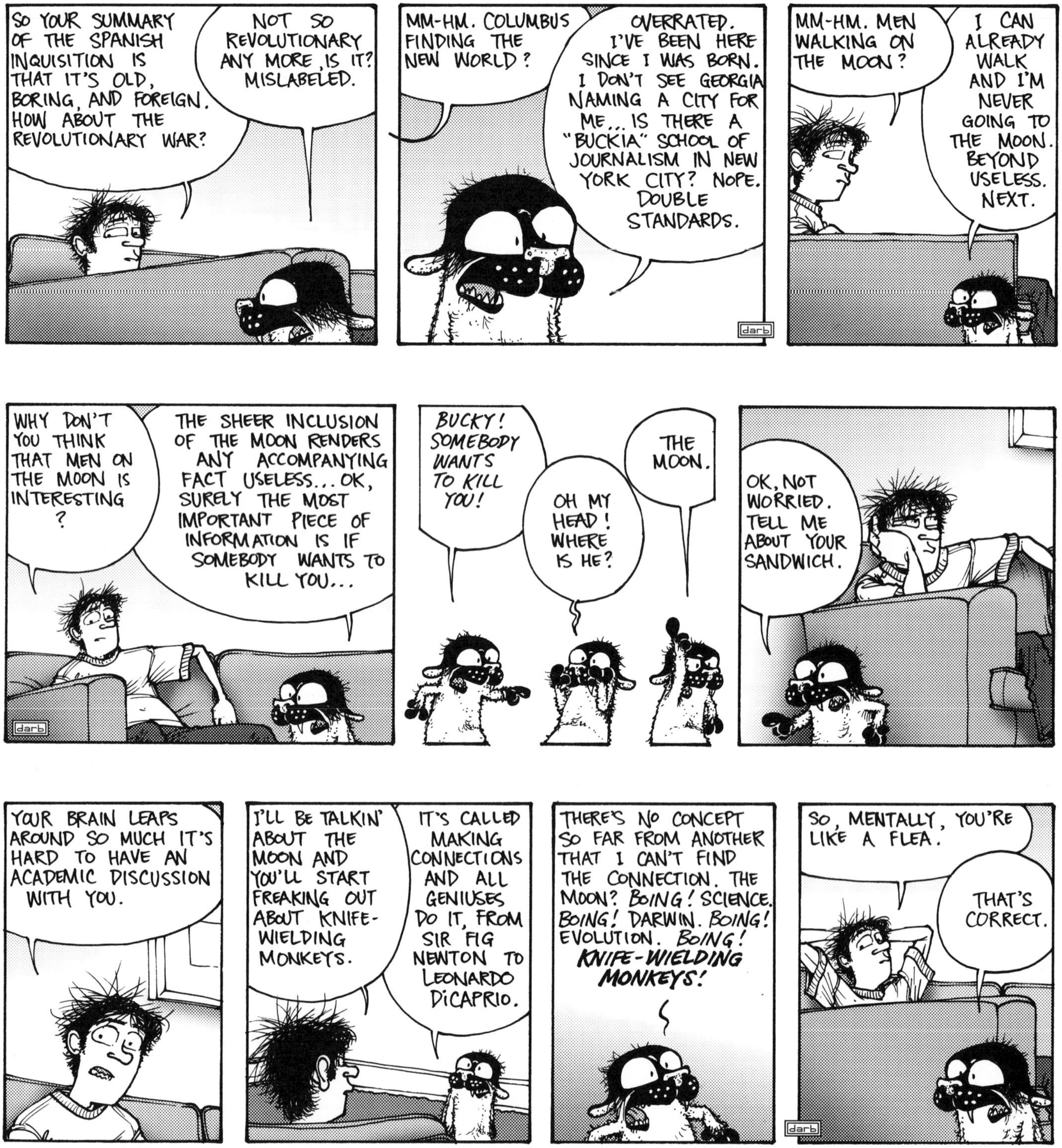
SO YOUR SUMMARY OF THE SPANISH INQUISITION IS THAT IT'S OLD, BORING, AND FOREIGN. HOW ABOUT THE REVOLUTIONARY WAR?
NOT SO REVOLUTIONARY ANY MORE, IS IT? MISLABELED.
MM-HM. COLUMBUS FINDING THE NEW WORLD?
OVERRATED. I'VE BEEN HERE SINCE I WAS BORN. I DON'T SEE GEORGIA NAMING A CITY FOR ME... IS THERE A "BUCKIA" SCHOOL OF JOURNALISM IN NEW YORK CITY? NOPE. DOUBLE STANDARDS.
MM-HM. MEN WALKING ON THE MOON?
I CAN ALREADY WALK AND I'M NEVER GOING TO THE MOON. BEYOND USELESS. NEXT.
darb
WHY DON'T YOU THINK THAT MEN ON THE MOON IS INTERESTING?
THE SHEER INCLUSION OF THE MOON RENDERS ANY ACCOMPANYING FACT USELESS... OK, SURELY THE MOST IMPORTANT PIECE OF INFORMATION IS IF SOMEBODY WANTS TO KILL YOU...
BUCKY! SOMEBODY WANTS TO KILL YOU!
OH MY HEAD! WHERE IS HE?
THE MOON.
OK, NOT WORRIED. TELL ME ABOUT YOUR SANDWICH.
darb
YOUR BRAIN LEAPS AROUND SO MUCH IT'S HARD TO HAVE AN ACADEMIC DISCUSSION WITH YOU.
I'LL BE TALKIN' ABOUT THE MOON AND YOU'LL START FREAKING OUT ABOUT KNIFE-WIELDING MONKEYS.
IT'S CALLED MAKING CONNECTIONS AND ALL GENIUSES DO IT, FROM SIR FIG NEWTON TO LEONARDO DICAPRIO.
THERE'S NO CONCEPT SO FAR FROM ANOTHER THAT I CAN'T FIND THE CONNECTION. THE MOON? BOING! SCIENCE. BOING! DARWIN. BOING! EVOLUTION. BOING! KNIFE-WIELDING MONKEYS!
SO, MENTALLY, YOU'RE LIKE A FLEA.
THAT'S CORRECT.
darb

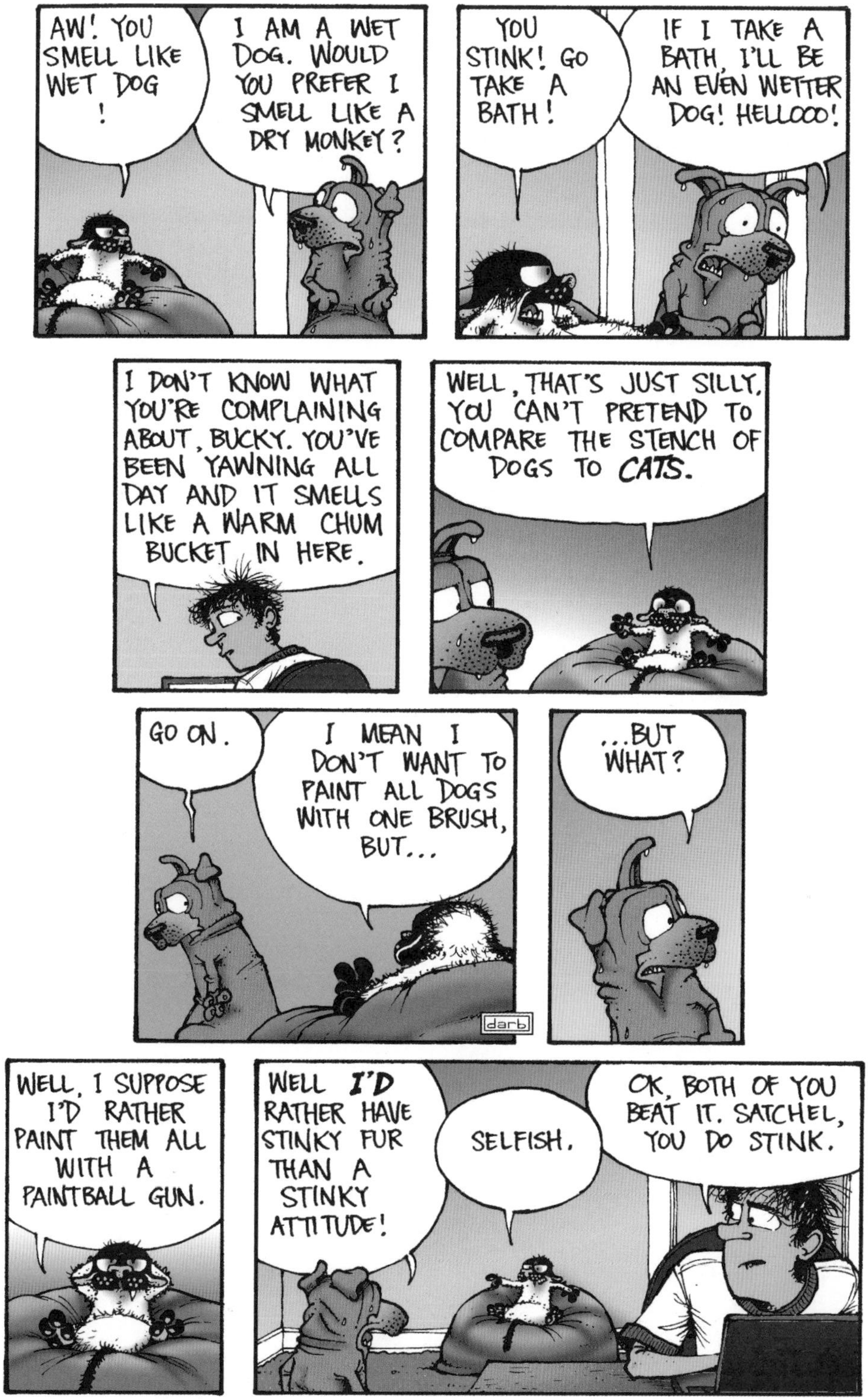
AW! YOU SMELL LIKE WET DOG !
I AM A WET DOG. WOULD YOU PREFER I SMELL LIKE A DRY MONKEY?
YOU STINK! GO TAKE A BATH!
IF I TAKE A BATH, I'LL BE AN EVEN WETTER DOG! HELLOOO!
I DON'T KNOW WHAT YOU'RE COMPLAINING ABOUT, BUCKY. YOU'VE BEEN YAWNING ALL DAY AND IT SMELLS LIKE A WARM CHUM BUCKET IN HERE.
WELL, THAT'S JUST SILLY. YOU CAN'T PRETEND TO COMPARE THE STENCH OF DOGS TO CATS.
GO ON.
I MEAN I DON'T WANT TO PAINT ALL DOGS WITH ONE BRUSH, BUT...
darb
...BUT WHAT?
WELL, I SUPPOSE I'D RATHER PAINT THEM ALL WITH A PAINTBALL GUN.
WELL I'D RATHER HAVE STINKY FUR THAN A STINKY ATTITUDE!
SELFISH.
OK, BOTH OF YOU BEAT IT. SATCHEL, YOU DO STINK.

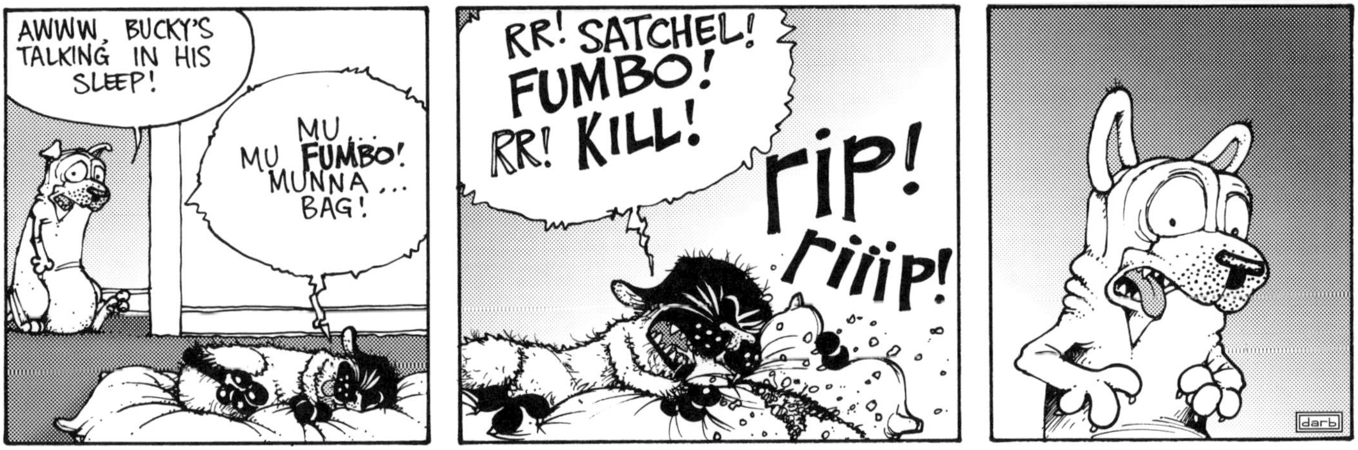
AWWW, BUCKY'S TALKING IN HIS SLEEP!
MU... MU FUMBO! MUNNA... BAG!
RR! SATCHEL! FUMBO! RR! KILL!
rip! riiip!
darb

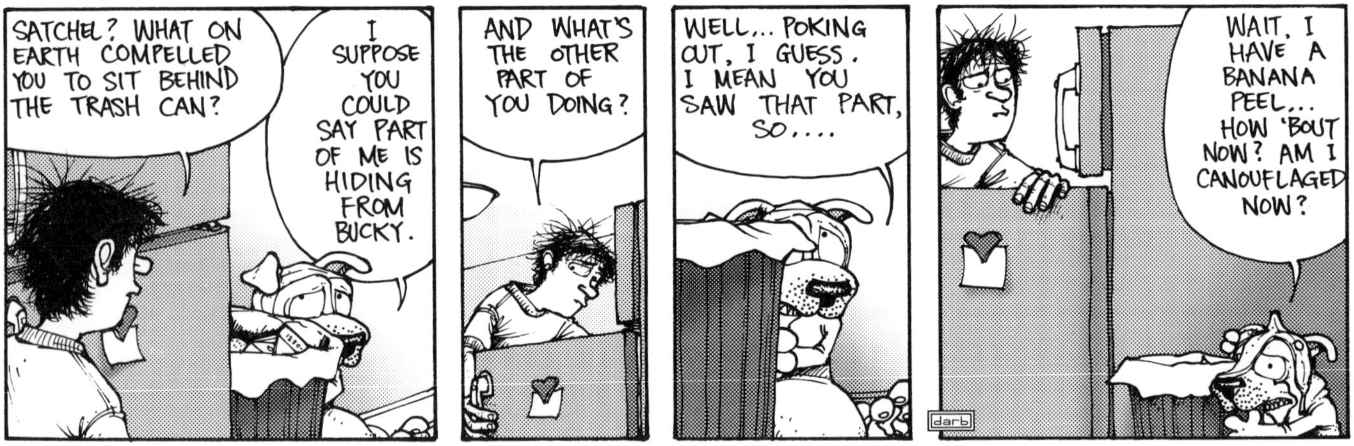
SATCHEL? WHAT ON EARTH COMPELLED YOU TO SIT BEHIND THE TRASH CAN?
I SUPPOSE YOU COULD SAY PART OF ME IS HIDING FROM BUCKY.
AND WHAT'S THE OTHER PART OF YOU DOING?
WELL... POKING OUT, I GUESS. I MEAN YOU SAW THAT PART, SO....
WAIT, I HAVE A BANANA PEEL... HOW 'BOUT NOW? AM I CANOUFLAGED NOW?
darb

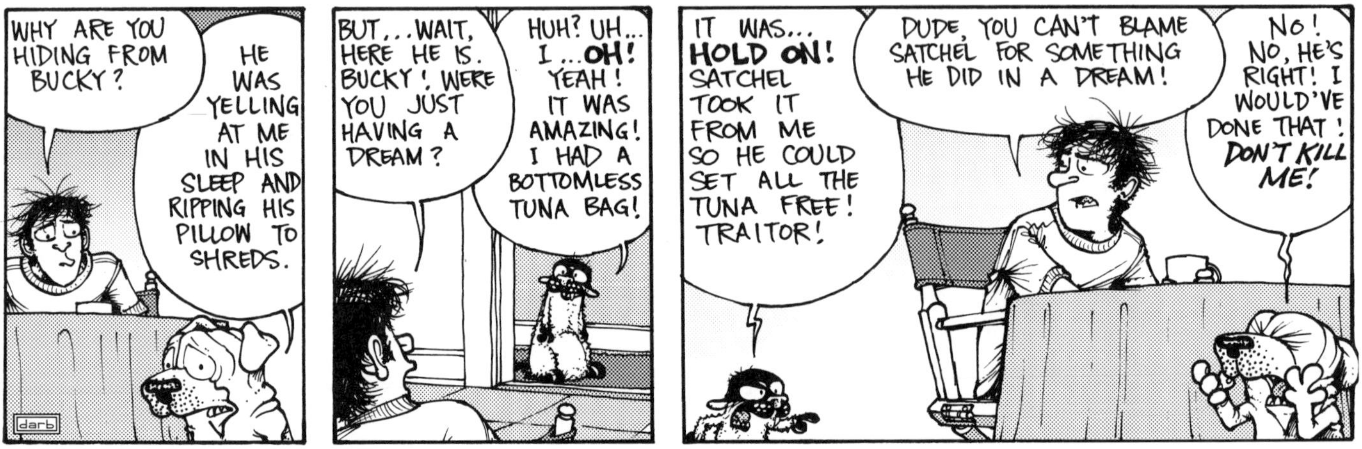
WHY ARE YOU HIDING FROM BUCKY?
HE WAS YELLING AT ME IN HIS SLEEP AND RIPPING HIS PILLOW TO SHREDS.
BUT... WAIT, HERE HE IS. BUCKY! WERE YOU JUST HAVING A DREAM?
HUH? UH... I... OH! YEAH! IT WAS AMAZING! I HAD A BOTTOMLESS TUNA BAG!
IT WAS... HOLD ON! SATCHEL TOOK IT FROM ME SO HE COULD SET ALL THE TUNA FREE! TRAITOR!
DUDE, YOU CAN'T BLAME SATCHEL FOR SOMETHING HE DID IN A DREAM!
NO! NO, HE'S RIGHT! I WOULD'VE DONE THAT! DON'T KILL ME!
darb

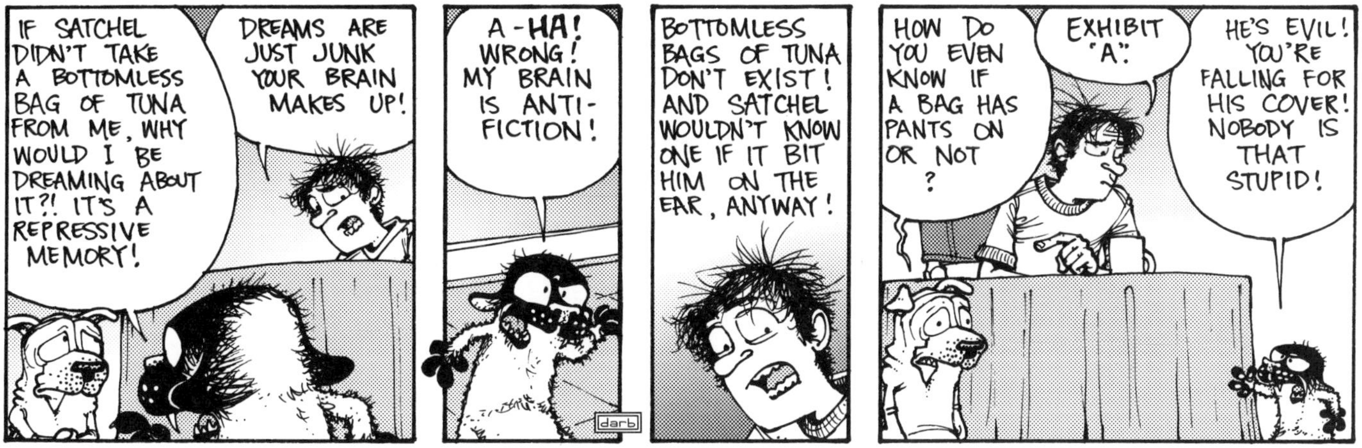
IF SATCHEL DIDN'T TAKE A BOTTOMLESS BAG OF TUNA FROM ME, WHY WOULD I BE DREAMING ABOUT IT?! IT'S A REPRESSIVE MEMORY!
DREAMS ARE JUST JUNK YOUR BRAIN MAKES UP!
A-HA! WRONG! MY BRAIN IS ANTI-FICTION!
BOTTOMLESS BAGS OF TUNA DON'T EXIST! AND SATCHEL WOULDN'T KNOW ONE IF IT BIT HIM ON THE EAR, ANYWAY!
HOW DO YOU EVEN KNOW IF A BAG HAS PANTS ON OR NOT?
EXHIBIT "A".
HE'S EVIL! YOU'RE FALLING FOR HIS COVER! NOBODY IS THAT STUPID!
darb

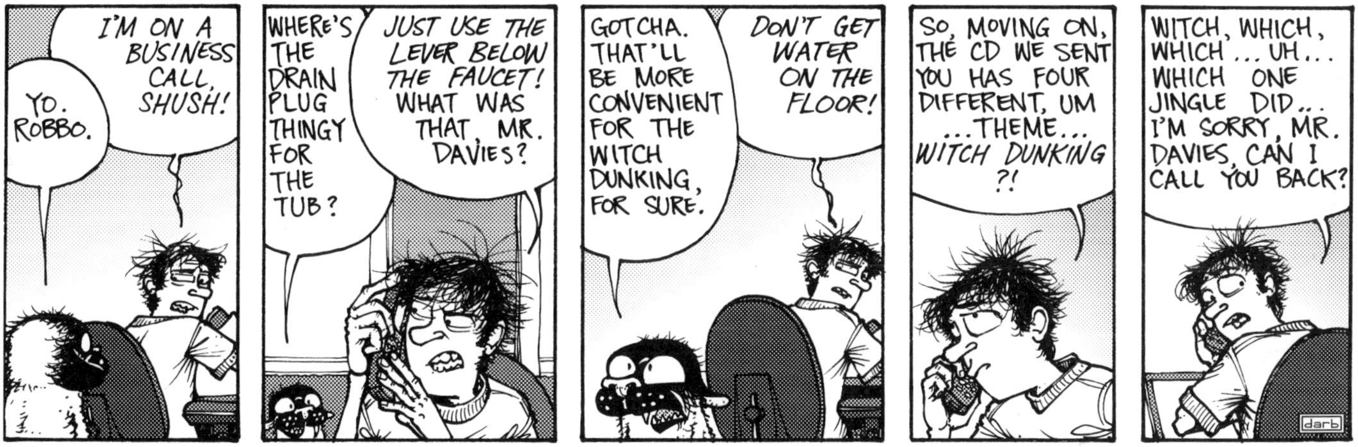
YO. ROBBO.
I'M ON A BUSINESS CALL, SHUSH!
WHERE'S THE DRAIN PLUG THINGY FOR THE TUB?
JUST USE THE LEVER BELOW THE FAUCET! WHAT WAS THAT, MR. DAVIES?
GOTCHA. THAT'LL BE MORE CONVENIENT FOR THE WITCH DUNKING, FOR SURE.
DON'T GET WATER ON THE FLOOR!
SO, MOVING ON, THE CD WE SENT YOU HAS FOUR DIFFERENT, UM ...THEME... WITCH DUNKING?!
WITCH, WHICH, WHICH... UH... WHICH ONE JINGLE DID... I'M SORRY, MR. DAVIES, CAN I CALL YOU BACK?
darb

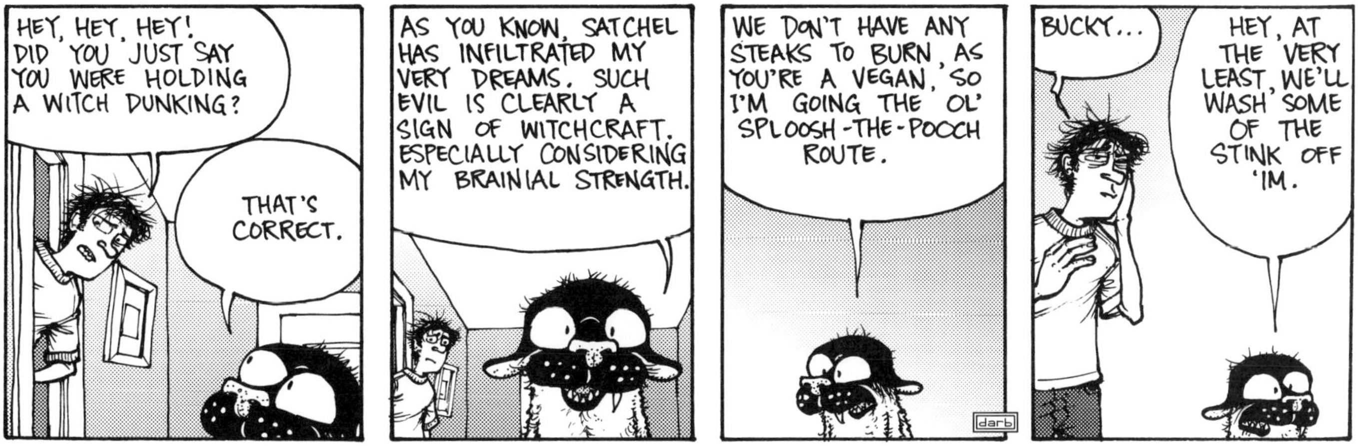
HEY, HEY, HEY! DID YOU JUST SAY YOU WERE HOLDING A WITCH DUNKING?
THAT'S CORRECT.
AS YOU KNOW, SATCHEL HAS INFILTRATED MY VERY DREAMS. SUCH EVIL IS CLEARLY A SIGN OF WITCHCRAFT. ESPECIALLY CONSIDERING MY BRAINIAL STRENGTH.
WE DON'T HAVE ANY STEAKS TO BURN, AS YOU'RE A VEGAN, SO I'M GOING THE OL' SPLOOSH-THE-POOCH ROUTE.
darb
BUCKY...
HEY, AT THE VERY LEAST, WE'LL WASH SOME OF THE STINK OFF 'IM.

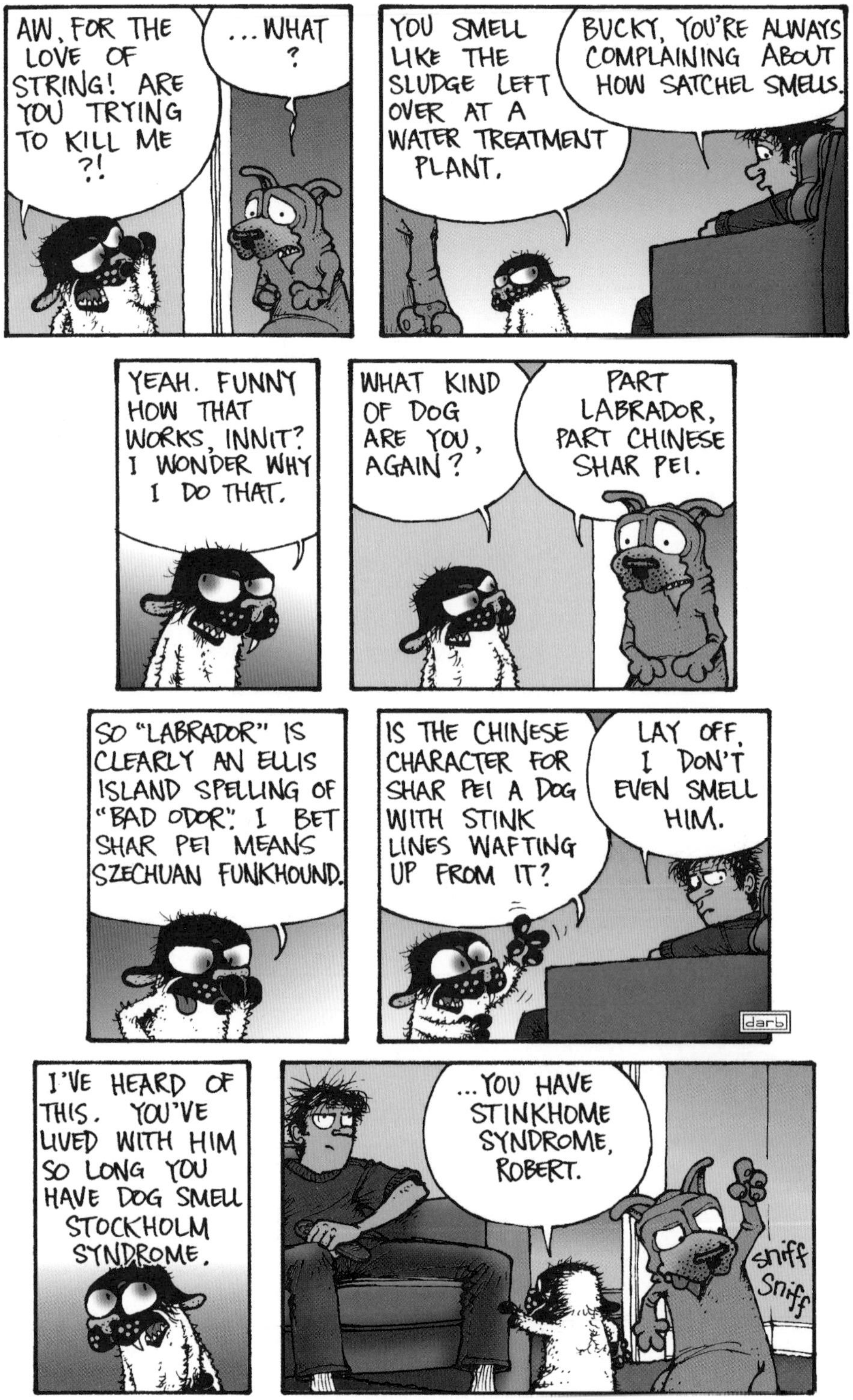
AW, FOR THE LOVE OF STRING! ARE YOU TRYING TO KILL ME ?!
...WHAT ?
YOU SMELL LIKE THE SLUDGE LEFT OVER AT A WATER TREATMENT PLANT.
BUCKY, YOU'RE ALWAYS COMPLAINING ABOUT HOW SATCHEL SMELLS.
YEAH. FUNNY HOW THAT WORKS, INNIT? I WONDER WHY I DO THAT.
WHAT KIND OF DOG ARE YOU, AGAIN?
PART LABRADOR, PART CHINESE SHAR PEI.
SO "LABRADOR" IS CLEARLY AN ELLIS ISLAND SPELLING OF "BAD ODOR". I BET SHAR PEI MEANS SZECHUAN FUNKHOUND.
IS THE CHINESE CHARACTER FOR SHAR PEI A DOG WITH STINK LINES WAFTING UP FROM IT?
LAY OFF. I DON'T EVEN SMELL HIM.
darb
I'VE HEARD OF THIS. YOU'VE LIVED WITH HIM SO LONG YOU HAVE DOG SMELL STOCKHOLM SYNDROME.
...YOU HAVE STINKHOME SYNDROME, ROBERT.
sniff
sniff

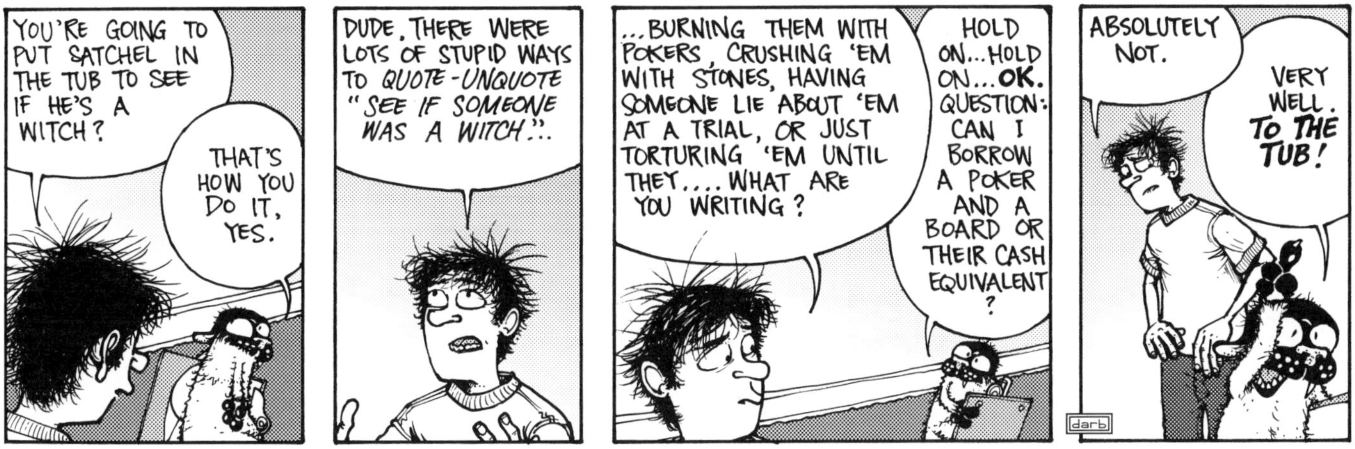
YOU'RE GOING TO PUT SATCHEL IN THE TUB TO SEE IF HE'S A WITCH?
THAT'S HOW YOU DO IT, YES.
DUDE, THERE WERE LOTS OF STUPID WAYS TO *QUOTE-UNQUOTE* *"SEE IF SOMEONE WAS A WITCH"*...
...BURNING THEM WITH POKERS, CRUSHING 'EM WITH STONES, HAVING SOMEONE LIE ABOUT 'EM AT A TRIAL, OR JUST TORTURING 'EM UNTIL THEY.... WHAT ARE YOU WRITING?
HOLD ON...HOLD ON...**OK.** QUESTION: CAN I BORROW A POKER AND A BOARD OR THEIR CASH EQUIVALENT?
ABSOLUTELY NOT.
VERY WELL. ***TO THE TUB!***
darb

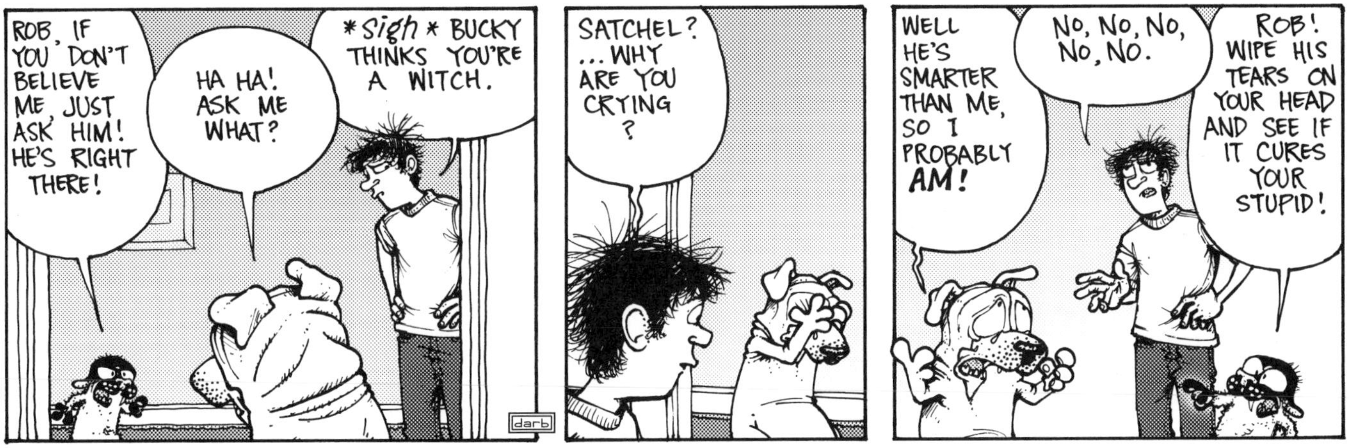
ROB, IF YOU DON'T BELIEVE ME, JUST ASK HIM! HE'S RIGHT THERE!
HA HA! ASK ME WHAT?
sigh BUCKY THINKS YOU'RE A WITCH.
darb
SATCHEL? ...WHY ARE YOU CRYING?
WELL HE'S SMARTER THAN ME, SO I PROBABLY **AM!**
NO, NO, NO, NO, NO.
ROB! WIPE HIS TEARS ON YOUR HEAD AND SEE IF IT CURES YOUR STUPID!

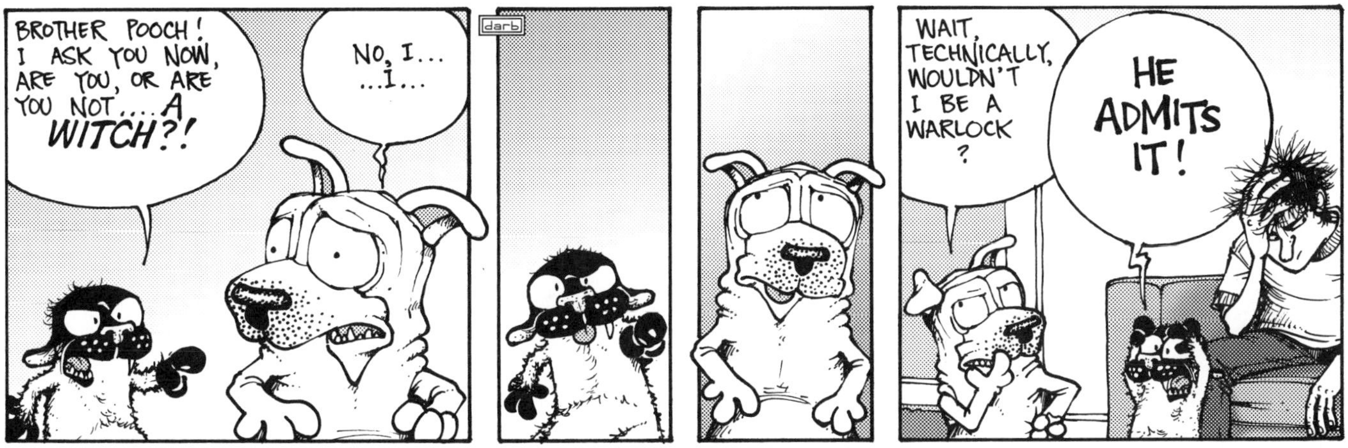
BROTHER POOCH! I ASK YOU NOW, ARE YOU, OR ARE YOU NOT.... ***A WITCH?!***
NO, I... ...I...
darb
WAIT, TECHNICALLY, WOULDN'T I BE A WARLOCK?
HE ADMITS IT!

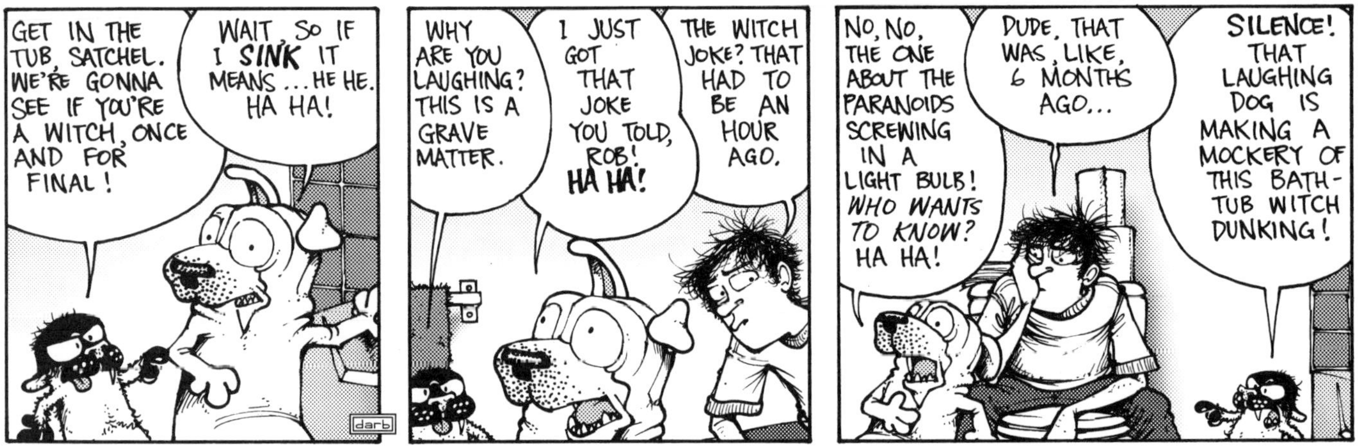
GET IN THE TUB, SATCHEL. WE'RE GONNA SEE IF YOU'RE A WITCH, ONCE AND FOR FINAL!
WAIT, SO IF I SINK IT MEANS... HE HE. HA HA!
WHY ARE YOU LAUGHING? THIS IS A GRAVE MATTER.
I JUST GOT THAT JOKE YOU TOLD, ROB! HA HA!
THE WITCH JOKE? THAT HAD TO BE AN HOUR AGO.
NO, NO, THE ONE ABOUT THE PARANOIDS SCREWING IN A LIGHT BULB! WHO WANTS TO KNOW? HA HA!
DUDE, THAT WAS, LIKE, 6 MONTHS AGO...
SILENCE! THAT LAUGHING DOG IS MAKING A MOCKERY OF THIS BATH-TUB WITCH DUNKING!
darb

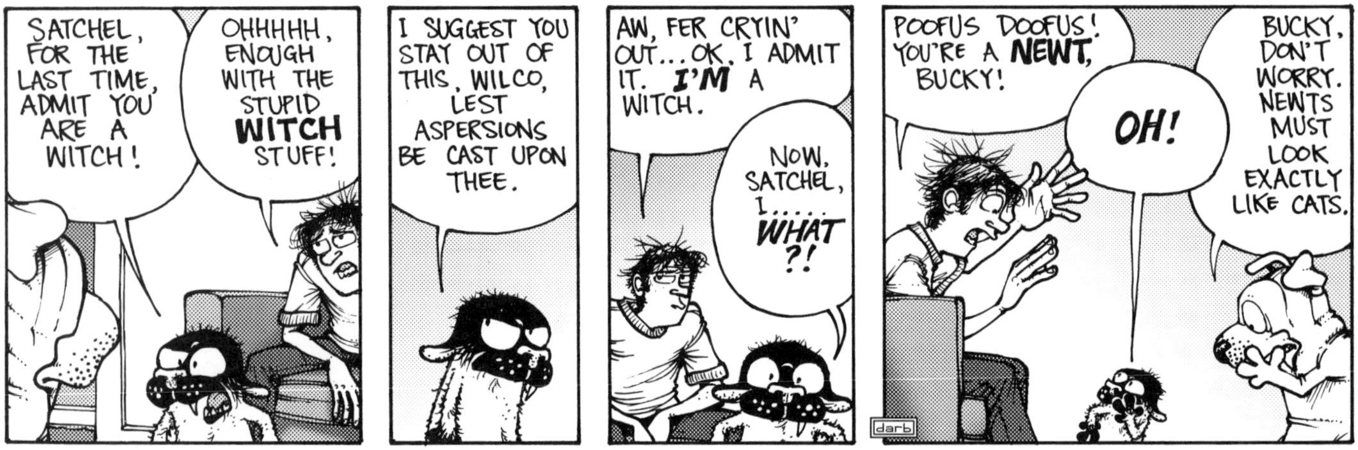
SATCHEL, FOR THE LAST TIME, ADMIT YOU ARE A WITCH!
OHHHHH, ENOUGH WITH THE STUPID WITCH STUFF!
I SUGGEST YOU STAY OUT OF THIS, WILCO, LEST ASPERSIONS BE CAST UPON THEE.
AW, FER CRYIN' OUT... OK, I ADMIT IT. I'M A WITCH.
NOW, SATCHEL, I..... WHAT?!
POOFUS DOOFUS! YOU'RE A NEWT, BUCKY!
OH!
BUCKY, DON'T WORRY. NEWTS MUST LOOK EXACTLY LIKE CATS.
darb

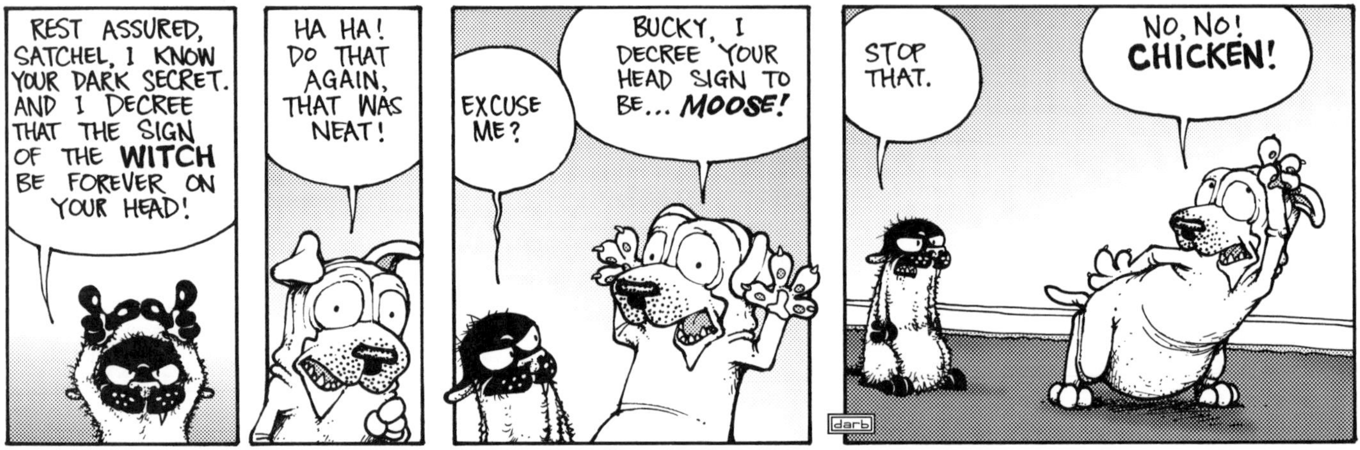
REST ASSURED, SATCHEL, I KNOW YOUR DARK SECRET. AND I DECREE THAT THE SIGN OF THE WITCH BE FOREVER ON YOUR HEAD!
HA HA! DO THAT AGAIN, THAT WAS NEAT!
EXCUSE ME?
BUCKY, I DECREE YOUR HEAD SIGN TO BE... MOOSE!
STOP THAT.
NO, NO! CHICKEN!
darb

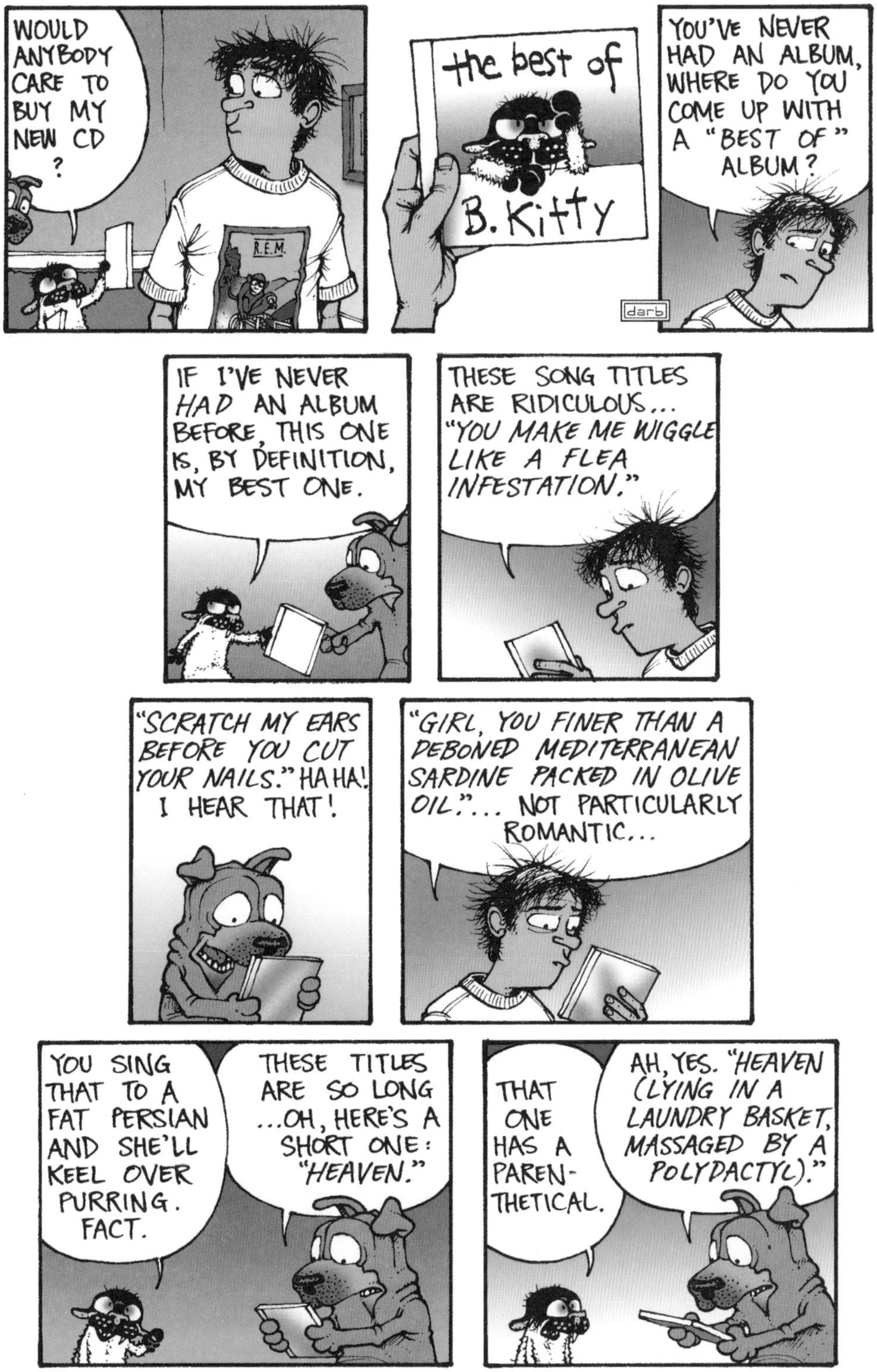
WOULD ANYBODY CARE TO BUY MY NEW CD ?
R.E.M.
the best of B. Kitty
darb
YOU'VE NEVER HAD AN ALBUM, WHERE DO YOU COME UP WITH A "BEST OF" ALBUM?
IF I'VE NEVER HAD AN ALBUM BEFORE, THIS ONE IS, BY DEFINITION, MY BEST ONE.
THESE SONG TITLES ARE RIDICULOUS... "YOU MAKE ME WIGGLE LIKE A FLEA INFESTATION."
"SCRATCH MY EARS BEFORE YOU CUT YOUR NAILS." HA HA! I HEAR THAT!
"GIRL, YOU FINER THAN A DEBONED MEDITERRANEAN SARDINE PACKED IN OLIVE OIL."... NOT PARTICULARLY ROMANTIC...
YOU SING THAT TO A FAT PERSIAN AND SHE'LL KEEL OVER PURRING. FACT.
THESE TITLES ARE SO LONG ...OH, HERE'S A SHORT ONE: "HEAVEN."
THAT ONE HAS A PAREN-THETICAL.
AH, YES. "HEAVEN (LYING IN A LAUNDRY BASKET, MASSAGED BY A POLYDACTYL)."

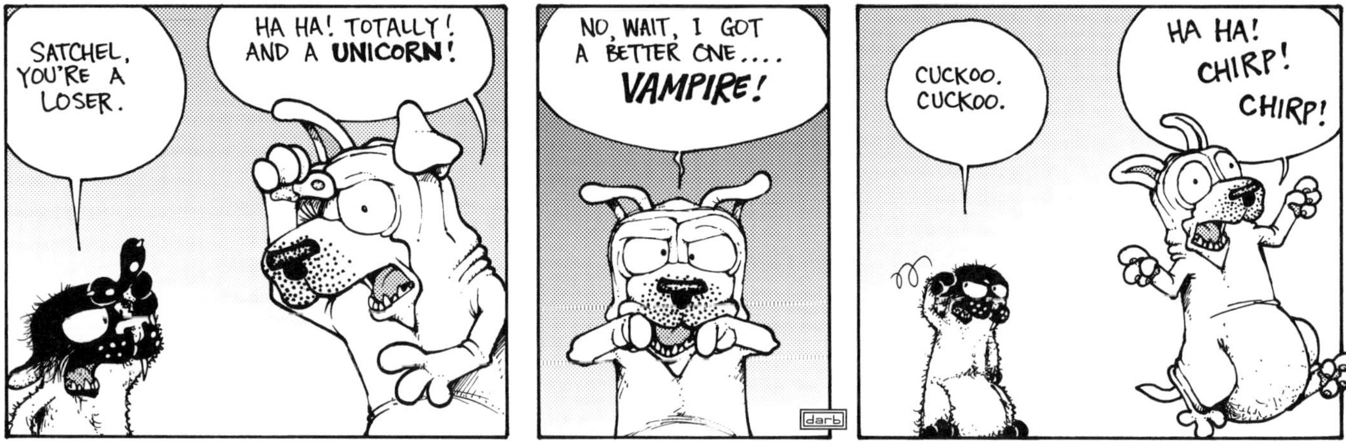
SATCHEL, YOU'RE A LOSER.
HA HA! TOTALLY! AND A **UNICORN**!
NO, WAIT, I GOT A BETTER ONE.... **VAMPIRE!**
darb
CUCKOO. CUCKOO.
HA HA! CHIRP! CHIRP!

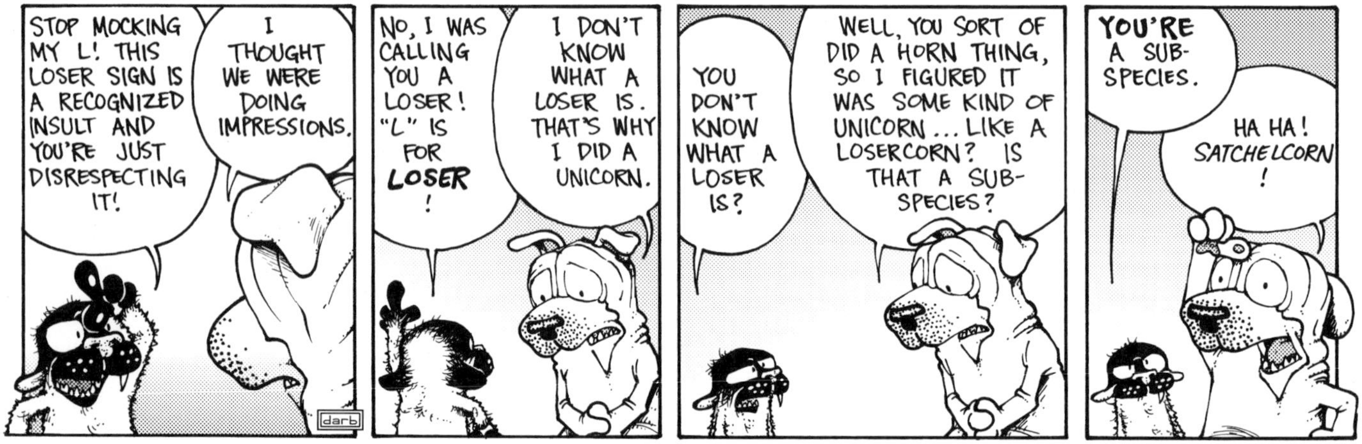
STOP MOCKING MY L! THIS LOSER SIGN IS A RECOGNIZED INSULT AND YOU'RE JUST DISRESPECTING IT!
I THOUGHT WE WERE DOING IMPRESSIONS.
darb
NO, I WAS CALLING YOU A LOSER! "L" IS FOR **LOSER**!
I DON'T KNOW WHAT A LOSER IS. THAT'S WHY I DID A UNICORN.
YOU DON'T KNOW WHAT A LOSER IS?
WELL, YOU SORT OF DID A HORN THING, SO I FIGURED IT WAS SOME KIND OF UNICORN... LIKE A LOSERCORN? IS THAT A SUB-SPECIES?
YOU'RE A SUB-SPECIES.
HA HA! *SATCHELCORN*!

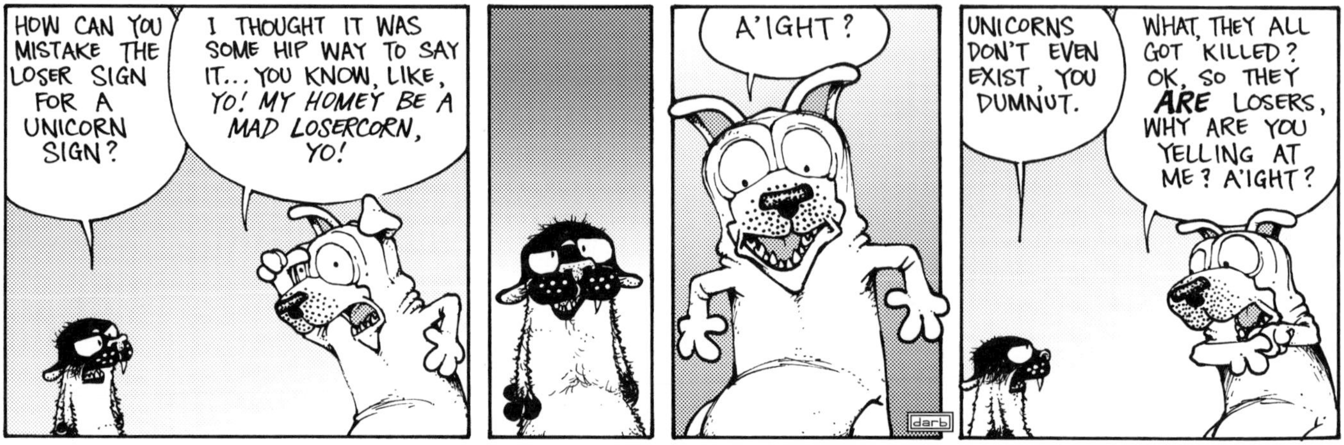
HOW CAN YOU MISTAKE THE LOSER SIGN FOR A UNICORN SIGN?
I THOUGHT IT WAS SOME HIP WAY TO SAY IT... YOU KNOW, LIKE, *YO! MY HOMEY BE A MAD LOSERCORN, YO!*
A'IGHT?
darb
UNICORNS DON'T EVEN EXIST, YOU DUMNUT.
WHAT, THEY ALL GOT KILLED? OK, SO THEY **ARE** LOSERS, WHY ARE YOU YELLING AT ME? A'IGHT?

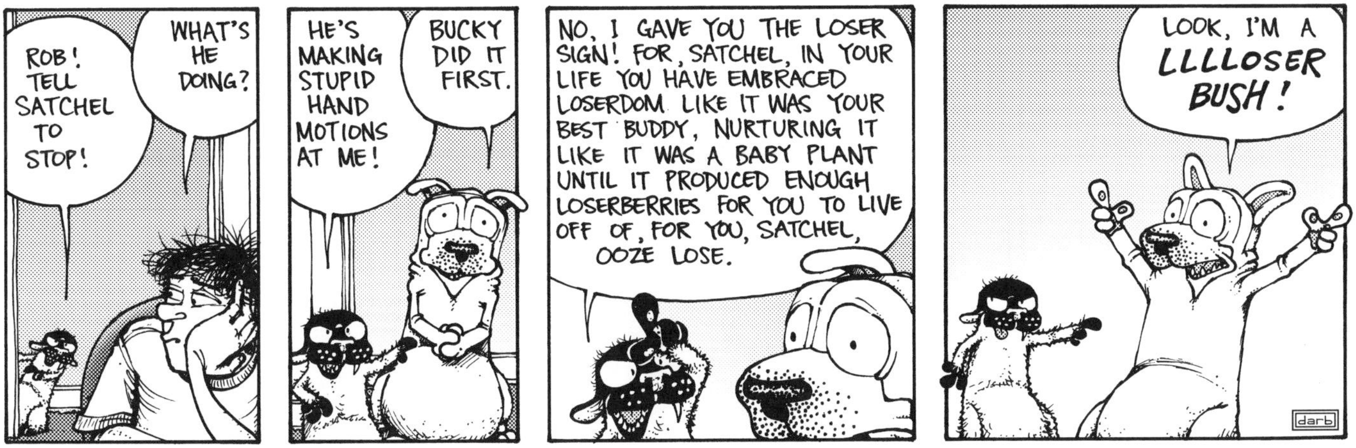
ROB! TELL SATCHEL TO STOP!
WHAT'S HE DOING?
HE'S MAKING STUPID HAND MOTIONS AT ME!
BUCKY DID IT FIRST.
NO, I GAVE YOU THE LOSER SIGN! FOR, SATCHEL, IN YOUR LIFE YOU HAVE EMBRACED LOSERDOM LIKE IT WAS YOUR BEST BUDDY, NURTURING IT LIKE IT WAS A BABY PLANT UNTIL IT PRODUCED ENOUGH LOSERBERRIES FOR YOU TO LIVE OFF OF, FOR YOU, SATCHEL, OOZE LOSE.
LOOK, I'M A LLLLOSER BUSH!
darb

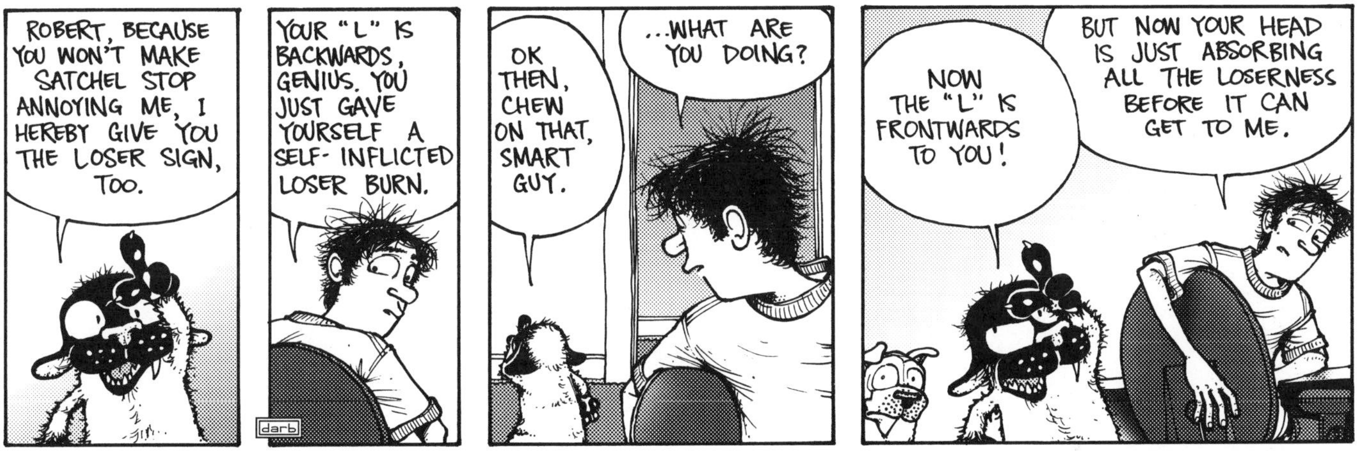
ROBERT, BECAUSE YOU WON'T MAKE SATCHEL STOP ANNOYING ME, I HEREBY GIVE YOU THE LOSER SIGN, TOO.
darb
YOUR "L" IS BACKWARDS, GENIUS. YOU JUST GAVE YOURSELF A SELF-INFLICTED LOSER BURN.
OK THEN, CHEW ON THAT, SMART GUY.
...WHAT ARE YOU DOING?
NOW THE "L" IS FRONTWARDS TO YOU!
BUT NOW YOUR HEAD IS JUST ABSORBING ALL THE LOSERNESS BEFORE IT CAN GET TO ME.

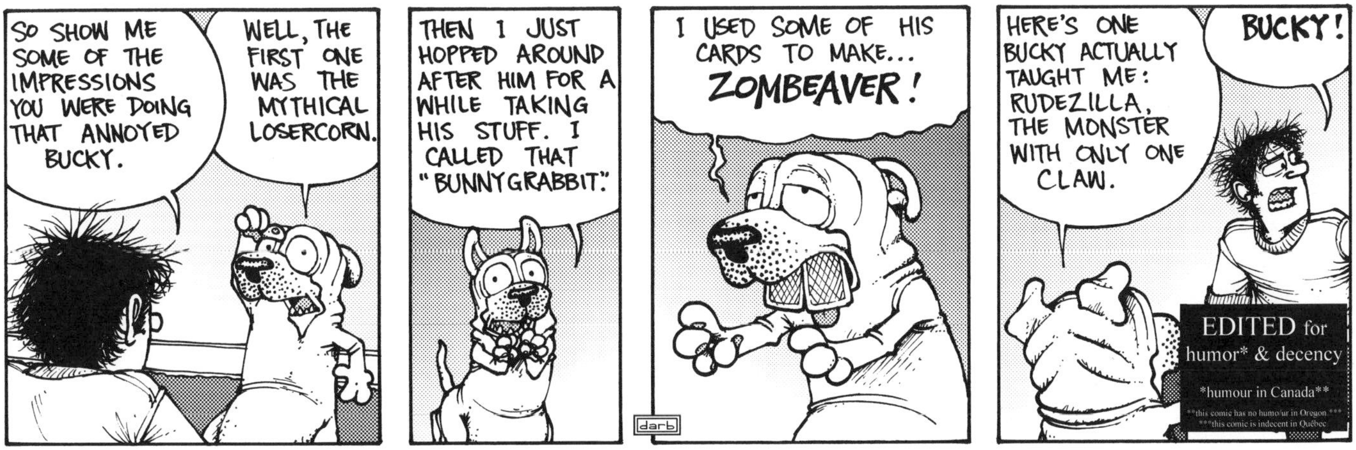
SO SHOW ME SOME OF THE IMPRESSIONS YOU WERE DOING THAT ANNOYED BUCKY.
WELL, THE FIRST ONE WAS THE MYTHICAL LOSERCORN.
THEN I JUST HOPPED AROUND AFTER HIM FOR A WHILE TAKING HIS STUFF. I CALLED THAT "BUNNYGRABBIT."
darb
I USED SOME OF HIS CARDS TO MAKE... ZOMBEAVER!
HERE'S ONE BUCKY ACTUALLY TAUGHT ME: RUDEZILLA, THE MONSTER WITH ONLY ONE CLAW.
BUCKY!
EDITED for humor* & decency
*humour in Canada**
this comic has no humo/ur in Oregon.*
***this comic is indecent in Québec.

WHOA. LAME TV SHOW.

NO, I RECORDED MY PROGRAM, SO I'M FAST-FORWARDING THE ADS.

DOESN'T THAT GO AGAINST YOUR PROFESSIONAL OATH?

MY WHAT?

WHATEVER YOU CALL THE OATH YOU TOOK WHEN YOU GOT A JOB IN ADVERTISING. LIKE THAT OATH HIPPO CRITICS TAKE.

...UHH...

OR IS THAT JUST A HIPPO THING? LIKE, IS THERE A HIPPO CABBIE OATH AND A HIPPO CASHIER OATH AND SO ON AND SO ON?

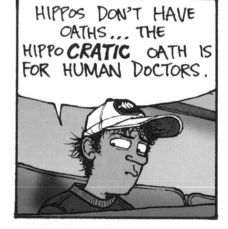

HIPPOS DON'T HAVE OATHS... THE HIPPO**CRATIC** OATH IS FOR HUMAN DOCTORS.

OH YEAH? SO DO HUMAN ACCOUNTANTS TAKE THE MONKEY PLUMBER OATH?

AND HEY, CAN YOU RECOMMEND ANY GOOD CATERERS? THEY HAVE TO HAVE TAKEN THEIR NAKED MOLE RAT CIVIL ENGINEER OATH, OF COURSE.

CLEARLY YOU DON'T UNDERSTAND WHAT HIPPOCRATIC MEANS.

OH MY. DOESN'T BEING RUDE TO A CONSUMER GO AGAINST AN ADMAN'S BEAVER DENTIST OATH?

darb

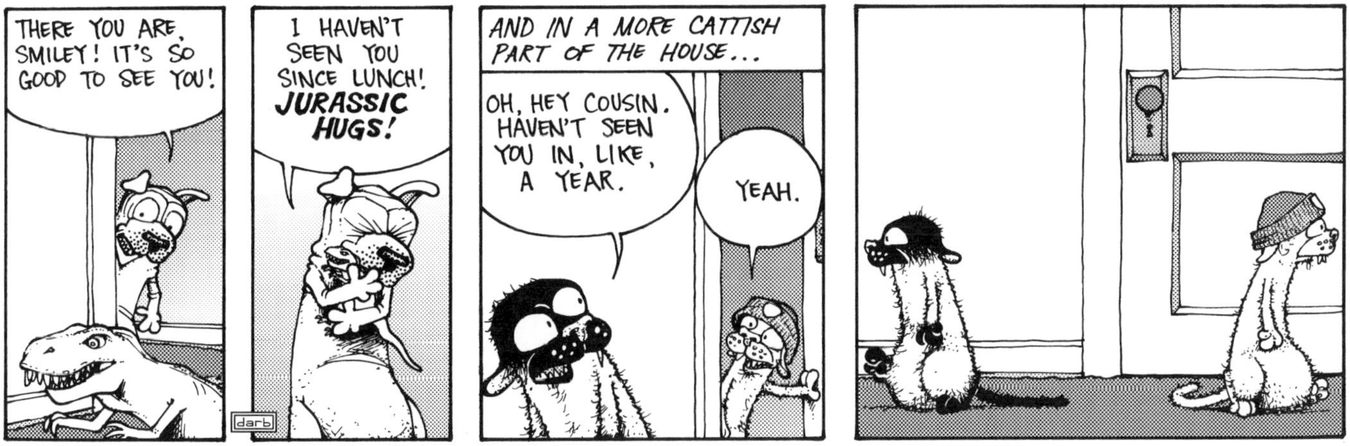
THERE YOU ARE, SMILEY! IT'S SO GOOD TO SEE YOU!
I HAVEN'T SEEN YOU SINCE LUNCH! **JURASSIC HUGS!**
darb
AND IN A MORE CATTISH PART OF THE HOUSE...
OH, HEY COUSIN. HAVEN'T SEEN YOU IN, LIKE, A YEAR.
YEAH.

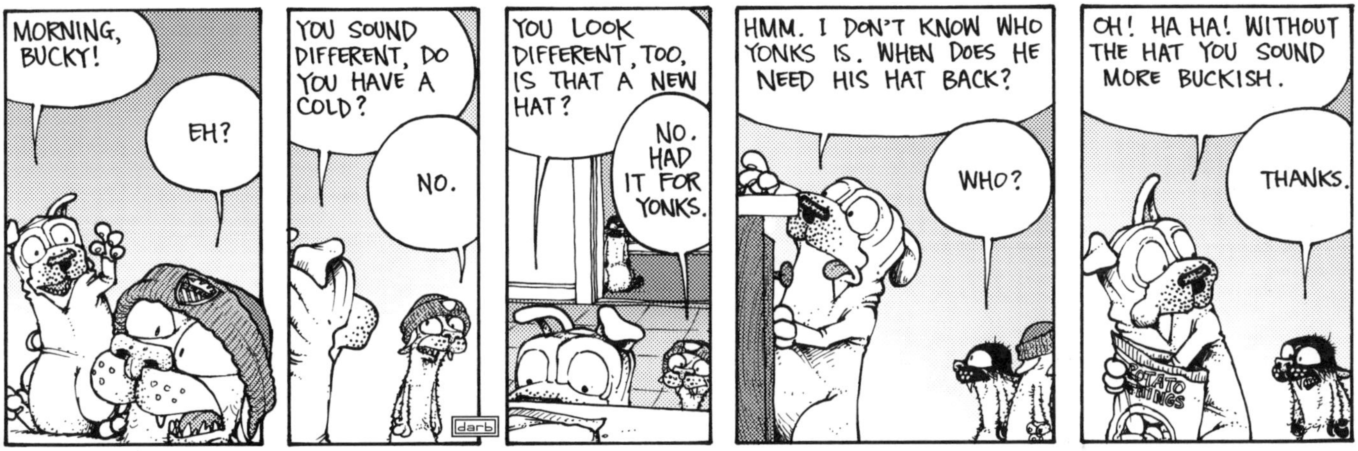
MORNING, BUCKY!
EH?
YOU SOUND DIFFERENT, DO YOU HAVE A COLD?
NO.
darb
YOU LOOK DIFFERENT, TOO, IS THAT A NEW HAT?
NO. HAD IT FOR YONKS.
HMM. I DON'T KNOW WHO YONKS IS. WHEN DOES HE NEED HIS HAT BACK?
WHO?
OH! HA HA! WITHOUT THE HAT YOU SOUND MORE BUCKISH.
THANKS.
POTATO THINGS

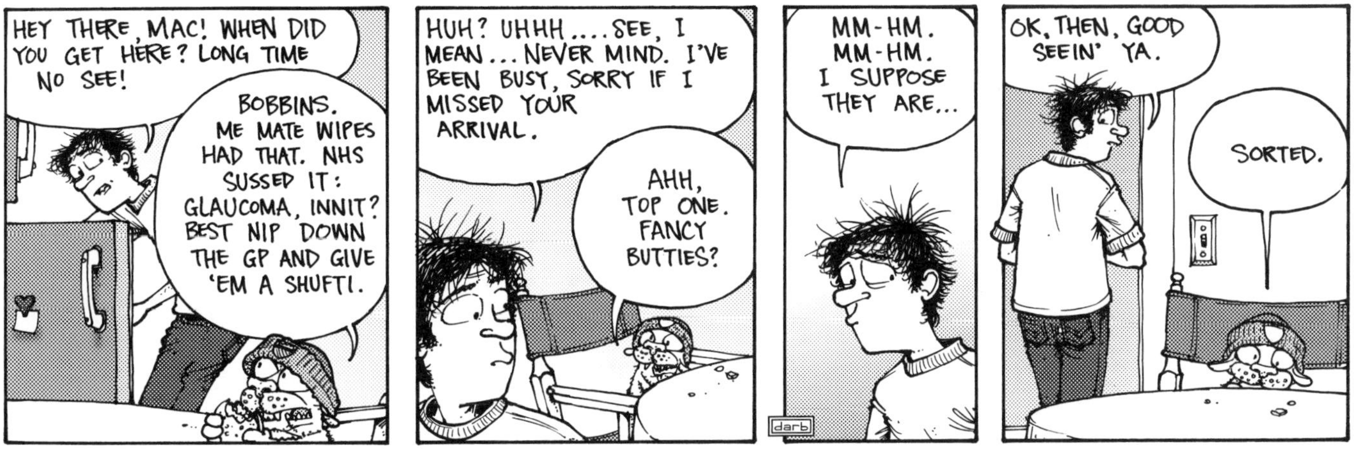
HEY THERE, MAC! WHEN DID YOU GET HERE? LONG TIME NO SEE!
BOBBINS. ME MATE WIPES HAD THAT. NHS SUSSED IT: GLAUCOMA, INNIT? BEST NIP DOWN THE GP AND GIVE 'EM A SHUFTI.
HUH? UHHH.... SEE, I MEAN... NEVER MIND. I'VE BEEN BUSY, SORRY IF I MISSED YOUR ARRIVAL.
AHH, TOP ONE. FANCY BUTTIES?
MM-HM. MM-HM. I SUPPOSE THEY ARE...
darb
OK, THEN, GOOD SEEIN' YA.
SORTED.

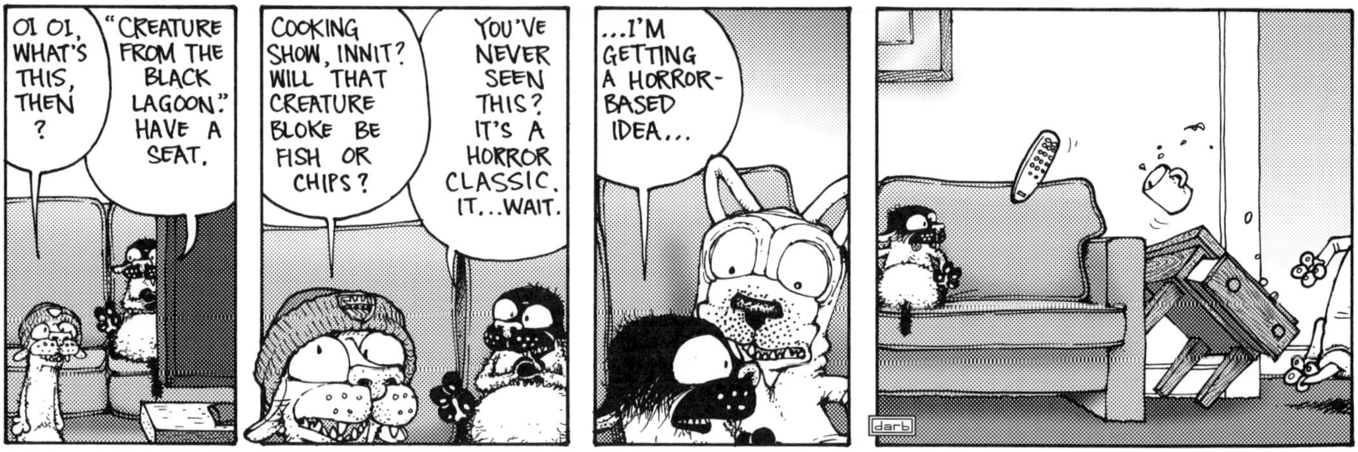
OI OI, WHAT'S THIS, THEN ?
"CREATURE FROM THE BLACK LAGOON." HAVE A SEAT.
COOKING SHOW, INNIT? WILL THAT CREATURE BLOKE BE FISH OR CHIPS?
YOU'VE NEVER SEEN THIS? IT'S A HORROR CLASSIC. IT...WAIT.
...I'M GETTING A HORROR-BASED IDEA...
darb

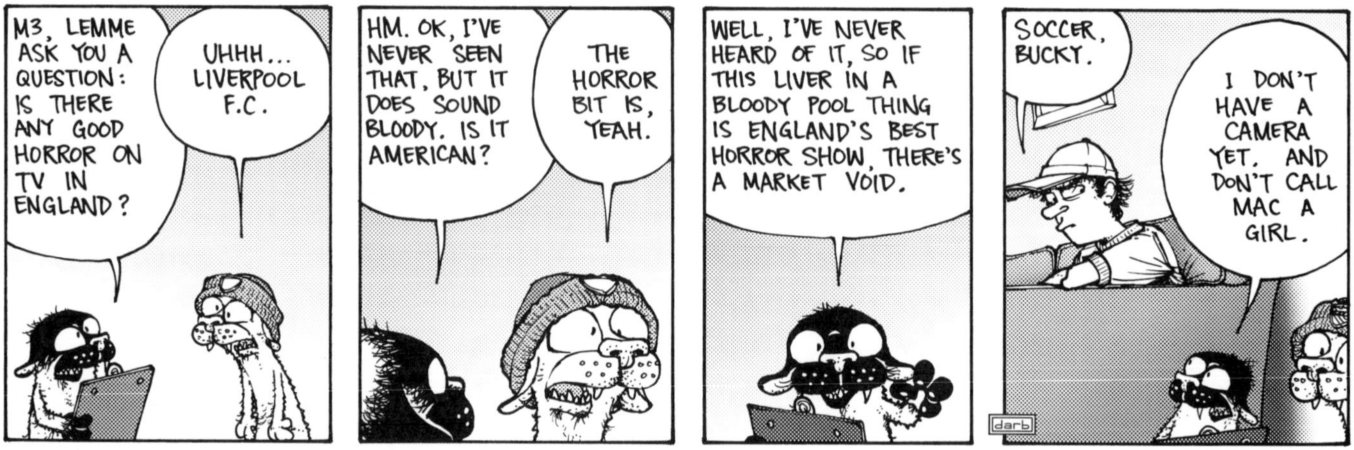
M3, LEMME ASK YOU A QUESTION: IS THERE ANY GOOD HORROR ON TV IN ENGLAND?
UHHH... LIVERPOOL F.C.
HM. OK, I'VE NEVER SEEN THAT, BUT IT DOES SOUND BLOODY. IS IT AMERICAN?
THE HORROR BIT IS, YEAH.
WELL, I'VE NEVER HEARD OF IT, SO IF THIS LIVER IN A BLOODY POOL THING IS ENGLAND'S BEST HORROR SHOW, THERE'S A MARKET VOID.
SOCCER, BUCKY.
I DON'T HAVE A CAMERA YET. AND DON'T CALL MAC A GIRL.
darb

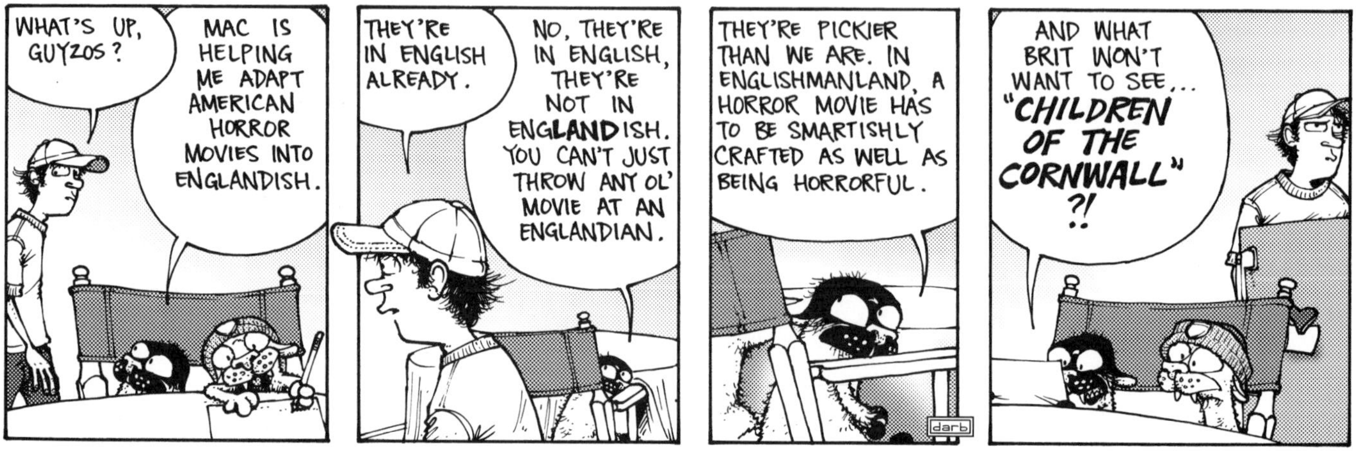
WHAT'S UP, GUYZOS?
MAC IS HELPING ME ADAPT AMERICAN HORROR MOVIES INTO ENGLANDISH.
THEY'RE IN ENGLISH ALREADY.
NO, THEY'RE IN ENGLISH, THEY'RE NOT IN ENGLANDISH. YOU CAN'T JUST THROW ANY OL' MOVIE AT AN ENGLANDIAN.
THEY'RE PICKIER THAN WE ARE. IN ENGLISHMANLAND, A HORROR MOVIE HAS TO BE SMARTISHLY CRAFTED AS WELL AS BEING HORRORFUL.
darb
AND WHAT BRIT WON'T WANT TO SEE... "CHILDREN OF THE CORNWALL"?!

COULD I HAVE JUST 5 MINUTES OF YOUR TIME FOR A BUSINESS OPPORTUNITY?

NO.

YOU WANT THE FULL 10, GOTCHA. I'D LIKE TO GIVE YOU THE OPPORTUNITY TO INVEST IN THE BOOK I'M WRITING.

NO.

BEFORE YOU SAY NO! I'M AUTHORIZED TO INFORM YOU THAT THIS BOOK IS A GUARANTEED #1 BEST-SELLER.

IN THE INTEREST OF SPEEDING THIS ALONG, I'LL ASK HOW YOU KNOW THAT.

FEAST YOUR EYES ON THE TOP OF THE COVER...

OPRAH'S PICK OF THE YEAR:

HOW ARE YOU GONNA GET OPRAH TO PICK YOUR BOOK?

THAT'S THE GENIUS BIT. SHE DOESN'T HAVE TO. OPRAH'S PICK OF THE YEAR IS THE FIRST PART OF THE TITLE!

OPRAH'S PICK OF THE YEAR

darb

AND THE TEXT WILL BE LIFTED FROM OTHER UBER-FAMOUS BOOKS, SO PEOPLE WILL LOVE IT.

YOU DON'T SEE ANY COPYRIGHT ISSUES WITH THAT?

HUH? NO, I CAN COPY TOTALLY RIGHT. NO ISSUES.

HARRY DaVINCI AND THE LORD OF THE 30 MINUTE MEALS

SO YOUR PLAN IS IDIOTPROOF, EH?

DON'T EVEN WORRY ABOUT THAT, SATCHEL ISN'T ALLOWED NEAR IT.

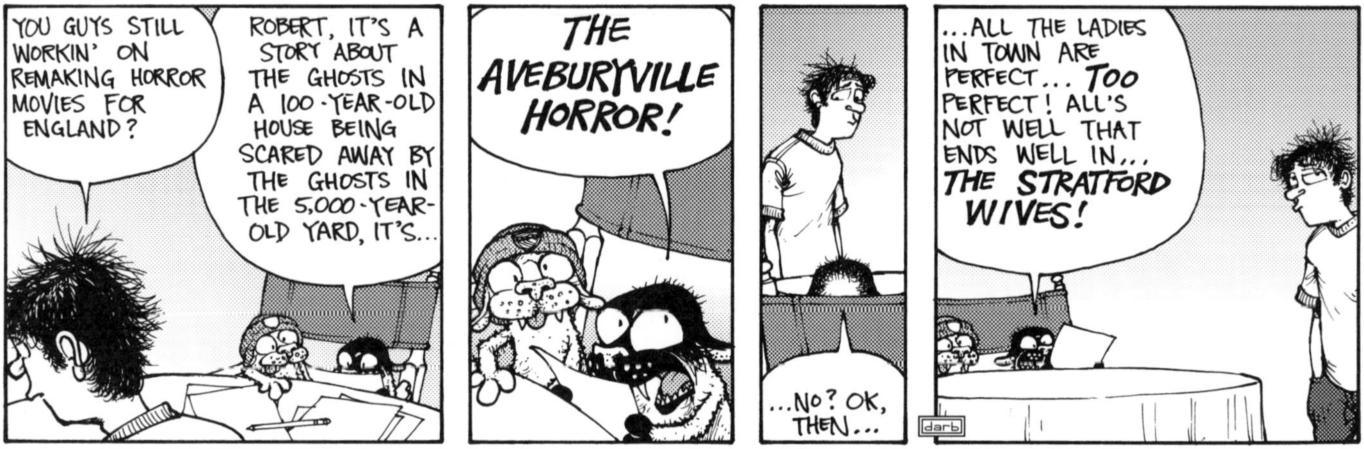
YOU GUYS STILL WORKIN' ON REMAKING HORROR MOVIES FOR ENGLAND?
ROBERT, IT'S A STORY ABOUT THE GHOSTS IN A 100-YEAR-OLD HOUSE BEING SCARED AWAY BY THE GHOSTS IN THE 5,000-YEAR-OLD YARD, IT'S...
THE AVEBURYVILLE HORROR!
...NO? OK, THEN...
...ALL THE LADIES IN TOWN ARE PERFECT... TOO PERFECT! ALL'S NOT WELL THAT ENDS WELL IN... THE STRATFORD WIVES!
darb

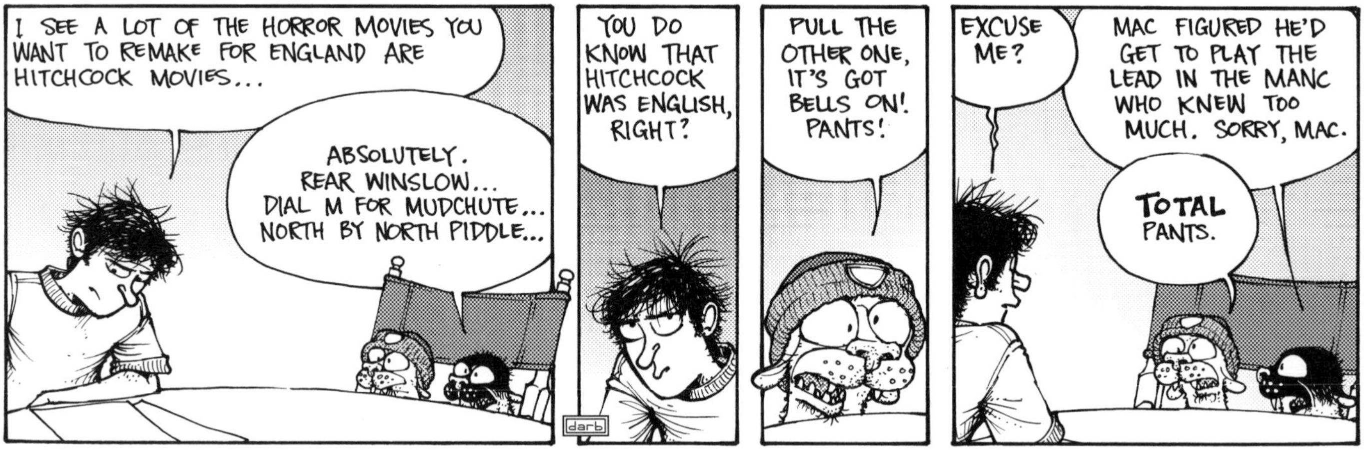
I SEE A LOT OF THE HORROR MOVIES YOU WANT TO REMAKE FOR ENGLAND ARE HITCHCOCK MOVIES...
ABSOLUTELY. REAR WINSLOW... DIAL M FOR MUDCHUTE... NORTH BY NORTH PIDDLE...
darb
YOU DO KNOW THAT HITCHCOCK WAS ENGLISH, RIGHT?
PULL THE OTHER ONE, IT'S GOT BELLS ON! PANTS!
EXCUSE ME?
MAC FIGURED HE'D GET TO PLAY THE LEAD IN THE MANC WHO KNEW TOO MUCH. SORRY, MAC.
TOTAL PANTS.

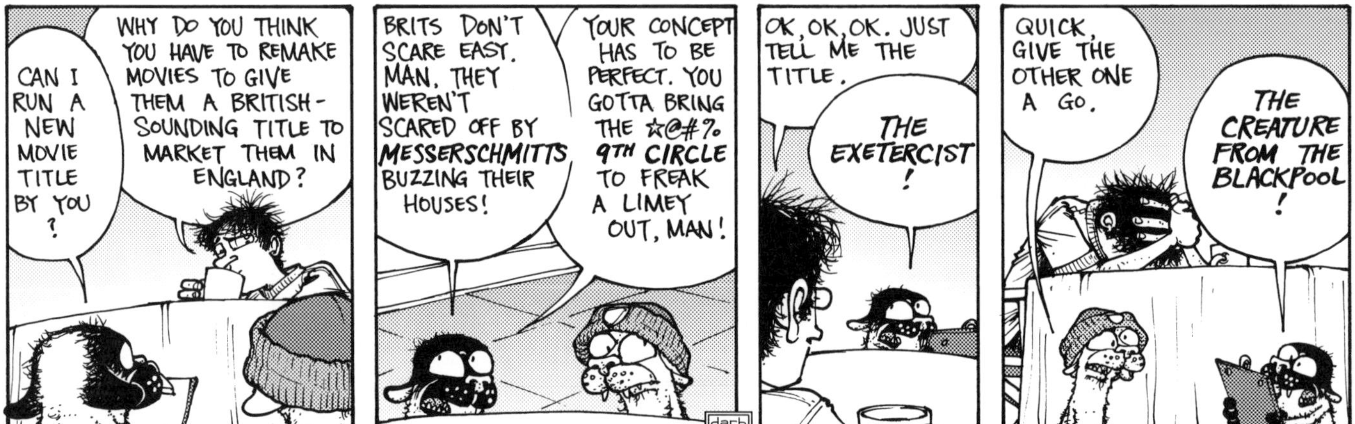
CAN I RUN A NEW MOVIE TITLE BY YOU?
WHY DO YOU THINK YOU HAVE TO REMAKE MOVIES TO GIVE THEM A BRITISH-SOUNDING TITLE TO MARKET THEM IN ENGLAND?
BRITS DON'T SCARE EASY. MAN, THEY WEREN'T SCARED OFF BY MESSERSCHMITTS BUZZING THEIR HOUSES!
YOUR CONCEPT HAS TO BE PERFECT. YOU GOTTA BRING THE ☆@#% 9TH CIRCLE TO FREAK A LIMEY OUT, MAN!
darb
OK, OK, OK. JUST TELL ME THE TITLE.
THE EXETERCIST!
QUICK, GIVE THE OTHER ONE A GO.
THE CREATURE FROM THE BLACKPOOL!

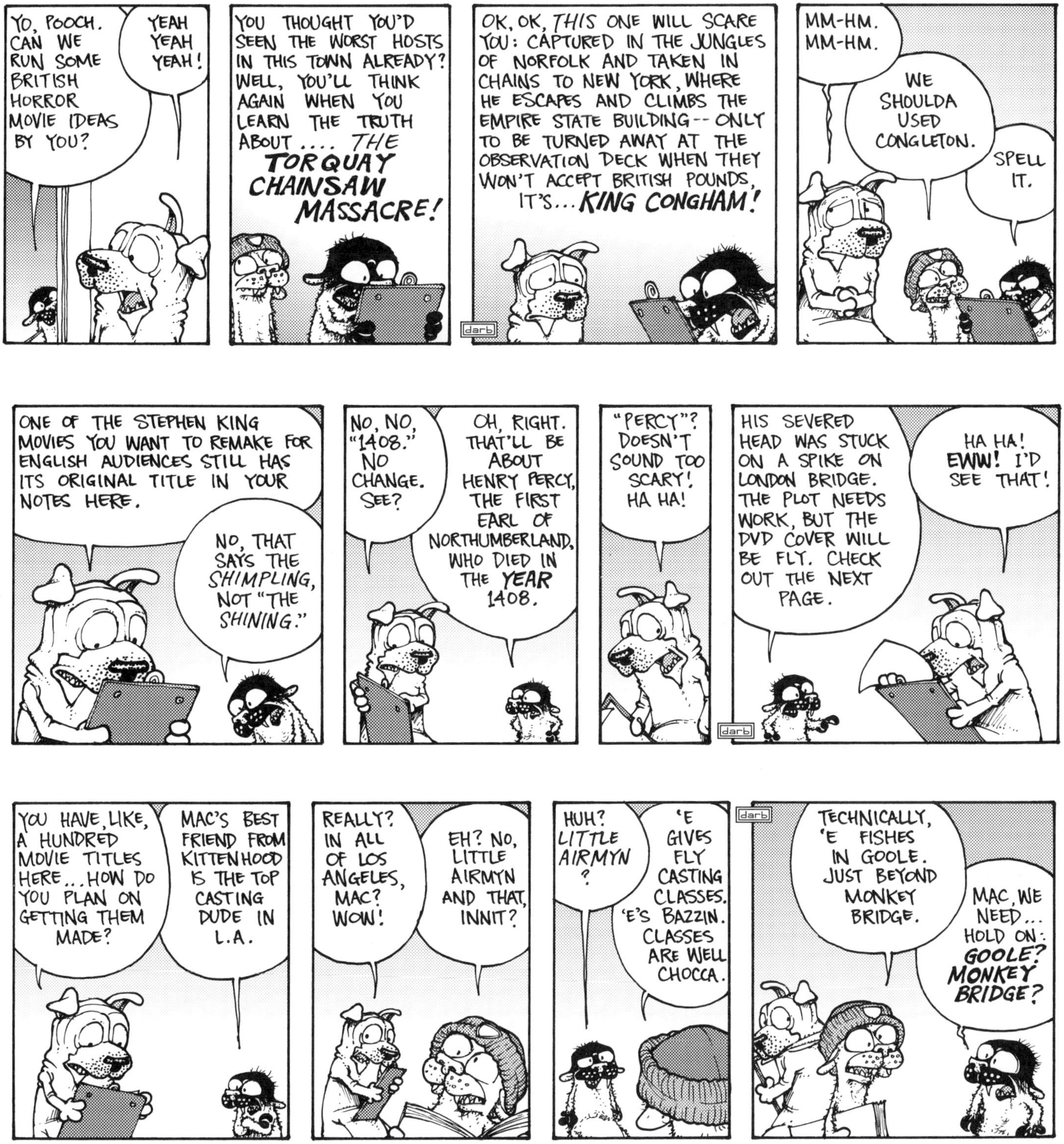
YO, POOCH. CAN WE RUN SOME BRITISH HORROR MOVIE IDEAS BY YOU?
YEAH YEAH YEAH!
YOU THOUGHT YOU'D SEEN THE WORST HOSTS IN THIS TOWN ALREADY? WELL, YOU'LL THINK AGAIN WHEN YOU LEARN THE TRUTH ABOUT .... THE TORQUAY CHAINSAW MASSACRE!
darb
OK, OK, THIS ONE WILL SCARE YOU: CAPTURED IN THE JUNGLES OF NORFOLK AND TAKEN IN CHAINS TO NEW YORK, WHERE HE ESCAPES AND CLIMBS THE EMPIRE STATE BUILDING -- ONLY TO BE TURNED AWAY AT THE OBSERVATION DECK WHEN THEY WON'T ACCEPT BRITISH POUNDS, IT'S... KING CONGHAM!
MM-HM. MM-HM.
WE SHOULDA USED CONGLETON.
SPELL IT.
ONE OF THE STEPHEN KING MOVIES YOU WANT TO REMAKE FOR ENGLISH AUDIENCES STILL HAS ITS ORIGINAL TITLE IN YOUR NOTES HERE.
NO, THAT SAYS THE SHIMPLING, NOT "THE SHINING."
NO, NO, "1408." NO CHANGE. SEE?
OH, RIGHT. THAT'LL BE ABOUT HENRY PERCY, THE FIRST EARL OF NORTHUMBERLAND, WHO DIED IN THE YEAR 1408.
"PERCY"? DOESN'T SOUND TOO SCARY! HA HA!
HIS SEVERED HEAD WAS STUCK ON A SPIKE ON LONDON BRIDGE. THE PLOT NEEDS WORK, BUT THE DVD COVER WILL BE FLY. CHECK OUT THE NEXT PAGE.
HA HA! EWW! I'D SEE THAT!
darb
YOU HAVE, LIKE, A HUNDRED MOVIE TITLES HERE... HOW DO YOU PLAN ON GETTING THEM MADE?
MAC'S BEST FRIEND FROM KITTENHOOD IS THE TOP CASTING DUDE IN L.A.
REALLY? IN ALL OF LOS ANGELES, MAC? WOW!
EH? NO, LITTLE AIRMYN AND THAT, INNIT?
HUH? LITTLE AIRMYN?
'E GIVES FLY CASTING CLASSES. 'E'S BAZZIN. CLASSES ARE WELL CHOCCA.
darb
TECHNICALLY, 'E FISHES IN GOOLE. JUST BEYOND MONKEY BRIDGE.
MAC, WE NEED... HOLD ON: GOOLE? MONKEY BRIDGE?

HMM. I THINK MY TAN MAY HAVE WORN OFF TOO MUCH TO WEAR SHORTS.

THIS "TAN" YOU SPEAK OF... WHEN WAS THIS?

I GOT A LITTLE TAN THIS SUMMER.

ARE YOU KIDDING? YOU'RE WHITER THAN AN IRISH SUNBLOCK TESTER!

THE LOCAL KIDS' NICKNAME FOR YOU IS FROSTY THE ADMAN.

NASA GAUGES THE BRIGHTNESS OF A STAR BY ITS APPARENT ROBERTUDE.

LOOK WHO'S TALKING! MOST OF YOU IS WHITE!

BUT THAT'S A FASHION STATEMENT. UNDER THIS GORGEOUS FUR COAT, I'M A MANLY PUCE.

DO MOTHS FLOCK TO YOU IN THE DARKNESS?

FINISHED?

darb

IS IT TRUE THAT BENJAMIN MOORE NIXED THEIR BETA ROB WILCO COLOR AFTER SEVERAL FOCUS GROUP MEMBERS GOT BURNED RETINAS?

WHERE ARE MY PANTS?

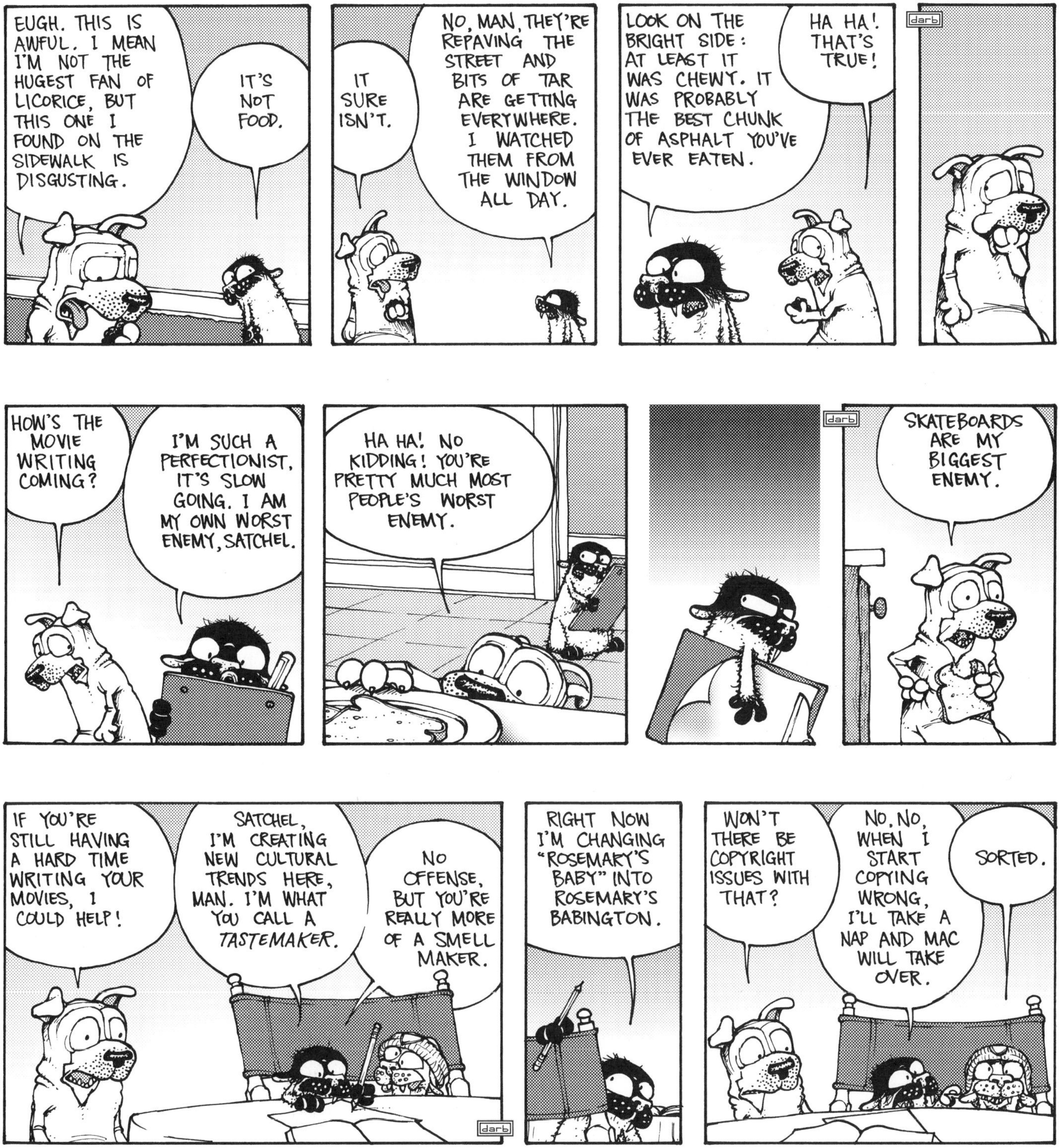
EUGH. THIS IS AWFUL. I MEAN I'M NOT THE HUGEST FAN OF LICORICE, BUT THIS ONE I FOUND ON THE SIDEWALK IS DISGUSTING.
IT'S NOT FOOD.
IT SURE ISN'T.
NO, MAN, THEY'RE REPAVING THE STREET AND BITS OF TAR ARE GETTING EVERYWHERE. I WATCHED THEM FROM THE WINDOW ALL DAY.
LOOK ON THE BRIGHT SIDE: AT LEAST IT WAS CHEWY. IT WAS PROBABLY THE BEST CHUNK OF ASPHALT YOU'VE EVER EATEN.
HA HA! THAT'S TRUE!
darb
HOW'S THE MOVIE WRITING COMING?
I'M SUCH A PERFECTIONIST, IT'S SLOW GOING. I AM MY OWN WORST ENEMY, SATCHEL.
HA HA! NO KIDDING! YOU'RE PRETTY MUCH MOST PEOPLE'S WORST ENEMY.
darb
SKATEBOARDS ARE MY BIGGEST ENEMY.
IF YOU'RE STILL HAVING A HARD TIME WRITING YOUR MOVIES, I COULD HELP!
SATCHEL, I'M CREATING NEW CULTURAL TRENDS HERE, MAN. I'M WHAT YOU CALL A *TASTEMAKER*.
NO OFFENSE, BUT YOU'RE REALLY MORE OF A SMELL MAKER.
darb
RIGHT NOW I'M CHANGING "ROSEMARY'S BABY" INTO ROSEMARY'S BABINGTON.
WON'T THERE BE COPYRIGHT ISSUES WITH THAT?
NO, NO, WHEN I START COPYING WRONG, I'LL TAKE A NAP AND MAC WILL TAKE OVER.
SORTED.

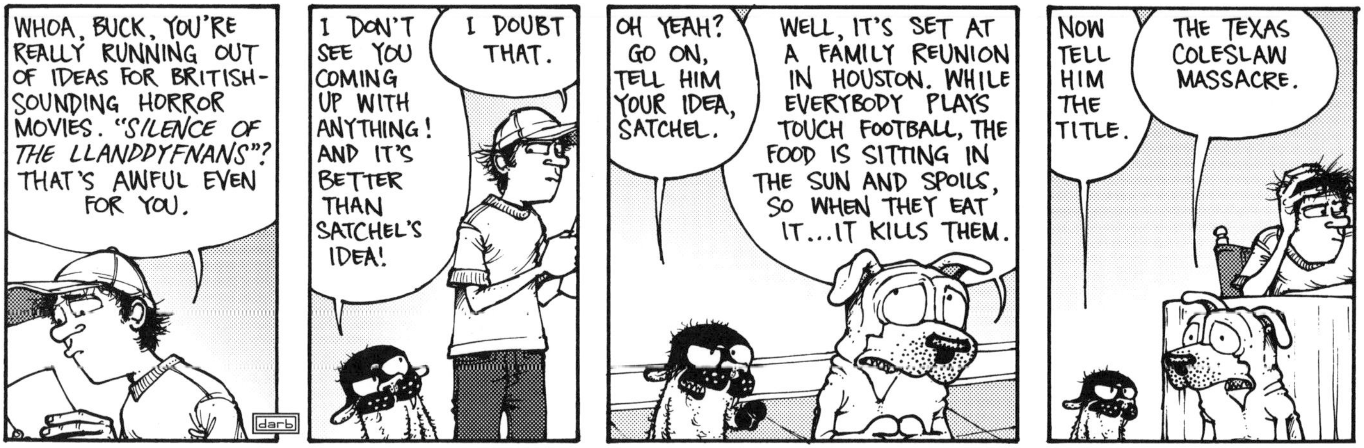
WHOA, BUCK, YOU'RE REALLY RUNNING OUT OF IDEAS FOR BRITISH-SOUNDING HORROR MOVIES. "*SILENCE OF THE LLANDDYFNANS*"? THAT'S AWFUL EVEN FOR YOU.
I DON'T SEE YOU COMING UP WITH ANYTHING! AND IT'S BETTER THAN SATCHEL'S IDEA!
I DOUBT THAT.
OH YEAH? GO ON, TELL HIM YOUR IDEA, SATCHEL.
WELL, IT'S SET AT A FAMILY REUNION IN HOUSTON. WHILE EVERYBODY PLAYS TOUCH FOOTBALL, THE FOOD IS SITTING IN THE SUN AND SPOILS, SO WHEN THEY EAT IT... IT KILLS THEM.
NOW TELL HIM THE TITLE.
THE TEXAS COLESLAW MASSACRE.

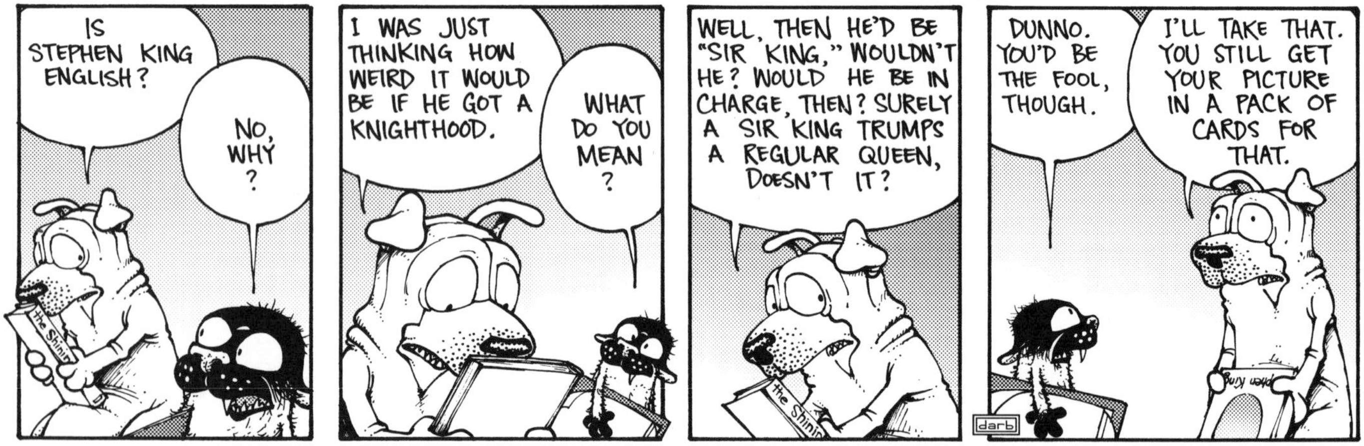
IS STEPHEN KING ENGLISH?
NO, WHY?
I WAS JUST THINKING HOW WEIRD IT WOULD BE IF HE GOT A KNIGHTHOOD.
WHAT DO YOU MEAN?
WELL, THEN HE'D BE "SIR KING," WOULDN'T HE? WOULD HE BE IN CHARGE, THEN? SURELY A SIR KING TRUMPS A REGULAR QUEEN, DOESN'T IT?
DUNNO. YOU'D BE THE FOOL, THOUGH.
I'LL TAKE THAT. YOU STILL GET YOUR PICTURE IN A PACK OF CARDS FOR THAT.

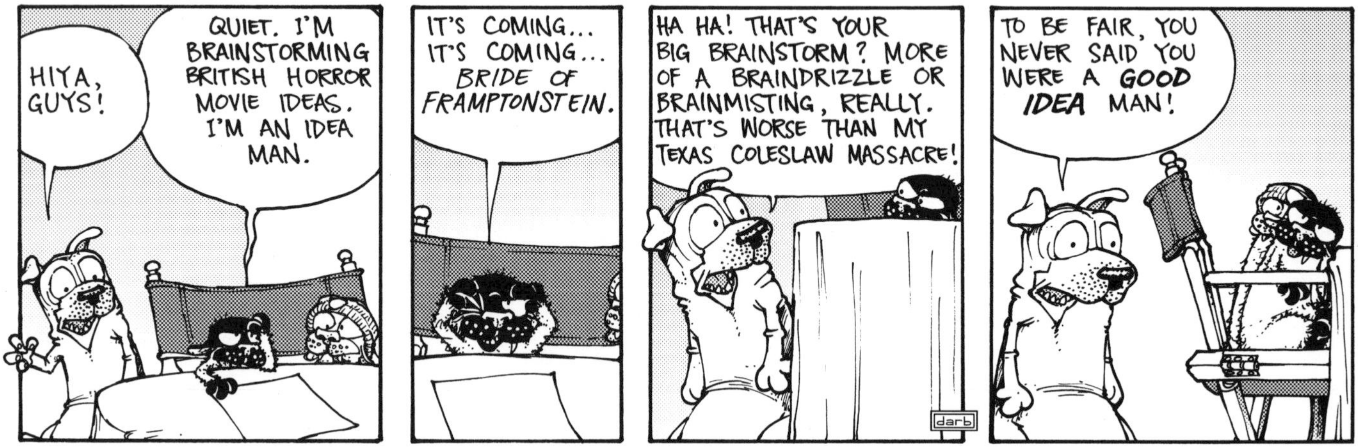
HIYA, GUYS!
QUIET. I'M BRAINSTORMING BRITISH HORROR MOVIE IDEAS. I'M AN IDEA MAN.
IT'S COMING... IT'S COMING... *BRIDE OF FRAMPTONSTEIN.*
HA HA! THAT'S YOUR BIG BRAINSTORM? MORE OF A BRAINDRIZZLE OR BRAINMISTING, REALLY. THAT'S WORSE THAN MY TEXAS COLESLAW MASSACRE!
TO BE FAIR, YOU NEVER SAID YOU WERE A **GOOD IDEA** MAN!

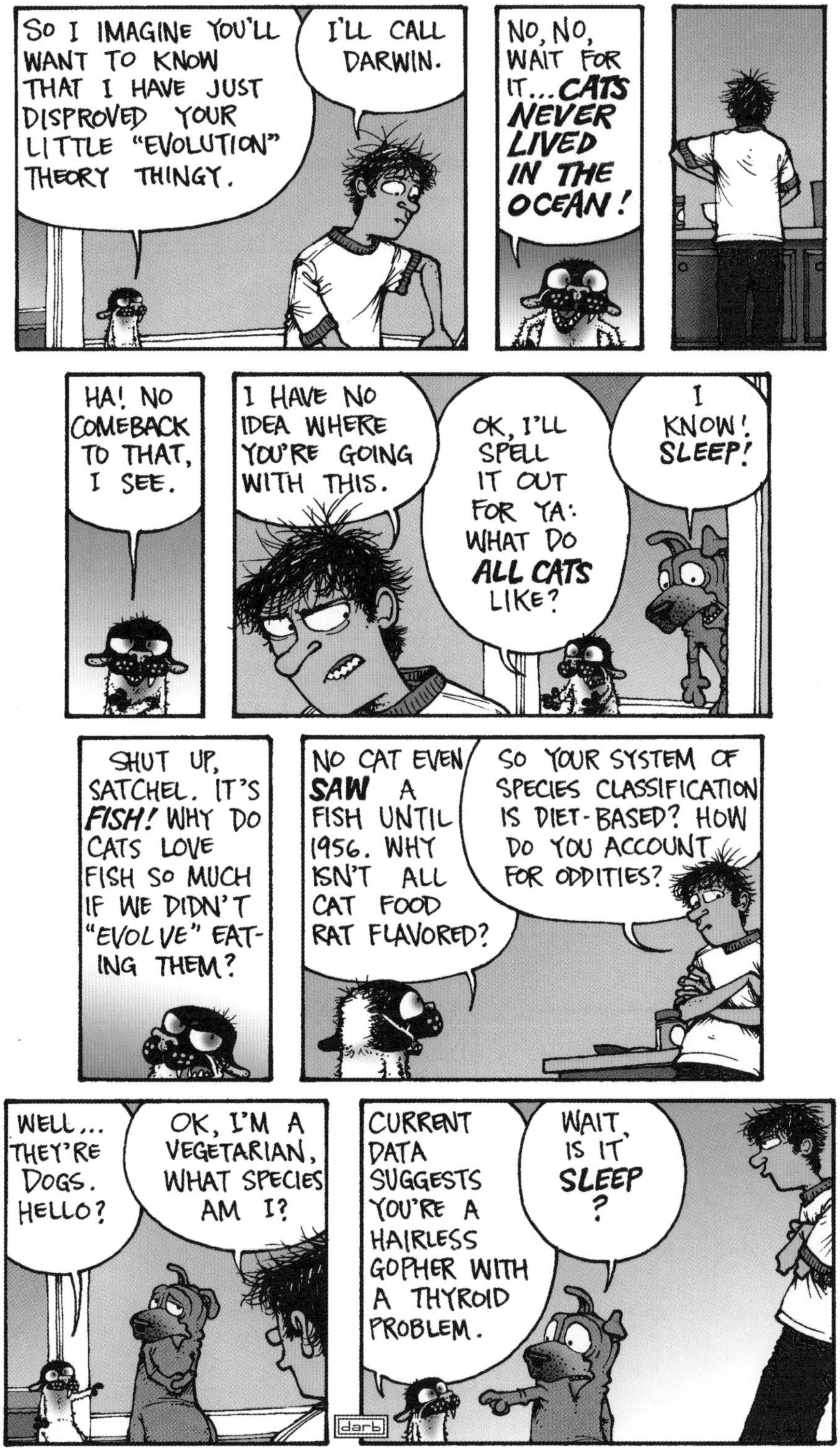
SO I IMAGINE YOU'LL WANT TO KNOW THAT I HAVE JUST DISPROVED YOUR LITTLE "EVOLUTION" THEORY THINGY.
I'LL CALL DARWIN.
NO, NO, WAIT FOR IT... CATS NEVER LIVED IN THE OCEAN!
HA! NO COMEBACK TO THAT, I SEE.
I HAVE NO IDEA WHERE YOU'RE GOING WITH THIS.
OK, I'LL SPELL IT OUT FOR YA: WHAT DO ALL CATS LIKE?
I KNOW! SLEEP!
SHUT UP, SATCHEL. IT'S FISH! WHY DO CATS LOVE FISH SO MUCH IF WE DIDN'T "EVOLVE" EATING THEM?
NO CAT EVEN SAW A FISH UNTIL 1956. WHY ISN'T ALL CAT FOOD RAT FLAVORED?
SO YOUR SYSTEM OF SPECIES CLASSIFICATION IS DIET-BASED? HOW DO YOU ACCOUNT FOR ODDITIES?
WELL... THEY'RE DOGS. HELLO?
OK, I'M A VEGETARIAN, WHAT SPECIES AM I?
CURRENT DATA SUGGESTS YOU'RE A HAIRLESS GOPHER WITH A THYROID PROBLEM.
WAIT, IS IT SLEEP?
darb

SO IT TURNS OUT MY FOCUS GROUP DIDN'T LIKE ENGLISH-THEMED HORROR MOVIES.

WHO WAS IN YOUR FOCUS GROUP?

SATCHEL, CHUBBY HUGGS AND FOODAR.

THAT'S IT, THEN, EH? NO MORE MOVIE ADAPTATIONS.

NO, NO, NO, I'M SAYING AUDIENCES WANT COMEDIES.

...AND BY THAT YOU MEAN?

WEEKEND AT BURNLEY'S.

WORKIN' ON YOUR BRITISH MOVIES? WHERE'S MAC?

HE HAD TO GO TAKE CARE OF SOMETHING AT HIS LAUNDROMAT.

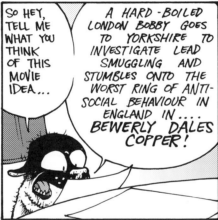
SO HEY, TELL ME WHAT YOU THINK OF THIS MOVIE IDEA...

A HARD-BOILED LONDON BOBBY GOES TO YORKSHIRE TO INVESTIGATE LEAD SMUGGLING AND STUMBLES ONTO THE WORST RING OF ANTI-SOCIAL BEHAVIOUR IN ENGLAND IN.... BEWERLY DALES COPPER!

WELL?

WAIT, MAC HAS A LAUNDROMAT?

FREE KEITH

DID BUCKY TELL YOU HE'S ADAPTING COMEDIES INTO BRITISH NOW?

YEAH. BAD ADAPTATIONS PART DUH.

UHHHHHH

DUH LIKE DEUX... IT MEANS "TWO" ...NO?...

ALWAYS A BIT AWKWARD WHEN YOU JOKE ABOUT SOMEONE BEING DUMB AND THE OTHER DUDE DOESN'T GET THE JOKE.

HA HA! WHAT DID BUCKY NOT GET, NOW?

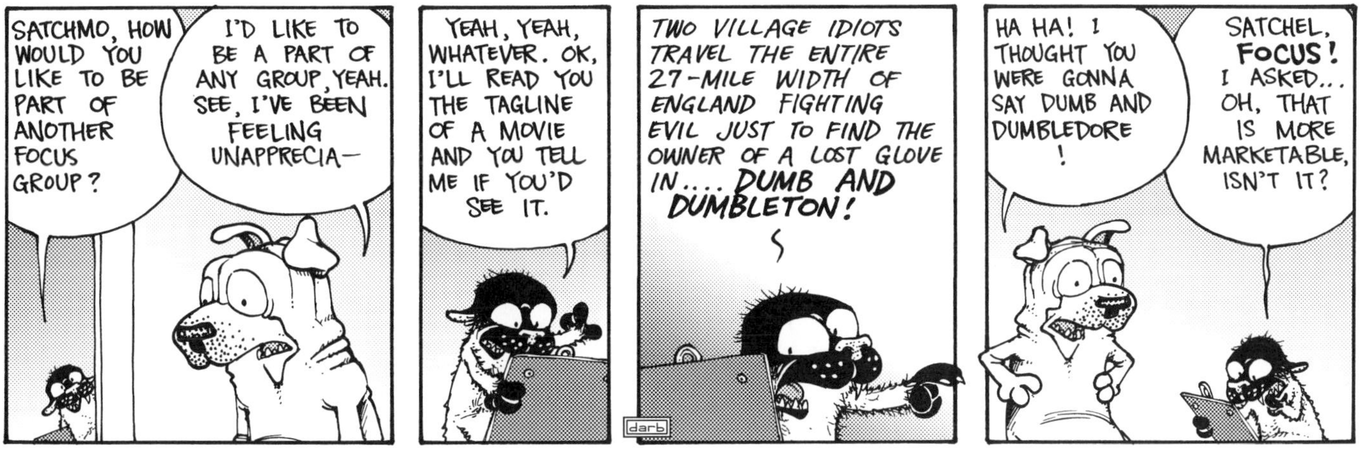
SATCHMO, HOW WOULD YOU LIKE TO BE PART OF ANOTHER FOCUS GROUP?
I'D LIKE TO BE A PART OF ANY GROUP, YEAH. SEE, I'VE BEEN FEELING UNAPPRECIA—
YEAH, YEAH, WHATEVER. OK, I'LL READ YOU THE TAGLINE OF A MOVIE AND YOU TELL ME IF YOU'D SEE IT.
TWO VILLAGE IDIOTS TRAVEL THE ENTIRE 27-MILE WIDTH OF ENGLAND FIGHTING EVIL JUST TO FIND THE OWNER OF A LOST GLOVE IN.... DUMB AND DUMBLETON!
HA HA! I THOUGHT YOU WERE GONNA SAY DUMB AND DUMBLEDORE!
SATCHEL, FOCUS! I ASKED... OH, THAT IS MORE MARKETABLE, ISN'T IT?
darb

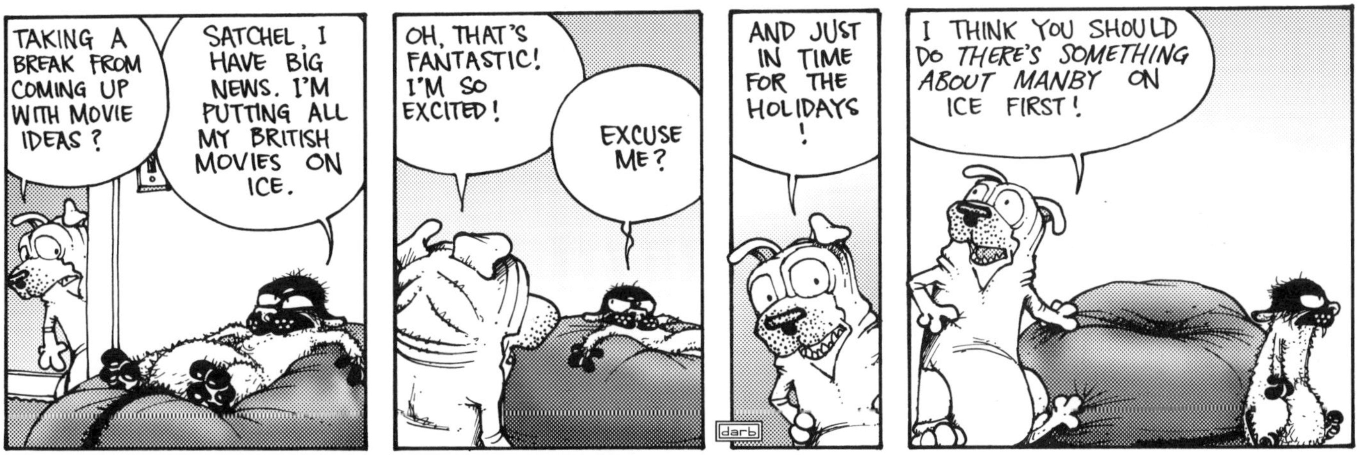
TAKING A BREAK FROM COMING UP WITH MOVIE IDEAS?
SATCHEL, I HAVE BIG NEWS. I'M PUTTING ALL MY BRITISH MOVIES ON ICE.
OH, THAT'S FANTASTIC! I'M SO EXCITED!
EXCUSE ME?
AND JUST IN TIME FOR THE HOLIDAYS!
I THINK YOU SHOULD DO THERE'S SOMETHING ABOUT MANBY ON ICE FIRST!
darb

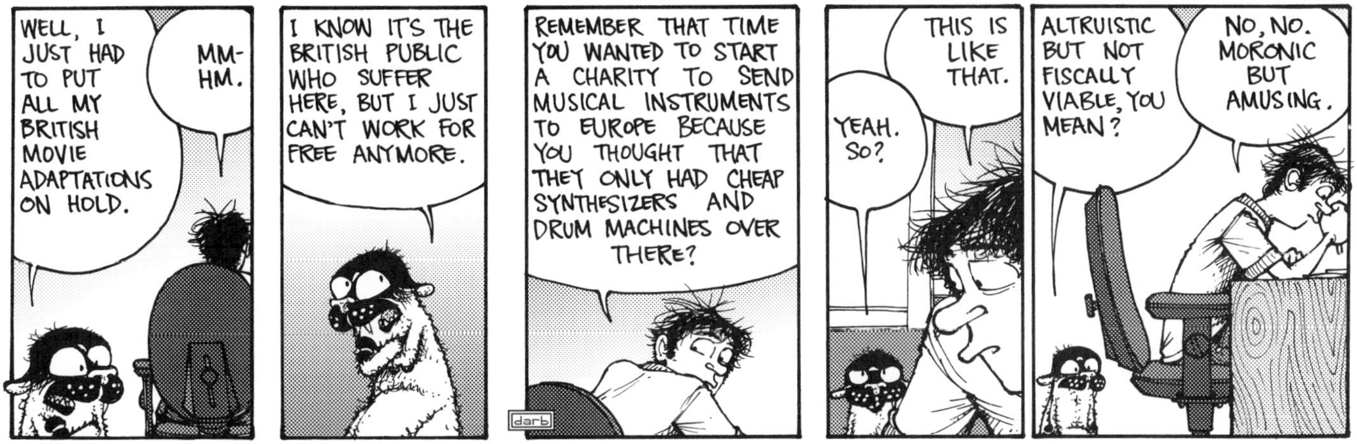
WELL, I JUST HAD TO PUT ALL MY BRITISH MOVIE ADAPTATIONS ON HOLD.
MM-HM.
I KNOW IT'S THE BRITISH PUBLIC WHO SUFFER HERE, BUT I JUST CAN'T WORK FOR FREE ANYMORE.
REMEMBER THAT TIME YOU WANTED TO START A CHARITY TO SEND MUSICAL INSTRUMENTS TO EUROPE BECAUSE YOU THOUGHT THAT THEY ONLY HAD CHEAP SYNTHESIZERS AND DRUM MACHINES OVER THERE?
YEAH. SO?
THIS IS LIKE THAT.
ALTRUISTIC BUT NOT FISCALLY VIABLE, YOU MEAN?
NO, NO. MORONIC BUT AMUSING.
darb

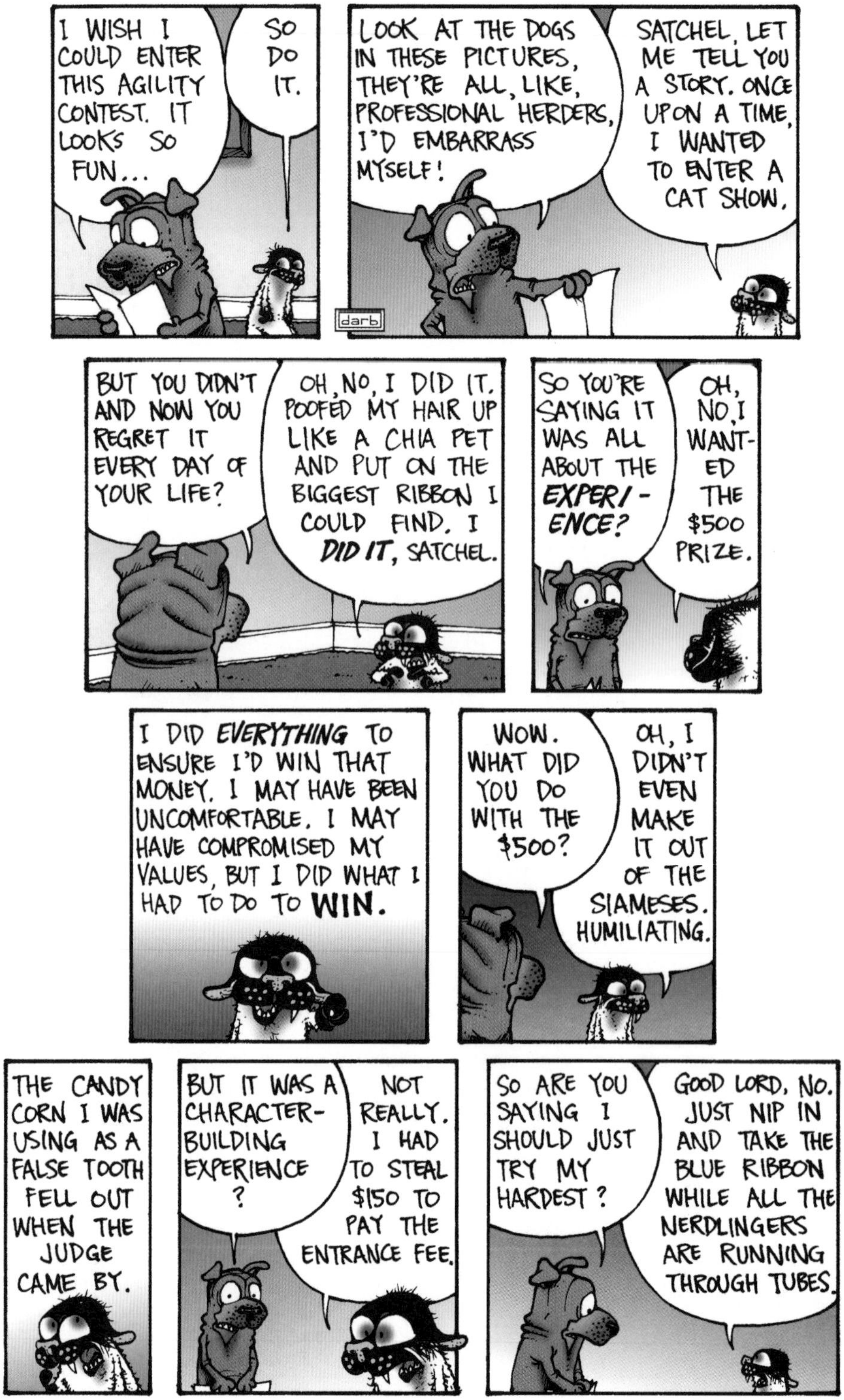
I WISH I COULD ENTER THIS AGILITY CONTEST. IT LOOKS SO FUN...
SO DO IT.
LOOK AT THE DOGS IN THESE PICTURES, THEY'RE ALL, LIKE, PROFESSIONAL HERDERS, I'D EMBARRASS MYSELF!
SATCHEL, LET ME TELL YOU A STORY. ONCE UPON A TIME, I WANTED TO ENTER A CAT SHOW.
darb
BUT YOU DIDN'T AND NOW YOU REGRET IT EVERY DAY OF YOUR LIFE?
OH, NO, I DID IT. POOFED MY HAIR UP LIKE A CHIA PET AND PUT ON THE BIGGEST RIBBON I COULD FIND. I DID IT, SATCHEL.
SO YOU'RE SAYING IT WAS ALL ABOUT THE EXPERIENCE?
OH, NO, I WANTED THE $500 PRIZE.
I DID EVERYTHING TO ENSURE I'D WIN THAT MONEY. I MAY HAVE BEEN UNCOMFORTABLE. I MAY HAVE COMPROMISED MY VALUES, BUT I DID WHAT I HAD TO DO TO WIN.
WOW. WHAT DID YOU DO WITH THE $500?
OH, I DIDN'T EVEN MAKE IT OUT OF THE SIAMESES. HUMILIATING.
THE CANDY CORN I WAS USING AS A FALSE TOOTH FELL OUT WHEN THE JUDGE CAME BY.
BUT IT WAS A CHARACTER-BUILDING EXPERIENCE?
NOT REALLY. I HAD TO STEAL $150 TO PAY THE ENTRANCE FEE.
SO ARE YOU SAYING I SHOULD JUST TRY MY HARDEST?
GOOD LORD, NO. JUST NIP IN AND TAKE THE BLUE RIBBON WHILE ALL THE NERDLINGERS ARE RUNNING THROUGH TUBES.

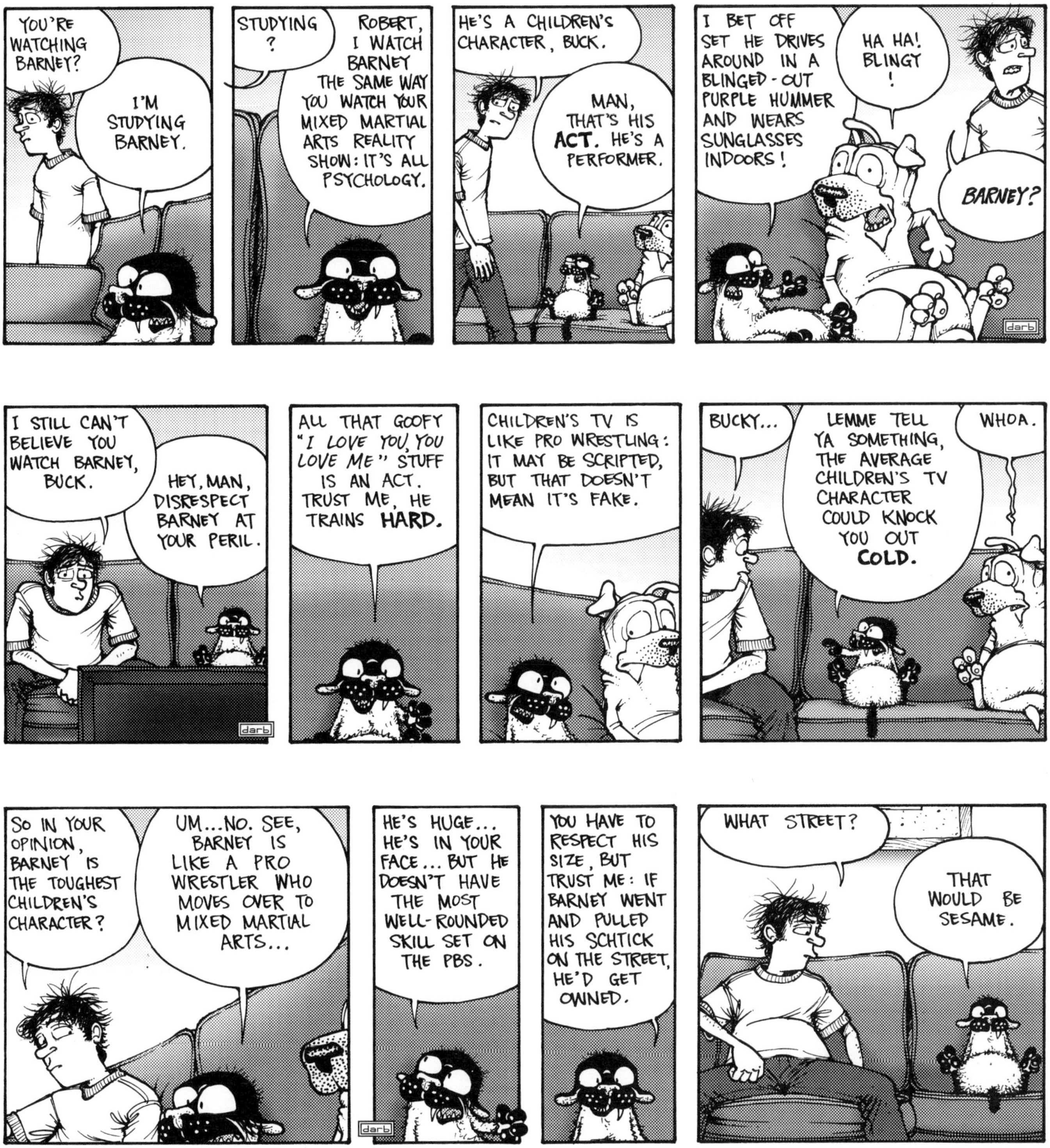
YOU'RE WATCHING BARNEY?
I'M STUDYING BARNEY.
STUDYING ?
ROBERT, I WATCH BARNEY THE SAME WAY YOU WATCH YOUR MIXED MARTIAL ARTS REALITY SHOW: IT'S ALL PSYCHOLOGY.
HE'S A CHILDREN'S CHARACTER, BUCK.
MAN, THAT'S HIS ACT. HE'S A PERFORMER.
I BET OFF SET HE DRIVES AROUND IN A BLINGED-OUT PURPLE HUMMER AND WEARS SUNGLASSES INDOORS!
HA HA! BLINGY !
BARNEY?
darb
I STILL CAN'T BELIEVE YOU WATCH BARNEY, BUCK.
HEY, MAN, DISRESPECT BARNEY AT YOUR PERIL.
darb
ALL THAT GOOFY "I LOVE YOU, YOU LOVE ME" STUFF IS AN ACT. TRUST ME, HE TRAINS HARD.
CHILDREN'S TV IS LIKE PRO WRESTLING: IT MAY BE SCRIPTED, BUT THAT DOESN'T MEAN IT'S FAKE.
BUCKY...
LEMME TELL YA SOMETHING, THE AVERAGE CHILDREN'S TV CHARACTER COULD KNOCK YOU OUT COLD.
WHOA.
SO IN YOUR OPINION, BARNEY IS THE TOUGHEST CHILDREN'S CHARACTER?
UM...NO. SEE, BARNEY IS LIKE A PRO WRESTLER WHO MOVES OVER TO MIXED MARTIAL ARTS...
darb
HE'S HUGE... HE'S IN YOUR FACE... BUT HE DOESN'T HAVE THE MOST WELL-ROUNDED SKILL SET ON THE PBS.
YOU HAVE TO RESPECT HIS SIZE, BUT TRUST ME: IF BARNEY WENT AND PULLED HIS SCHTICK ON THE STREET, HE'D GET OWNED.
WHAT STREET?
THAT WOULD BE SESAME.

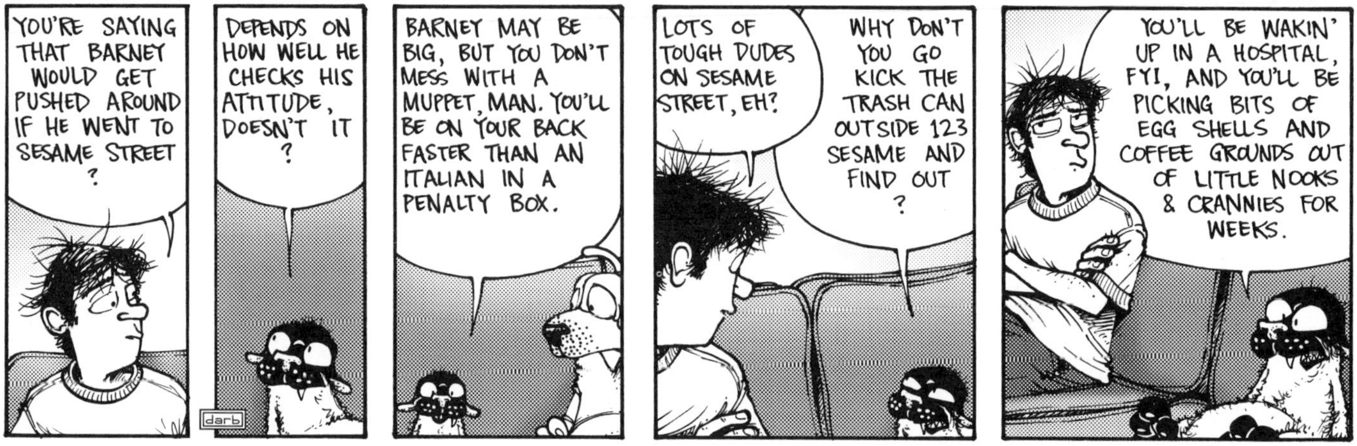
YOU'RE SAYING THAT BARNEY WOULD GET PUSHED AROUND IF HE WENT TO SESAME STREET?
DEPENDS ON HOW WELL HE CHECKS HIS ATTITUDE, DOESN'T IT?
darb
BARNEY MAY BE BIG, BUT YOU DON'T MESS WITH A MUPPET, MAN. YOU'LL BE ON YOUR BACK FASTER THAN AN ITALIAN IN A PENALTY BOX.
LOTS OF TOUGH DUDES ON SESAME STREET, EH?
WHY DON'T YOU GO KICK THE TRASH CAN OUTSIDE 123 SESAME AND FIND OUT?
YOU'LL BE WAKIN' UP IN A HOSPITAL, FYI, AND YOU'LL BE PICKING BITS OF EGG SHELLS AND COFFEE GROUNDS OUT OF LITTLE NOOKS & CRANNIES FOR WEEKS.

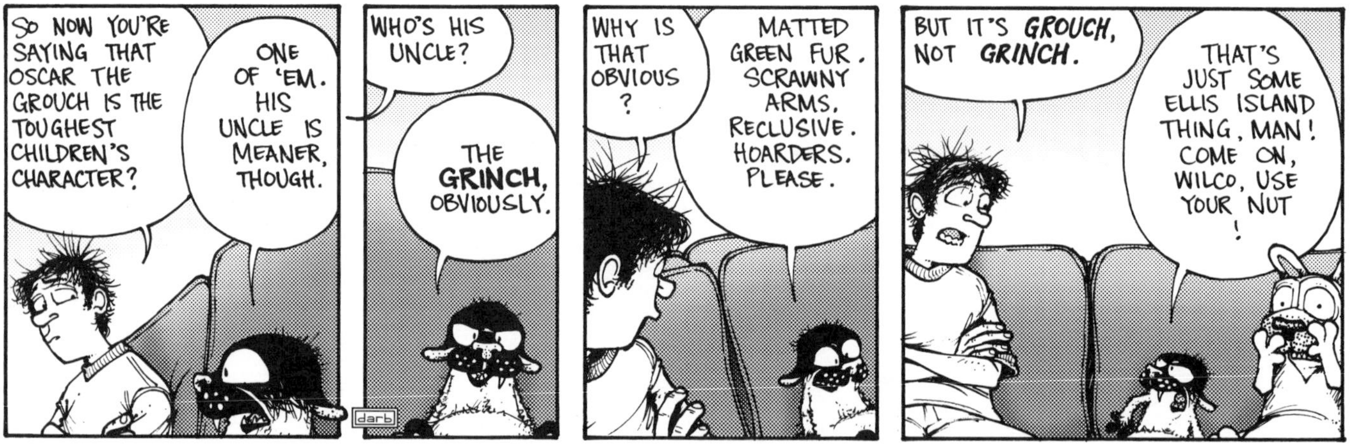
SO NOW YOU'RE SAYING THAT OSCAR THE GROUCH IS THE TOUGHEST CHILDREN'S CHARACTER?
ONE OF 'EM. HIS UNCLE IS MEANER, THOUGH.
WHO'S HIS UNCLE?
THE **GRINCH,** OBVIOUSLY.
darb
WHY IS THAT OBVIOUS?
MATTED GREEN FUR. SCRAWNY ARMS. RECLUSIVE. HOARDERS. PLEASE.
BUT IT'S **GROUCH,** NOT **GRINCH.**
THAT'S JUST SOME ELLIS ISLAND THING, MAN! COME ON, WILCO, USE YOUR NUT!

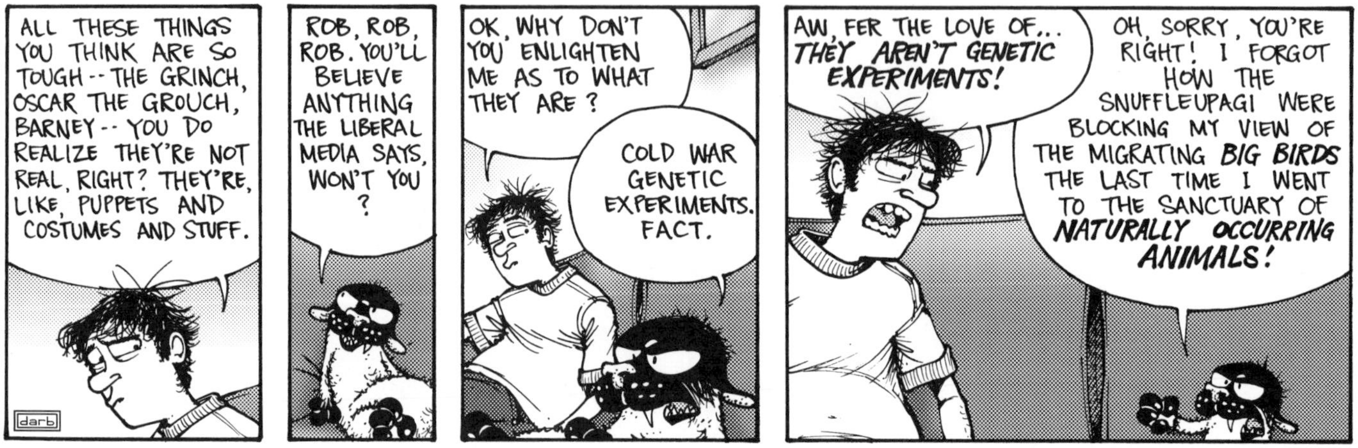
ALL THESE THINGS YOU THINK ARE SO TOUGH -- THE GRINCH, OSCAR THE GROUCH, BARNEY -- YOU DO REALIZE THEY'RE NOT REAL, RIGHT? THEY'RE, LIKE, PUPPETS AND COSTUMES AND STUFF.
darb
ROB, ROB, ROB. YOU'LL BELIEVE ANYTHING THE LIBERAL MEDIA SAYS, WON'T YOU?
OK, WHY DON'T YOU ENLIGHTEN ME AS TO WHAT THEY ARE?
COLD WAR GENETIC EXPERIMENTS. FACT.
AW, FER THE LOVE OF... ***THEY AREN'T GENETIC EXPERIMENTS!***
OH, SORRY, YOU'RE RIGHT! I FORGOT HOW THE SNUFFLEUPAGI WERE BLOCKING MY VIEW OF THE MIGRATING ***BIG BIRDS*** THE LAST TIME I WENT TO THE SANCTUARY OF ***NATURALLY OCCURRING ANIMALS!***

CHECK THESE TICKETS OUT. FRONT ROW, BABY!

TO WHAT?

ONLY *EDDIE LIZZARD*, THE WORLD'S FUNNIEST VERTEBRATE. READ 'EM AND WEEP.

OH! IS THE EXTRA ONE FOR ME?

YOU? YOU DON'T GET ANYTHING OUT OF COMEDY. I MIGHT AS WELL GIVE A MIME A MEGAPHONE.

AW... THEN WHO ARE YOU GONNA—

LOOK OUT FOR THE BALL!

HEY YOU! PUT THOSE DOWN! THOSE ARE MINE!

HEY! BRING THOSE BACK! THOSE AREN'T YOURS!

THERE BUT FOR THE LACK OF GRACE OF DOG, GO I.

SORRY.

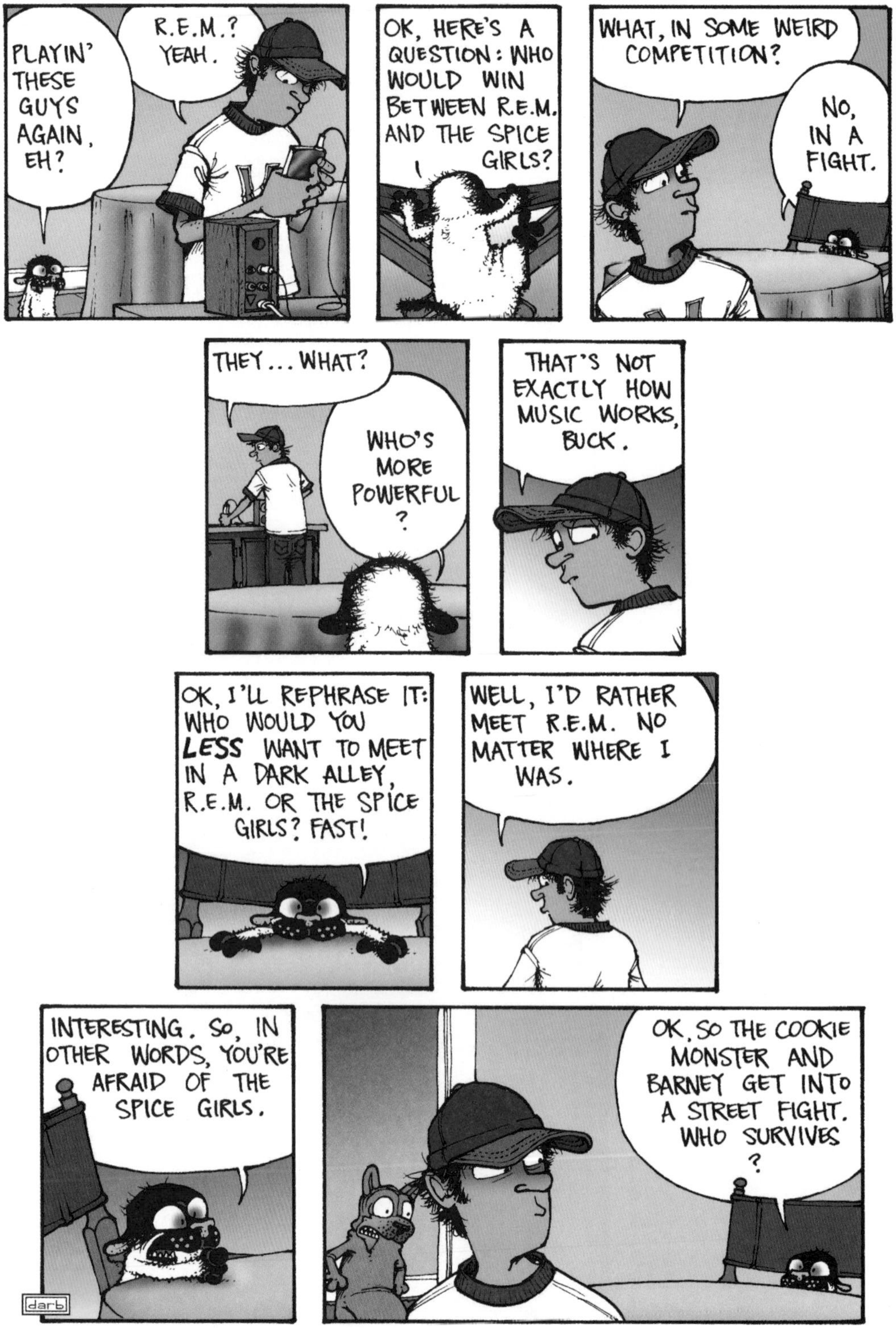
PLAYIN' THESE GUYS AGAIN, EH?
R.E.M.? YEAH.
OK, HERE'S A QUESTION: WHO WOULD WIN BETWEEN R.E.M. AND THE SPICE GIRLS?
WHAT, IN SOME WEIRD COMPETITION?
NO, IN A FIGHT.
THEY... WHAT?
WHO'S MORE POWERFUL?
THAT'S NOT EXACTLY HOW MUSIC WORKS, BUCK.
OK, I'LL REPHRASE IT: WHO WOULD YOU LESS WANT TO MEET IN A DARK ALLEY, R.E.M. OR THE SPICE GIRLS? FAST!
WELL, I'D RATHER MEET R.E.M. NO MATTER WHERE I WAS.
INTERESTING. SO, IN OTHER WORDS, YOU'RE AFRAID OF THE SPICE GIRLS.
darb
OK, SO THE COOKIE MONSTER AND BARNEY GET INTO A STREET FIGHT. WHO SURVIVES?

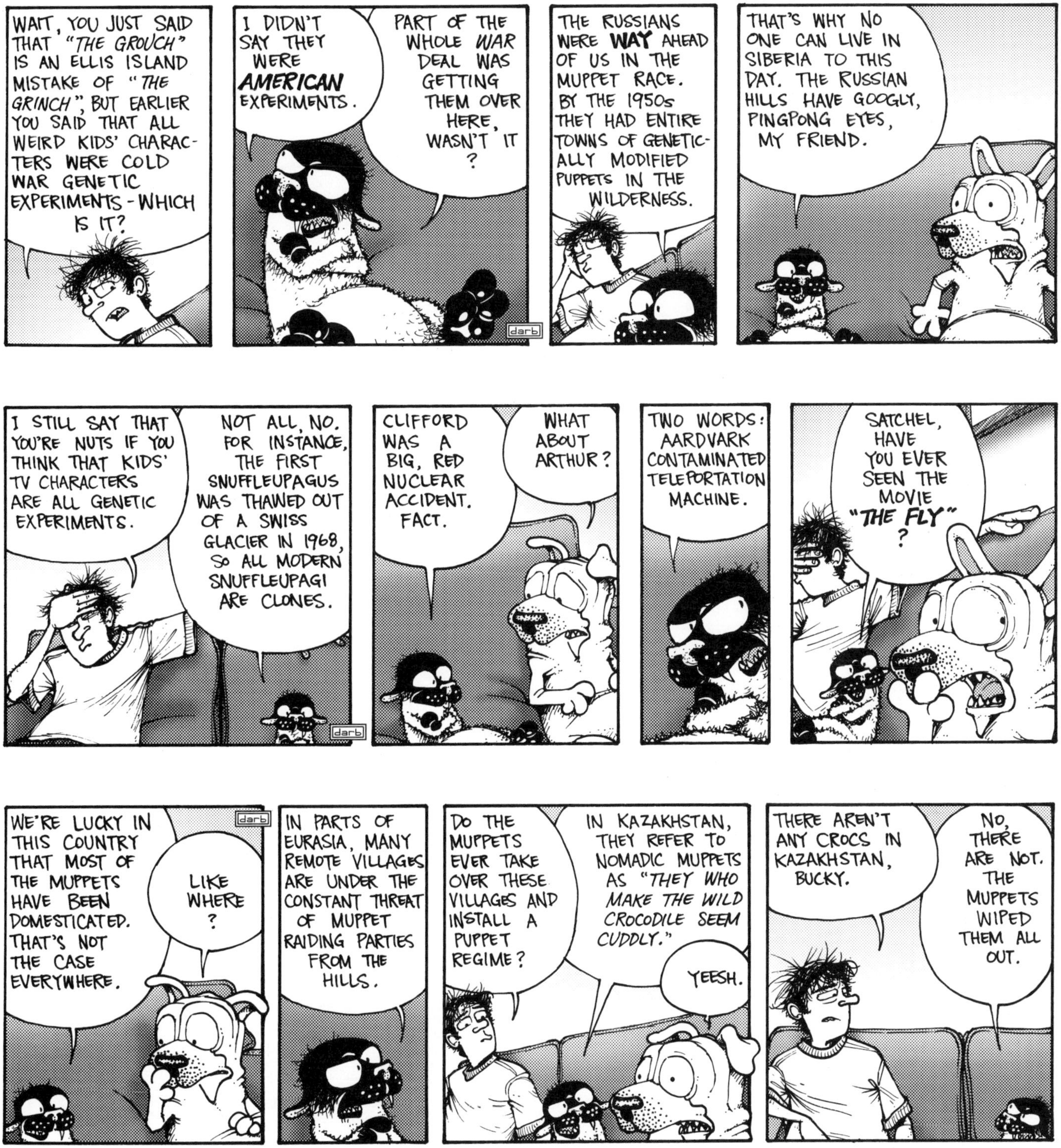
WAIT, YOU JUST SAID THAT "THE GROUCH" IS AN ELLIS ISLAND MISTAKE OF "THE GRINCH", BUT EARLIER YOU SAID THAT ALL WEIRD KIDS' CHARACTERS WERE COLD WAR GENETIC EXPERIMENTS - WHICH IS IT?
I DIDN'T SAY THEY WERE AMERICAN EXPERIMENTS.
PART OF THE WHOLE WAR DEAL WAS GETTING THEM OVER HERE, WASN'T IT?
darb
THE RUSSIANS WERE WAY AHEAD OF US IN THE MUPPET RACE. BY THE 1950s THEY HAD ENTIRE TOWNS OF GENETICALLY MODIFIED PUPPETS IN THE WILDERNESS.
THAT'S WHY NO ONE CAN LIVE IN SIBERIA TO THIS DAY. THE RUSSIAN HILLS HAVE GOOGLY, PINGPONG EYES, MY FRIEND.
I STILL SAY THAT YOU'RE NUTS IF YOU THINK THAT KIDS' TV CHARACTERS ARE ALL GENETIC EXPERIMENTS.
NOT ALL, NO. FOR INSTANCE, THE FIRST SNUFFLEUPAGUS WAS THAWED OUT OF A SWISS GLACIER IN 1968, SO ALL MODERN SNUFFLEUPAGI ARE CLONES.
darb
CLIFFORD WAS A BIG, RED NUCLEAR ACCIDENT. FACT.
WHAT ABOUT ARTHUR?
TWO WORDS: AARDVARK CONTAMINATED TELEPORTATION MACHINE.
SATCHEL, HAVE YOU EVER SEEN THE MOVIE "THE FLY"?
WE'RE LUCKY IN THIS COUNTRY THAT MOST OF THE MUPPETS HAVE BEEN DOMESTICATED. THAT'S NOT THE CASE EVERYWHERE.
darb
LIKE WHERE?
IN PARTS OF EURASIA, MANY REMOTE VILLAGES ARE UNDER THE CONSTANT THREAT OF MUPPET RAIDING PARTIES FROM THE HILLS.
DO THE MUPPETS EVER TAKE OVER THESE VILLAGES AND INSTALL A PUPPET REGIME?
IN KAZAKHSTAN, THEY REFER TO NOMADIC MUPPETS AS "THEY WHO MAKE THE WILD CROCODILE SEEM CUDDLY."
YEESH.
THERE AREN'T ANY CROCS IN KAZAKHSTAN, BUCKY.
NO, THERE ARE NOT. THE MUPPETS WIPED THEM ALL OUT.

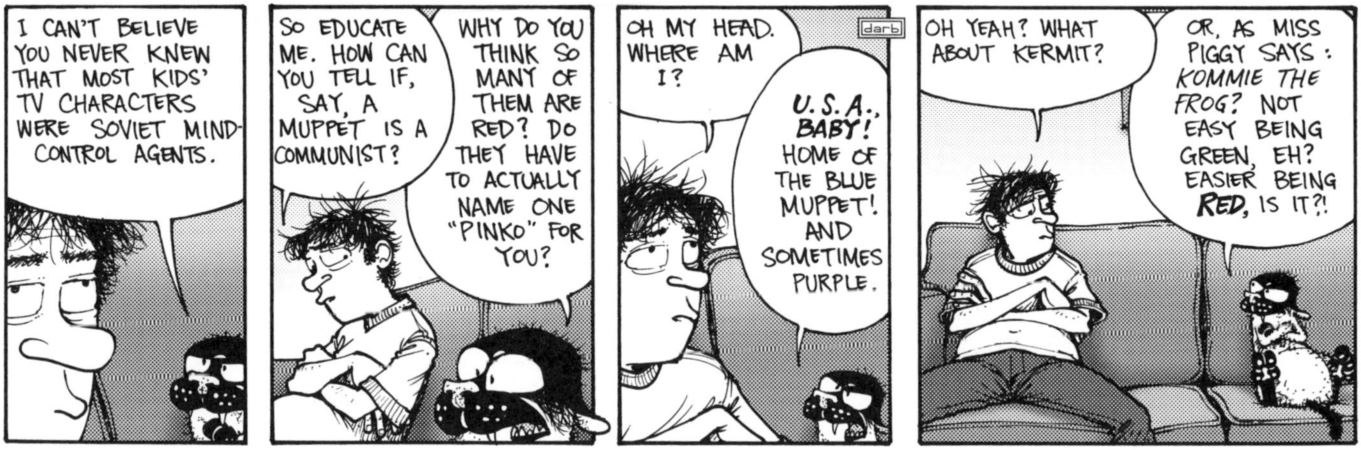
I CAN'T BELIEVE YOU NEVER KNEW THAT MOST KIDS' TV CHARACTERS WERE SOVIET MIND-CONTROL AGENTS.
SO EDUCATE ME. HOW CAN YOU TELL IF, SAY, A MUPPET IS A COMMUNIST?
WHY DO YOU THINK SO MANY OF THEM ARE RED? DO THEY HAVE TO ACTUALLY NAME ONE "PINKO" FOR YOU?
darb
OH MY HEAD. WHERE AM I?
U.S.A., BABY! HOME OF THE BLUE MUPPET! AND SOMETIMES PURPLE.
OH YEAH? WHAT ABOUT KERMIT?
OR, AS MISS PIGGY SAYS: KOMMIE THE FROG? NOT EASY BEING GREEN, EH? EASIER BEING RED, IS IT?!

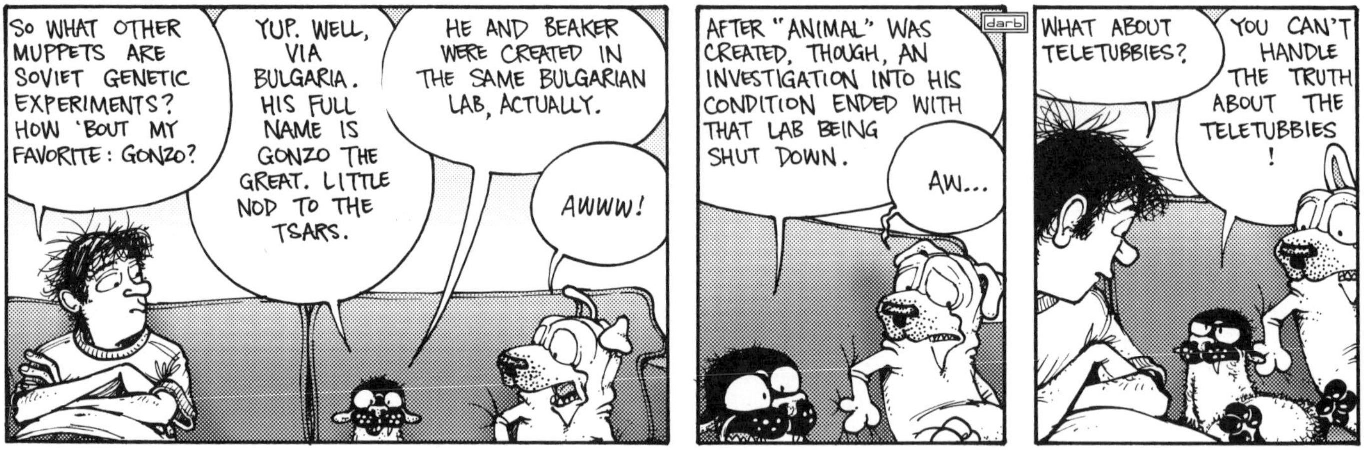
SO WHAT OTHER MUPPETS ARE SOVIET GENETIC EXPERIMENTS? HOW 'BOUT MY FAVORITE: GONZO?
YUP. WELL, VIA BULGARIA. HIS FULL NAME IS GONZO THE GREAT. LITTLE NOD TO THE TSARS.
HE AND BEAKER WERE CREATED IN THE SAME BULGARIAN LAB, ACTUALLY.
AWWW!
darb
AFTER "ANIMAL" WAS CREATED, THOUGH, AN INVESTIGATION INTO HIS CONDITION ENDED WITH THAT LAB BEING SHUT DOWN.
AW...
WHAT ABOUT TELETUBBIES?
YOU CAN'T HANDLE THE TRUTH ABOUT THE TELETUBBIES!

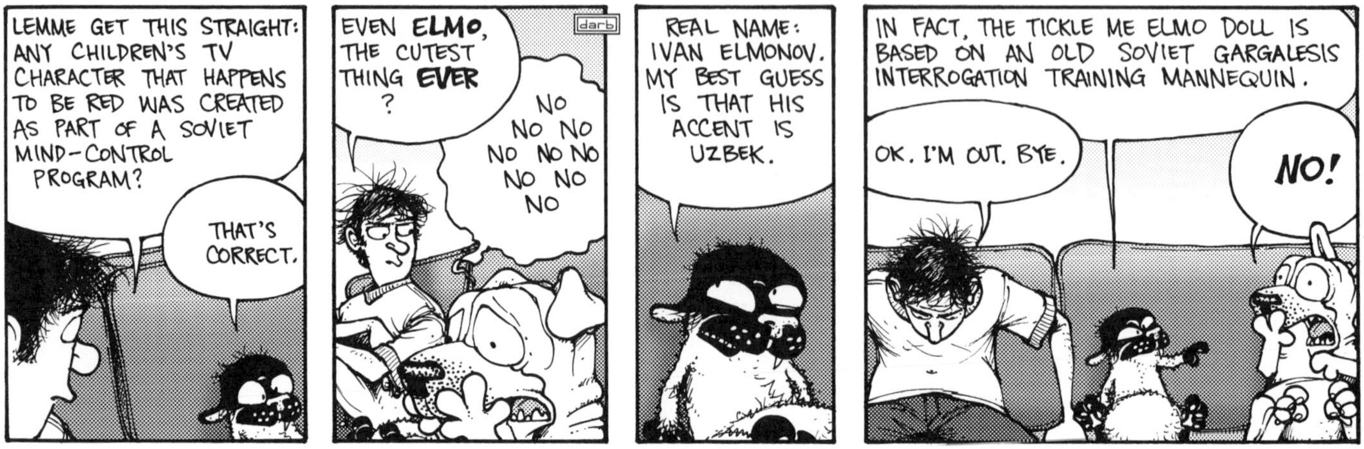
LEMME GET THIS STRAIGHT: ANY CHILDREN'S TV CHARACTER THAT HAPPENS TO BE RED WAS CREATED AS PART OF A SOVIET MIND-CONTROL PROGRAM?
THAT'S CORRECT.
darb
EVEN ELMO, THE CUTEST THING EVER?
NO NO NO NO NO NO NO NO NO
REAL NAME: IVAN ELMONOV. MY BEST GUESS IS THAT HIS ACCENT IS UZBEK.
IN FACT, THE TICKLE ME ELMO DOLL IS BASED ON AN OLD SOVIET GARGALESIS INTERROGATION TRAINING MANNEQUIN.
OK. I'M OUT. BYE.
NO!

HM. I WAS GOING TO THE STORE, BUT I CAN'T REMEMBER WHAT I NEEDED.

HAIR PIECE?

WHAT? I DON'T NEED A HAIR PIECE.

WELL...

WHAT DOES THAT MEAN?

WELL THAT WOULD DEPEND ON WHAT THE PIECE LOOKS LIKE, WOULDN'T IT?

HUH?

LET'S BE HONEST, ANY COMMERCIALLY AVAILABLE HAIR PIECE IS GONNA BE AN IMPROVEMENT FOR YOU.

YOUR HAIR MAKES YOU LOOK LIKE SOME *SCARE-YOU-STRAIGHT* CAMPAIGN "AFTER" PICTURE.

I MEAN, NOBODY GOES INTO A CANDY STORE AND SAYS, "*I WANT A DIRT-FLAVORED CANDY,*" RIGHT?

AND NOBODY WALKS INTO A WIG STORE AND SAYS, "*I WANT A ROB WILCO.*"

darb

MAYBE I'LL REMEMBER WHAT I NEED WHEN I GET THERE.

DEODORANT!

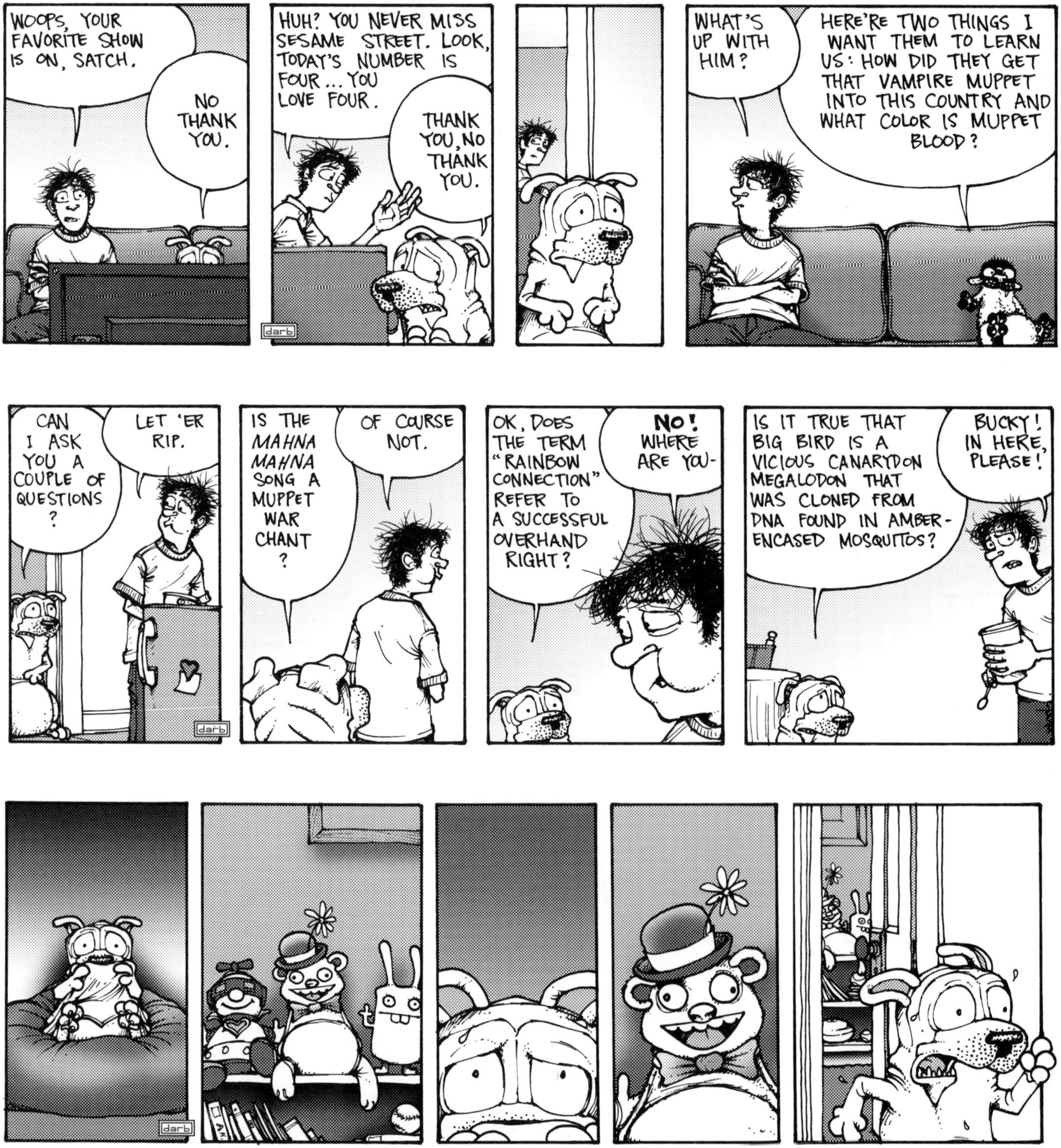
WOOPS, YOUR FAVORITE SHOW IS ON, SATCH.
NO THANK YOU.
HUH? YOU NEVER MISS SESAME STREET. LOOK, TODAY'S NUMBER IS FOUR... YOU LOVE FOUR.
THANK YOU, NO THANK YOU.
WHAT'S UP WITH HIM?
HERE'RE TWO THINGS I WANT THEM TO LEARN US: HOW DID THEY GET THAT VAMPIRE MUPPET INTO THIS COUNTRY AND WHAT COLOR IS MUPPET BLOOD?
CAN I ASK YOU A COUPLE OF QUESTIONS?
LET 'ER RIP.
IS THE MAHNA MAHNA SONG A MUPPET WAR CHANT?
OF COURSE NOT.
OK, DOES THE TERM "RAINBOW CONNECTION" REFER TO A SUCCESSFUL OVERHAND RIGHT?
NO! WHERE ARE YOU-
IS IT TRUE THAT BIG BIRD IS A VICIOUS CANARYDON MEGALODON THAT WAS CLONED FROM DNA FOUND IN AMBER-ENCASED MOSQUITOS?
BUCKY! IN HERE, PLEASE!
darb

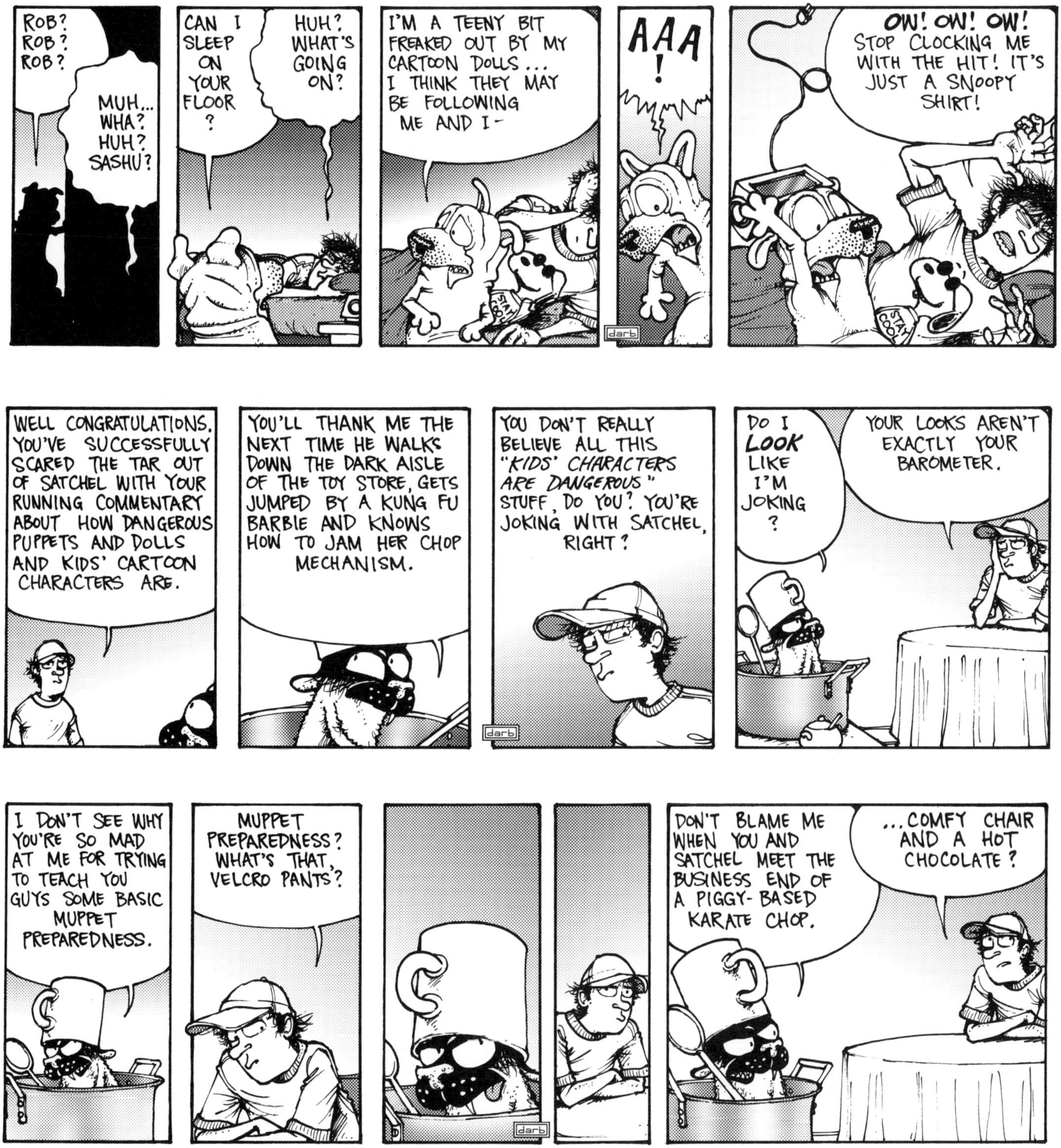
ROB? ROB? ROB?
MUH... WHA? HUH? SASHU?
CAN I SLEEP ON YOUR FLOOR?
HUH? WHAT'S GOING ON?
I'M A TEENY BIT FREAKED OUT BY MY CARTOON DOLLS... I THINK THEY MAY BE FOLLOWING ME AND I–
AAA!
OW! OW! OW! STOP CLOCKING ME WITH THE HIT! IT'S JUST A SNOOPY SHIRT!
WELL CONGRATULATIONS. YOU'VE SUCCESSFULLY SCARED THE TAR OUT OF SATCHEL WITH YOUR RUNNING COMMENTARY ABOUT HOW DANGEROUS PUPPETS AND DOLLS AND KIDS' CARTOON CHARACTERS ARE.
YOU'LL THANK ME THE NEXT TIME HE WALKS DOWN THE DARK AISLE OF THE TOY STORE, GETS JUMPED BY A KUNG FU BARBIE AND KNOWS HOW TO JAM HER CHOP MECHANISM.
YOU DON'T REALLY BELIEVE ALL THIS "KIDS' CHARACTERS ARE DANGEROUS" STUFF, DO YOU? YOU'RE JOKING WITH SATCHEL, RIGHT?
DO I LOOK LIKE I'M JOKING?
YOUR LOOKS AREN'T EXACTLY YOUR BAROMETER.
I DON'T SEE WHY YOU'RE SO MAD AT ME FOR TRYING TO TEACH YOU GUYS SOME BASIC MUPPET PREPAREDNESS.
MUPPET PREPAREDNESS? WHAT'S THAT, VELCRO PANTS?
DON'T BLAME ME WHEN YOU AND SATCHEL MEET THE BUSINESS END OF A PIGGY-BASED KARATE CHOP.
...COMFY CHAIR AND A HOT CHOCOLATE?

OOF... I ATE SOMETHING THAT DIDN'T AGREE WITH ME.

YEAH, I DO THAT ALL THE TIME. THE TRICK IS TO SNEAK UP ON IT FROM BEHIND.

NO, I MEAN IT HURT MY STOMACH.

THAT'S WHY I AMBUSH THEM. IT MINIMIZES RISK.

NO, IT WAS JUST A LITTLE LUMP OF BLUE CHEESE. I THOUGHT IT WAS FRENCH, BUT IT TURNS OUT IT WAS JUST ROTTEN.

WHAT'S BLUE CHEESE?

CHEESE WITH MOLD ON IT.

WHAT? YOU EAT MOLDY CHEESE?

HEY, IT'S REVERED IN FRANCE.

SO ARE CLOWNS AND PUPPETS, BUT YOU'RE NOT SUPPOSED TO EAT 'EM.

YOU DOGS HAVE NO RULES ABOUT WHAT YOU CAN EAT! YOU'RE GOING FOOD ROGUE!

IF DOGS COULD UNHINGE THEIR JAWS LIKE SNAKES, I'D COME IN HERE ONE DAY AND YOU'D HAVE THE SOFA STICKIN' OUT OF YOUR MOUTH!

darb

IF IT WAS UP TO ME, DOGS WOULD BE ILLEGAL. LIKE LEAD SPOONS.

I CAN NEVER TELL IF YOU'RE JOKING OR SERIOUS...

HUMOR IS FOR THE WEAK, SATCHEL.

HA HA! GOOD ONE.

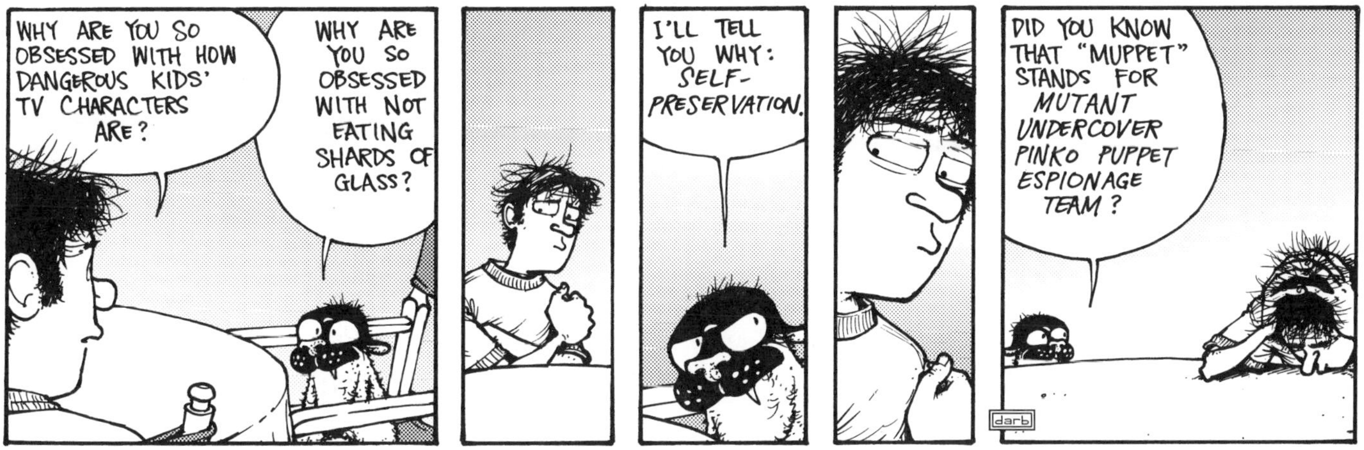
WHY ARE YOU SO OBSESSED WITH HOW DANGEROUS KIDS' TV CHARACTERS ARE?
WHY ARE YOU SO OBSESSED WITH NOT EATING SHARDS OF GLASS?
I'LL TELL YOU WHY: SELF-PRESERVATION.
DID YOU KNOW THAT "MUPPET" STANDS FOR MUTANT UNDERCOVER PINKO PUPPET ESPIONAGE TEAM?
darb

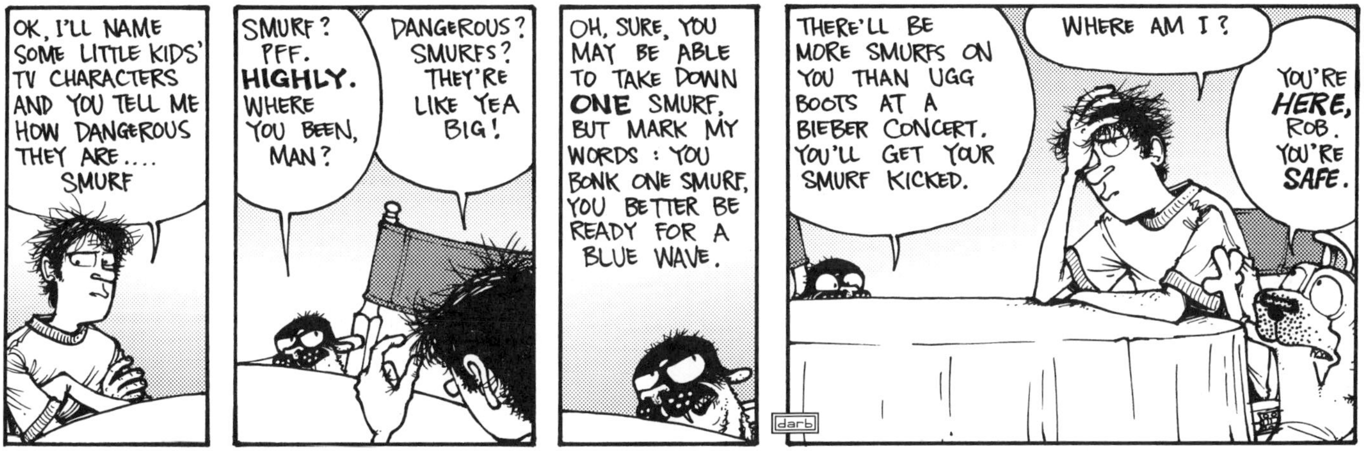
OK, I'LL NAME SOME LITTLE KIDS' TV CHARACTERS AND YOU TELL ME HOW DANGEROUS THEY ARE.... SMURF
SMURF? PFF. HIGHLY. WHERE YOU BEEN, MAN?
DANGEROUS? SMURFS? THEY'RE LIKE YEA BIG!
OH, SURE, YOU MAY BE ABLE TO TAKE DOWN ONE SMURF, BUT MARK MY WORDS: YOU BONK ONE SMURF, YOU BETTER BE READY FOR A BLUE WAVE.
darb
THERE'LL BE MORE SMURFS ON YOU THAN UGG BOOTS AT A BIEBER CONCERT. YOU'LL GET YOUR SMURF KICKED.
WHERE AM I?
YOU'RE HERE, ROB. YOU'RE SAFE.

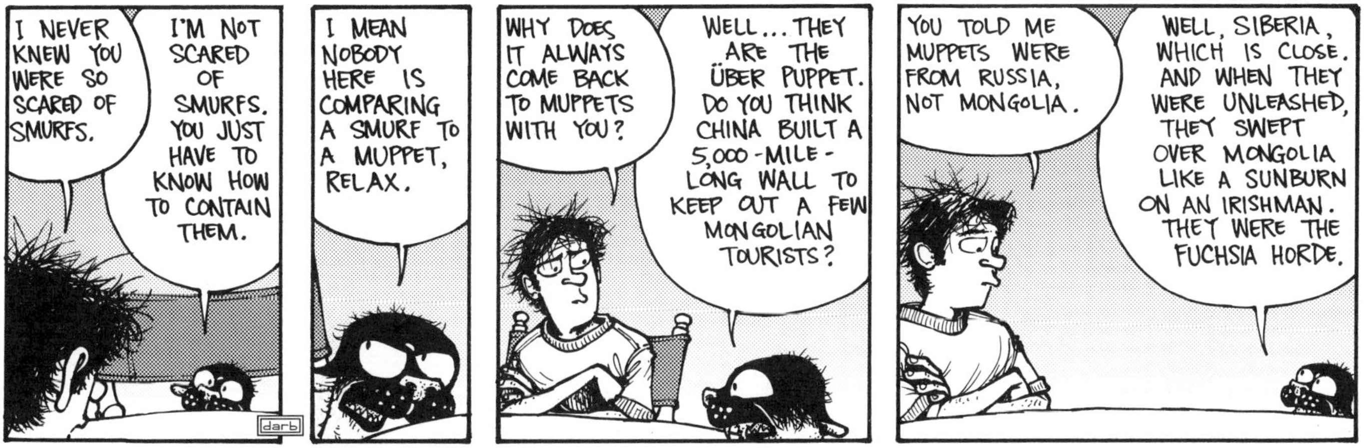
I NEVER KNEW YOU WERE SO SCARED OF SMURFS.
I'M NOT SCARED OF SMURFS. YOU JUST HAVE TO KNOW HOW TO CONTAIN THEM.
darb
I MEAN NOBODY HERE IS COMPARING A SMURF TO A MUPPET, RELAX.
WHY DOES IT ALWAYS COME BACK TO MUPPETS WITH YOU?
WELL... THEY ARE THE ÜBER PUPPET. DO YOU THINK CHINA BUILT A 5,000-MILE-LONG WALL TO KEEP OUT A FEW MONGOLIAN TOURISTS?
YOU TOLD ME MUPPETS WERE FROM RUSSIA, NOT MONGOLIA.
WELL, SIBERIA, WHICH IS CLOSE. AND WHEN THEY WERE UNLEASHED, THEY SWEPT OVER MONGOLIA LIKE A SUNBURN ON AN IRISHMAN. THEY WERE THE FUCHSIA HORDE.

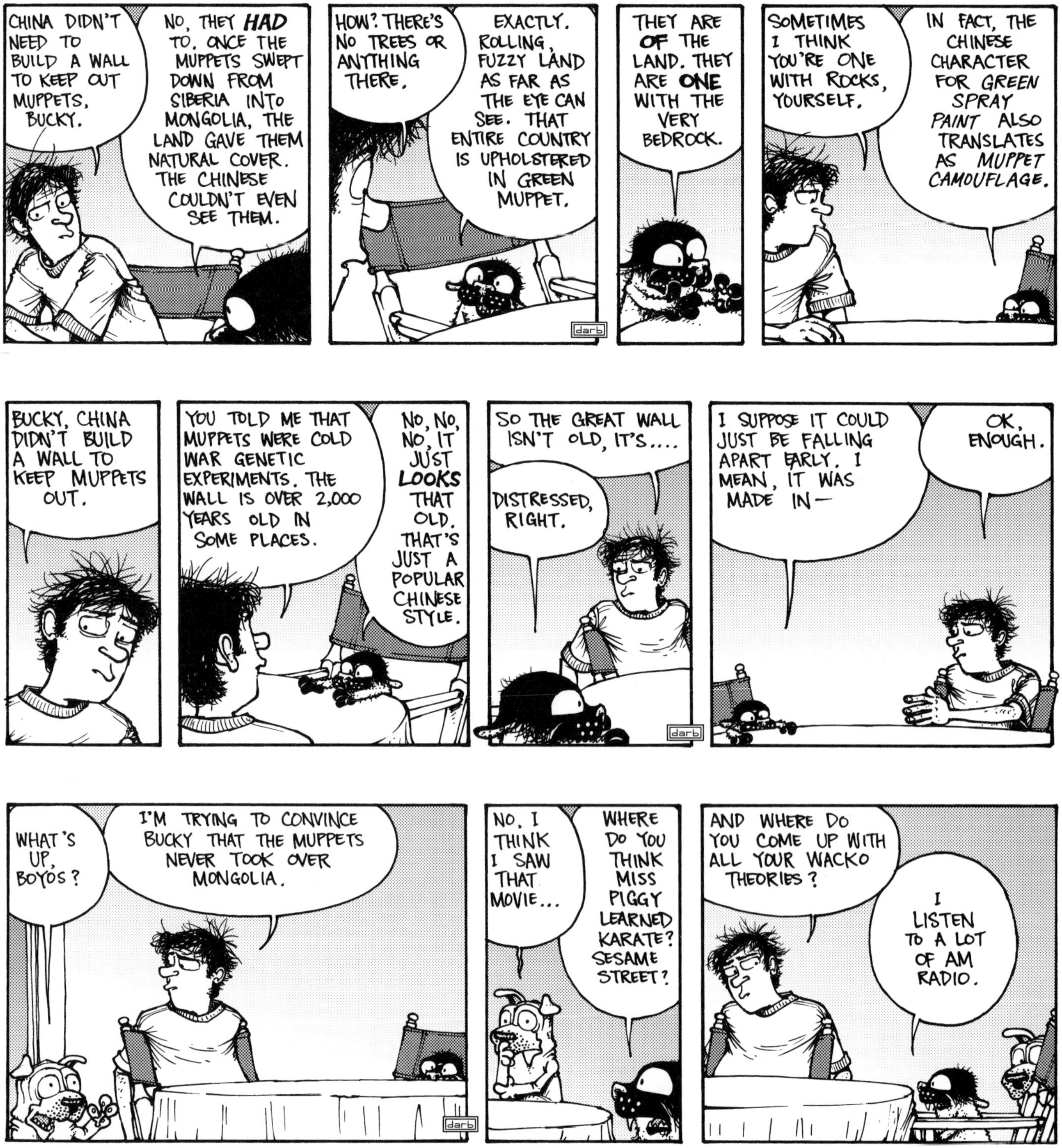
CHINA DIDN'T NEED TO BUILD A WALL TO KEEP OUT MUPPETS, BUCKY.
NO, THEY **HAD** TO. ONCE THE MUPPETS SWEPT DOWN FROM SIBERIA INTO MONGOLIA, THE LAND GAVE THEM NATURAL COVER. THE CHINESE COULDN'T EVEN SEE THEM.
HOW? THERE'S NO TREES OR ANYTHING THERE.
EXACTLY. ROLLING, FUZZY LAND AS FAR AS THE EYE CAN SEE. THAT ENTIRE COUNTRY IS UPHOLSTERED IN GREEN MUPPET.
darb
THEY ARE **OF** THE LAND. THEY ARE **ONE** WITH THE VERY BEDROCK.
SOMETIMES I THINK YOU'RE ONE WITH ROCKS, YOURSELF.
IN FACT, THE CHINESE CHARACTER FOR *GREEN SPRAY PAINT* ALSO TRANSLATES AS *MUPPET CAMOUFLAGE*.
BUCKY, CHINA DIDN'T BUILD A WALL TO KEEP MUPPETS OUT.
YOU TOLD ME THAT MUPPETS WERE COLD WAR GENETIC EXPERIMENTS. THE WALL IS OVER 2,000 YEARS OLD IN SOME PLACES.
NO, NO, NO, IT JUST **LOOKS** THAT OLD. THAT'S JUST A POPULAR CHINESE STYLE.
SO THE GREAT WALL ISN'T OLD, IT'S....
DISTRESSED, RIGHT.
darb
I SUPPOSE IT COULD JUST BE FALLING APART EARLY. I MEAN, IT WAS MADE IN—
OK, ENOUGH.
WHAT'S UP, BOYOS?
I'M TRYING TO CONVINCE BUCKY THAT THE MUPPETS NEVER TOOK OVER MONGOLIA.
darb
NO, I THINK I SAW THAT MOVIE...
WHERE DO YOU THINK MISS PIGGY LEARNED KARATE? SESAME STREET?
AND WHERE DO YOU COME UP WITH ALL YOUR WACKO THEORIES?
I LISTEN TO A LOT OF AM RADIO.

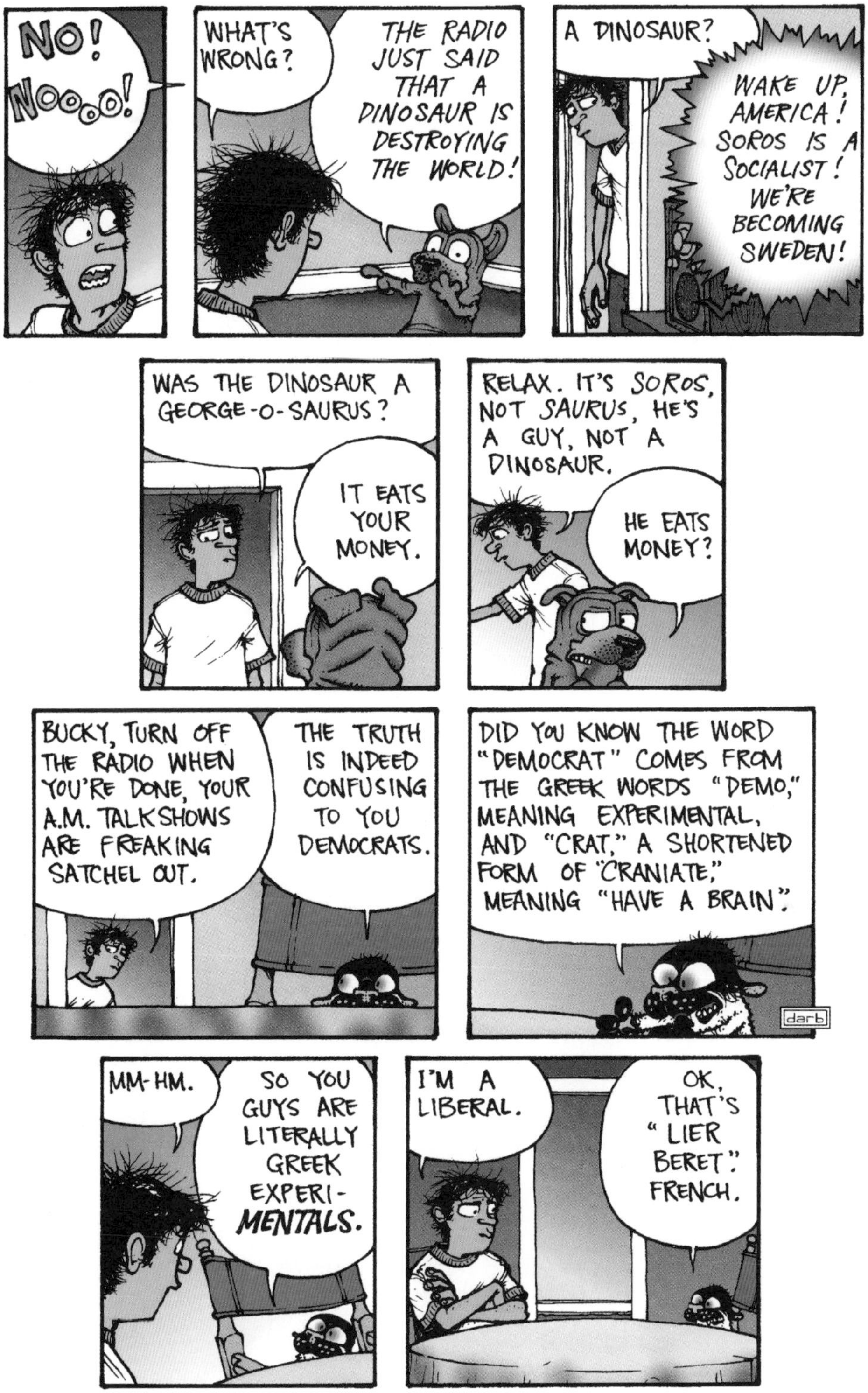
NO! NOOOOO!
WHAT'S WRONG?
THE RADIO JUST SAID THAT A DINOSAUR IS DESTROYING THE WORLD!
A DINOSAUR?
WAKE UP, AMERICA! SOROS IS A SOCIALIST! WE'RE BECOMING SWEDEN!
WAS THE DINOSAUR A GEORGE-O-SAURUS?
IT EATS YOUR MONEY.
RELAX. IT'S SOROS, NOT SAURUS, HE'S A GUY, NOT A DINOSAUR.
HE EATS MONEY?
BUCKY, TURN OFF THE RADIO WHEN YOU'RE DONE, YOUR A.M. TALKSHOWS ARE FREAKING SATCHEL OUT.
THE TRUTH IS INDEED CONFUSING TO YOU DEMOCRATS.
DID YOU KNOW THE WORD "DEMOCRAT" COMES FROM THE GREEK WORDS "DEMO," MEANING EXPERIMENTAL, AND "CRAT," A SHORTENED FORM OF "CRANIATE," MEANING "HAVE A BRAIN".
darb
MM-HM.
SO YOU GUYS ARE LITERALLY GREEK EXPERI-MENTALS.
I'M A LIBERAL.
OK, THAT'S "LIER BERET". FRENCH.

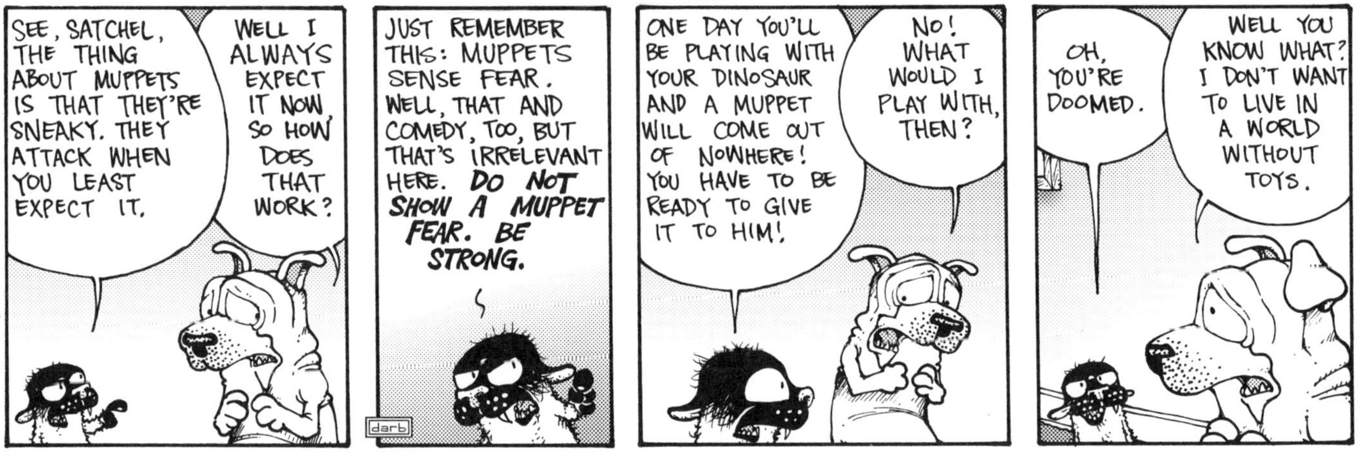
SEE, SATCHEL, THE THING ABOUT MUPPETS IS THAT THEY'RE SNEAKY. THEY ATTACK WHEN YOU LEAST EXPECT IT.
WELL I ALWAYS EXPECT IT NOW, SO HOW DOES THAT WORK?
JUST REMEMBER THIS: MUPPETS SENSE FEAR. WELL, THAT AND COMEDY, TOO, BUT THAT'S IRRELEVANT HERE. DO NOT SHOW A MUPPET FEAR. BE STRONG.
ONE DAY YOU'LL BE PLAYING WITH YOUR DINOSAUR AND A MUPPET WILL COME OUT OF NOWHERE! YOU HAVE TO BE READY TO GIVE IT TO HIM!
NO! WHAT WOULD I PLAY WITH, THEN?
OH, YOU'RE DOOMED.
WELL YOU KNOW WHAT? I DON'T WANT TO LIVE IN A WORLD WITHOUT TOYS.
darb

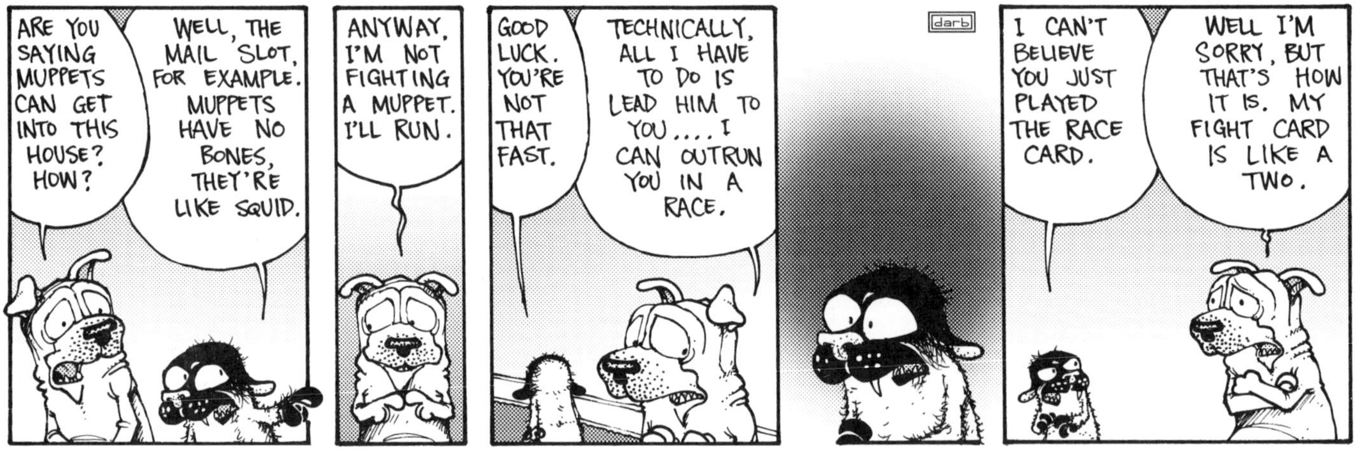
ARE YOU SAYING MUPPETS CAN GET INTO THIS HOUSE? HOW?
WELL, THE MAIL SLOT, FOR EXAMPLE. MUPPETS HAVE NO BONES, THEY'RE LIKE SQUID.
ANYWAY, I'M NOT FIGHTING A MUPPET. I'LL RUN.
GOOD LUCK. YOU'RE NOT THAT FAST.
TECHNICALLY, ALL I HAVE TO DO IS LEAD HIM TO YOU.... I CAN OUTRUN YOU IN A RACE.
darb
I CAN'T BELIEVE YOU JUST PLAYED THE RACE CARD.
WELL I'M SORRY, BUT THAT'S HOW IT IS. MY FIGHT CARD IS LIKE A TWO.

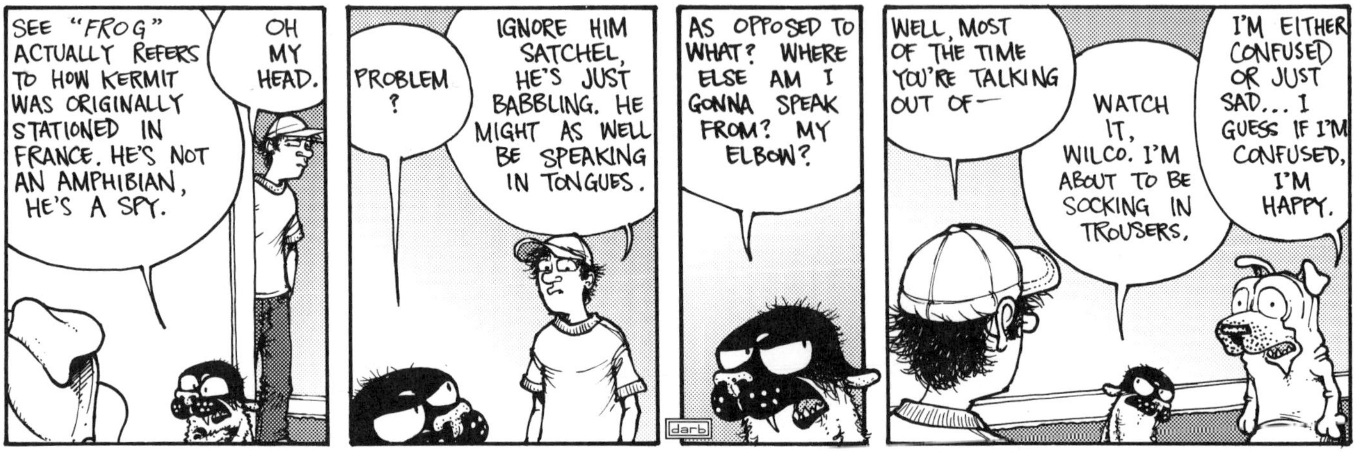
SEE "FROG" ACTUALLY REFERS TO HOW KERMIT WAS ORIGINALLY STATIONED IN FRANCE. HE'S NOT AN AMPHIBIAN, HE'S A SPY.
OH MY HEAD.
PROBLEM?
IGNORE HIM SATCHEL, HE'S JUST BABBLING. HE MIGHT AS WELL BE SPEAKING IN TONGUES.
AS OPPOSED TO WHAT? WHERE ELSE AM I GONNA SPEAK FROM? MY ELBOW?
darb
WELL, MOST OF THE TIME YOU'RE TALKING OUT OF—
WATCH IT, WILCO. I'M ABOUT TO BE SOCKING IN TROUSERS.
I'M EITHER CONFUSED OR JUST SAD... I GUESS IF I'M CONFUSED, I'M HAPPY.

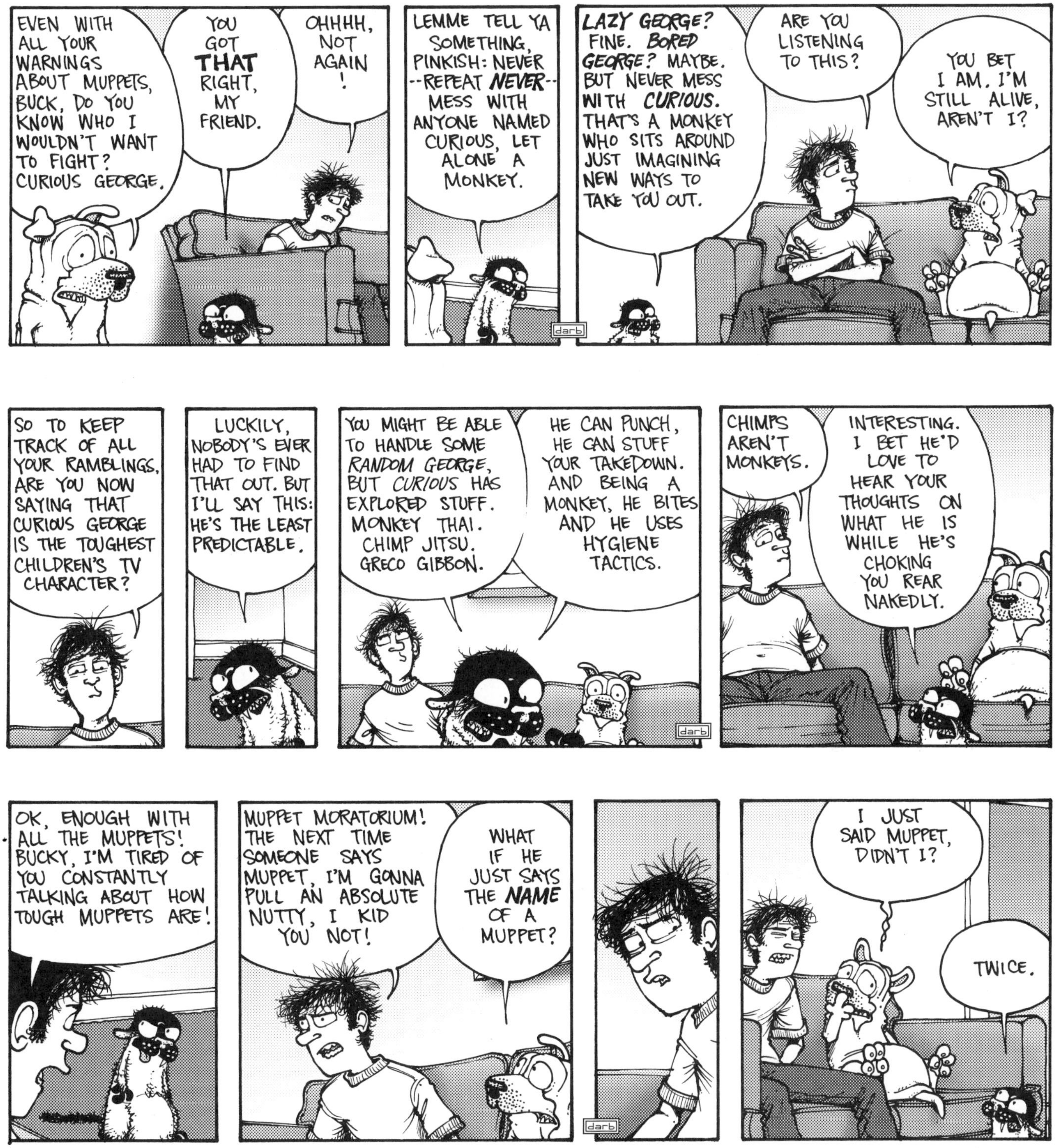
EVEN WITH ALL YOUR WARNINGS ABOUT MUPPETS, BUCK, DO YOU KNOW WHO I WOULDN'T WANT TO FIGHT? CURIOUS GEORGE.
YOU GOT **THAT** RIGHT, MY FRIEND.
OHHHH, NOT AGAIN!
LEMME TELL YA SOMETHING, PINKISH: NEVER --REPEAT ***NEVER***-- MESS WITH ANYONE NAMED CURIOUS, LET ALONE A MONKEY.
darb
LAZY GEORGE? FINE. ***BORED GEORGE?*** MAYBE. BUT NEVER MESS WITH ***CURIOUS.*** THAT'S A MONKEY WHO SITS AROUND JUST IMAGINING NEW WAYS TO TAKE YOU OUT.
ARE YOU LISTENING TO THIS?
YOU BET I AM. I'M STILL ALIVE, AREN'T I?
SO TO KEEP TRACK OF ALL YOUR RAMBLINGS, ARE YOU NOW SAYING THAT CURIOUS GEORGE IS THE TOUGHEST CHILDREN'S TV CHARACTER?
LUCKILY, NOBODY'S EVER HAD TO FIND THAT OUT. BUT I'LL SAY THIS: HE'S THE LEAST PREDICTABLE.
YOU MIGHT BE ABLE TO HANDLE SOME *RANDOM GEORGE*, BUT *CURIOUS* HAS EXPLORED STUFF. MONKEY THAI. CHIMP JITSU. GRECO GIBBON.
HE CAN PUNCH, HE CAN STUFF YOUR TAKEDOWN. AND BEING A MONKEY, HE BITES AND HE USES HYGIENE TACTICS.
darb
CHIMPS AREN'T MONKEYS.
INTERESTING. I BET HE'D LOVE TO HEAR YOUR THOUGHTS ON WHAT HE IS WHILE HE'S CHOKING YOU REAR NAKEDLY.
OK, ENOUGH WITH ALL THE MUPPETS! BUCKY, I'M TIRED OF YOU CONSTANTLY TALKING ABOUT HOW TOUGH MUPPETS ARE!
MUPPET MORATORIUM! THE NEXT TIME SOMEONE SAYS MUPPET, I'M GONNA PULL AN ABSOLUTE NUTTY, I KID YOU NOT!
WHAT IF HE JUST SAYS THE ***NAME*** OF A MUPPET?
darb
I JUST SAID MUPPET, DIDN'T I?
TWICE.

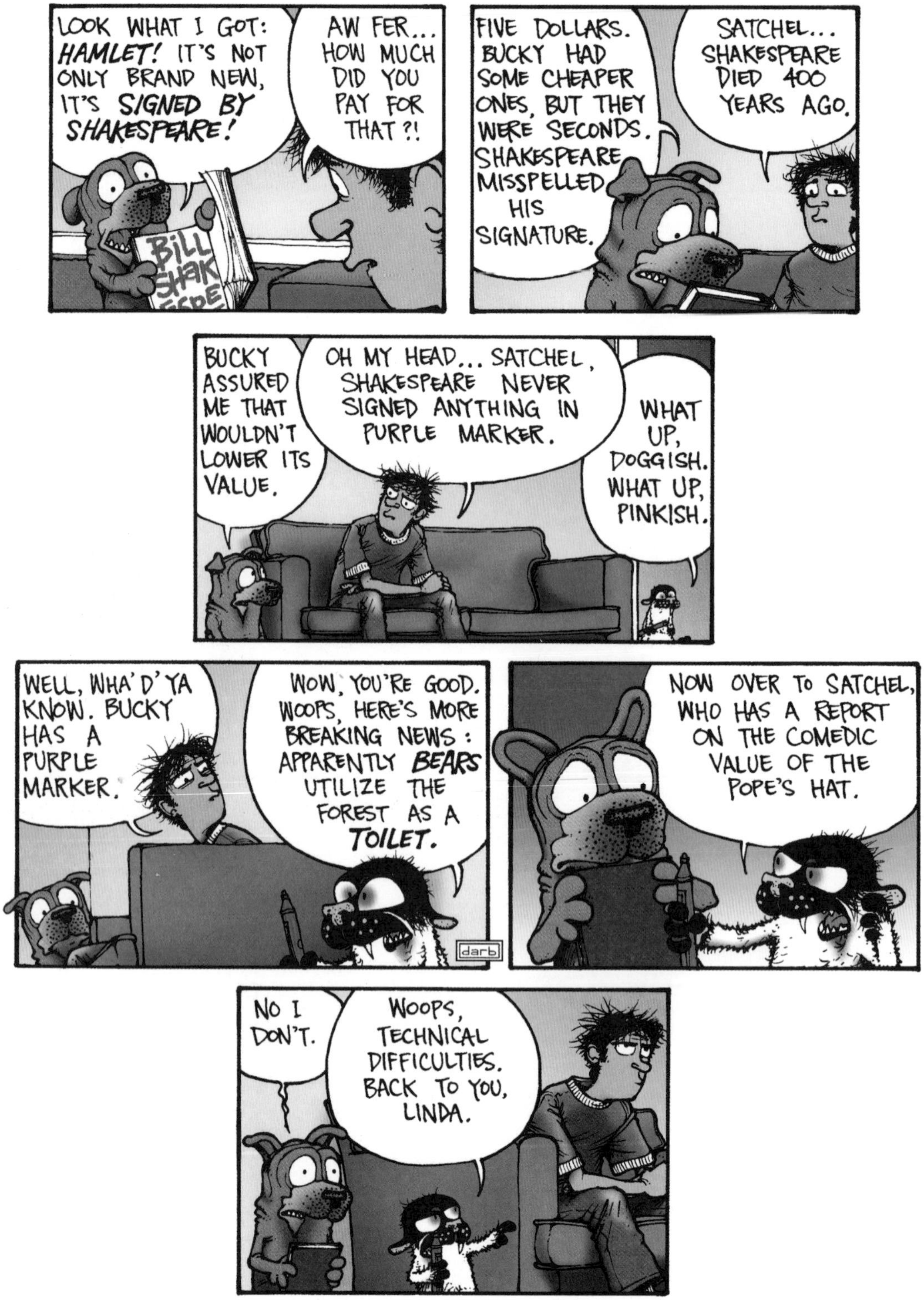
LOOK WHAT I GOT: HAMLET! IT'S NOT ONLY BRAND NEW, IT'S SIGNED BY SHAKESPEARE!
BILL SHAK
AW FER... HOW MUCH DID YOU PAY FOR THAT?!
FIVE DOLLARS. BUCKY HAD SOME CHEAPER ONES, BUT THEY WERE SECONDS. SHAKESPEARE MISSPELLED HIS SIGNATURE.
SATCHEL... SHAKESPEARE DIED 400 YEARS AGO.
BUCKY ASSURED ME THAT WOULDN'T LOWER ITS VALUE.
OH MY HEAD... SATCHEL, SHAKESPEARE NEVER SIGNED ANYTHING IN PURPLE MARKER.
WHAT UP, DOGGISH. WHAT UP, PINKISH.
WELL, WHA'D'YA KNOW. BUCKY HAS A PURPLE MARKER.
WOW, YOU'RE GOOD. WOOPS, HERE'S MORE BREAKING NEWS: APPARENTLY BEARS UTILIZE THE FOREST AS A TOILET.
darb
NOW OVER TO SATCHEL, WHO HAS A REPORT ON THE COMEDIC VALUE OF THE POPE'S HAT.
NO I DON'T.
WOOPS, TECHNICAL DIFFICULTIES. BACK TO YOU, LINDA.

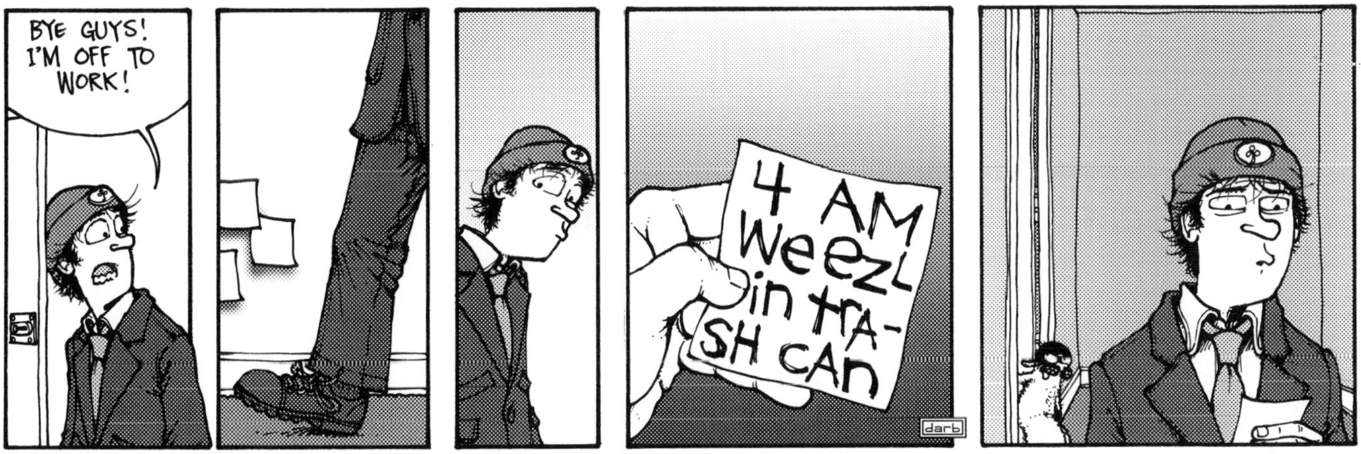
BYE GUYS! I'M OFF TO WORK!
4 AM Weezl in tra-sh can
darb

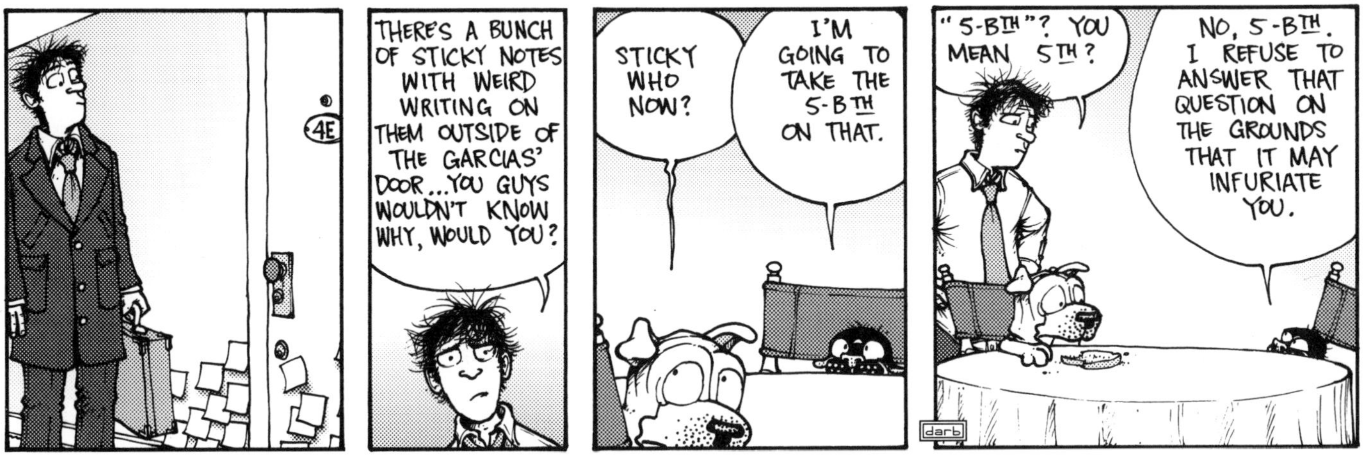
4E
THERE'S A BUNCH OF STICKY NOTES WITH WEIRD WRITING ON THEM OUTSIDE OF THE GARCIAS' DOOR... YOU GUYS WOULDN'T KNOW WHY, WOULD YOU?
STICKY WHO NOW?
I'M GOING TO TAKE THE 5-BTH ON THAT.
darb
"5-BTH"? YOU MEAN 5TH?
NO, 5-BTH. I REFUSE TO ANSWER THAT QUESTION ON THE GROUNDS THAT IT MAY INFURIATE YOU.

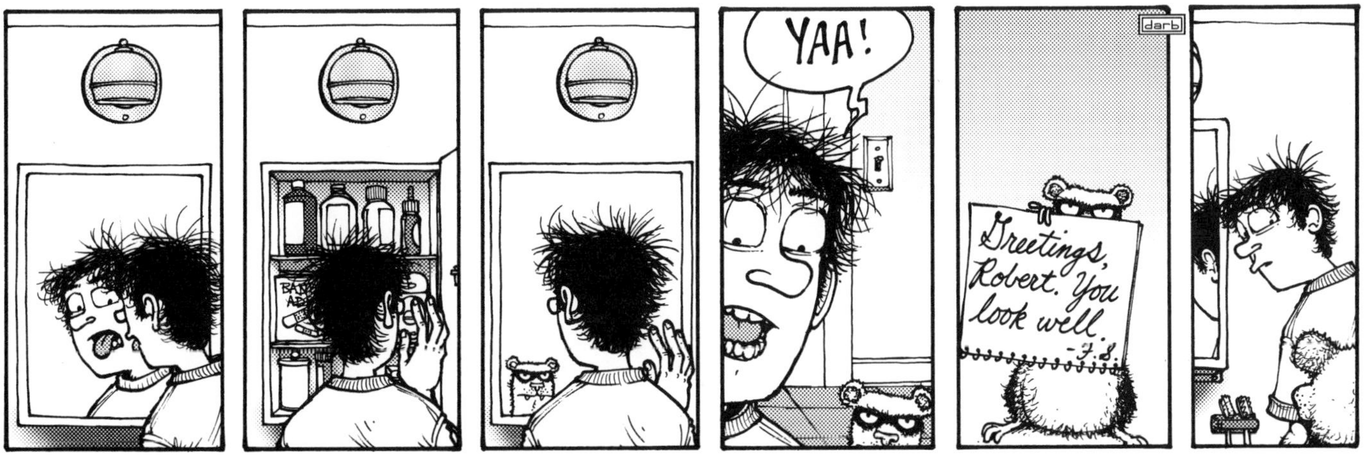
YAA!
darb
Greetings, Robert. You look well.

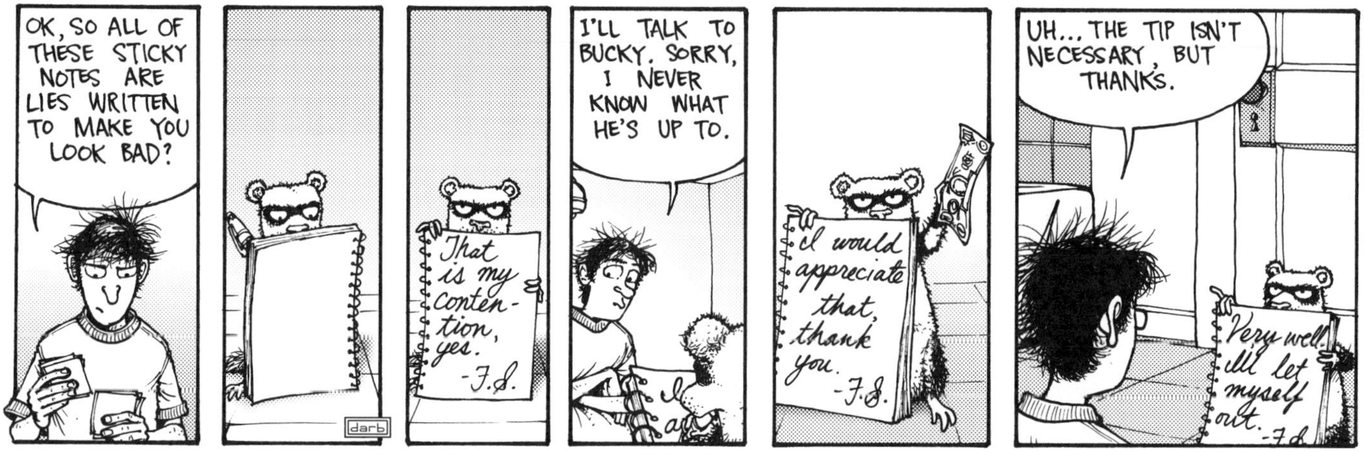
OK, SO ALL OF THESE STICKY NOTES ARE LIES WRITTEN TO MAKE YOU LOOK BAD?
darb
That is my contention, yes. -F.S.
I'LL TALK TO BUCKY. SORRY, I NEVER KNOW WHAT HE'S UP TO.
I would appreciate that, thank you. -F.S.
UH... THE TIP ISN'T NECESSARY, BUT THANKS.
Very well. I'll let myself out. -F.S.

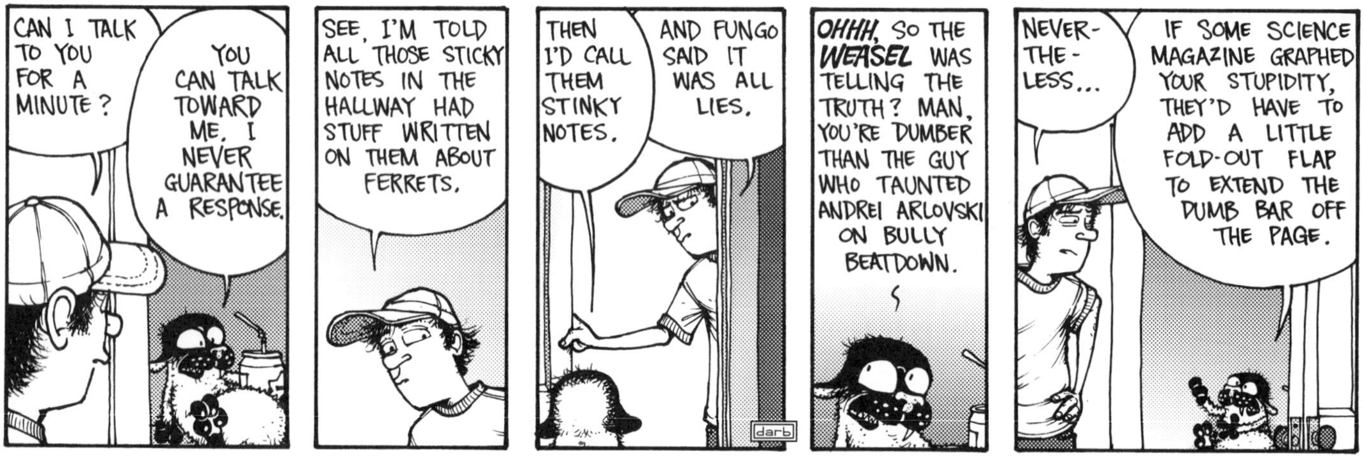
CAN I TALK TO YOU FOR A MINUTE?
YOU CAN TALK TOWARD ME. I NEVER GUARANTEE A RESPONSE.
SEE, I'M TOLD ALL THOSE STICKY NOTES IN THE HALLWAY HAD STUFF WRITTEN ON THEM ABOUT FERRETS.
THEN I'D CALL THEM STINKY NOTES.
AND FUNGO SAID IT WAS ALL LIES.
darb
OHHH, SO THE WEASEL WAS TELLING THE TRUTH? MAN, YOU'RE DUMBER THAN THE GUY WHO TAUNTED ANDREI ARLOVSKI ON BULLY BEATDOWN.
NEVER-THE-LESS...
IF SOME SCIENCE MAGAZINE GRAPHED YOUR STUPIDITY, THEY'D HAVE TO ADD A LITTLE FOLD-OUT FLAP TO EXTEND THE DUMB BAR OFF THE PAGE.

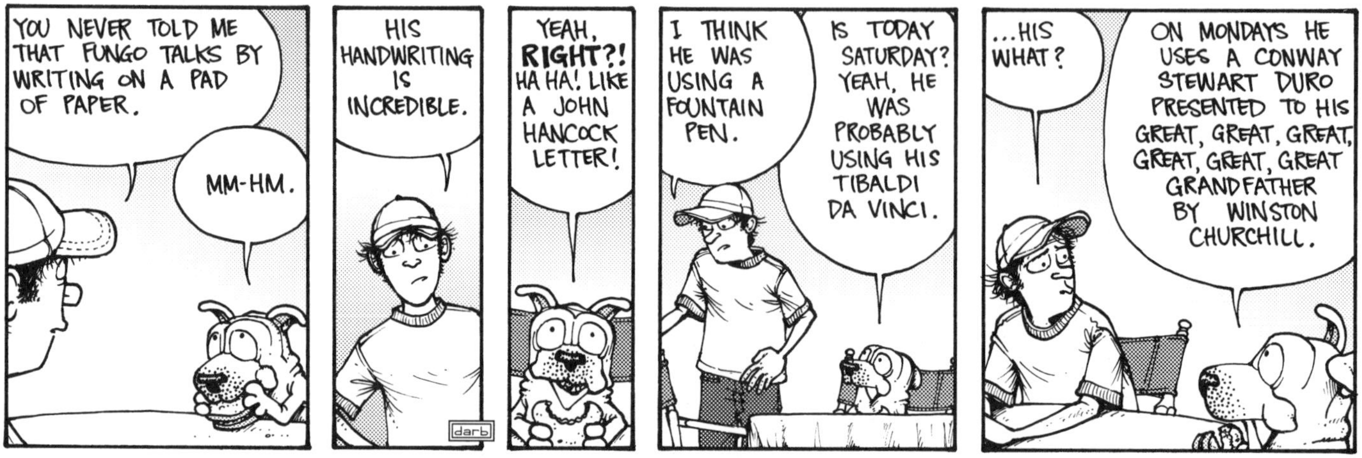
YOU NEVER TOLD ME THAT FUNGO TALKS BY WRITING ON A PAD OF PAPER.
MM-HM.
HIS HANDWRITING IS INCREDIBLE.
darb
YEAH, RIGHT?! HA HA! LIKE A JOHN HANCOCK LETTER!
I THINK HE WAS USING A FOUNTAIN PEN.
IS TODAY SATURDAY? YEAH, HE WAS PROBABLY USING HIS TIBALDI DA VINCI.
...HIS WHAT?
ON MONDAYS HE USES A CONWAY STEWART DURO PRESENTED TO HIS GREAT, GREAT, GREAT, GREAT, GREAT, GREAT GRANDFATHER BY WINSTON CHURCHILL.

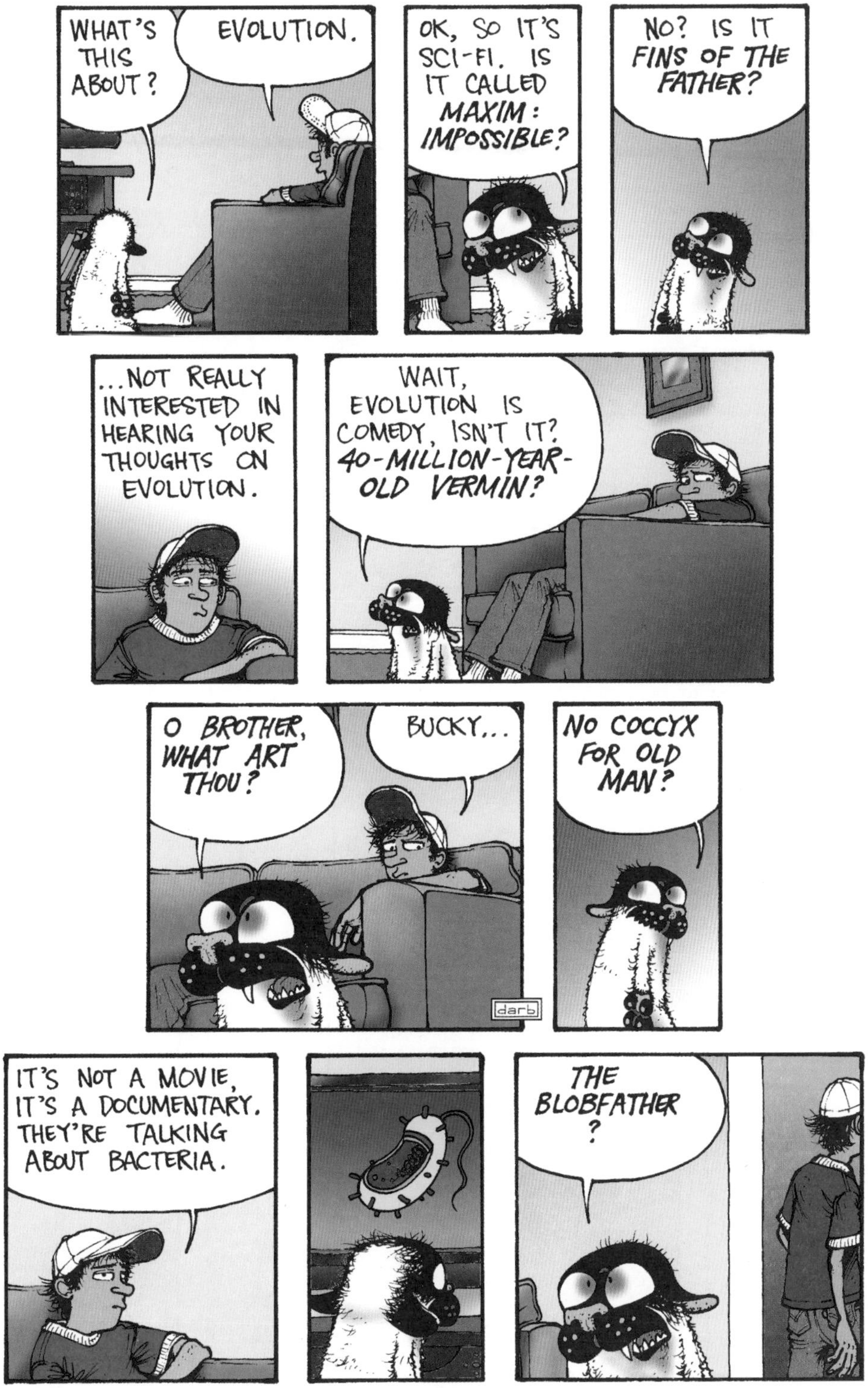
WHAT'S THIS ABOUT?
EVOLUTION.
OK, SO IT'S SCI-FI. IS IT CALLED MAXIM: IMPOSSIBLE?
NO? IS IT FINS OF THE FATHER?
...NOT REALLY INTERESTED IN HEARING YOUR THOUGHTS ON EVOLUTION.
WAIT, EVOLUTION IS COMEDY, ISN'T IT? 40-MILLION-YEAR-OLD VERMIN?
O BROTHER, WHAT ART THOU?
BUCKY...
darb
NO COCCYX FOR OLD MAN?
IT'S NOT A MOVIE, IT'S A DOCUMENTARY. THEY'RE TALKING ABOUT BACTERIA.
THE BLOBFATHER?

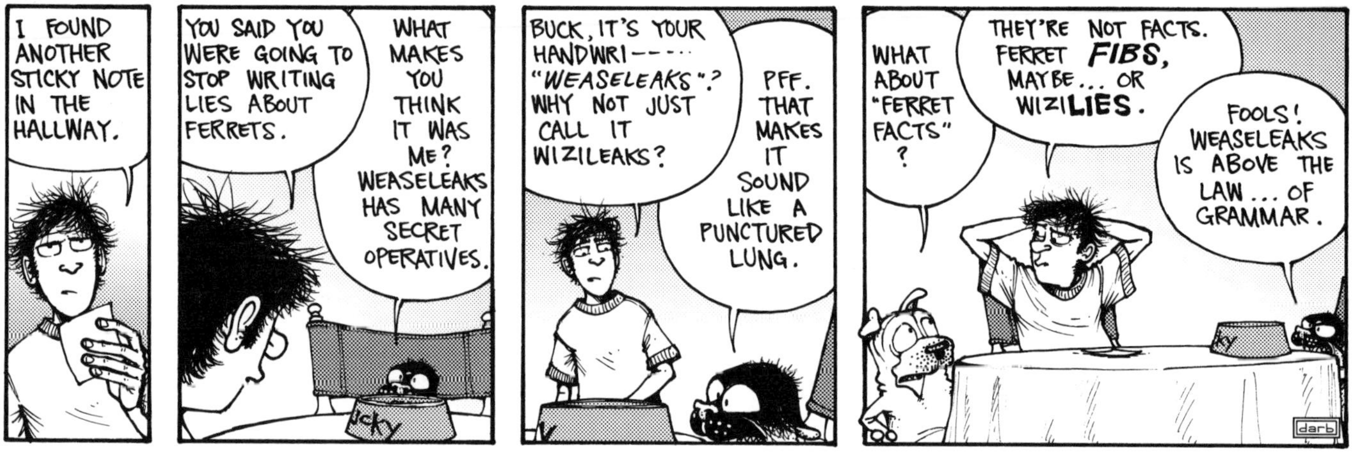
I FOUND ANOTHER STICKY NOTE IN THE HALLWAY.
YOU SAID YOU WERE GOING TO STOP WRITING LIES ABOUT FERRETS.
WHAT MAKES YOU THINK IT WAS ME? WEASELEAKS HAS MANY SECRET OPERATIVES.
BUCK, IT'S YOUR HANDWRI----- "WEASELEAKS"? WHY NOT JUST CALL IT WIZILEAKS?
PFF. THAT MAKES IT SOUND LIKE A PUNCTURED LUNG.
WHAT ABOUT "FERRET FACTS"?
THEY'RE NOT FACTS. FERRET FIBS, MAYBE... OR WIZILIES.
FOOLS! WEASELEAKS IS ABOVE THE LAW... OF GRAMMAR.
darb

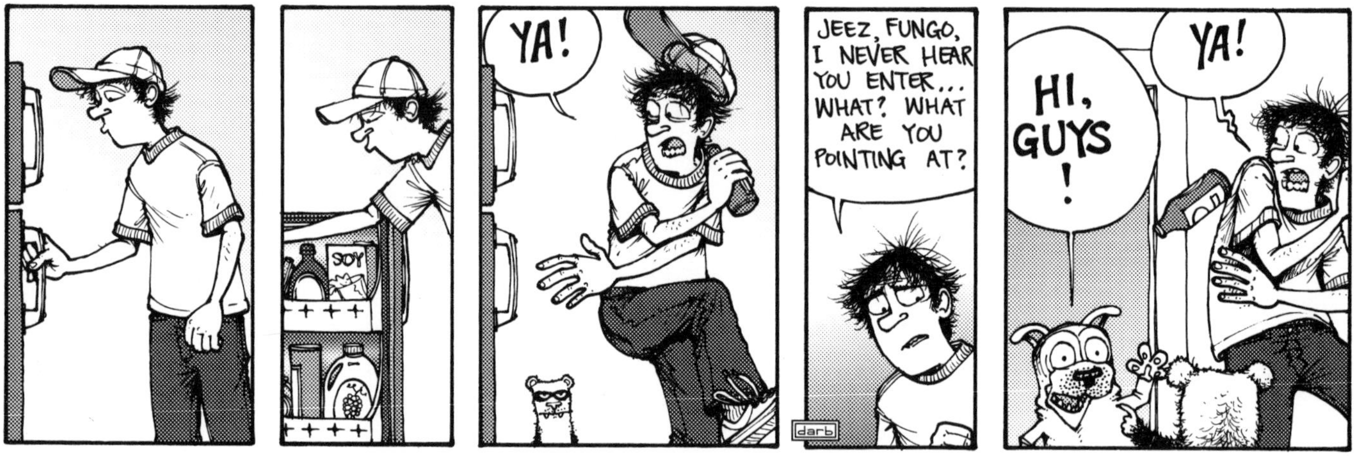
SOY
YA!
darb
JEEZ, FUNGO, I NEVER HEAR YOU ENTER... WHAT? WHAT ARE YOU POINTING AT?
HI, GUYS!
YA!

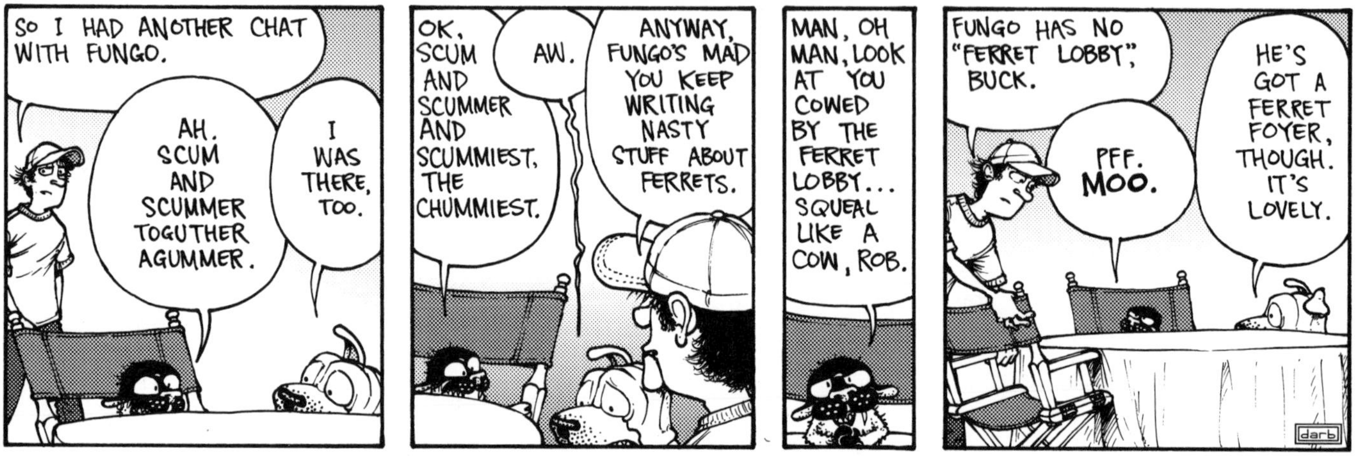
SO I HAD ANOTHER CHAT WITH FUNGO.
AH. SCUM AND SCUMMER TOGUTHER AGUMMER.
I WAS THERE, TOO.
OK, SCUM AND SCUMMER AND SCUMMIEST, THE CHUMMIEST.
AW.
ANYWAY, FUNGO'S MAD YOU KEEP WRITING NASTY STUFF ABOUT FERRETS.
MAN, OH MAN, LOOK AT YOU COWED BY THE FERRET LOBBY... SQUEAL LIKE A COW, ROB.
FUNGO HAS NO "FERRET LOBBY," BUCK.
PFF. MOO.
HE'S GOT A FERRET FOYER, THOUGH. IT'S LOVELY.
darb

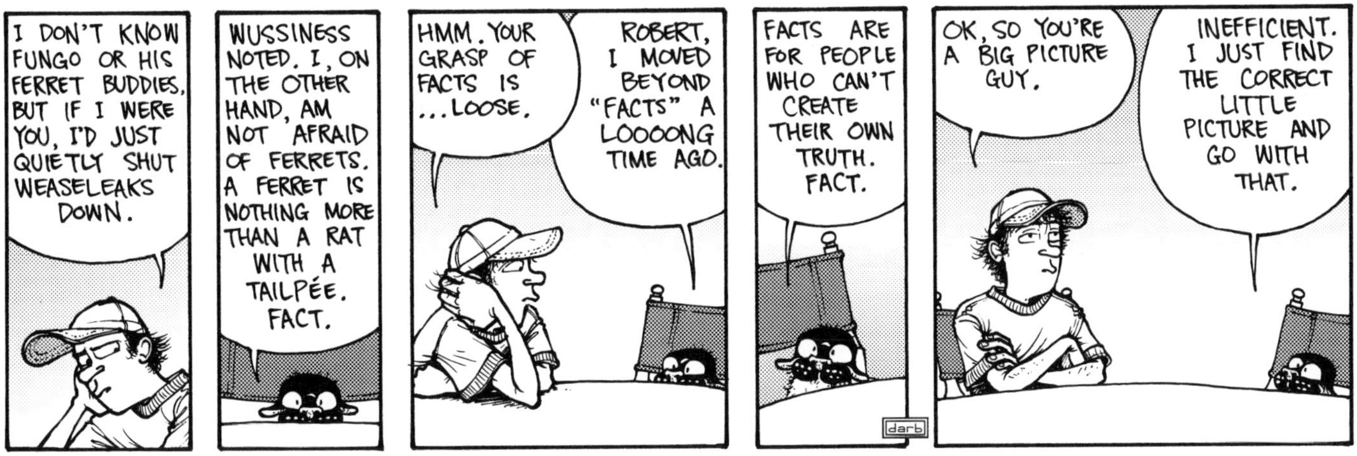
I DON'T KNOW FUNGO OR HIS FERRET BUDDIES, BUT IF I WERE YOU, I'D JUST QUIETLY SHUT WEASELEAKS DOWN.
WUSSINESS NOTED. I, ON THE OTHER HAND, AM NOT AFRAID OF FERRETS. A FERRET IS NOTHING MORE THAN A RAT WITH A TAILPÉE. FACT.
HMM. YOUR GRASP OF FACTS IS ...LOOSE.
ROBERT, I MOVED BEYOND "FACTS" A LOOOONG TIME AGO.
FACTS ARE FOR PEOPLE WHO CAN'T CREATE THEIR OWN TRUTH. FACT.
OK, SO YOU'RE A BIG PICTURE GUY.
INEFFICIENT. I JUST FIND THE CORRECT LITTLE PICTURE AND GO WITH THAT.
darb

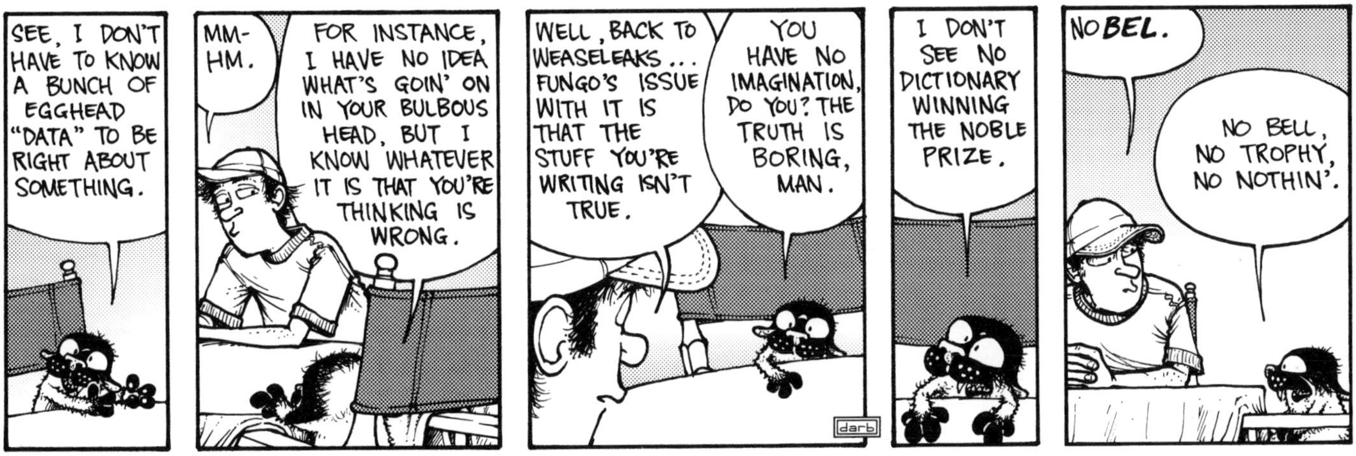
SEE, I DON'T HAVE TO KNOW A BUNCH OF EGGHEAD "DATA" TO BE RIGHT ABOUT SOMETHING.
MM-HM.
FOR INSTANCE, I HAVE NO IDEA WHAT'S GOIN' ON IN YOUR BULBOUS HEAD, BUT I KNOW WHATEVER IT IS THAT YOU'RE THINKING IS WRONG.
WELL, BACK TO WEASELEAKS... FUNGO'S ISSUE WITH IT IS THAT THE STUFF YOU'RE WRITING ISN'T TRUE.
YOU HAVE NO IMAGINATION, DO YOU? THE TRUTH IS BORING, MAN.
I DON'T SEE NO DICTIONARY WINNING THE NOBLE PRIZE.
NO*BEL*.
NO BELL, NO TROPHY, NO NOTHIN'.
darb

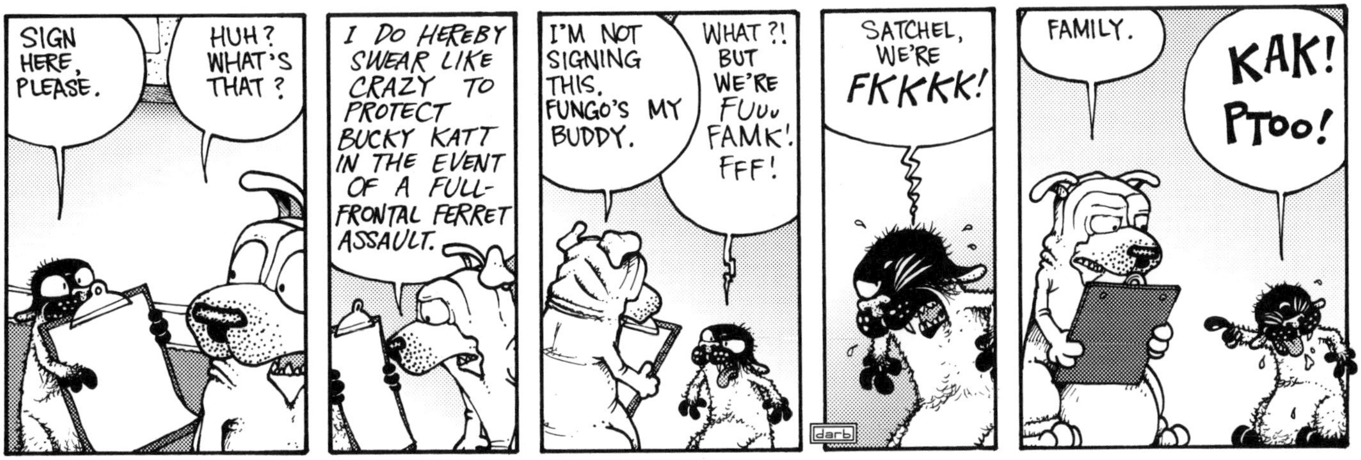
SIGN HERE, PLEASE.
HUH? WHAT'S THAT?
I DO HEREBY SWEAR LIKE CRAZY TO PROTECT BUCKY KATT IN THE EVENT OF A FULL-FRONTAL FERRET ASSAULT.
I'M NOT SIGNING THIS. FUNGO'S MY BUDDY.
WHAT?! BUT WE'RE FUuu FAMK! FFF!
SATCHEL, WE'RE FKKKK!
FAMILY.
KAK! PTOO!
darb

LIKE MY NEW BRUSH? ROB GOT IT FOR ME AT THE STORE.
PFF. IT'S USELESS TO YOU. IT'S NOT GONNA HELP YOUR APPEARANCE. YOU MIGHT AS WELL GIVE A MIME A CELLPHONE.
I DUNNO... IF YOU BOUGHT THEM ONE OF THOSE FANCY IPHONES, THEY COULD AT LEAST SURF THE INTERNET.
IN FACT, I BET THE MAP FUNCTION WOULD BE PRETTY USEFUL TO A MIME. IT'S NOT LIKE THEY CAN JUST ASK SOMEONE FOR DIRECTIONS.
Hey-O Doggie
PROBABLY GOT A CAMERA IN IT... MIME'D LIKE THAT.
AND OH! HOW DID I FORGET TEXTING? I BET A MIME WOULD TEXT LIKE A TEENAGE DRIVER!
darb
...MP3 PLAYER... I THINK AN IPHONE WOULD BE A GREAT PRESENT FOR A MIME.
WOULD YOU SHUT UP?
HEY, IF I HAD AN IPHONE, I WOULDN'T WANT TO TALK TO YOU, EITHER!

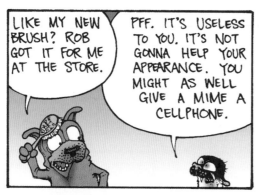

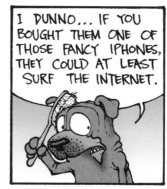

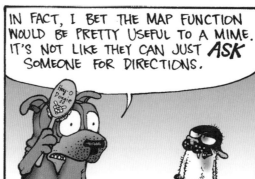

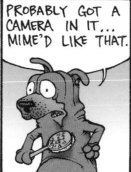

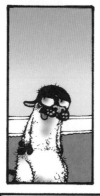

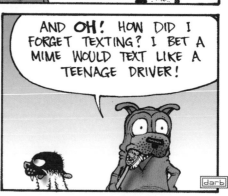

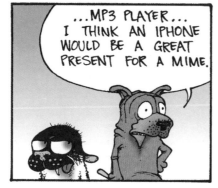

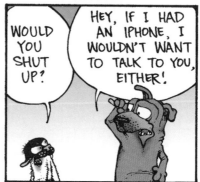

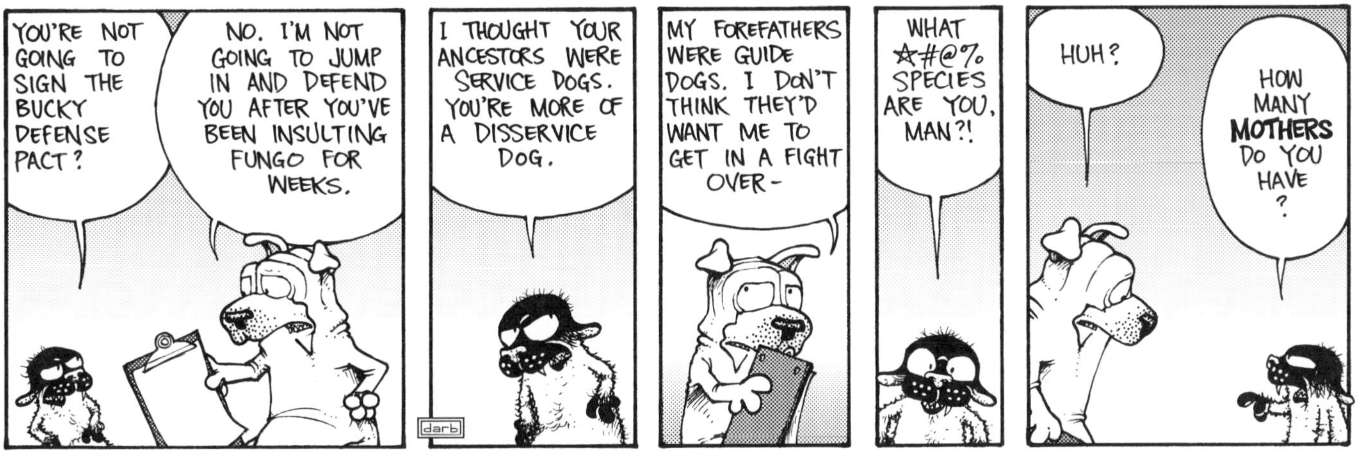
YOU'RE NOT GOING TO SIGN THE BUCKY DEFENSE PACT?
NO. I'M NOT GOING TO JUMP IN AND DEFEND YOU AFTER YOU'VE BEEN INSULTING FUNGO FOR WEEKS.
I THOUGHT YOUR ANCESTORS WERE SERVICE DOGS. YOU'RE MORE OF A DISSERVICE DOG.
darb
MY FOREFATHERS WERE GUIDE DOGS. I DON'T THINK THEY'D WANT ME TO GET IN A FIGHT OVER-
WHAT ☆#@% SPECIES ARE YOU, MAN?!
HUH?
HOW MANY **MOTHERS** DO YOU HAVE?

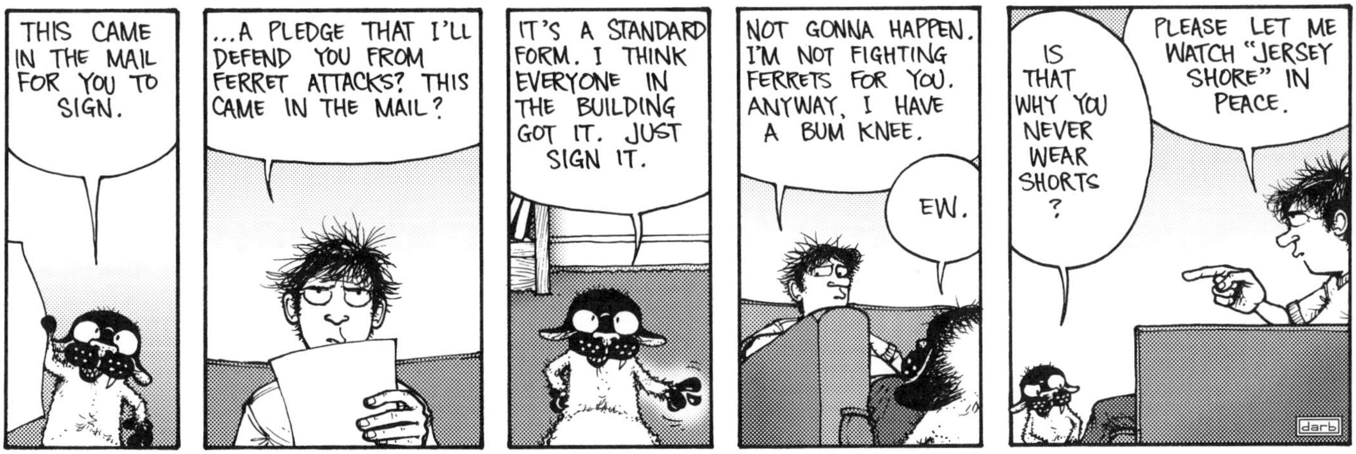
THIS CAME IN THE MAIL FOR YOU TO SIGN.
...A PLEDGE THAT I'LL DEFEND YOU FROM FERRET ATTACKS? THIS CAME IN THE MAIL?
IT'S A STANDARD FORM. I THINK EVERYONE IN THE BUILDING GOT IT. JUST SIGN IT.
NOT GONNA HAPPEN. I'M NOT FIGHTING FERRETS FOR YOU. ANYWAY, I HAVE A BUM KNEE.
EW.
IS THAT WHY YOU NEVER WEAR SHORTS?
PLEASE LET ME WATCH "JERSEY SHORE" IN PEACE.
darb

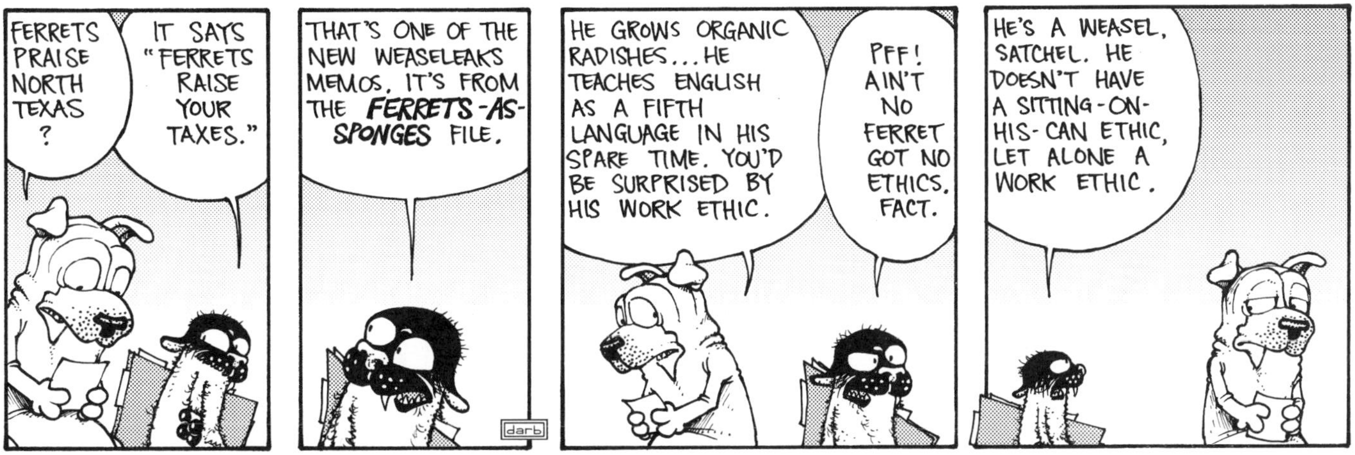
FERRETS PRAISE NORTH TEXAS?
IT SAYS "FERRETS RAISE YOUR TAXES."
THAT'S ONE OF THE NEW WEASELEAKS MEMOS, IT'S FROM THE ***FERRETS-AS-SPONGES*** FILE.
darb
HE GROWS ORGANIC RADISHES... HE TEACHES ENGLISH AS A FIFTH LANGUAGE IN HIS SPARE TIME. YOU'D BE SURPRISED BY HIS WORK ETHIC.
PFF! AIN'T NO FERRET GOT NO ETHICS. FACT.
HE'S A WEASEL, SATCHEL. HE DOESN'T HAVE A SITTING-ON-HIS-CAN ETHIC, LET ALONE A WORK ETHIC.

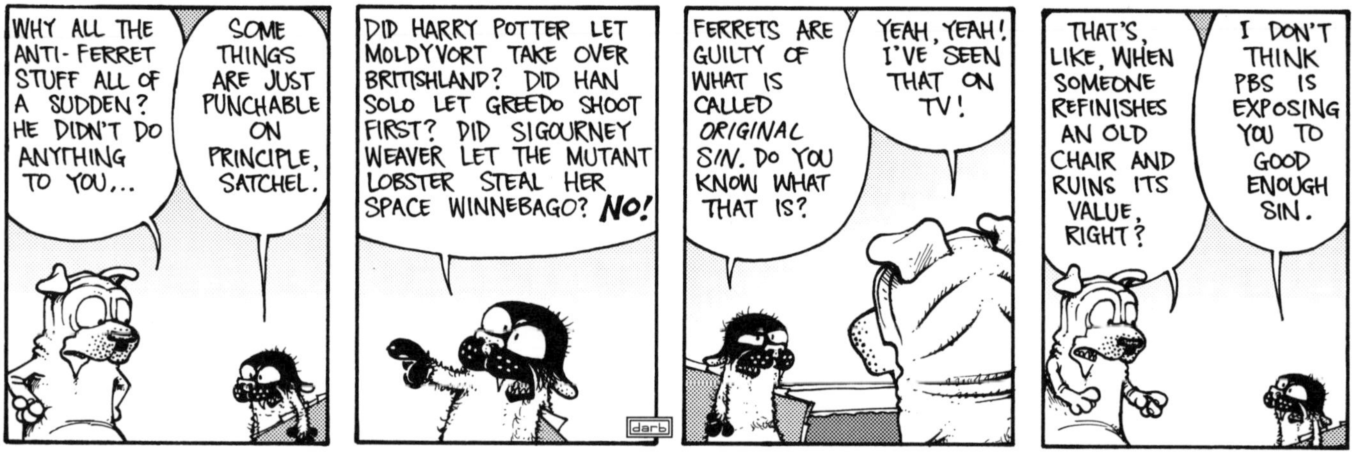
WHY ALL THE ANTI-FERRET STUFF ALL OF A SUDDEN? HE DIDN'T DO ANYTHING TO YOU...
SOME THINGS ARE JUST PUNCHABLE ON PRINCIPLE, SATCHEL.
DID HARRY POTTER LET MOLDYVORT TAKE OVER BRITISHLAND? DID HAN SOLO LET GREEDO SHOOT FIRST? DID SIGOURNEY WEAVER LET THE MUTANT LOBSTER STEAL HER SPACE WINNEBAGO? NO!
FERRETS ARE GUILTY OF WHAT IS CALLED ORIGINAL SIN. DO YOU KNOW WHAT THAT IS?
YEAH, YEAH! I'VE SEEN THAT ON TV!
THAT'S, LIKE, WHEN SOMEONE REFINISHES AN OLD CHAIR AND RUINS ITS VALUE, RIGHT?
I DON'T THINK PBS IS EXPOSING YOU TO GOOD ENOUGH SIN.

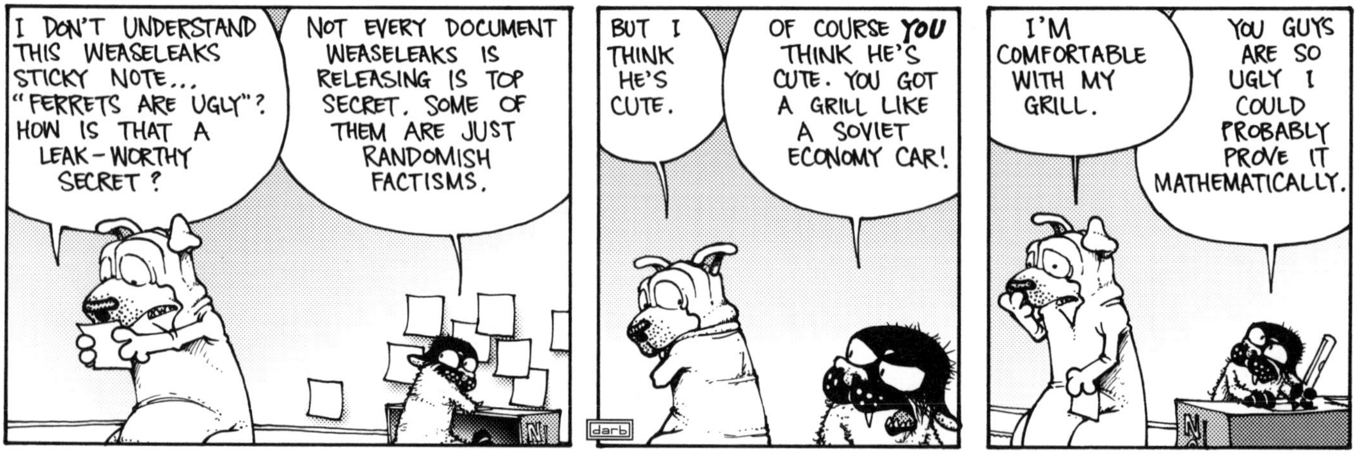
I DON'T UNDERSTAND THIS WEASELEAKS STICKY NOTE... "FERRETS ARE UGLY"? HOW IS THAT A LEAK-WORTHY SECRET?
NOT EVERY DOCUMENT WEASELEAKS IS RELEASING IS TOP SECRET. SOME OF THEM ARE JUST RANDOMISH FACTISMS.
BUT I THINK HE'S CUTE.
OF COURSE YOU THINK HE'S CUTE. YOU GOT A GRILL LIKE A SOVIET ECONOMY CAR!
I'M COMFORTABLE WITH MY GRILL.
YOU GUYS ARE SO UGLY I COULD PROBABLY PROVE IT MATHEMATICALLY.

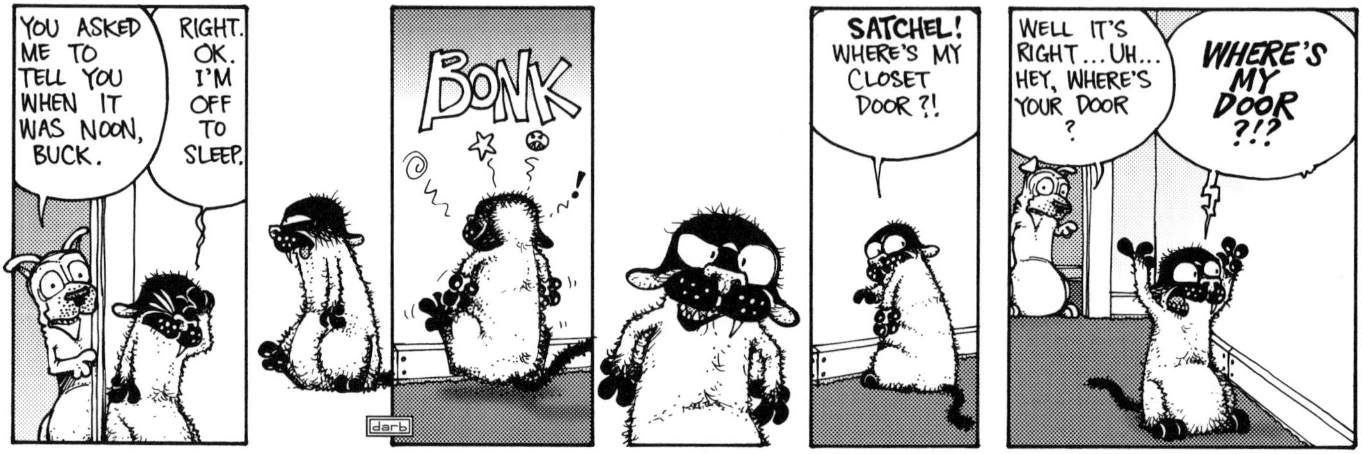
YOU ASKED ME TO TELL YOU WHEN IT WAS NOON, BUCK.
RIGHT. OK. I'M OFF TO SLEEP.
BONK
SATCHEL! WHERE'S MY CLOSET DOOR?!
WELL IT'S RIGHT... UH... HEY, WHERE'S YOUR DOOR?
WHERE'S MY DOOR?!?

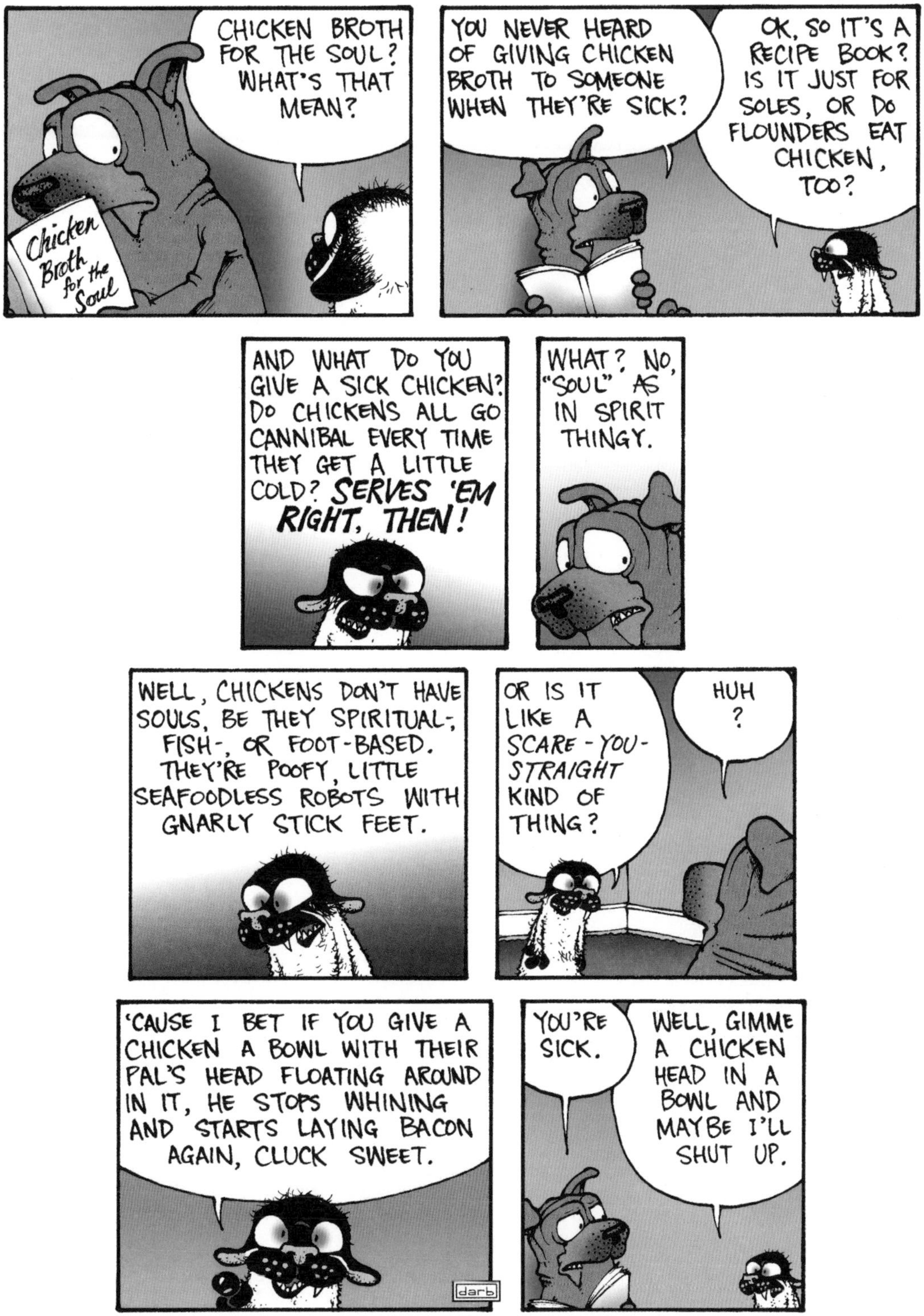
CHICKEN BROTH FOR THE SOUL? WHAT'S THAT MEAN?
Chicken Broth for the Soul
YOU NEVER HEARD OF GIVING CHICKEN BROTH TO SOMEONE WHEN THEY'RE SICK?
OK, SO IT'S A RECIPE BOOK? IS IT JUST FOR SOLES, OR DO FLOUNDERS EAT CHICKEN, TOO?
AND WHAT DO YOU GIVE A SICK CHICKEN? DO CHICKENS ALL GO CANNIBAL EVERY TIME THEY GET A LITTLE COLD? SERVES 'EM RIGHT, THEN!
WHAT? NO, "SOUL" AS IN SPIRIT THINGY.
WELL, CHICKENS DON'T HAVE SOULS, BE THEY SPIRITUAL-, FISH-, OR FOOT-BASED. THEY'RE POOFY, LITTLE SEAFOODLESS ROBOTS WITH GNARLY STICK FEET.
OR IS IT LIKE A SCARE-YOU-STRAIGHT KIND OF THING?
HUH?
'CAUSE I BET IF YOU GIVE A CHICKEN A BOWL WITH THEIR PAL'S HEAD FLOATING AROUND IN IT, HE STOPS WHINING AND STARTS LAYING BACON AGAIN, CLUCK SWEET.
darb
YOU'RE SICK.
WELL, GIMME A CHICKEN HEAD IN A BOWL AND MAYBE I'LL SHUT UP.

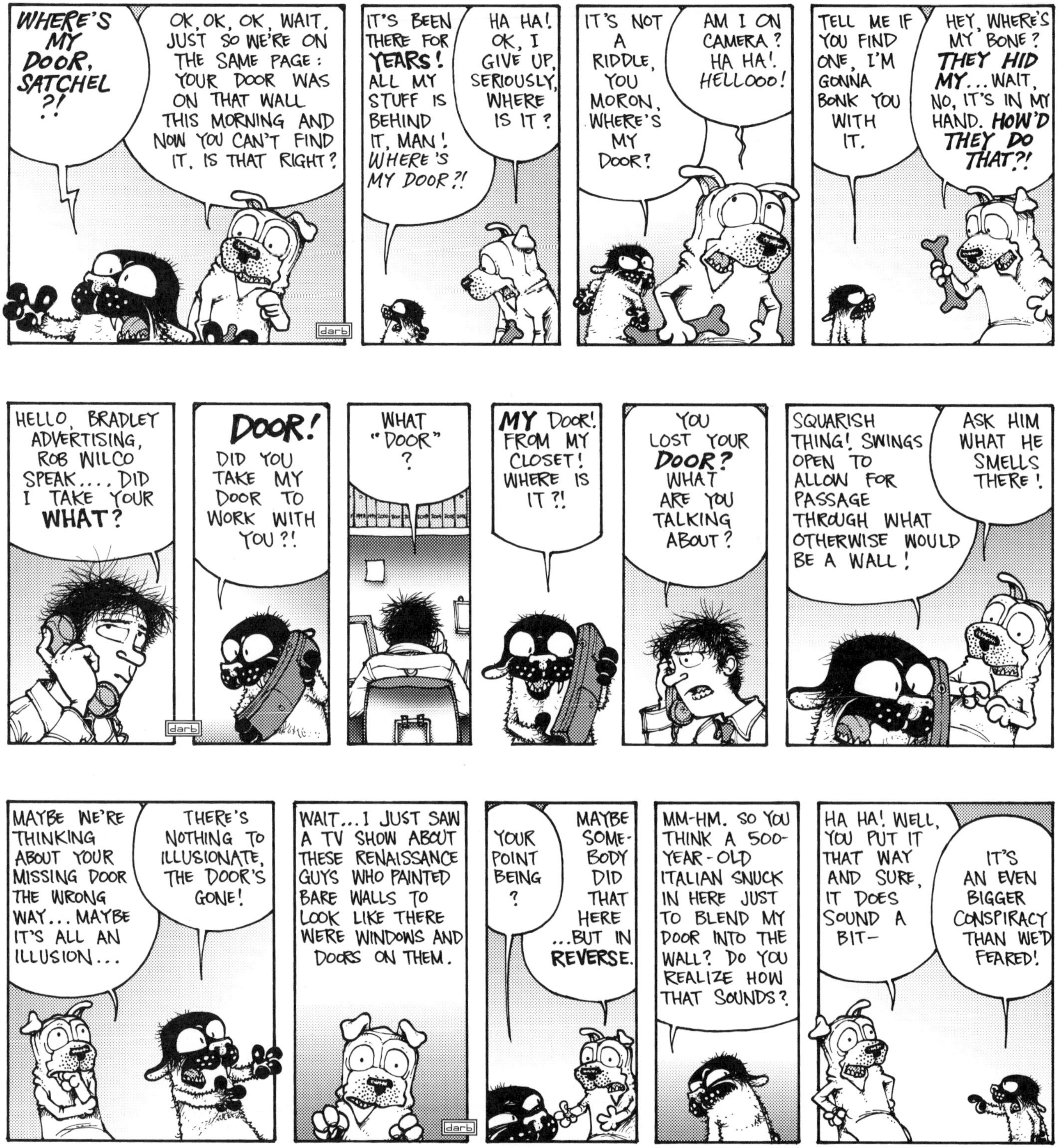
WHERE'S MY DOOR, SATCHEL ?!
OK, OK, OK, WAIT, JUST SO WE'RE ON THE SAME PAGE: YOUR DOOR WAS ON THAT WALL THIS MORNING AND NOW YOU CAN'T FIND IT. IS THAT RIGHT?
darb
IT'S BEEN THERE FOR YEARS! ALL MY STUFF IS BEHIND IT, MAN! WHERE'S MY DOOR?!
HA HA! OK, I GIVE UP, SERIOUSLY, WHERE IS IT?
IT'S NOT A RIDDLE, YOU MORON, WHERE'S MY DOOR?
AM I ON CAMERA? HA HA! HELLOOO!
TELL ME IF YOU FIND ONE, I'M GONNA BONK YOU WITH IT.
HEY, WHERE'S MY BONE? THEY HID MY... WAIT, NO, IT'S IN MY HAND. HOW'D THEY DO THAT?!
HELLO, BRADLEY ADVERTISING, ROB WILCO SPEAK.... DID I TAKE YOUR WHAT?
darb
DOOR! DID YOU TAKE MY DOOR TO WORK WITH YOU?!
WHAT "DOOR"?
MY DOOR! FROM MY CLOSET! WHERE IS IT?!
YOU LOST YOUR DOOR? WHAT ARE YOU TALKING ABOUT?
SQUARISH THING! SWINGS OPEN TO ALLOW FOR PASSAGE THROUGH WHAT OTHERWISE WOULD BE A WALL!
ASK HIM WHAT HE SMELLS THERE!
MAYBE WE'RE THINKING ABOUT YOUR MISSING DOOR THE WRONG WAY... MAYBE IT'S ALL AN ILLUSION...
THERE'S NOTHING TO ILLUSIONATE, THE DOOR'S GONE!
WAIT... I JUST SAW A TV SHOW ABOUT THESE RENAISSANCE GUYS WHO PAINTED BARE WALLS TO LOOK LIKE THERE WERE WINDOWS AND DOORS ON THEM.
darb
MAYBE SOME-BODY DID THAT HERE ...BUT IN REVERSE.
YOUR POINT BEING?
MM-HM. SO YOU THINK A 500-YEAR-OLD ITALIAN SNUCK IN HERE JUST TO BLEND MY DOOR INTO THE WALL? DO YOU REALIZE HOW THAT SOUNDS?
HA HA! WELL, YOU PUT IT THAT WAY AND SURE, IT DOES SOUND A BIT—
IT'S AN EVEN BIGGER CONSPIRACY THAN WE'D FEARED!

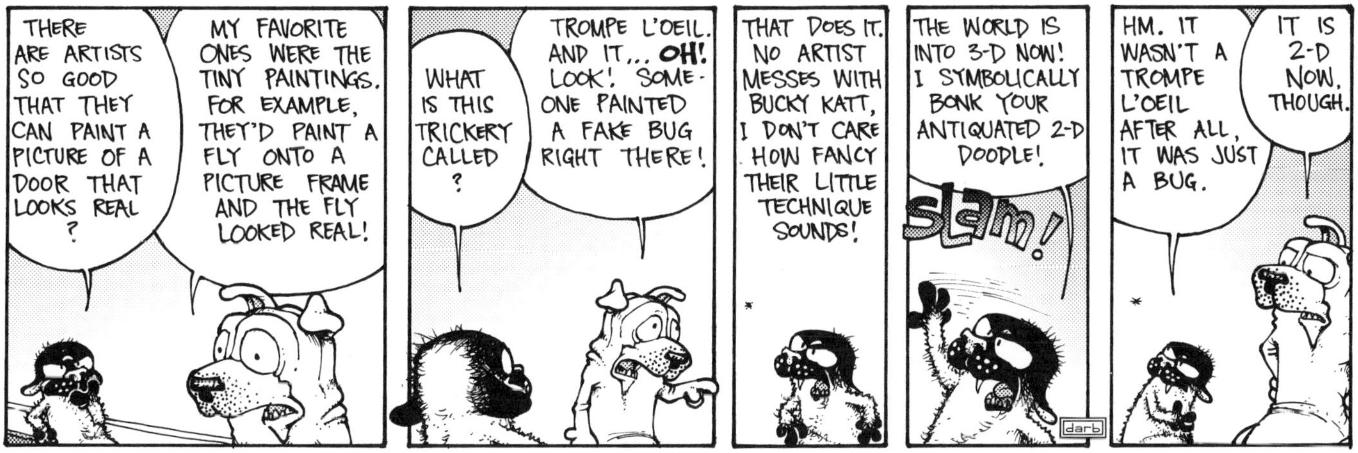
THERE ARE ARTISTS SO GOOD THAT THEY CAN PAINT A PICTURE OF A DOOR THAT LOOKS REAL?
MY FAVORITE ONES WERE THE TINY PAINTINGS. FOR EXAMPLE, THEY'D PAINT A FLY ONTO A PICTURE FRAME AND THE FLY LOOKED REAL!
WHAT IS THIS TRICKERY CALLED?
TROMPE L'OEIL. AND IT... OH! LOOK! SOMEONE PAINTED A FAKE BUG RIGHT THERE!
THAT DOES IT. NO ARTIST MESSES WITH BUCKY KATT, I DON'T CARE HOW FANCY THEIR LITTLE TECHNIQUE SOUNDS!
THE WORLD IS INTO 3-D NOW! I SYMBOLICALLY BONK YOUR ANTIQUATED 2-D DOODLE!
SLAM!
HM. IT WASN'T A TROMPE L'OEIL AFTER ALL, IT WAS JUST A BUG.
IT IS 2-D NOW, THOUGH.
darb

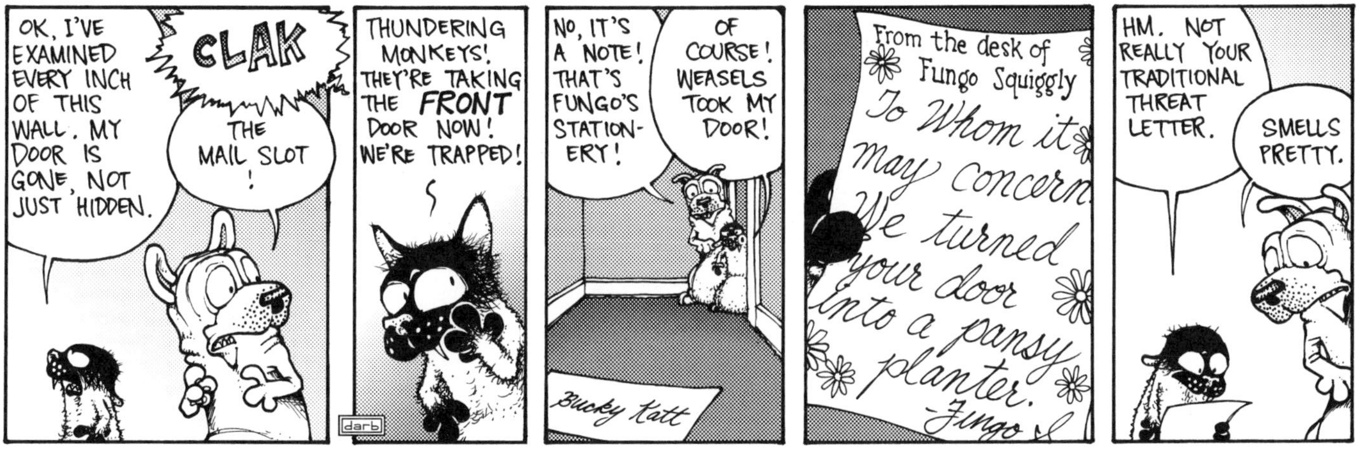
OK, I'VE EXAMINED EVERY INCH OF THIS WALL. MY DOOR IS GONE, NOT JUST HIDDEN.
CLAK
THE MAIL SLOT!
THUNDERING MONKEYS! THEY'RE TAKING THE FRONT DOOR NOW! WE'RE TRAPPED!
NO, IT'S A NOTE! THAT'S FUNGO'S STATIONERY!
OF COURSE! WEASELS TOOK MY DOOR!
Bucky Katt
From the desk of Fungo Squiggly
To Whom it may concern: We turned your door into a pansy planter.
-Fungo
HM. NOT REALLY YOUR TRADITIONAL THREAT LETTER.
SMELLS PRETTY.
darb

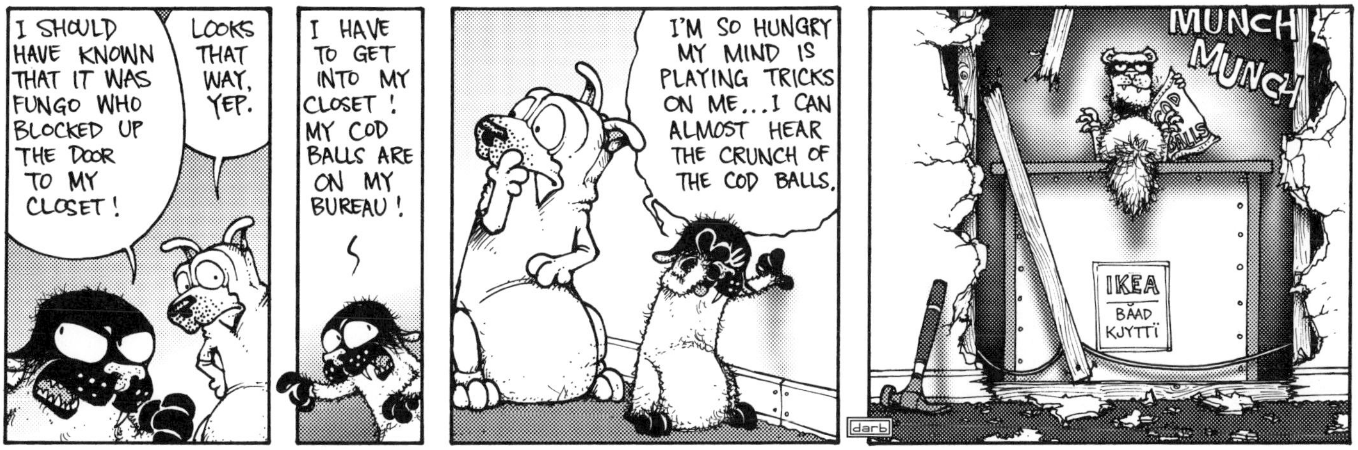
I SHOULD HAVE KNOWN THAT IT WAS FUNGO WHO BLOCKED UP THE DOOR TO MY CLOSET!
LOOKS THAT WAY, YEP.
I HAVE TO GET INTO MY CLOSET! MY COD BALLS ARE ON MY BUREAU!
I'M SO HUNGRY MY MIND IS PLAYING TRICKS ON ME... I CAN ALMOST HEAR THE CRUNCH OF THE COD BALLS.
MUNCH MUNCH
COD BALLS
IKEA
BÄAD KJYTTÏ
darb

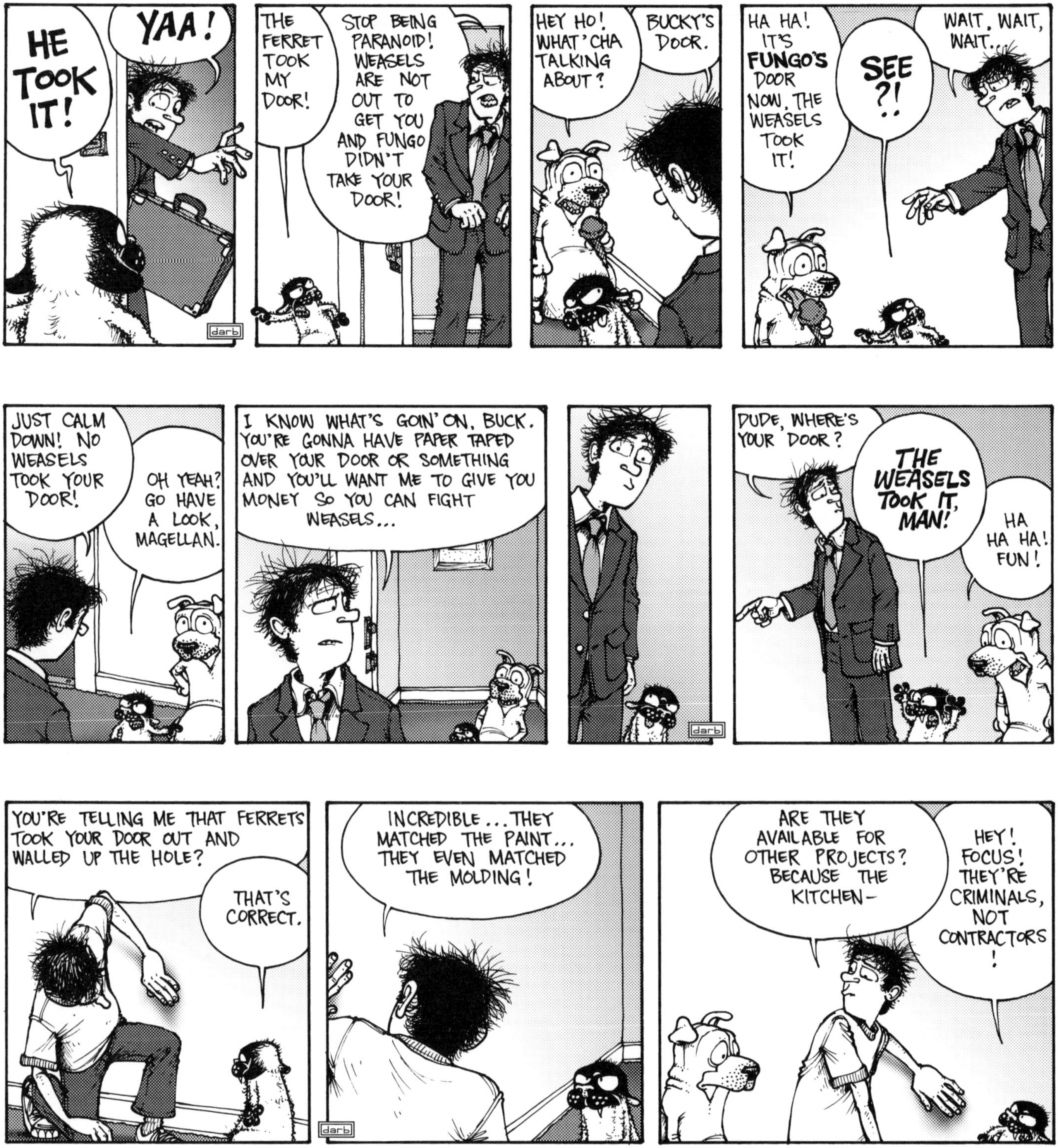
HE TOOK IT!
YAA!
THE FERRET TOOK MY DOOR!
STOP BEING PARANOID! WEASELS ARE NOT OUT TO GET YOU AND FUNGO DIDN'T TAKE YOUR DOOR!
HEY HO! WHAT'CHA TALKING ABOUT?
BUCKY'S DOOR.
HA HA! IT'S FUNGO'S DOOR NOW. THE WEASELS TOOK IT!
SEE?!
WAIT, WAIT, WAIT...
darb
JUST CALM DOWN! NO WEASELS TOOK YOUR DOOR!
OH YEAH? GO HAVE A LOOK, MAGELLAN.
I KNOW WHAT'S GOIN' ON, BUCK. YOU'RE GONNA HAVE PAPER TAPED OVER YOUR DOOR OR SOMETHING AND YOU'LL WANT ME TO GIVE YOU MONEY SO YOU CAN FIGHT WEASELS...
DUDE, WHERE'S YOUR DOOR?
THE WEASELS TOOK IT, MAN!
HA HA HA! FUN!
darb
YOU'RE TELLING ME THAT FERRETS TOOK YOUR DOOR OUT AND WALLED UP THE HOLE?
THAT'S CORRECT.
INCREDIBLE... THEY MATCHED THE PAINT... THEY EVEN MATCHED THE MOLDING!
ARE THEY AVAILABLE FOR OTHER PROJECTS? BECAUSE THE KITCHEN–
HEY! FOCUS! THEY'RE CRIMINALS, NOT CONTRACTORS!
darb

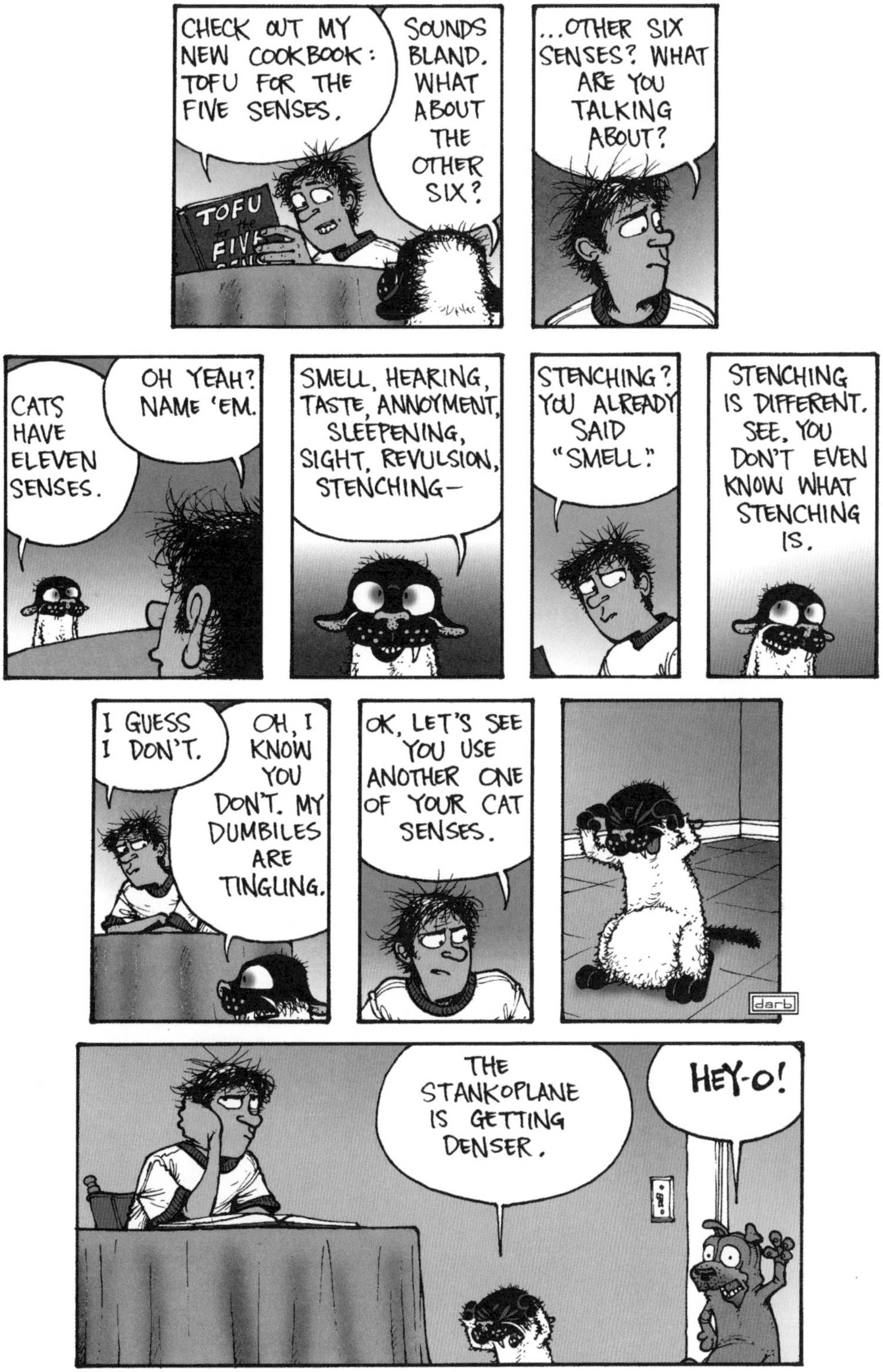
CHECK OUT MY NEW COOKBOOK: TOFU FOR THE FIVE SENSES.
TOFU
SOUNDS BLAND. WHAT ABOUT THE OTHER SIX?
...OTHER SIX SENSES? WHAT ARE YOU TALKING ABOUT?
CATS HAVE ELEVEN SENSES.
OH YEAH? NAME 'EM.
SMELL, HEARING, TASTE, ANNOYMENT, SLEEPENING, SIGHT, REVULSION, STENCHING—
STENCHING? YOU ALREADY SAID "SMELL."
STENCHING IS DIFFERENT. SEE, YOU DON'T EVEN KNOW WHAT STENCHING IS.
I GUESS I DON'T.
OH, I KNOW YOU DON'T. MY DUMBILES ARE TINGLING.
OK, LET'S SEE YOU USE ANOTHER ONE OF YOUR CAT SENSES.
darb
THE STANKOPLANE IS GETTING DENSER.
HEY-O!

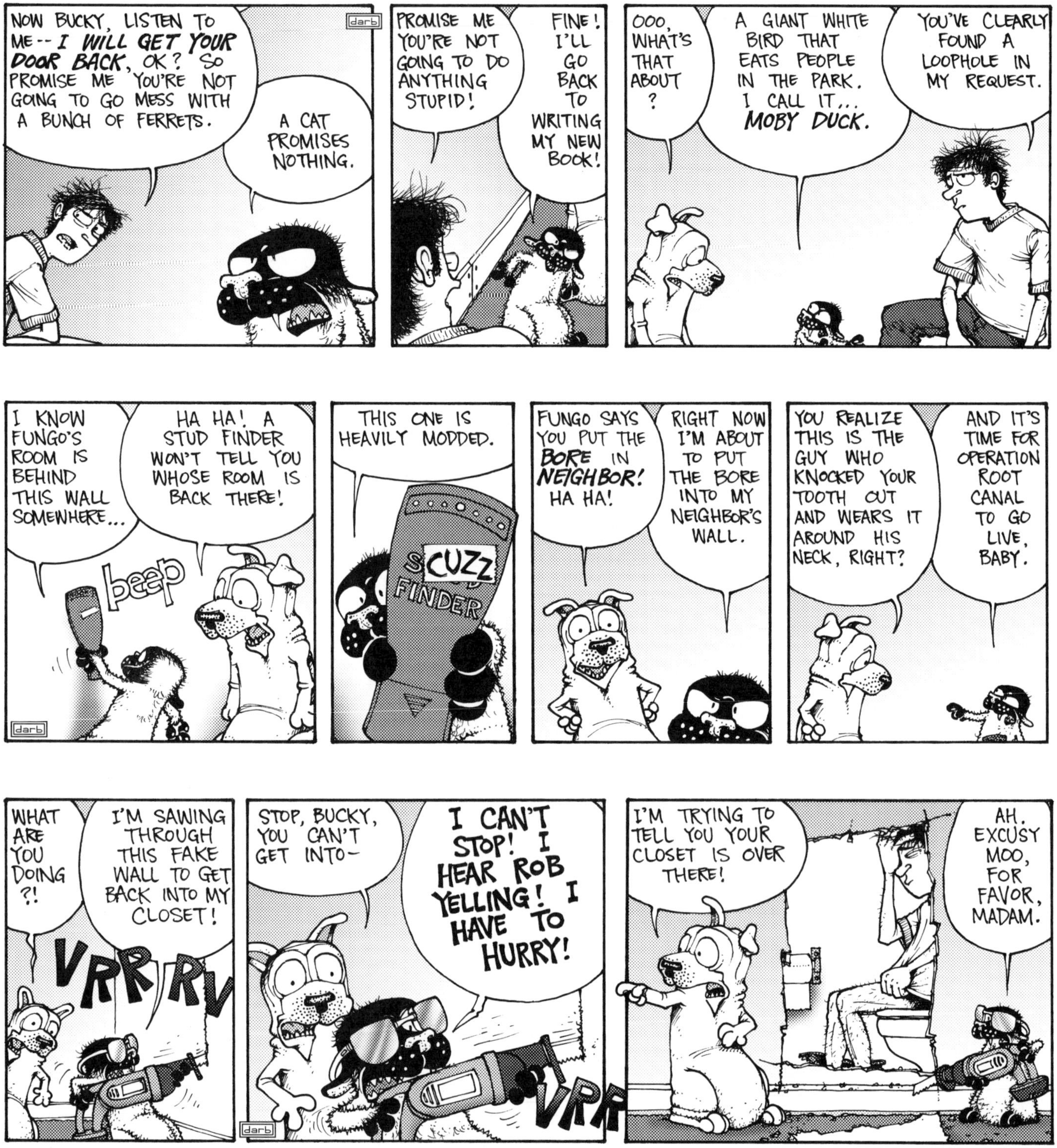

darb
NOW BUCKY, LISTEN TO ME-- I WILL GET YOUR DOOR BACK, OK? SO PROMISE ME YOU'RE NOT GOING TO GO MESS WITH A BUNCH OF FERRETS.
A CAT PROMISES NOTHING.
PROMISE ME YOU'RE NOT GOING TO DO ANYTHING STUPID!
FINE! I'LL GO BACK TO WRITING MY NEW BOOK!
OOO, WHAT'S THAT ABOUT?
A GIANT WHITE BIRD THAT EATS PEOPLE IN THE PARK. I CALL IT... MOBY DUCK.
YOU'VE CLEARLY FOUND A LOOPHOLE IN MY REQUEST.
I KNOW FUNGO'S ROOM IS BEHIND THIS WALL SOMEWHERE...
beep
HA HA! A STUD FINDER WON'T TELL YOU WHOSE ROOM IS BACK THERE!
darb
THIS ONE IS HEAVILY MODDED.
SCUZZ FINDER
FUNGO SAYS YOU PUT THE BORE IN NEIGHBOR! HA HA!
RIGHT NOW I'M ABOUT TO PUT THE BORE INTO MY NEIGHBOR'S WALL.
YOU REALIZE THIS IS THE GUY WHO KNOCKED YOUR TOOTH OUT AND WEARS IT AROUND HIS NECK, RIGHT?
AND IT'S TIME FOR OPERATION ROOT CANAL TO GO LIVE, BABY.
WHAT ARE YOU DOING?!
I'M SAWING THROUGH THIS FAKE WALL TO GET BACK INTO MY CLOSET!
VRRRRV
darb
STOP, BUCKY, YOU CAN'T GET INTO-
I CAN'T STOP! I HEAR ROB YELLING! I HAVE TO HURRY!
VRR
I'M TRYING TO TELL YOU YOUR CLOSET IS OVER THERE!
AH. EXCUSY MOO, FOR FAVOR, MADAM.

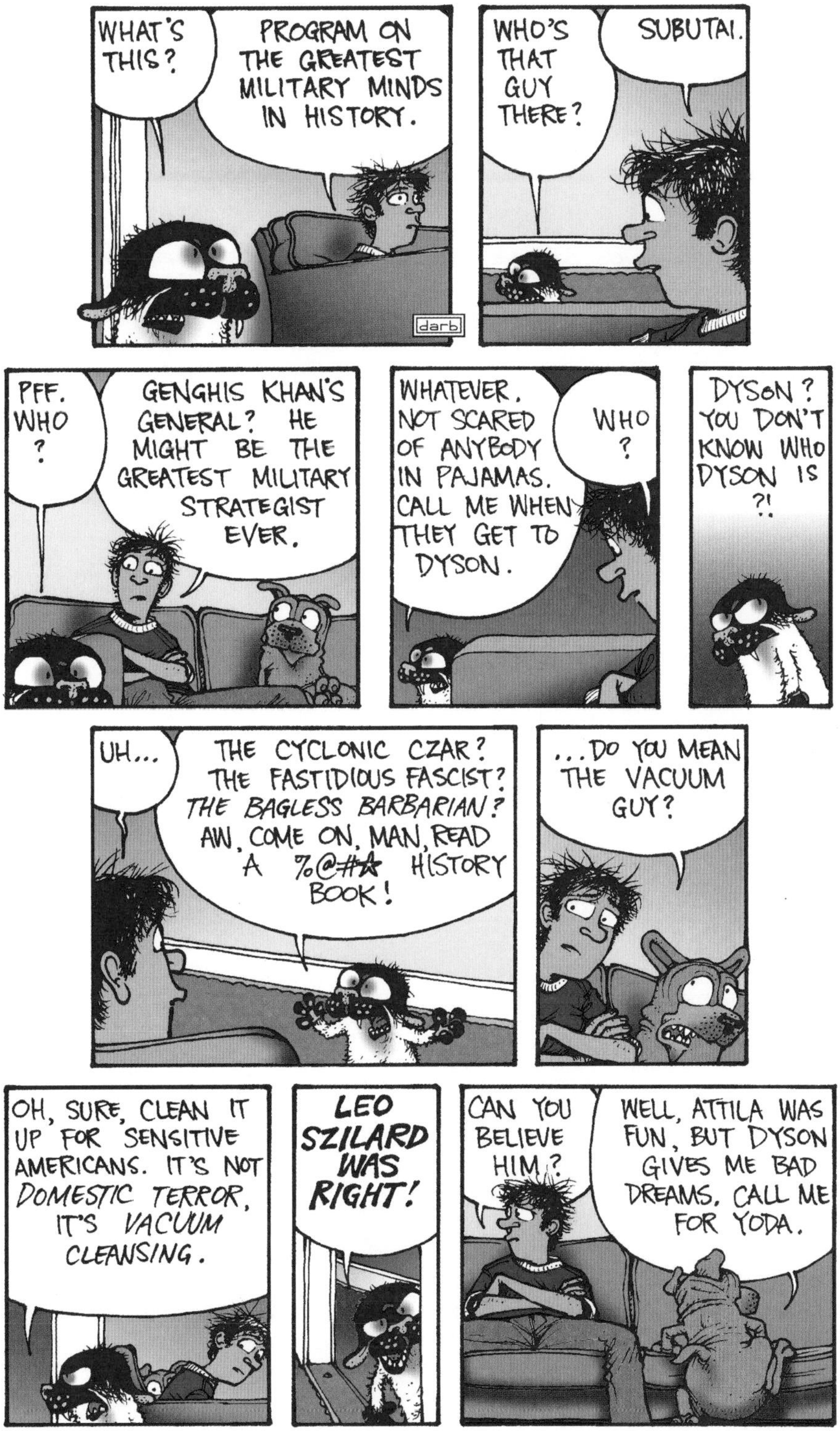

WHAT'S THIS?
PROGRAM ON THE GREATEST MILITARY MINDS IN HISTORY.
darb
WHO'S THAT GUY THERE?
SUBUTAI.
PFF. WHO?
GENGHIS KHAN'S GENERAL? HE MIGHT BE THE GREATEST MILITARY STRATEGIST EVER.
WHATEVER. NOT SCARED OF ANYBODY IN PAJAMAS. CALL ME WHEN THEY GET TO DYSON.
WHO?
DYSON? YOU DON'T KNOW WHO DYSON IS?!
UH...
THE CYCLONIC CZAR? THE FASTIDIOUS FASCIST? *THE BAGLESS BARBARIAN?* AW, COME ON, MAN, READ A %@#☆ HISTORY BOOK!
...DO YOU MEAN THE VACUUM GUY?
OH, SURE, CLEAN IT UP FOR SENSITIVE AMERICANS. IT'S NOT *DOMESTIC TERROR,* IT'S *VACUUM CLEANSING.*
LEO SZILARD WAS RIGHT!
CAN YOU BELIEVE HIM?
WELL, ATTILA WAS FUN, BUT DYSON GIVES ME BAD DREAMS. CALL ME FOR YODA.

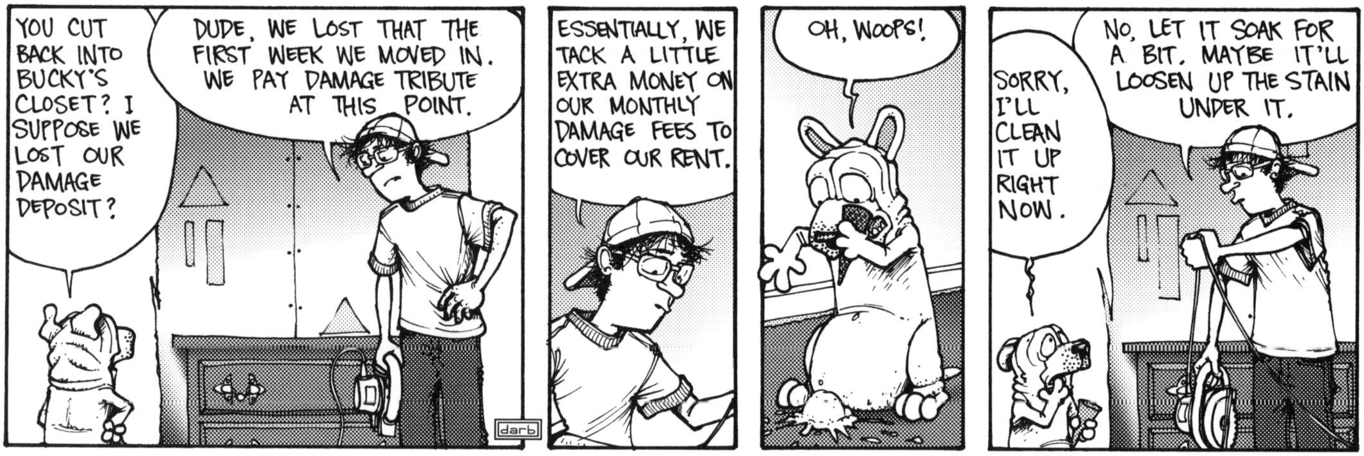
YOU CUT BACK INTO BUCKY'S CLOSET? I SUPPOSE WE LOST OUR DAMAGE DEPOSIT?
DUDE, WE LOST THAT THE FIRST WEEK WE MOVED IN. WE PAY DAMAGE TRIBUTE AT THIS POINT.
ESSENTIALLY, WE TACK A LITTLE EXTRA MONEY ON OUR MONTHLY DAMAGE FEES TO COVER OUR RENT.
OH, WOOPS!
SORRY, I'LL CLEAN IT UP RIGHT NOW.
NO, LET IT SOAK FOR A BIT. MAYBE IT'LL LOOSEN UP THE STAIN UNDER IT.
darb

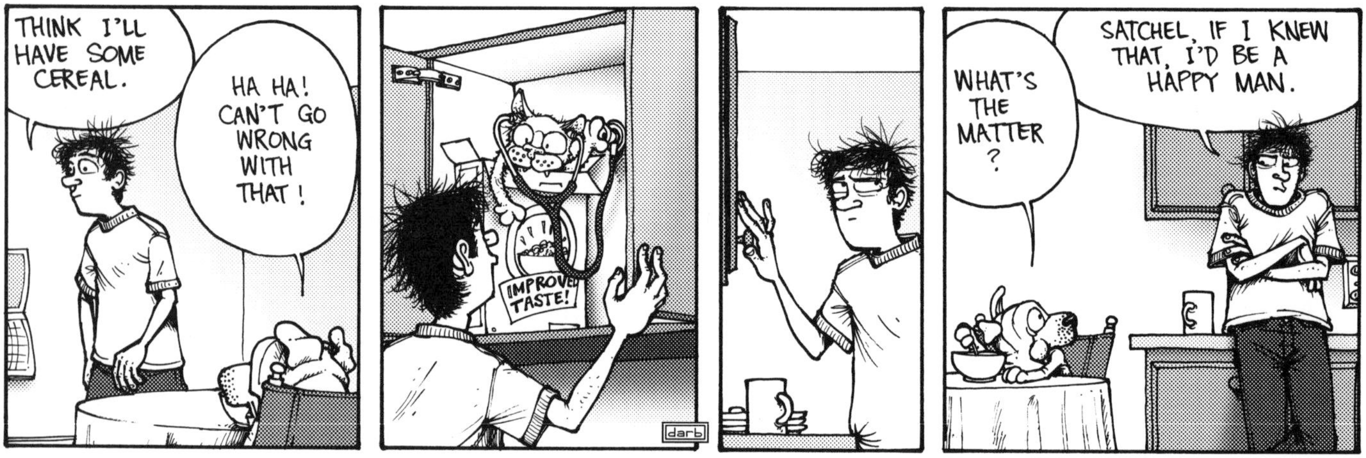
THINK I'LL HAVE SOME CEREAL.
HA HA! CAN'T GO WRONG WITH THAT!
IMPROVE TASTE!
darb
WHAT'S THE MATTER?
SATCHEL, IF I KNEW THAT, I'D BE A HAPPY MAN.

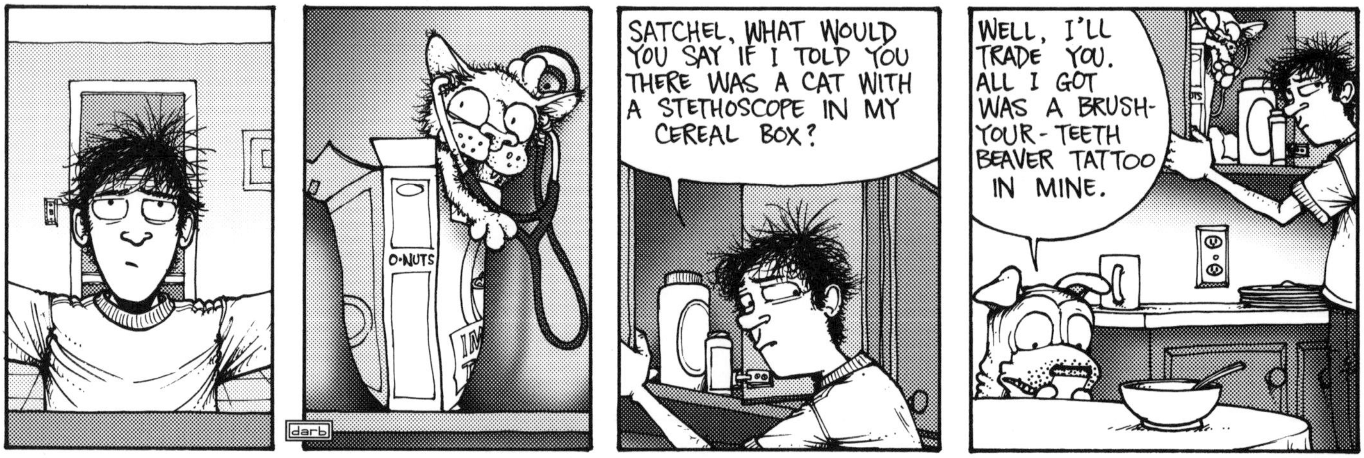
O-NUTS
darb
SATCHEL, WHAT WOULD YOU SAY IF I TOLD YOU THERE WAS A CAT WITH A STETHOSCOPE IN MY CEREAL BOX?
WELL, I'LL TRADE YOU. ALL I GOT WAS A BRUSH-YOUR-TEETH BEAVER TATTOO IN MINE.

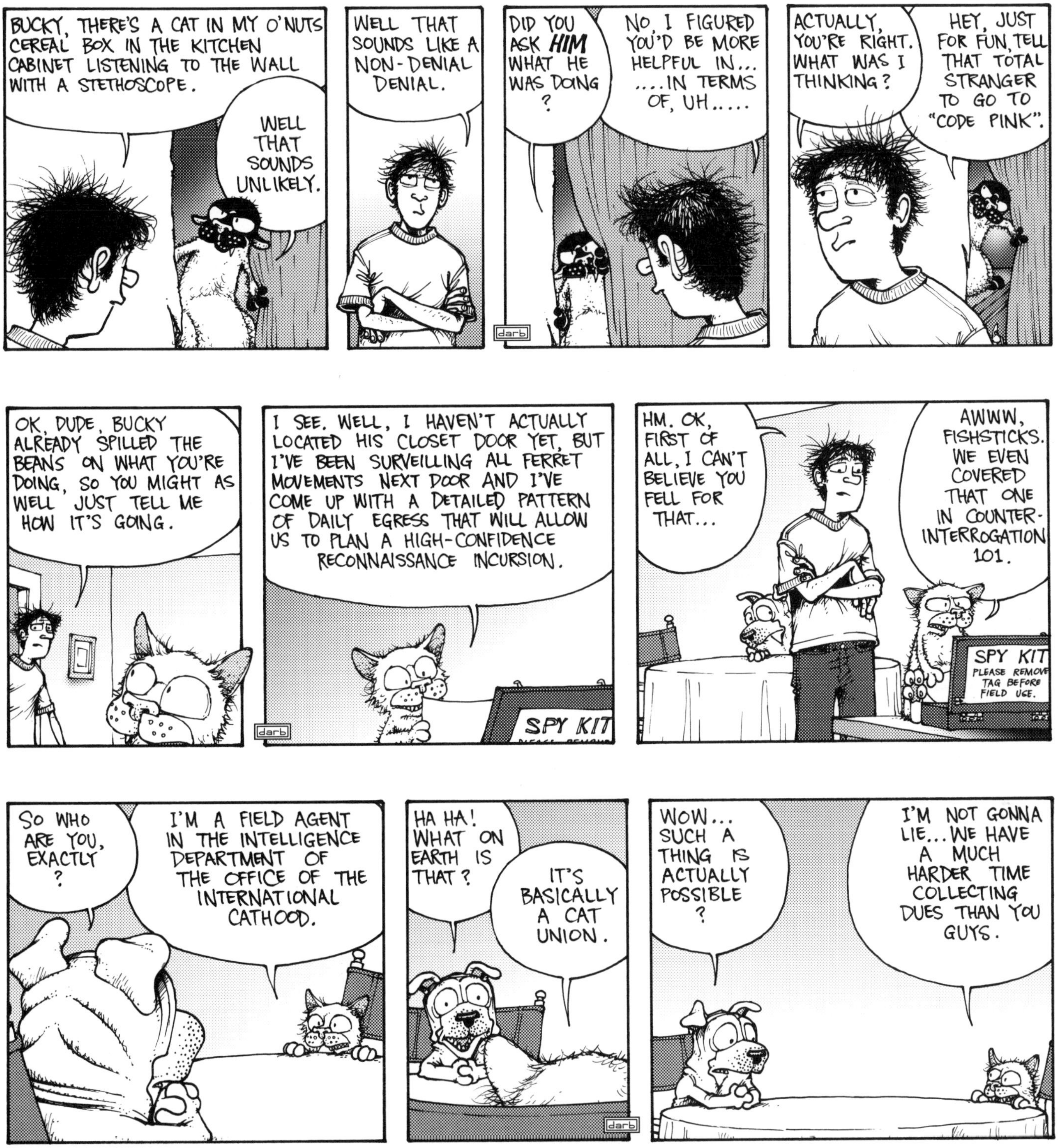
BUCKY, THERE'S A CAT IN MY O'NUTS CEREAL BOX IN THE KITCHEN CABINET LISTENING TO THE WALL WITH A STETHOSCOPE.
WELL THAT SOUNDS UNLIKELY.
WELL THAT SOUNDS LIKE A NON-DENIAL DENIAL.
DID YOU ASK **HIM** WHAT HE WAS DOING?
NO, I FIGURED YOU'D BE MORE HELPFUL IN... ....IN TERMS OF, UH.....
darb
ACTUALLY, YOU'RE RIGHT. WHAT WAS I THINKING?
HEY, JUST FOR FUN, TELL THAT TOTAL STRANGER TO GO TO "CODE PINK".
OK, DUDE, BUCKY ALREADY SPILLED THE BEANS ON WHAT YOU'RE DOING, SO YOU MIGHT AS WELL JUST TELL ME HOW IT'S GOING.
darb
I SEE. WELL, I HAVEN'T ACTUALLY LOCATED HIS CLOSET DOOR YET, BUT I'VE BEEN SURVEILLING ALL FERRET MOVEMENTS NEXT DOOR AND I'VE COME UP WITH A DETAILED PATTERN OF DAILY EGRESS THAT WILL ALLOW US TO PLAN A HIGH-CONFIDENCE RECONNAISSANCE INCURSION.
SPY KIT
HM. OK, FIRST OF ALL, I CAN'T BELIEVE YOU FELL FOR THAT...
AWWW, FISHSTICKS. WE EVEN COVERED THAT ONE IN COUNTER-INTERROGATION 101.
SPY KIT
PLEASE REMOVE TAG BEFORE FIELD USE.
SO WHO ARE YOU, EXACTLY?
I'M A FIELD AGENT IN THE INTELLIGENCE DEPARTMENT OF THE OFFICE OF THE INTERNATIONAL CATHOOD.
HA HA! WHAT ON EARTH IS THAT?
IT'S BASICALLY A CAT UNION.
darb
WOW... SUCH A THING IS ACTUALLY POSSIBLE?
I'M NOT GONNA LIE... WE HAVE A MUCH HARDER TIME COLLECTING DUES THAN YOU GUYS.

Panel 1: OK, SO YOU'RE HERE TO FIND BUCKY'S DOOR, BUT WHO ARE YOU?

Panel 2: SECRET AGENT BOB JIMBOB.

Panel 3: HA HA! YOU EVEN SAY YOUR NAME LIKE A SECRET AGENT!
HOW SO?

Panel 4: YOU KNOW... LIKE "BOND... JAMES BOND."
WHO'S BOND JAMES BOND?

Panel 5: NO, HIS NAME IS JUST JAMES BOND, BUT HE SAYS IT LIKE "BOND... JAMES BOND."
TO SAY MY NAME LIKE THAT, I'D HAVE TO SAY "JIMBOB... BOB JIMBOB." SO I DON'T SEE YOUR POINT.

Panel 6: YOU'RE STILL HERE?
I HAVEN'T COMPLETED MY MISSION YET.

Panel 7: WHAT'S YOUR NAME?
SECRET AGENT BOB JIMBOB.

Panel 8: DO ALL YOU SPY GUYS SAY YOUR NAME LIKE JAMES BOND?
NO, NO, HIS FIRST NAME IS BOB, HIS SECOND NAME IS JIMBOB.
ACTUALLY, JIMBOB IS MY LAST NAME, MY SECOND NAME IS JIM.

Panel 9: ....BOB JIM JIMBOB?
JUNIOR.

Panel 10: HEY, BUCK! DO YOU KNOW WHAT YOUR SPY FRIEND'S NAME IS?
OF COURSE I DO, AND I'M NOT TELLING **YOU** WHAT IT IS!

Panel 11: NO, HE ALREADY TOLD ME, IT'S *BOB JIMBOB*. IT'S LIKE A PALINDROME!
WHAT?! MAN, YOU'RE NOT SUPPOSED TO DIVULGE YOUR NAME!
UHHHHH... OOPS. THINK YOU'RE RIGHT. HANG ON, I'LL CHECK THE HANDBOOK.

Panel 12: I CAN'T BELIEVE YOU HAVE A SPY HANDBOOK.
WANNA SEE IT? IT'S GOT COOL SPY PICTURES.
AW, FER... **PUT IT AWAY, MAN!**

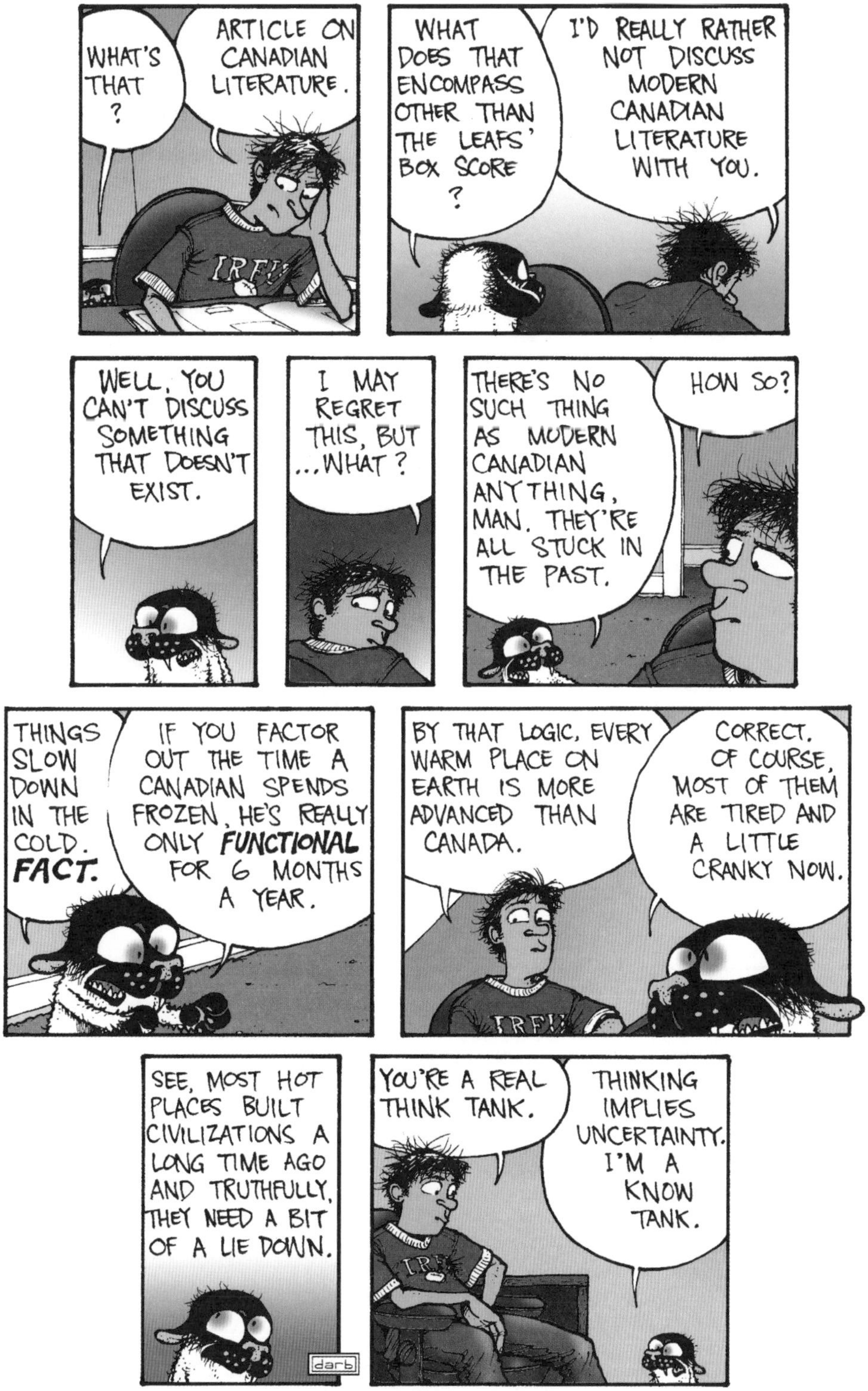
WHAT'S THAT ?
ARTICLE ON CANADIAN LITERATURE.
WHAT DOES THAT ENCOMPASS OTHER THAN THE LEAFS' BOX SCORE ?
I'D REALLY RATHER NOT DISCUSS MODERN CANADIAN LITERATURE WITH YOU.
WELL, YOU CAN'T DISCUSS SOMETHING THAT DOESN'T EXIST.
I MAY REGRET THIS, BUT ...WHAT ?
THERE'S NO SUCH THING AS MODERN CANADIAN ANYTHING, MAN. THEY'RE ALL STUCK IN THE PAST.
HOW SO?
THINGS SLOW DOWN IN THE COLD. FACT.
IF YOU FACTOR OUT THE TIME A CANADIAN SPENDS FROZEN, HE'S REALLY ONLY FUNCTIONAL FOR 6 MONTHS A YEAR.
BY THAT LOGIC, EVERY WARM PLACE ON EARTH IS MORE ADVANCED THAN CANADA.
CORRECT. OF COURSE, MOST OF THEM ARE TIRED AND A LITTLE CRANKY NOW.
SEE, MOST HOT PLACES BUILT CIVILIZATIONS A LONG TIME AGO AND TRUTHFULLY, THEY NEED A BIT OF A LIE DOWN.
darb
YOU'RE A REAL THINK TANK.
THINKING IMPLIES UNCERTAINTY. I'M A KNOW TANK.

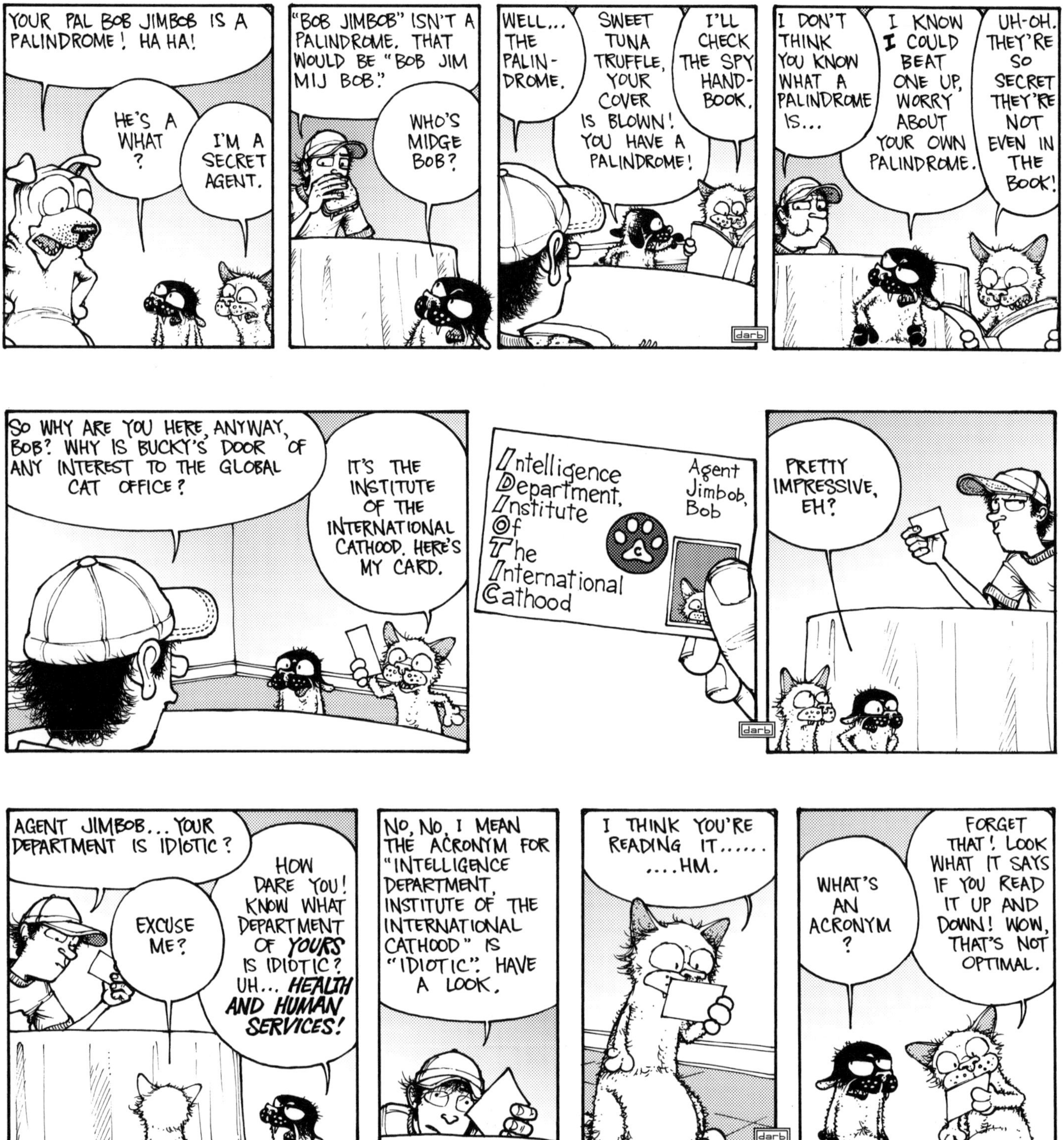
YOUR PAL BOB JIMBOB IS A PALINDROME! HA HA!
HE'S A WHAT?
I'M A SECRET AGENT.
"BOB JIMBOB" ISN'T A PALINDROME. THAT WOULD BE "BOB JIM MIJ BOB."
WHO'S MIDGE BOB?
WELL... THE PALINDROME.
SWEET TUNA TRUFFLE, YOUR COVER IS BLOWN! YOU HAVE A PALINDROME!
I'LL CHECK THE SPY HANDBOOK.
I DON'T THINK YOU KNOW WHAT A PALINDROME IS...
I KNOW I COULD BEAT ONE UP, WORRY ABOUT YOUR OWN PALINDROME.
UH-OH. THEY'RE SO SECRET THEY'RE NOT EVEN IN THE BOOK!
SO WHY ARE YOU HERE, ANYWAY, BOB? WHY IS BUCKY'S DOOR OF ANY INTEREST TO THE GLOBAL CAT OFFICE?
IT'S THE INSTITUTE OF THE INTERNATIONAL CATHOOD. HERE'S MY CARD.
Intelligence
Department,
Institute
Of
The
International
Cathood
Agent Jimbob, Bob
PRETTY IMPRESSIVE, EH?
AGENT JIMBOB... YOUR DEPARTMENT IS IDIOTIC?
EXCUSE ME?
HOW DARE YOU! KNOW WHAT DEPARTMENT OF YOURS IS IDIOTIC? UH... HEALTH AND HUMAN SERVICES!
NO, NO, I MEAN THE ACRONYM FOR "INTELLIGENCE DEPARTMENT, INSTITUTE OF THE INTERNATIONAL CATHOOD" IS "IDIOTIC". HAVE A LOOK.
I THINK YOU'RE READING IT...... ....HM.
WHAT'S AN ACRONYM?
FORGET THAT! LOOK WHAT IT SAYS IF YOU READ IT UP AND DOWN! WOW, THAT'S NOT OPTIMAL.

THIS PROGRAM AGAIN? YOU'RE OBSESSED WITH THE MONGOLS! YOU'RE GENGHIS CONSUMED!

DIFFERENT PROGRAM.

ARE YOU A HORDE HOARDER, ROBERT?

YOU'RE NOT IMPRESSED BY THE MONGOLS?

UH, NO. EQUESTRIANS AREN'T SCARY, NO MATTER HOW CRANKY THEY ARE.

THEY ONLY CONQUERED THE LARGEST CONTIGUOUS EMPIRE IN HISTORY.

HOW HARD CAN IT HAVE BEEN? THEY DIDN'T EVEN BOTHER GETTING OUT OF THEIR PAJAMAS.

THEY CHEATED, ANYWAY. YOU EVER SMELLED A HORSE? IT MAKES YOU DIZZY, AND DIZZY PEOPLE ARE EASY TO CONQUER. LOOK AT THE BELGIANS.

HOW DO HORSES.... *BELGIANS?*

NEW THINGS ARE DANGEROUS. LIKE THROWING A TACO AT A SCOTSMAN: IT'S NEW. IT'S SPICY. HE'LL FREAK OUT.

darb

MAN, A JAR OF NEWMAN'S SALSA WOULD PROBABLY KILL AN IRISHMAN. *THEIR SYSTEM ISN'T USED TO IT.*

NOT A GOOD ANALOGY.

OK, THEN, LIKE HOW YOU FEEL WHEN A GIRL TALKS TO YOU.

HA HA! OOOO.

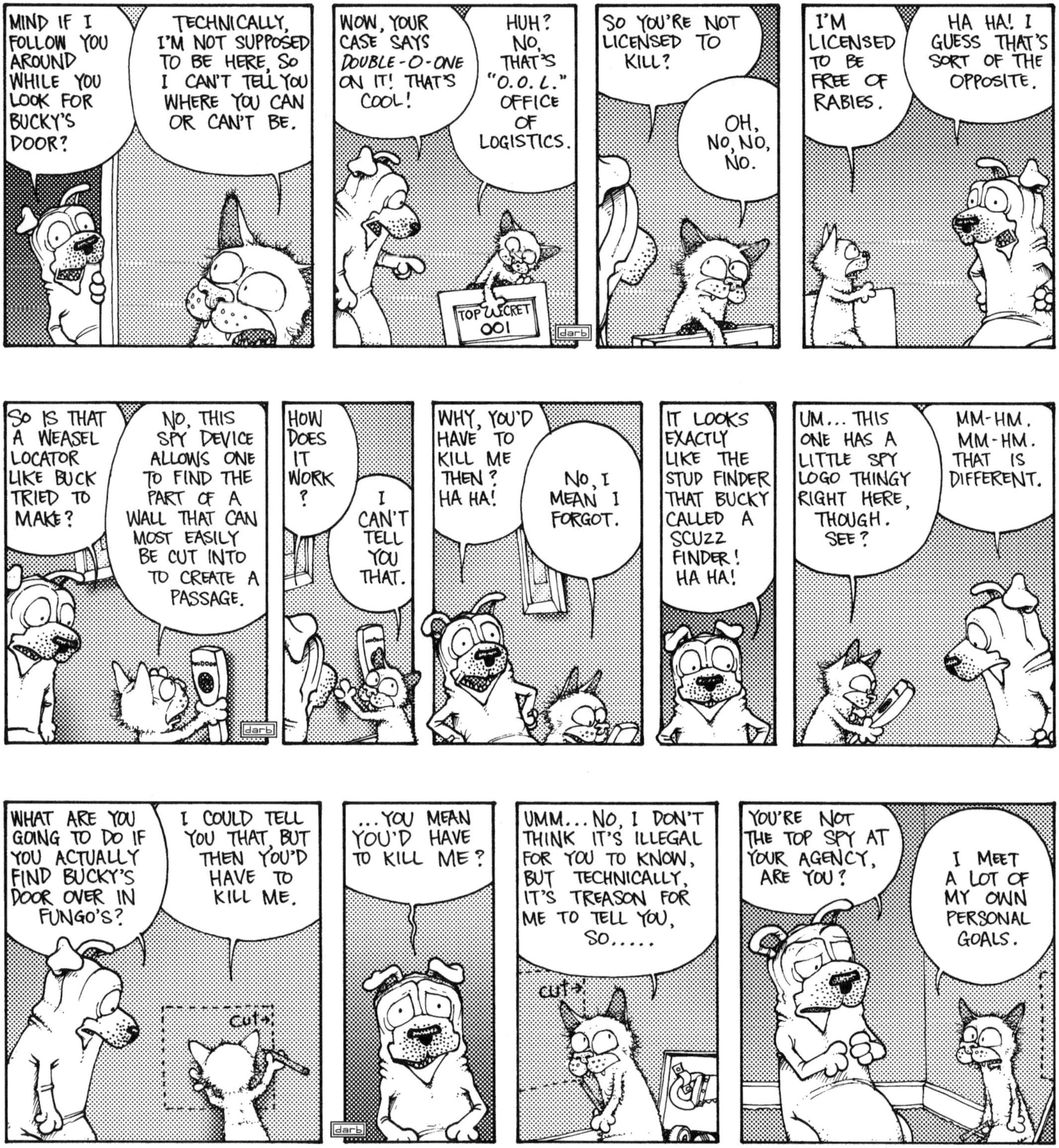
MIND IF I FOLLOW YOU AROUND WHILE YOU LOOK FOR BUCKY'S DOOR?
TECHNICALLY, I'M NOT SUPPOSED TO BE HERE, SO I CAN'T TELL YOU WHERE YOU CAN OR CAN'T BE.
WOW, YOUR CASE SAYS *DOUBLE-O-ONE* ON IT! THAT'S COOL!
HUH? NO, THAT'S "O.O.L." OFFICE OF LOGISTICS.
TOP SECRET 001
darb
SO YOU'RE NOT LICENSED TO KILL?
OH, NO, NO, NO.
I'M LICENSED TO BE FREE OF RABIES.
HA HA! I GUESS THAT'S SORT OF THE OPPOSITE.
SO IS THAT A WEASEL LOCATOR LIKE BUCK TRIED TO MAKE?
NO, THIS SPY DEVICE ALLOWS ONE TO FIND THE PART OF A WALL THAT CAN MOST EASILY BE CUT INTO TO CREATE A PASSAGE.
darb
HOW DOES IT WORK?
I CAN'T TELL YOU THAT.
WHY, YOU'D HAVE TO KILL ME THEN? HA HA!
NO, I MEAN I FORGOT.
IT LOOKS EXACTLY LIKE THE STUD FINDER THAT BUCKY CALLED A SCUZZ FINDER! HA HA!
UM... THIS ONE HAS A LITTLE SPY LOGO THINGY RIGHT HERE, THOUGH. SEE?
MM-HM. MM-HM. THAT IS DIFFERENT.
WHAT ARE YOU GOING TO DO IF YOU ACTUALLY FIND BUCKY'S DOOR OVER IN FUNGO'S?
I COULD TELL YOU THAT, BUT THEN YOU'D HAVE TO KILL ME.
CUT→
darb
...YOU MEAN YOU'D HAVE TO KILL ME?
UMM... NO, I DON'T THINK IT'S ILLEGAL FOR YOU TO KNOW, BUT TECHNICALLY, IT'S TREASON FOR ME TO TELL YOU, SO.....
CUT→
YOU'RE NOT THE TOP SPY AT YOUR AGENCY, ARE YOU?
I MEET A LOT OF MY OWN PERSONAL GOALS.

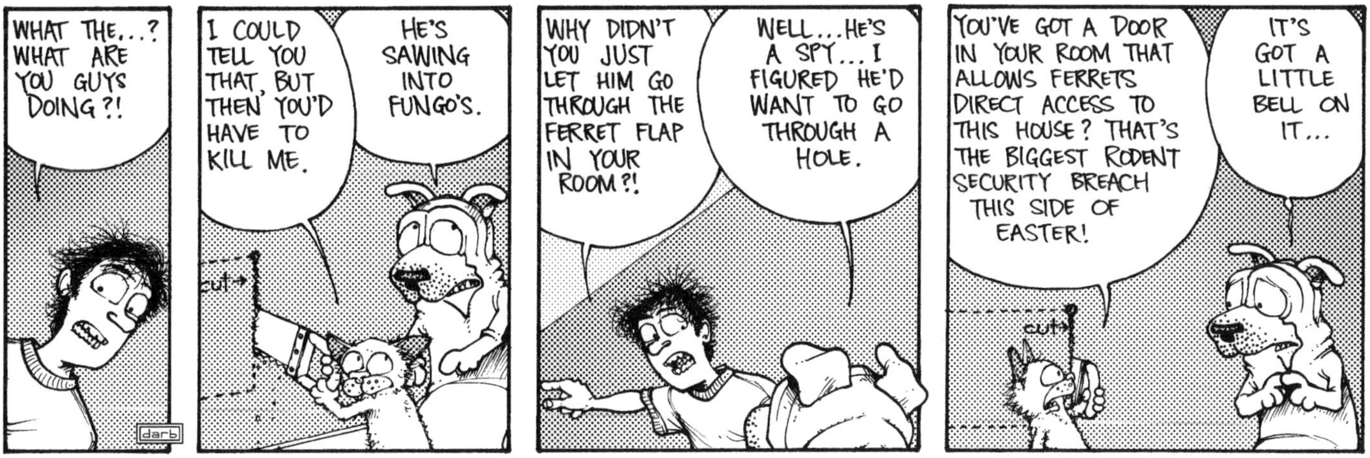
WHAT THE...? WHAT ARE YOU GUYS DOING?!
I COULD TELL YOU THAT, BUT THEN YOU'D HAVE TO KILL ME.
HE'S SAWING INTO FUNGO'S.
WHY DIDN'T YOU JUST LET HIM GO THROUGH THE FERRET FLAP IN YOUR ROOM?!
WELL...HE'S A SPY... I FIGURED HE'D WANT TO GO THROUGH A HOLE.
YOU'VE GOT A DOOR IN YOUR ROOM THAT ALLOWS FERRETS DIRECT ACCESS TO THIS HOUSE? THAT'S THE BIGGEST RODENT SECURITY BREACH THIS SIDE OF EASTER!
IT'S GOT A LITTLE BELL ON IT...

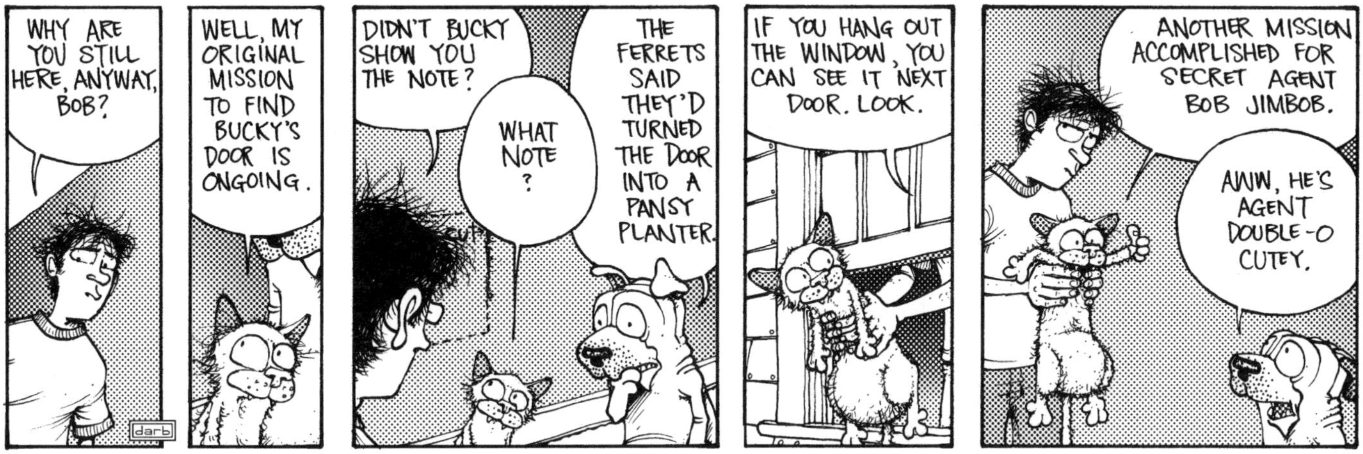
WHY ARE YOU STILL HERE, ANYWAY, BOB?
WELL, MY ORIGINAL MISSION TO FIND BUCKY'S DOOR IS ONGOING.
DIDN'T BUCKY SHOW YOU THE NOTE?
WHAT NOTE?
THE FERRETS SAID THEY'D TURNED THE DOOR INTO A PANSY PLANTER.
IF YOU HANG OUT THE WINDOW, YOU CAN SEE IT NEXT DOOR. LOOK.
ANOTHER MISSION ACCOMPLISHED FOR SECRET AGENT BOB JIMBOB.
AWW, HE'S AGENT DOUBLE-O CUTEY.

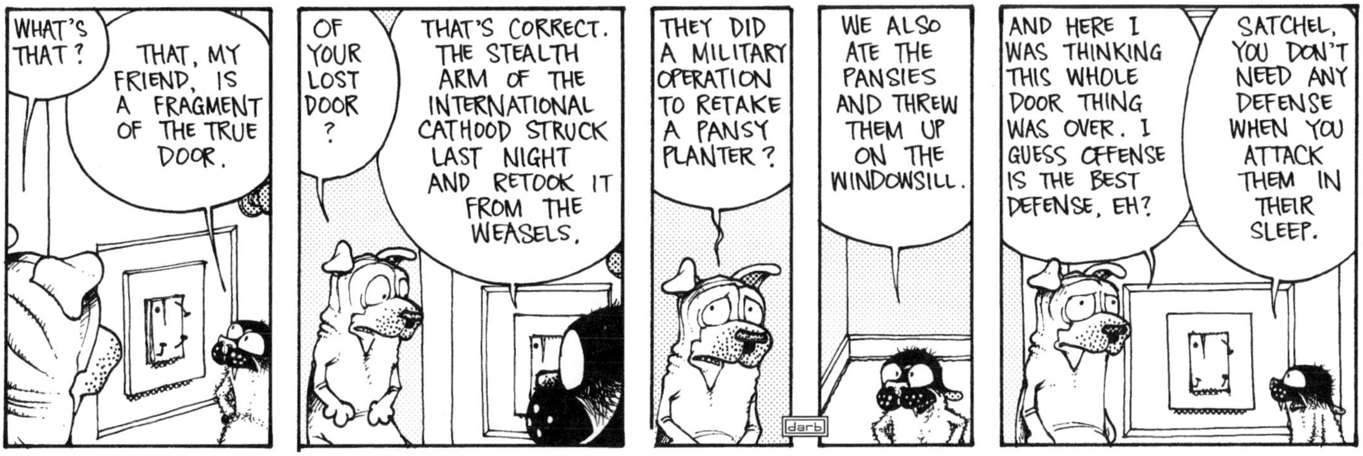
WHAT'S THAT?
THAT, MY FRIEND, IS A FRAGMENT OF THE TRUE DOOR.
OF YOUR LOST DOOR?
THAT'S CORRECT. THE STEALTH ARM OF THE INTERNATIONAL CATHOOD STRUCK LAST NIGHT AND RETOOK IT FROM THE WEASELS.
THEY DID A MILITARY OPERATION TO RETAKE A PANSY PLANTER?
WE ALSO ATE THE PANSIES AND THREW THEM UP ON THE WINDOWSILL.
AND HERE I WAS THINKING THIS WHOLE DOOR THING WAS OVER. I GUESS OFFENSE IS THE BEST DEFENSE, EH?
SATCHEL, YOU DON'T NEED ANY DEFENSE WHEN YOU ATTACK THEM IN THEIR SLEEP.

WHERE ARE YOU GOIN'?

FUNGO'S. HE'S GOT A BUDDY FROM VIETNAM IN TOWN.

WHAT'S HIS STORY?

HE'S A CA PHE COFFEE BEAN PROCESSOR.

WHAT'S THAT?

HE GETS PAID TO EAT COFFEE BEANS.

LOVELY. NOT JUST A WEASEL, A JACKED-UP WEASEL.

NO, HE DOESN'T DIGEST THE COFFEE, IT PASSES THROUGH HIM AND THEN PEOPLE RECOLLECT THE BEANS TO ROAST THEM TO MAKE COFFEE.

darb

IT'S CONSIDERED QUITE A DELICACY IN HANOI.

I KNOW WHAT YOU'RE—

PUT ME DOWN FOR A POUND.

OH! WELL, THAT'S VERY OPEN-MINDED OF—

AFTER THIS, I'LL NEVER HAVE TO BUY ROB ANOTHER BIRTHDAY PRESENT.

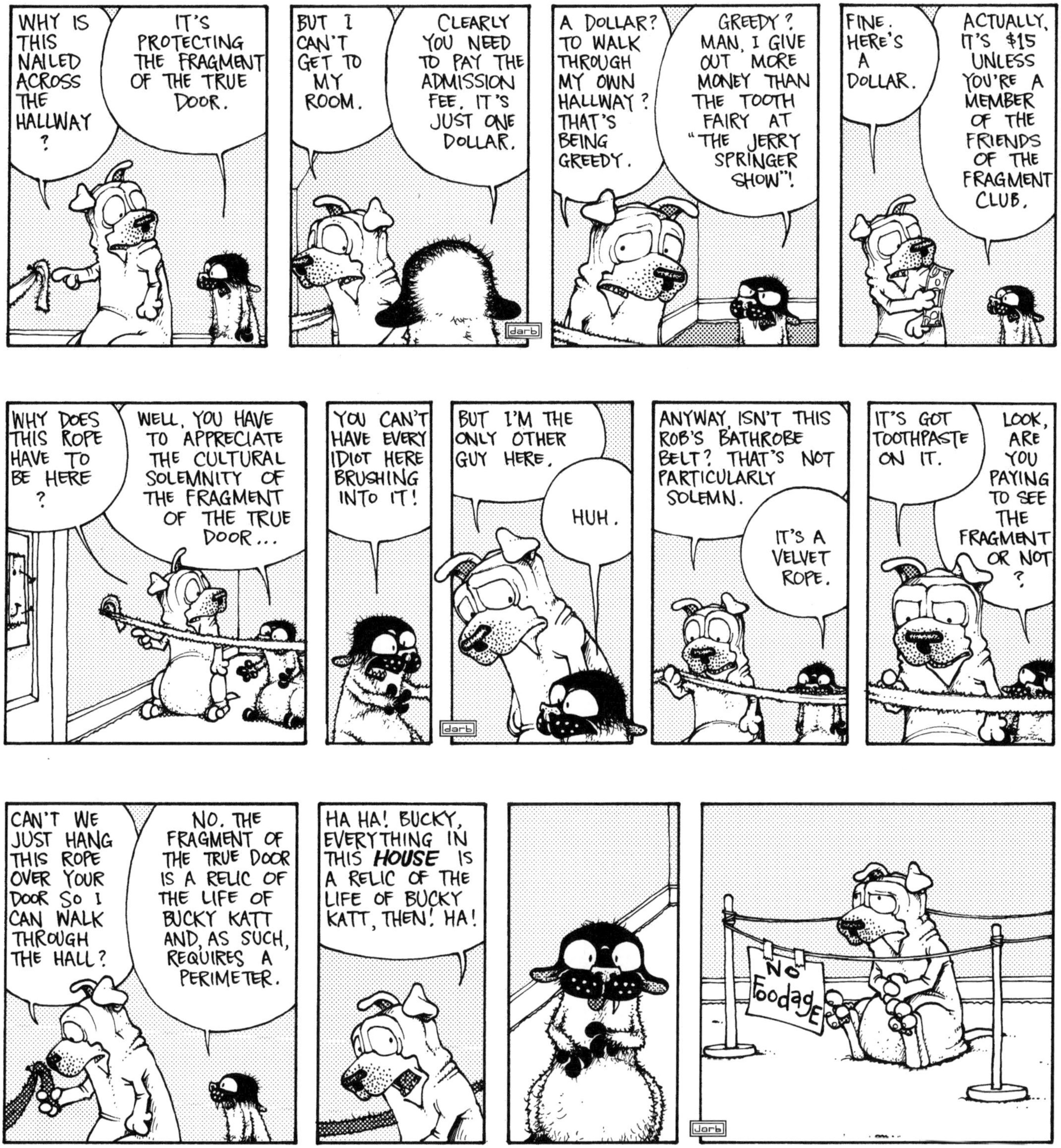
WHY IS THIS NAILED ACROSS THE HALLWAY?
IT'S PROTECTING THE FRAGMENT OF THE TRUE DOOR.
BUT I CAN'T GET TO MY ROOM.
CLEARLY YOU NEED TO PAY THE ADMISSION FEE. IT'S JUST ONE DOLLAR.
A DOLLAR? TO WALK THROUGH MY OWN HALLWAY? THAT'S BEING GREEDY.
GREEDY? MAN, I GIVE OUT MORE MONEY THAN THE TOOTH FAIRY AT "THE JERRY SPRINGER SHOW"!
FINE. HERE'S A DOLLAR.
ACTUALLY, IT'S $15 UNLESS YOU'RE A MEMBER OF THE FRIENDS OF THE FRAGMENT CLUB.
WHY DOES THIS ROPE HAVE TO BE HERE?
WELL, YOU HAVE TO APPRECIATE THE CULTURAL SOLEMNITY OF THE FRAGMENT OF THE TRUE DOOR...
YOU CAN'T HAVE EVERY IDIOT HERE BRUSHING INTO IT!
BUT I'M THE ONLY OTHER GUY HERE.
HUH.
ANYWAY, ISN'T THIS ROB'S BATHROBE BELT? THAT'S NOT PARTICULARLY SOLEMN.
IT'S A VELVET ROPE.
IT'S GOT TOOTHPASTE ON IT.
LOOK, ARE YOU PAYING TO SEE THE FRAGMENT OR NOT?
CAN'T WE JUST HANG THIS ROPE OVER YOUR DOOR SO I CAN WALK THROUGH THE HALL?
NO. THE FRAGMENT OF THE TRUE DOOR IS A RELIC OF THE LIFE OF BUCKY KATT AND, AS SUCH, REQUIRES A PERIMETER.
HA HA! BUCKY, EVERYTHING IN THIS HOUSE IS A RELIC OF THE LIFE OF BUCKY KATT, THEN! HA!
NO FoodagE
darb

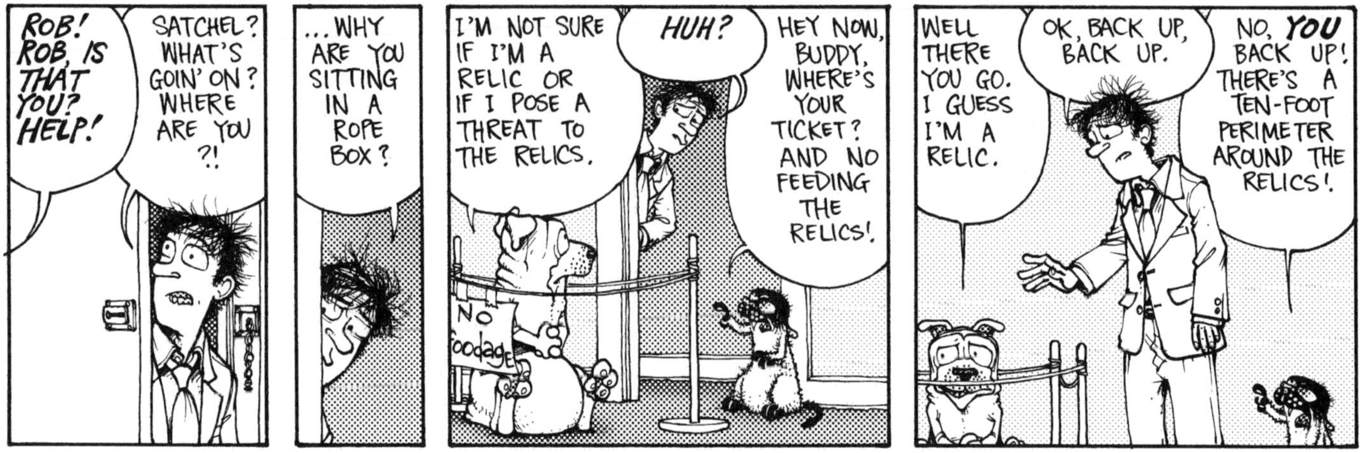
ROB! ROB, IS THAT YOU? HELP!
SATCHEL? WHAT'S GOIN' ON? WHERE ARE YOU ?!
...WHY ARE YOU SITTING IN A ROPE BOX?
I'M NOT SURE IF I'M A RELIC OR IF I POSE A THREAT TO THE RELICS.
HUH?
HEY NOW, BUDDY, WHERE'S YOUR TICKET? AND NO FEEDING THE RELICS!
NO FOODAGE
WELL THERE YOU GO. I GUESS I'M A RELIC.
OK, BACK UP, BACK UP.
NO, YOU BACK UP! THERE'S A TEN-FOOT PERIMETER AROUND THE RELICS!

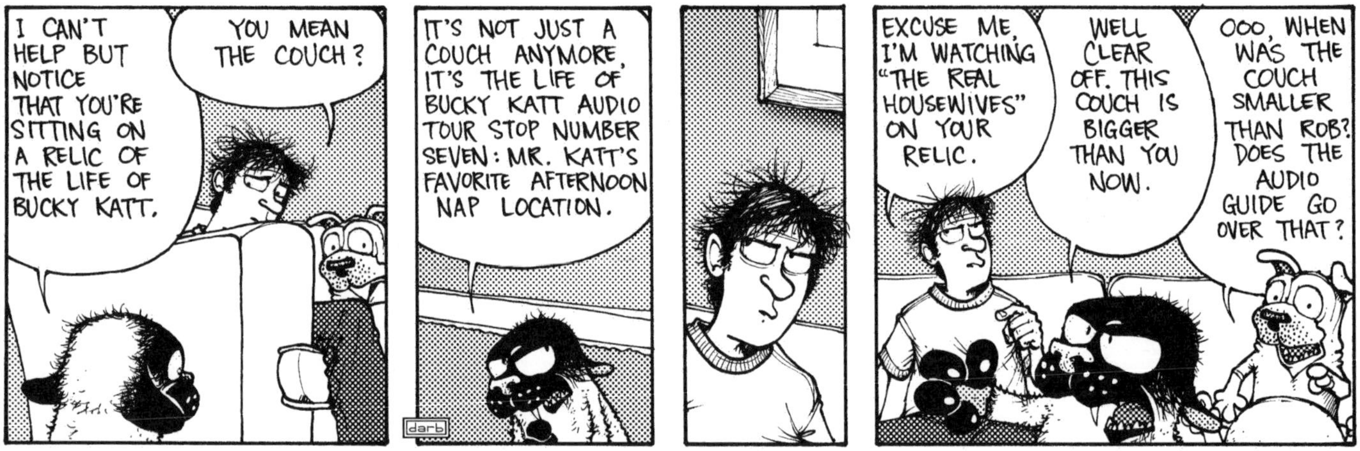
I CAN'T HELP BUT NOTICE THAT YOU'RE SITTING ON A RELIC OF THE LIFE OF BUCKY KATT.
YOU MEAN THE COUCH?
IT'S NOT JUST A COUCH ANYMORE, IT'S THE LIFE OF BUCKY KATT AUDIO TOUR STOP NUMBER SEVEN: MR. KATT'S FAVORITE AFTERNOON NAP LOCATION.
darb
EXCUSE ME, I'M WATCHING "THE REAL HOUSEWIVES" ON YOUR RELIC.
WELL CLEAR OFF. THIS COUCH IS BIGGER THAN YOU NOW.
OOO, WHEN WAS THE COUCH SMALLER THAN ROB? DOES THE AUDIO GUIDE GO OVER THAT?

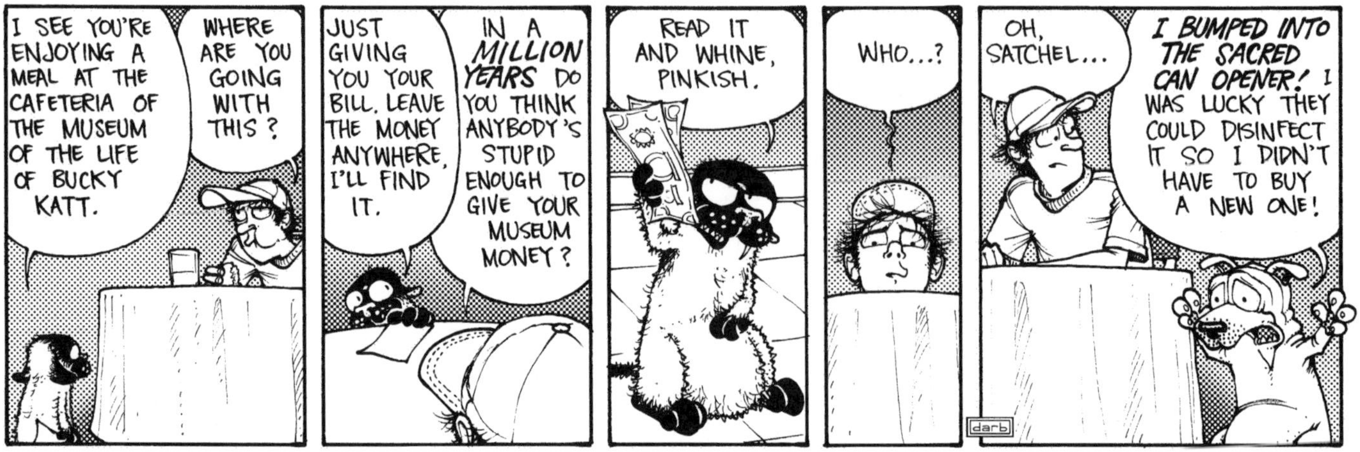
I SEE YOU'RE ENJOYING A MEAL AT THE CAFETERIA OF THE MUSEUM OF THE LIFE OF BUCKY KATT.
WHERE ARE YOU GOING WITH THIS?
JUST GIVING YOU YOUR BILL. LEAVE THE MONEY ANYWHERE, I'LL FIND IT.
IN A MILLION YEARS DO YOU THINK ANYBODY'S STUPID ENOUGH TO GIVE YOUR MUSEUM MONEY?
READ IT AND WHINE, PINKISH.
WHO...?
OH, SATCHEL...
I BUMPED INTO THE SACRED CAN OPENER! I WAS LUCKY THEY COULD DISINFECT IT SO I DIDN'T HAVE TO BUY A NEW ONE!
darb